Storytelling Across Worlds: Transmedia for Creatives and Producers

Praise for *Storytelling Across Worlds*

"For anyone interested in transmedia storytelling this book is a fantastic starting point – stimulating, observant, and insightful. It's a panoramic view of this fascinating new arena of storytelling."

— Carlton Cuse, Writer/Executive Producer/Showrunner *LOST*, *Bates Motel*

"Storytelling Across Worlds" acknowledges that, increasingly, all media is transmedia. As part of working in television, I've found myself creating webisodes, podcasts, games, comic books, motion comics, short stories, fictionalized twitter feeds and web sites set within the parent shows' fictional worlds. This book draws on contemporary examples to provide perspective on this huge, and somehow still growing, creative world. Any book would be challenged to get its arms around a topic that is defined by its unconstrained scope. This one grabs transmedia in a mighty hug and doesn't let go."

— Jane Espenson, Television writer/producer: *Buffy The Vampire Slayer*,
Battlestar Galactica, *Once Upon A Time*, *Husbands*

"How often in life have you been warned that "there are rules"? *Storytelling Across Worlds* delightfully dispenses with antiquated narrative limitations by throwing open the endless possibilities of sophisticated narrative through transmedia storytelling as the actual, practical bedrock of modern entertainment. With this book, the authors have crafted an elegant and masterful dissection of narrative's new world order."

—Vlad Woylnetz, President of Production, Cineflix, Executive Producer *Torchwood*,
Executive in Charge of Production *Mad Men*, *Breaking Bad*, & *Walking Dead*

Storytelling Across Worlds: Transmedia for Creatives and Producers

Tom Dowd
Michael Niederman
Michael Fry
Josef Steiff

Focal Press
Taylor & Francis Group

NEW YORK AND LONDON

First published 2013
by Focal Press
70 Blanchard Rd Suite 402
Burlington, MA 01803

Simultaneously published in the UK
by Focal Press
2 Park Square, Milton Park, Abingdon, Oxon OX14 4RN

Focal Press is an imprint of the Taylor & Francis Group, an informa business

Library of Congress Cataloging in Publication Data
Dowd, Tom, 1964-
Storytelling Across Worlds: Transmedia for Creatives and Producers / Tom Dowd, Michael Niederman, Michael Fry, and Josef Steiff.
    pages cm
ISBN 978-0-240-82411-6 (pbk.)
1. Mass media–Marketing. 2. Convergence (Telecommunication) I. Niederman, Michael, 1958-
II. Fry, Micheal, 1966- III. Steiff, Josef, 1957- IV. Title.

P96.M36D69 2013
659.13'4—dc23

                                                                        2012039089

ISBN: 978-0-240-82411-6 (pbk)
ISBN: 978-0-240-82475-8 (ebk)

Typeset in Bembo Std Regular,
by MPS Limited, Chennai, India
www.adi-mps.com

Printed and bound in the United States of America by Sheridan Books, Inc. (a Sheridan Group Company).

Contents

Preface   *xiii*

List of Figures   *xvii*

Part 1   Understanding Transmedia Storytelling   **1**

Chapter 1   One Story   **3**

What Is Transmedia?   3

The Producers Guild Definition   4

Transmedia, Intellectual Property and Franchises   5

Stumbling Toward Transmedia   6

Transmedia Storytelling for Producers   7

The Role of the Transmedia Producer   8

    Finding the Idea   9

    Determining the Scope/Setting the Budget   9

    Building the Team   10

    Setting the Schedule   10

    Overseeing Production   11

Audience, Presentation and Platforms   11

    Presentation and Platform   12

Transmedia for Creatives   20

    A Story for All Screens   20

One World, Many Stories   21

Adaptation vs. Extension vs. Expansion   22

    Adaptation   22

    Extension   23

    Expansion   23

Where to Start   24

    Finding the Starting Concept   24

Reboot and Reinvention   25

Cornerstone Platform/Property   27

    Story and Medium   27

    Audience and Medium   29

    Development, Production and Medium   29

Engagement and Participation   30

Chapter 2   Worldbuilding and Key Story Elements   **33**

The Challenge of Transmedia Development   34

Development Processes   36

    Bottom-Up Creation   36

    Top-Down Crafting   38

Contents

Weaving the Universe   38
     Economic Issues   39
     Cultural Impact   39
     Cast of Characters   39
     Platform Implications   40
     Two Weaving Examples   40
Story Universe vs. The Storyworld   41
Building Blocks   42
     Physical Geography   43
     Culture   44
     History   44
     Mythology and Cosmology   44
Key Story Elements   48
     Story/Theme   48
     Plot   50
     Characters   51
     Setting   54
Style/Tone   54
More to Explore   55

Chapter 3   Storytelling and Narrative Continuity   **56**
Driving the Story   57
Genre Types   58
Plotting Points and Curves   60
World Out of Balance   61
The Beginning and End of Our Universe   62
     Entry Points   63
     Entry Into *LOST*   64
     Entry Into *Avatar*   64
     Managing Multiple Entry Points   64
     Endings   65
Narrative Coherence   66
Continuity, Canon, and Consistency   69
     Continuity   69
     Canon   72

Part 2   Many Media   **77**

Chapter 4   Motion Pictures and Visual Storytelling   **79**
How Fast? Speed   80
How Much? Duration   80
How Big? Shot Size   82
Why Film?   82

Basics of Film Storytelling and Structure   82
  Story Structures   83
Turning the Plot Curve Upside Down   84
Three-Act Structure in Film   87
Key Transmedia Elements and Motion Pictures   88
  Theme/Story   88
  Plot   89
  Character   89
  Setting   90
  Style/Tone   90
Presenting a Visual Story with Words   91
  Loglines   91
  Outlines   91
Story Summaries   92
  Synopsis   92
  Treatments   93
Scripts/Screenplays   93
  Proposals   94
Film Production Realities   95
A Film's Life Cycle   96
  Development   96
  Preproduction   96
  Production   97
  Postproduction   97
  Marketing/Exhibition/Distribution   97
Film Franchises and Sequels   99
Film and Transmedia   99
  Visual Storytelling   99
Film and Other Media   100
Interview: Phil Hay   101

Chapter 5   Television and Serialized Storytelling   **111**
Basics of Television Storytelling   112
  Structured Acts   113
  A Story … and a B Story, C Story, D and Sometimes E!   114
  Act Breaks and Bridging the Gaps   114
  Episodic vs. Serialized Storytelling   116
  Arcs: The Long and Short of It   117
  Procedurals and the Best of Both Worlds   120
Formats and How Long It Takes   121
  Spirals of Conflict   122
  It's All About the Timing   122
Why Television Loves Genres   123

Key Transmedia Elements and Television 124
   Theme/Story 124
   Plot 125
   Character 125
   Setting 126
   Style/Tone 126
Television Production Realities 127
   A Season at a Time 128
   Franchises 129
Spin-Offs 130
Revival 131
The Remake/Reboot 131
Television and Transmedia 132
   The History 132
   Case Studies 134
   Why Aren't We All *LOST*? 138
A Modest Proposal … A Transmedia Network 139
   The CBS Dramatic Universe – Possible? 139
   Making It All Work Together 140
Interview: Carlton Cuse 141

Chapter 6 Video Games and Interactive Storytelling 152
The State of Video Game Development 152
Participatory Content, for the Win 154
Basics of Game Design and Storytelling 155
   Gameplay and Story Working Together 156
   Game – Story – Game – Story is a Familiar Pattern 157
Key Transmedia Elements and Video Games 158
   Theme/Story 158
   Plot 159
   Character 160
   Setting 160
   Style/Tone 161
Video Game Storytelling Structure 161
   The Story Written vs. The Story Played 163
   Interactive Stories 164
   The Complexities of Branching Stories 164
The Concepts of Agency and Affordance 168
   Agency and Affordance and the Transmedia Property 169
Character, Action, and the Expression of Character 170
   Action and Gameplay 171
   Character Motivation 172
Dialogue and Conversation 174
   Example: *Mass Effect* Conversations 174

Game Production Realities   175
Production Time and Timing   176
Production Methodologies   176
    Agile Development   177
    Iterative Development (Cerny Method)   177
    Waterfall Model   177
Developers and Publishers   178
Licensing   179
The Game Production Process   179
    Game Production Scheduling and Milestones   180
Video Games and Transmedia   186
    Role-Playing Games, World Building and Story Extension   186
    Video Games and Other Media   188
    Video Games and Television   191
Interview: Jordan Weisman   194

Chapter 7   Other Forms of Storytelling   **201**
Intellectual Properties that Started as Novels, Comics or New Media   201
    Novels   201
    "Comics" (Comics, Graphic Novels, Manga)   202
    New Media Content (Internet-based)   204
Cultural Artifacts   205
    Toys, Food, Advertising and News as a Source   206
Does Anybody Just Make a Universe for the Hell of it?   207
Other Forms of Narrative Extension   207
Conventional Additions   207
    Fan Fiction   207
    Cosplay   208
    Fan Conventions   208
Unconventional Additions   208
    Slash Fiction/Fan Media Pornography   208
    Fan "Canon" Videos …   208
Batman and *Naruto* Face the Challenges of Size and Longevity   210
Naruto/Naruto Shippuden   210
    Origin: Manga   210
    Anime   210
    Films   210
    Video Games   211
    All Sorts of Alternative Media   211
    Why has *Naruto* been so Successful?   211
    Naruto's Core Story/Arc Dynamics   211
Batman   212
    Origins: Comics   212
    First Transformation   212

Contents

Re-Emergence into Mainstream Popular Culture 212
So What Happened to the Movies? 213
Interview: Anthony Del Col 215

Chapter 8   Choosing Properties and Forms **225**
Fan Base 225
Wizard of Oz 225
Nancy Drew 226
Fred 227
Developed Universe 227
Lord of the Rings 228
The Walking Dead 228
Chronicles of Narnia 229
His Dark Materials 229
Economic Factors 230
The Graphic Novel Craze 230
The Internet Craze 231
Cheap has Value 231
Author's Pull 231
Stephen King 232
George R. R. Martin 232
Orson Scott Card 232
J. K. Rowling 233
Final Thoughts on an Existing Property 233
The Expectation and Impact of Extension and Expansion 233
A Final Thought: The Blurring of Ownership 235

Part 3   Managing the Story **237**

Chapter 9   Managing the Transmedia Property **239**
Maintaining the Brand 239
Marvel and Story Extension 241
Feedback and Conversation 241
Brand Loyalty, Across Platforms 241
Release Schedule 242
Factors in Scheduling the Release of a Television Series 243
Factors in Scheduling the Release of a Film 244
Factors in Scheduling the Release of a Game 244
Factors in Scheduling the Release of a Graphic Novel 245
Release Sequence 246
Marketing 247
The Gift of Fire 248
Licensing and Rights Management 249
Trademarks and Copyright 249

The Approval Process 254
Who's in Charge? 256
Fans, Fandom and Fan Culture 257
Connections 257
Conversations 258
Technical Management 258
Technical Solutions 259
Internal vs. External Needs 260
Local Network 260
Remote Access 260
Document Storage and Sharing 260
Database Software 261
Wikis 261
Project and Multipurpose Sites 261

Chapter 10   The Transmedia Intellectual Property Bible **263**
Building the Bible 264
Story, Rules and Underlying Assumptions 264
Authors 266
Elements of the Bible 266
Sharing the Bible 277
Updating the Bible, Maintaining the Franchise 277
The Transmedia Intellectual Property Bible as a Static Document 277
The Bible as a Dynamic Digital Document 279
Maintaining the Continuity Bible Consistently 279

Part 4   End Matters **281**

Chapter 11   Wrap Up **283**

Appendix A   Motion Picture Platform Bible **285**

Appendix B   Television Platform Bible **289**

Appendix C   Video Game Platform Bible **293**

Appendix D   Platform Bibles for Other Forms of Storytelling **303**

Appendix E   Sample Trademark Licensing Agreement **310**

**Appendix F   The Producer's Guild of America "Code of Credits"
Definition of Transmedia Producer** **315**

Appendix G   Suggested Readings **316**

Index *318*

Preface

Transmedia storytelling represents a process where integral elements of a fiction get dispersed systematically across multiple delivery channels for the purpose of creating a unified and coordinated entertainment experience. Ideally, each medium makes its own unique contribution to the unfolding of the story. So, for example, in the Matrix franchise, key bits of information are conveyed through three live action films, a series of animated shorts, two collections of comic book stories, and several video games. There is no one single source or ur-text where one can turn to gain all of the information needed to comprehend the Matrix universe.

—Henry Jenkins ("Transmedia Storytelling 101," accessed April 25, 2012, http://www.henryjenkins.org/2007/03/transmedia_storytelling_101.html)

Transmedia storytelling is storytelling writ large, across multiple platforms, media, and story words. The modern narrative property cannot exist in one form alone. Freely absorbing multiple channels of media constantly, today's audience has an almost insatiable desire for *more* of its current favorite property or franchise. From film to television to games to webisodes to novels to alternate-reality games to comic books, and beyond, any major media property that expects to stand out from the crowd has to do so on multiple platforms. Traditional single media or simple adaptations – where the storyline from one media piece is adapted into another medium – are rapidly becoming old school. In its place is the idea (and ideal) of transmedia storytelling, where one broadly-conceived, engaging story is told across multiple media, with each platform telling its own contained story, but at the same time only part of the larger story. (The Producers Guild of America, a trade organization whose members are television, motion picture, and new media producers, recently recognized the new above-the-line credit of "Transmedia Producer" in acknowledgment of the field's rapid development.)

Watch the movie, and you experience one complete, satisfying story, but that's only part of the larger possibilities. Now play the game or read the novels, and learn more about what else is going on in and around the story. You may even see some of the events from the film in a different light. For producers and property-rights holders, transmedia storytelling is the avenue to multiple-platform monetization of the larger story, and for "creatives" (writers and other creative contributors) it is the art of world building and the opportunity to tell stories, reveal characters, and explore worlds as never before.

Times have changed. We live in a time when we are all connected by technology of one kind or another. We absorb information from multiple, parallel channels constantly. True multi-tasking may or may not be a real thing, but it often feels like we're absorbing all of these channels simultaneously in one great wave of information. We're not, but it feels like we are.

One of the reasons we, the authors, sat down to create this book is not only our own involvement in transmedia creation, but our experience discussing transmedia and transmedia storytelling with our graduate and undergraduate students. The deeper we take them into Alice's rabbit hole, the more excited they become. Not only do they realize that this is something that they *want*, but that it has been, subconsciously for some, what they *expect*. When there isn't a video game tie-in to a blockbuster movie or when they can't find more stories about their favorite television series on bookstore shelves (virtual or physical), they're surprised and disappointed. The fact that some of their favorite franchises have had cross-media support has conditioned them to expect it from all of them, especially the ones that excite them the most.

Our students have been filmmakers, television writers and producers, video game designers, aspiring novelists … media creators of all flavors. But we've also spoken to industry professionals of all shapes, sizes and backgrounds about transmedia and though their eyes collectively light up over the subject, there is a haze of uncertainty and confusion that quickly settles in. More than one media producer expressed to us that they wished a book like we intend existed when they were trying to explain transmedia to other more traditionally entrenched producers and executives.

We suspect this book has the most value for newcomers to the realm of transmedia storytelling, but we hope seasoned creators and producers can find value as well. We intend this book as a practical primer (albeit introductory) on the conceptualization, structuring, writing, execution, management and marketing of a transmedia property that manifests on multiple media and shares a single interwoven story. Frankly, in order to fully understand the transmedia storytelling creation process one has to be versed well enough in all of the media involved, and all of the processes involved. The task is probably too large for one book to cover completely. In fact, the scope of this project – and the thinking involved (yes, there was some) – required four authors, each with particular knowledge, experience and insight into the different areas the book covers.

Even with that we fully recognize that this book does not, and cannot, cover everything – past, present or future – in transmedia storytelling. This means that invariably some property or franchise, some transmedia storytelling project or expression (undoubtedly your favorite and the one you think is the *most important* example of the form) will get the short shrift, or be insultingly ignored entirely. For that, we apologize in advance, but we knew going in that we were going to have to make significant content and coverage choices and decided to focus on the larger, mass-media transmedia storytelling franchises and possibilities.

One way we thought about this was that we were focusing on transmedia projects "writ large." Others, such as transmedia producer/creator Andrea Phillips (*Perplex City*, *Routes*) would place this book firmly in the "West Coast" or "Hollywood" camp of transmedia, versus the more indie, intimate, personally interactive "East Coast" transmedia. While we hope that this characterization won't fuel something rivaling the East Coast–West Coast hip-hop wars, we would agree with her. We're also going to avoid wading into the academic end of transmedia analysis and theory too deeply, but some of it will be necessary (and we do open the book with a quote from Henry Jenkins.) Some of that discourse will be useful, but this book is about doing, not just considering.

This book is for everyone curious about transmedia storytelling in one form or another, coming at it from nearly any medium. We're going to focus primarily on motion pictures, television, and video games as the primary launch medium (or "mothership" – but more on that in a bit), but delve into other areas such as novels, webisodes, graphic novels, and so on. The three chapters on motion pictures, television, and video games in Part 2 of the book respectively exist to provide practitioners and managers who may exist in one of those fields, but don't fully know the others, a basic overview and introduction of the structures and practices of these other areas while exploring the presence of transmedia storytelling in each area. Thus far, creatives and producers have focused on single areas of production – motion pictures, television, or video games. For those going to participate in or supervise the creation of a transmedia property, a minimum understanding of all the important media is required. Each field has its seminal works on theory (and we'll point you at them) for additional detail and understanding. For the heavy lifting, however, we *strongly* encourage recruitment of experts in the individual media areas who live and breathe those platforms. Film is not television, television is not video games, and so on. What is normal, commonplace, assumed, or standard in one is not in the other. Some core ideas move laterally across media, but some basic conceptions do not. We encourage anyone involved in the transmedia production process to make use of such experts as much as possible, especially those with a multi-disciplinary mindset.

Transmedia storytelling is the new frontier. Don't let anyone tell you that the old rules don't apply anymore — many of them do — but many of them require a different critical, creative, and managerial eye to make work. We're in the early days of deliberate transmedia storytelling, so be prepared to explore and experiment. New thinking and new approaches are required, but the possibilities and the rewards are staggering.

Tom Dowd, Michael Fry,
Michael Niederman, and Josef Steiff.
Chicago, Summer 2012

List of Figures

Figure 3.1 *Plot points.   Ch3, p.60*

Figure 4.1 *Plot curve again.   Ch 4, p.84*

Figure 4.2 *Main character discomfort.   Ch 4, p.85*

Figure 4.3 *More plot points.   Ch 4, p.85*

Figure 4.4 *Three-act structure.   Ch 4, p.86*

Figure 4.5 *Another plot curve.   Ch4, p.86*

Figure 4.1.1 *Phil Hay.   Ch4, interview. p.101*

Figure 5.1 *Hour Long Arc.   Ch5, p.118*

Figure 5.2 *Season Arcs.   Ch5, p.119*

Figure 5.3 *Sitcom Arcs.   Ch5, p.121*

Figure 5.1.1 *Carlton Cuse.   Ch5, interview, p.141*

Figure 6.1 *Vanilla plot structure.   Ch6, p.162*

Figure 6.2 *The Three-Act Structure.   Ch6, p.162*

Figure 6.3 *The Story-Gameplay Structure.   Ch6, p.162*

Figure 6.4 *Vanilla plot structure.   Ch6, p.164*

Figure 6.5 *Simple branched structure.   Ch6, p.165*

Figure 6.6 *Complex branched structure.   Ch6, p.165*

Figure 6.7 *Branch with chokepoints structure.   Ch6, p.166*

Figure 6.8 *Parallel Structure diagram.   Ch6, p.166*

Figure 6.9 *Non-linear structure diagram.   Ch6, p.167*

Figure 6.10 *Master Effect conversation wheel.   Ch6, p.174*

Figure 6.11 *Conversation wheel close-up.   Ch6, p.175*

Figure 6.1.1 *Jordan Weisman.   Ch6, interview, p.195*

Figure 7.1.1 *Anthony Del Col.   Ch7, interview, p.215*

Part 1

Understanding Transmedia Storytelling

Chapter 1

One Story

With transmedia you're not repeating the same story on a movie screen, a TV screen, a novel and a videogame. You are using each one to tell a complete piece of your story and combined they can all become a deeper, richer and more immersive experience.

—Jeff Gomez, CEO, Starlight Runner Entertainment[1]

What Is Transmedia?

Transmedia has many definitions, some of them new, some of them legacy and some of them based in non-storytelling mediums, such as marketing, merchandizing, and advertising. In many of these definitions, transmedia is conceptually interchangeable with terms like "cross-media" "multimedia", "multiplatform storytelling", "franchise" or even "interactive media" – associations and uses that can make the concept of "transmedia" a bit confusing. The definition of a transmedia narrative property used by the Producers Guild of America (which we'll get to shortly) differs from the definition used by transmedia/alternate-reality game pioneers like Jordan Weisman, who see transmedia as the use of multiple media fragments to reveal a previously unknown, or unexpected, hidden story.

In this book, we are expressly talking about the process of storytelling, of building the transmedia narrative property (the end product) in all its forms. We are particularly looking at how to tell stories that come from and exist in a larger intellectual property universe carefully designed and built to allow multiple iterations, expressions, and platforms simultaneously and sequentially. Though there are implications in the delivery of transmedia stories that fall within the territory of marketing, we are principally concerned here with those aspects that directly relate to the creation of narrative. The term we're using is *transmedia storytelling*. It is a bit cumbersome, so we'll often just say transmedia. If we're meaning transmedia marketing, or some other use of transmedia, we'll specifically call that out. So, if you see transmedia it means transmedia storytelling.

[1] "5 Questions with Jeff Gomez, CEO, Starlight Runner Entertainment" accessed July 25, 2012, www.dmwmedia.com/news/2011/04/11

More and more, audiences want their entertainment experiences to transcend the medium itself and transmedia storytelling provides this by creating a unified and coordinated entertainment experience that builds from multiple encounters with the narrative and elements of the property's universe, each medium making its own unique contribution to the unfolding story.

The Producers Guild Definition

Our cornerstone is the motion picture Producers Guild of America's definition of a transmedia producer credit, established in 2010, which has more or less set the industry standard for transmedia:

> *A Transmedia Narrative project must consist of three or more narrative storylines existing within the same fictional universe.*

Producers Guild of America, Code of Credits – New Media[2]

(The entirety of the Code of Credits entry for transmedia producer is reproduced in Appendix F.)

The piece of language quoted above is interesting in that it specifically calls out a transmedia narrative project as having *three or more narrative storylines existing within the same universe*. It does not differentiate between how many platforms these discrete storylines must exist on, but we're going to operate under the distinction that a true transmedia narrative property has to utilize at least two different platforms – the more the better – to tell its stories.

The transmedia producer is responsible for a significant portion of the transmedia property's long-term planning, development, production and/or maintenance of story continuity across the multiple platforms and creation of original storylines for new platforms. This can include the creation and implementation of interactive endeavors to unite the audience of the property with the narrative, as long as they are related directly to the narrative presentation of the project and not simply marketing extensions. Media properties like *Glee*, *True Blood*, and *Game of Thrones* have been successful at developing interactive projects that engage their audiences through a variety of means, though not all of these have been transmedia storytelling.

For a property to be transmedia, it also has to be more than just adapting the same story to different media. Each expression has to tell a complete piece of a larger story. This is not an arbitrary decision – we as transmedia producers have to identify those aspects of the story or universe that are best served by the specific strengths of a particular medium. Our goal is to create multiple expressions of the story across various platforms that when taken as a whole create a deeper, richer and more immersive experience for the audience.

Transmedia is most conducive to those stories where there is a complex universe and rich backstory or mythology that can extend into an exploration of that universe via multiple (potentially interrelated) characters, each with their own stories that expand and deepen our understanding of that world. As Henry Jenkins pointed out in the Preface, *The Matrix* (Warner Brothers, 1999) is a good example of this. Our understanding of the property comes from information conveyed through three live-action films, a series of animated shorts, two collections of comic book stories and several video games. Much of the pleasure for the audience is in compiling this range of experiences and the story information gathered from each into a meaningful larger view of the universe, characters, conflicts and themes we call *The Matrix*. This said, not all stories should be a transmedia experience and one of our tasks as a transmedia producer is similar to that of all producers within individual mediums – figuring out whether this is the best possible expression for the story we want to tell.

This is one of the toughest lessons for novice producers – the temptation is to think any story can be told in any medium. But there are some forms of stories or story elements that work best as a live theatre and others that work

[2] accessed July 20, 2012, http://www.producersguild.org/?page=coc_nm#transmedia

best as novels and others that work as TV series and … you get the idea. The core elements of your story – character, conflict, and so on – all have to work in any of the media, however.

If we do have a property that does benefit from or work best with multiple expressions of the story, each individual expression must be a satisfying experience on its own terms and yet also make a contribution to the larger intellectual property narrative as well. In other words, we need to be able to watch J. J. Abram's 2009 and 2013 *Star Trek* (Paramount Pictures) films and have a complete coherent story experience, but at the same time, if we have read the prequel comic series *Star Trek: Countdown* (IDW, 2009) (which bridges the 2009 motion picture and the *Star Trek: The Next Generation* television series) or the *Star Trek Ongoing* (IDW, 2011 – present) comics (which bridges the 2009 and 2013 motion pictures *and* connects the new films with events seen in *Star Trek: The Original Series* in the 1960s), we learn additional narrative information that makes for a deeper and more complex understanding of the larger story. Transmedia guru Henry Jenkins has pointed out that this is similar to game designer Neil Young's concept of "additive comprehension" or the ways in which we compile information from each part of the story we encounter which then causes us to reconsider or revise our understanding of the larger narrative as a whole (Henry Jenkins, *Convergence Culture: Where Old and New Media Collides*, NYU Press, 2006).

Transmedia, Intellectual Property and Franchises

Before we dig much further in, we're going to lay out a set of definitions that hopefully make what comes after easier to understand. If you are hip-deep in media production and transmedia, you probably already know these terms and if not here they are.

According to the World Intellectual Property Organization (WIPO):

> *Intellectual property (IP) refers to creations of the mind: inventions, literary and artistic works and symbols, names, images and designs used in commerce.*

> *IP is divided into two categories: Industrial property, which includes inventions (patents), trademarks, industrial designs and geographic indications of source; and Copyright, which includes literary and artistic works such as novels, poems and plays, films, musical works, artistic works such as drawings, paintings, photographs and sculptures and architectural designs. Rights related to copyright include those of performing artists in their performances, producers of phonograms in their recordings and those of broadcasters in their radio and television programs.*

What is Intellectual Property[3]

The Stanford Encyclopedia of Philosophy further elaborates:

> *Intellectual property is generally characterized as non-physical property that is the product of original thought. Typically, rights do not surround the abstract non-physical entity; rather, intellectual property rights surround the control of physical manifestations or expressions of ideas. Intellectual property protects rights to ideas by protecting rights to produce and control physical instantiations of those ideas.*

Intellectual Property[4]

Both of these definitions/explanations focus heavily on the idea of legal rights associated with the dissemination, distribution, publication or control of otherwise intangible ideas. For us transmedia professionals (or aspiring) the majority of concepts and issues around intellectual property are outside our concern. When we talk about *intellectual properties*, or IP as it is often abbreviated, we're talking about a universe of story possibilities presentable and creatively expressible in a variety of media. Let's reiterate: when we talk about intellectual property we're talking

[3] accessed July 27, 2012, http://www.wipo.int/about-ip/en/
[4] accessed July 27, 2012, http://plato.stanford.edu/entries/intellectual-property/

about an overall or over-arching story that can be told in a number of media. And when we're talking about a story, we're not just talking about the simple expression of a story, like "Bob loves Alice, but Alice is actually leader of a band of rebellious ghosts seeking more fulfilling after-lives. Can true love prevail?," but rather all of the creative effort and expression that goes into it – what the story is about literally (rebellious ghosts), figuratively (the quest for true love) and thematically (what defines life and living), what actually happens in the story (the plot sequence and elements), the characters of Bob, Alice and whomever (or whatever) might be in the story, the world and setting the story takes place in (is it our realistic world, or something more heightened or stylized?) and the overall style and tone of the story (tongue-in-cheek? serious and gory?). For us, the intellectual property is all of the narrative-related creative components.

As transmedia-makers we care about all of these things because these are our building blocks. Our main project may directly tell the story of Bob and Alice, but we can create a tie-in novel that deals with Alice's backstory before she met Bob, or an interactive tablet game that focuses on Fizzle, her sarcastic but equally ghostly cat sidekick. We can tell other stories of other ghosts in the world, or if there's a ghostly version of our world we can tell stories there.

All these components, all these elements – *story/theme*, *plot*, *character*, *setting* and to some extent *style/tone* (which informs the other elements) – are valued parts of our intellectual property. If our property is solid, they are all working together to support each other and if they aren't, there will be problems. As transmedia-makers, we have to understand how all these parts fit together since in many ways it is a big three-dimensional puzzle; moving or changing one of the pieces in the wrong way could blow the whole thing apart.

Throughout the book we'll use the terms *intellectual property* and *property* synonymously. We'll use the terms *platform* or *medium* to refer to the type of expression of the property, such as motion picture, television series, video game, novel, comic book and so on. So a given intellectual property can have multiple expressions on a variety of platforms or media.

We'll also use the term *franchise*, and for a long time franchise and intellectual property basically meant the same thing. We're going to broaden the term franchise to include the intellectual property, all of the various platform expressions, all of the marketing … everything, the whole burrito related to the property and how the market experiences or access it. (And that's the last crappy food analogy we're going to use. We hope.)

Stumbling Toward Transmedia

While we can talk about the ideal transmedia development process as the careful planning and development of a larger narrative that has a coordinated presentation to its audience via multiple methods or storytelling platforms, the reality is that there are few great examples of that process … yet. Many of the properties we might call transmedia include iterations of story that were not conceived simultaneously, but rather were created sequentially. *Alien* (20th Century Fox, 1979) did not start out as larger intellectual property, but grew from the original motion picture to a sequel (*Aliens*, 20th Century Fox, 1986) that spawned its own sequel (*Alien³*, 20th Century Fox, 1992) and branched out into video games, comics, novels and additional films, and even crossed over into two other film franchises, *Aliens vs. Predator* (20th Century Fox, 2004) and *Prometheus* (20th Century Fox, 2012).

The process here is similar to building a house by adding rooms to a small existing structure (a shed perhaps?) rather than designing and creating a blueprint for all the house's rooms at once. Our goal in transmedia development is to design a house – not build a room and then keep adding to it. We want to treat transmedia as simultaneous development of its various (or at least its initial multiple) expressions rather than think of it as a sequential series of additions to the mythology, themes, conflicts and universe.

For all these reasons, you will see the term transmedia used in a variety of ways to refer to a variety of projects and intellectual properties, regardless of how they came about. At best, we can identify some of the ideal defining characteristics for transmedia, but the terminology is still in flux. The bottom line is that transmedia *storytelling* is about *story*, a story whose individual components have to capture the imagination and fully engage an audience who wants to discover a larger universe filled with narrative possibilities. And *transmedia storytelling* is what we are all about.

Transmedia Storytelling for Producers

We've just gone on somewhat about what transmedia storytelling is, isn't and might be to some. Since we're targeted this book at both producers and creatives currently working in different media it makes sense to first define what we mean by a "producer"… and that depends on what medium we're talking about. (We'll look at transmedia for creatives later in this chapter.)

Different media (and we're focusing on our "big three" here – motion pictures, television and video games) define the term "producer" differently and in fact they have different roles and responsibilities in each of those media. Though we're going to touch on each of those and their differences, in many ways we're really talking about any producer of transmedia narrative properties, which is to say any individual responsible for overseeing and managing one or more interconnected transmedia narrative projects. The credit/title of transmedia producer that we mentioned earlier is one bestowed by the Producers Guild of America and pertains to motion picture and television projects under their jurisdiction, but members of the Producers Guild aren't going to be the only managers, coordinators or facilitators of transmedia narrative properties.

First, let's look at the different roles of producers in each medium and then a look again at who a transmedia producer (as per the Producers Guild) or transmedia producer (not part of the Producers Guild) could be. Each of the examples below are quick-and-dirty explanations for those who may not know what each type of producer does in the different areas. (If you are in that medium as a producer, you know full well that your role and responsibility is far more complicated than we've depicted here, for brevity's sake.)

Motion picture producers: In motion pictures, the designations and roles for members of the producing team have evolved over the decades. Currently, there are several tiers of producer titles, but the ones most pertinent to us as transmedia storytellers are executive producer, producer (sometimes now referred to as creative producer but still credited as producer) and line producer.

The motion picture executive producer's role is primarily one of financial and organizational responsibility. It is also the executive producer's responsibility to act as a liaison to the producing studio, as well as any independent backers.

The (creative) producer finds the original idea, hires the scriptwriters and director, helps develop the story material into a producible script, and helps bring together the financing. The producer then coordinates and oversees the actual production of the motion picture with the assistance of the line producer, who keeps an eye on and manages the schedule and budget on a day-to-day basis. A motion picture producer has supervisory business and creative responsibilities for the production and has direct participation in the decision making, but is not an implementer of those decisions. Line producers will coordinate between departments, oversee logistics, and facilitate the day-to-day running of the production.

In smaller independent productions these different producing roles might be combined.

Television producers: There are actually different professional descriptions of the television producer depending on if they are working on a long-form (television movie) or series production. Long-form producers have roles and responsibilities very similar to their motion picture counterparts. Producers of television series have different responsibilities. The television series executive producer has the final responsibility for all of the business and creative aspects of the production and is responsible to the financial backers of the series. The executive producer is often also referred to as the showrunner, which in a nutshell explains his role and responsibility. On some series the head writer also receives the title of executive producer. Producers, as listed in television series credits, may have financial and budget responsibilities for the show, or they may be staff writers on the program. Producers with day-to-day production responsibilities are usually designated by the title coordinating producer or associate producer.

Video game producers: The exact role of a producer in video games varies somewhat depending on the company making the game. In some companies, the executive producer is the senior creative and production team member, with overall authority on the project. In some companies that responsibility is split between a creative director (creative) and executive producer (budgetary and coordination.) Again, depending on the company, and the relationship between the publisher (financial backer) of the project and the development studio (the production house), the executive producer may be working at the publisher, or may be on-staff at the developer, in which case the individual responsible at the publisher is known as the project or product manager. Producers are usually on-staff at the development house and are responsible for working with the production team on budget, scheduling and coordination issues. Sometimes, though, the publisher has a producer also attached to the project. Confused yet? Welcome to the game industry …

What this all means is that depending on which medium you are working in and which medium those you are working with are in, similar titles could very well mean different roles and responsibilities. So, understand that your title of producer in one medium may not entail the same responsibilities as someone titled producer in a different medium. We're singling out these particular producer roles because even though the Producers Guild has recognized the transmedia producer credit for their members, producers in other fields (particularly video games) are very often involved in transmedia storytelling projects. For the remainder of this section, however, we're going to roll all the "producers" out there together and use the term to refer to someone who, to use the Producers Guild definition is:

> *the person(s) responsible for a significant portion of a project's long-term planning, development, production and/or maintenance of narrative continuity across multiple platforms and creation of original storylines for new platforms. Transmedia producers also create and implement interactive endeavors to unite the audience of the property with the canonical narrative and this element should be considered as valid qualification for credit as long as they are related directly to the narrative presentation of a project.*

Producers Guild of America, Code of Credits – New Media[5]

The Role of the Transmedia Producer

Remembering that the language in the preceding section defines a transmedia narrative property or franchise as consisting of three or more narrative storylines existing in the same fictional universe on multiple platforms, it becomes very clear that someone who is a transmedia producer could be doing so from a great number of entry points. There's a commonality to the responsibilities of "producer" as well in the explanation of the different types of producers in motion pictures, television and video games that applies to the transmedia producer as well. Let's lay them out:

- Finding the idea
- Determining the scope/setting the budget

[5] accessed July 20, 2012, http://www.producersguild.org/?page=coc_nm#transmedia

- Building the team
- Setting the schedule
- Overseeing production

We address many of the bullet points above in sections throughout this book, but some we do not, or only lightly touch upon, because they are so specific to particular circumstances. We're going to look at each of them briefly in the following sections and then leave you to dig into details later on.

Finding the Idea

This usually comes about in one of two ways – you seek an original property to build a transmedia franchise from, or you are associated with an existing intellectual property that is expanding through transmedia storytelling. To a large extent in this book we're assuming the latter, but everything that we talk about pertains equally to what would make an original property or an existing one successful as a transmedia storytelling property. It does require careful analysis and consideration: transmedia storytelling does not happen by magic. You cannot simply decide to extend a property through transmedia storytelling and expect success, as the managerial, production and creative processes involved are complex and sometimes cumbersome. Frankly it's hard, and if it wasn't, everyone would be doing it successfully all the time, and they're not. We're not trying to dissuade anyone from undertaking a transmedia narrative project, but it is important to understand that the degree of difficulty (to toss in the obligatory sports metaphor) is notably higher than the already significant challenges present in producing a story-driven property in a single medium.

Hopefully this book will help you identify the elements of a successful transmedia storytelling property and understand what needs to be done to bring it to life.

Determining the Scope/Setting the Budget

How big, how many properties, how many stories … these are all difficult questions to ask and answer. This is somewhat of a cop-out answer, but so much depends on the particulars of the specific project. Understanding the realities of your budget and production realities will in and of itself answer many of the scope questions. A major motion picture of the summer blockbuster variety can cost upwards of $150 million, while limited-scope productions like *Paranormal Activity* (Paramount Pictures, 2007) can cost in the tens of thousands of dollars and still be very successful both commercially and artistically. A television series can likewise cost millions of dollars an episode, whereas the webisode series content of a transmedia project like *Collider* (www.colliderworld.com) costs magnitudes less. Video game development for a huge Playstation 3/Xbox 360/PC project like *Mass Effect 3* (Electronic Arts, 2012) can easily cost tens of millions of dollars (and then some), but a web-delivered or mobile game such as the *Doctor Who: The Mazes of Time* (BBC Worldwide, 2010) game for the iPad costs significantly less. Novels, comic books and graphic novels are all viable alternatives on a limited budget, but have differing levels of impact and different exposure patterns.

While budget and scope are production reality issues, the creative scope must also be considered as well. Transmedia storytelling projects can get narratively big and unwieldy quickly as multiple projects have to be cross-referenced for consistency and continuity. How much new story material will be created and how quickly? Who has to review and approve it all? How quickly does this approval process have to happen in order for the various projects to stay on schedule? Again, there are no simple answers. A screenplay might be relatively easy to vet, whereas as the contents of a novel are significantly denser … but a motion picture has visual and production design elements (costumes, makeup, etc.) that have to be reviewed. Who's going to do that and how quickly?

One obvious course of action in trying to overcome budgetary constraints is to reach out to production partners who are willing to take on part of the financial risk in return for some of the profits. These can be complex deals to achieve and may themselves be outside the scope of a brand-new transmedia franchise. It is easier to find production partners for properties with established track-records, or properties from producers with established track-records.

Building the Team

Perhaps the single most important thing a transmedia producer can do is find the right people for the right job. One of the purposes of this book is to introduce producers and creatives who currently exist in one of the common transmedia storytelling property mediums to enough aspects of the other mediums that they can carry on a conversation with other practitioners. But we're not trying to turn everyone who reads these pages into an expert at everything. Those who are truly multi-medium savants are few and far between, so we strongly advocate that the transmedia producer seek out those who are skilled in a particular medium to create for that medium.

Ideally, you want a team that has some inter-disciplinary knowledge or experience, but it is more important to make sure that the person hired to write your kick-ass screenplay knows how to write for motion pictures, and that the team that you hire to design your awesome iPad game has experience making video games. Don't fall into the trap of assuming too much overlap in the skill sets of those experienced in these different areas. Continuing the previous example, writing a great story for a motion picture is not the same as writing a great story for a video game, even though both are visual mediums that seem to have a great deal in common.

So, it is important that the team you assemble to oversee the transmedia storytelling properties is either comprised of those individually strong in the different areas, or have some multi-disciplinary knowledge themselves. It is also important that whoever on the transmedia property management team that is interfacing with those producing material in a particular medium is able to speak-the-speak of that medium. Being able to at least somewhat walk-the-walk and actually having some real production experience in that area is even better. Nothing is a substitute for actually making something in the medium.

Lastly, make sure the people you hire are passionate about your project, truly and deeply, since that passion manifests in what they produce. Their technical skills need to be up to snuff, but their energy level and love of your property have to match that. Be careful of production or development studios that can muster a great pitch for your project, but don't have a team backing them that matches that vim and vigor. You are handing off your baby, your prized possession, to acquaintances … spend the time making sure that they're the right people for the job.

Setting the Schedule

Knowing in what order to release the elements of a transmedia storytelling property is an art. You could go big and release the primary property and then trail any secondary or ancillary material a short time after it, and then release a medium-sized project a little time after that to keep interest up. Alternatively, you could release some smaller transmedia narrative pieces before the primary property to build anticipation and then debut the main project.

Many of the answers to these questions are determined by the realities of your projects and the realities of the markets you are releasing into. In many ways, this is more of a question of the marketing strategy that you choose for the property. We're stumbling into cart-before-the-horse or chicken-or-the-egg territory here, but how you decide to use transmedia to tell your story could affect your release schedule, but in all likelihood your marketing strategy will have as much impact as anything else. Will you need to fund and produce viral videos? Can your project be teased through a broad under-the-radar social media campaign? Do you want to release your webisodes all before the primary platform release, or just before and continue with more through the release? We'll get more into the marketing aspects of your transmedia property, but be prepared to find out that the release schedule and its impact on what projects you can produce, and vice-versa, is as complicated as producing the actual story material.

Understanding the timetables of the different mediums in production is one critical aspect of setting the schedule. (In Part Two we talk about how long it takes to make something in each major transmedia storytelling medium and how much risk there is in terms of production schedule.) Once you understand how long it is going to take to make each different project or expression you can create a schedule that staggers the production start times so that everything releases in relation to the other elements.

As an example, it is difficult to create video game tie-ins for major motion pictures because of the realities of production scheduling. Depending on the length of postproduction, the time from when a script is green-lit (approved for production) to when it launches in theatres can be significantly shorter than the time it takes to make a video game of comparable scale and scope. So, if you are making a big-budget action film the realities of production scheduling could require you to start the video game development *before* the studio approves your script for production. Clearly this could be problematic, both in terms of financing and of content creation if there isn't a final, or near-final, script available for the game developers to spring-board from. This means that either the scale and scope of the video game has to be narrowed to fit the production time, or the game's schedule has to be compressed and rushed, significantly increasing the risk of creating a flawed or inadequate game. If, however, the project was conceived as a true transmedia narrative property, the motion picture script and the game design could be developed simultaneously and synergistically with funding arranged for the entire project, not just the piecemeal elements as they ramp up into production. You can probably guess which approach we advocate.

Overseeing Production

Once the various transmedia narrative elements are in production, the best thing a transmedia producer can do is let his skilled teams do their job, while keeping an eye on them to insure that not only are they doing what they're supposed to be doing, but they're doing it well and at the level of quality the project demands. It is difficult for the transmedia producer to find the right balance of hands-off or hands-on interaction with the projects in production, and in truth how firm of a hand to apply will be based entirely on the projects, the teams and the producer. Please remember our warnings about making sure that whoever is providing feedback or guidance to a particular production team knows how to talk-the-talk in that area and has some relevant experience.

"Trust, but verify" is a great piece of advice when overseeing transmedia narrative productions, or really productions of any kind. If you've hired the right people for the job, you need to let them do their job … at the same time you need to be sure they're doing it the way it needs to be done, without constantly interfering with their process or progress. (If you really truly figure out a best practices way to do that, please let us know!)

Audience, Presentation and Platforms

Hopefully, as you are selecting or creating a transmedia narrative property you consider who the audience for this property is going to be. Nailing down who your audience is and how big an audience you are going for (with the overall property and with each element of it) will tell you a lot about how you're going to tell your stories.

First, unless you are venturing out into completely unknown market territory, look at what's come before you, both in traditional linear presentation and in transmedia narrative (if any). If there haven't been any transmedia narrative ventures in the area that you're looking at, you need to look at similar linear ventures in each of the mediums you're targeting. Deconstruct what's worked and what hasn't. Figure out if there were key elements that helped its success, or notable areas that contributed to its failure. Learn from the past.

Look at the demographics of those who consume the different types of media and the different genres presented by each. Is the belief that fantasy attracts a younger, more female audience true? Or that hard-core science fiction is predominantly male and older? You need to know. Don't be seduced by the apparent power of demographics, however – think about who *could* or *should* be a market for your property as well.

That said, if you are doing a show like ABC Television's *LOST* (2004–2010), you need to understand who watched that show, and why. You need to figure out who consumed that franchise's transmedia content, and why. You also need to understand why NBC's *The Event* (2010–2011) or Fox's *Alcatraz* (2012) failed to recreate the *LOST* formula. Was it the narrative? Was it the production? Was it the transmedia content (or lack thereof?) Were there other factors (time slot, current events, etc.) that contributed to the misfire?

Also start to understand how the audience you've chosen for your transmedia franchise consumes media. The old media ingestion patterns are changing … you're thinking of a television show, but does your target market still watch television as we've traditionally considered it? Clearly many still do watch television shows, but is it as habitual and reflexive as it used to be, or are viewers lured to that medium by exposure in other mediums that they spend more hours per week in? Are they social media followers or broadcasters? Focusing on the idea of the television series just as an example, does your audience view the airing of a new episode as a "must-see" time and date event that requires them to be ready to watch on their couch when the episode first airs, or are they time-shifters who record the show and then watch it at their convenience, or catch it on-demand or via some other off-time broadcast technology? Do you care? Do you want your show to be a continual burn where the conversation plays out over the time between episodes, or do you want the conversation – be it online or at the water cooler – to spike the day after the episode airs? What can you do to maximize that decision? Is there additional content you can release the day after to drive the spike, or other content to trickle out over the week to maintain the burn?

These are all strategies for managing the transmedia property that depend a great deal on the audience you are engaging. We talk more about engagement later in this chapter, but understand that knowing your audience is required for understanding how to engage them.

Presentation and Platform

When we say platform we're referring to the media delivery or presentation system. For example, a motion picture that shows in theatres and is then distributed via Blu-ray/DVD as well as Netflix and cable-on-demand is being presented on three platforms, with the greatest distinction being between the first and the last two as a group. The least distinction is between the last two, Netflix and cable-on-demand, because they are both video-on-demand systems accessible through the same, or similar technologies (living room TVs or set-top boxes, game consoles and home computers).

Given the blending of production and presentation technologies, some of the platform distinctions get rather blurry, especially since elsewhere in this book we'll be looking at the various platforms in terms of the storytelling impact, at which time you'll see the lines move all over the place.

We're seeing more and more secondary content effort put into so-called "second screen" experiences where a viewer at home can access additional behind-the-scenes or narrative content on their laptop or tablet while a television episode is airing. This isn't all that different, conceptually, from some of the on-screen, or picture-in-picture commentary or behind-the-scenes features available on Blu-ray or standard DVDs, but the technology behind it and the user experience are different.

Microsoft's Xbox SmartGlass technology is, as the maker described it in a press release on June 4, 2012 "an application for Windows 8, Windows Phone and other portable devices that connects phones, PCs and tablets with your Xbox console to make your entertainment smarter, more interactive and more fun." Is the platform the Xbox? Is it a movie DVD or Netflix stream playing on the Xbox, or is it the tablet used to manipulate the interactive content? How long before Sony comes out with a competitor for the PlayStation 3/PlayStation Network, and should we view that as a different platform? The answer is complicated.

Building on this example, we group the major video game consoles – the Microsoft Xbox, the Sony PlayStation 3, the Nintendo Wii/Wii U – into one platform often referred to simply as "game consoles," yet the home computer is often viewed as a separate platform due to the difference in the user location (office vs. living room) and the control input (keyboard/mouse vs. game controller). Given the increasing number of home theatre personal computers that sit in the living room, game consoles that sit on the desk or multi-platform games that are released on both game consoles and for the home computer, the platform distinction seems fuzzy (especially in terms of storytelling.)

The decision that a video game is going to be a platform for the transmedia franchise is, initially, a more important one than which game console, home computer, portable game system and so on is to be supported. That decision can be made later when it comes time to look into partnership and production realities. Initial platform decisions for transmedia franchises need to be made in terms of user experience not technology implementation.

So, what are the platforms to consider?

Motion Pictures

We're all pretty familiar with motion pictures and when we talk about them in this book, understand we are talking about the common cinema experience – a linearly presented audio/visual experience undertaken out of the home, in a movie theatre, with a crowd of (presumably) strangers. Budget is initially irrelevant and whether the movie was recorded on film or high-definition video or is being projected on film or digitally is irrelevant as well.

The important thing to understand about the medium is this:

- The audience has to learn about it from another source (though they may have learned about it from a trailer at another movie).
- The audience has to be engaged or interested enough to change their schedule to accommodate the time and place of the presentation.
- The audience has to be engaged enough to incur all of the associated costs (gas, parking, tickets, food, time, etc.) with the presentation.
- The experience is transitory, meaning that it occurs and is done. If the audience wants to repeat the experience they have to repeat the entire process. (Or experience the production again, albeit differently, with the Blu-ray/DVD or video-on-demand release.)
- The experience is passive – the audience watches and does not interact (shouting at the screen does not count).

- Setting and character elements are presented in an intense manner that tend to lock an audience's perception. (For example, many movie goers who go to see an adaptation of a favorite book report that after seeing the movie they see and hear the characters in the book as the actors they saw on screen.)

Yes, your motion picture can be experienced on Blu-ray/DVD or through video-on-demand, but those are secondary channels for the primary medium. If you are directly targeting Blu-ray/DVD or video-on-demand distribution your production decisions will probably be different, and more like those of television discussed next.

For more on motion pictures, see Chapter 3 of this book.

Television

We should all also be familiar with television and television series. We've also seen a significant shift in the presentation options for television series in recent years, with the experience transitioning from a "you must be ready on your couch at 9 pm" to anywhere, anytime, when-you-want-it viewing. When we're talking about a television series we're talking about episodic television, be it a limited duration mini-series or multi-season television series. If you are producing a made-for-TV movie, your production decisions probably have more in common with motion pictures than television series.

And if we're talking about episodic television as a format, we're really looking at a variety of possible platforms for content delivery. Short-form episodic content could be produced as webisodes for delivery through the Internet or a mobile platform. The traditional television series content is now delivered through "normal" broadcast or cable channels, via video-on-demand (especially with Netflix producing original content), or through various Internet broadcasting services, including Netflix, Hulu, Crackle and others. Regardless of the final delivery methodology, many of the important considerations are the same:

- The audience may have learned about it from another source entirely, or it may have been through advertising on the delivery channel.
- With the rise of on-demand viewing and time-shifting, the audience can alter their viewing patterns to match the rest of their schedule. This is a profound change from when the scheduling of when the viewer had to be in front of the television affected other scheduling decisions.
- Putting aside channel subscription costs, which viewers do not normally associate with the viewing of one particular episode or series, there is no immediately perceived financial cost to sitting down to watch a television show, so the required level of engagement to compel watching is reduced. This also means that it is easier to ignore or defer. Video-on-demand (VOD) or rental window decisions are made at the time of purchase so the return on dollars spent is immediate.
- Digital video recorders mean that television viewers can retain the broadcast program for as long as their technology permits. Some viewers let a number of episodes of their favorite show "pile up" and then watch them all in a mini-marathon.
- Related to the above point, some viewers of television series will wait until the program is released on Blu-ray/DVD and then watch the entire season or large chunks of it one after the other. One view of this phenomenon is that some viewers become impatient with the gap between episode broadcasts and want their absorption of the property to occur in bulk, as it were. One benefit of transmedia storytelling is that it can be used successfully to bridge those gaps and keep the audience sated longer.
- The experience itself is passive – the audience watches and does not interact (and, as we have said before, in motion pictures, shouting at the screen does not count). The presentation, if on disk or video-on-demand can

be interacted with in that pause or rewind can be used to alter the flow of presentation, but the content itself does not change.

- Setting and character elements are presented in an intense manner that tend to lock an audience's perception of the characters and story.

The increasing amount of additional material provided on Blu-ray/DVD releases of television series (regardless of their origin) reflects not only a value-added marketing perspective for increasing the buy-appeal of the product, but also of increasing the transmedia content. Note the inclusion of additional un-aired "between-the-episodes" scenes in the recent compilation releases of the current BBC *Doctor Who* series and the second-screen content provided during the original and repeat broadcasts of HBO's *Game of Thrones* (2011–present) series.

For more on television and television series, see Chapter 4 of this book.

Video Games

Frankly, video game development is probably the production area the majority of readers of this book know the least about. Compared to motion pictures and television, the medium is relatively new but has grown to rival both in terms of participation and awareness, cultural impact and even production budget and profits. Video games have platform fragmentation similar to the presentation of television series, but in some ways it is more profound because the primary distinctive element of video games – interaction and gameplay – differs significantly depending on where and how the game is played. When we talk about games, we're talking about console (Xbox, PlayStation 3, Wii), home computer (PC or Mac), portable (Nintendo 3DS or Sony PlayStation Vita), web-delivered (Flash, Java and most recently HTML5), or mobile (iOS or Android). There's a production problem associated with video games as well. While you can produce a motion picture for the theatre and you can convert it relatively easily for distribution via Blu-ray/DVD, broadcast television, or video-on-demand, the same it not true for video games. There is no easy way to translate a game between the different game platforms we just listed. Some are easier than others (Xbox to PC, for example, or iOS to Android depending on the production methodology), but in general different releases of the same game on different platforms require parallel or near-parallel development and production efforts. We just hit on an important thing to understand about this medium, but here are some others:

- The audience has to learn about it from another source.
- The audience is able to engage in the product when they choose (for the most part) either at home at their convenience, or out of the home at their convenience on a mobile or portable platform. Both of these, however, assume the game can be relatively easily stopped and then returned to (at that same point) some other time.
- Console and video games are relatively expensive – roughly a $60 price point for console games and roughly a $40–50 price point for the same game on the personal computer. This makes the purchase of the game an expensive proposition for some game players and requires budget planning and consideration if multiple high-profile or desired games are releasing relatively close to each other. Mobile and smaller console or personal computer games have lower price points (from free or $0.99 to less than $10 for mobile games, to roughly $40 for portable games) with those in the lower price range (especially on mobile) profiting (pardon the pun) from the impulse buy price point.
- Gamers expect long games. Large-scale role-playing games like *Skyrim* are expected to include 40+ hours of gameplay, while high-profile action titles like *Mass Effect 3* or the *Modern Warfare* series come under serious criticism if they take less than 12 hours to complete.

- Video games generally have "difficulty levels" which affects how hard or easy the game is, and can therefore radically change the experience. Additionally, some recent story-driven games explicitly call out a "story" or "cinema" mode as the description of one of the easy game difficulties.
- Multiplayer gaming, where game players can play directly against other players competitively or (less frequently) cooperatively using the Internet or dedicated services like Microsoft's Xbox Live or Sony's PlayStation Network, is becoming more and more expected.
- The experience is inherently interactive – video game players expect to feel like participants in the storytelling (whether they really are or not) and not just observers or along for the narrative ride. Games are about what the main character does, not what the player watches.

It is important to understand that video games, in terms of conception, production and to some extent distribution are very different beasts from motion pictures and television series. See Chapter 5 of this book for more on video game development.

Comic Books and Graphic Novels

Comic books and graphic novels are a great medium for transmedia storytelling, both as an intellectual property source and as a medium to extend the narrative. They are visually dynamic (be sure to check out the new generation of interactive comics available on tablets, like Marvel's Infinite Comics format), capable of powerful storytelling and relatively inexpensive to produce, market and distribute. Beyond the "big two" publishers of Marvel Comics (owned by Disney) and DC Comics (owned by Warner Brothers), there are scores of smaller and independent creators, studios and publishers able to partner with you to deliver your transmedia experience.

Some things to consider:

- The audience probably learned about it in connection to your transmedia franchise, or if they are comic book or graphic novel fans, they may have come across it without knowing the connection to your property and may now be drawn to it.
- The audience is able to engage in the product when and where they choose, especially with digital distribution to mobile and portable devices.
- The cost of entry is relatively affordable for a single comic book, to more expensive than a movie ticket or video-on-demand rental, but less than the cost of a Blu-ray/DVD seasonal boxed set.
- Comic book and graphic novel readers tend to be collectors and so there is additional attraction to having something permanent to return to in the future. The impact of digital distribution and mobile presentation on this aspect isn't yet known.
- In physical form the experience is passive, but the new-generation of interactive comics allows a linear interaction. The story doesn't change, but the viewer feels a degree of control over the presentation.

For more on comic books and graphic novels, see Chapter 6 of this book.

Novels

Hopefully your community still has a bookstore. Go there. Walk into the science fiction and fantasy section and look for what is probably the single largest sub-section there – the movie, TV and video game tie-in novels. There you'll find novels (and comics and graphic novels) set in the universes of *Star Wars*, *Star Trek*, *Doctor Who*, *Dungeons and Dragons*, *Underworld*, *Halo*, *Supernatural*, *Mass Effect*, *Warhammer: 40,000*, *Assassin's Creed*, *Gears of War*, and others, including continuations of canceled television series like *Buffy the Vampire Slayer*, *Stargate Atlantis*, and *Charmed*.

Some are adaptations of motion pictures or television episodes, but the majority of them are original stories. (Whether they are "official" stories and part of the franchise canon varies. See the section in Chapter 3 called Continuity, Canon and Consistency as to why that could be very important to a transmedia property.)

Even if your community doesn't have a bookstore, the growing popularity of dedicated e-readers and e-reader software for the various mobile platforms shows that the consumption of novels, especially adaptation and tie-ins (transmedia storytelling or not) remains high. Like comic books and graphic novels, traditional novels are a great way to extend and support your transmedia narrative relatively inexpensively and with significant impact and beyond the big publishers. There are scores of smaller and independent publishers able to partner with you to deliver your transmedia experience.

Some things to consider:

- The audience probably learned about it in connection to your transmedia franchise, or if they are avid readers they may have come across it without knowing the connection to your property and may now be drawn to it.
- The audience is able to engage in the product when and where they choose, especially with digital distribution to mobile and portable devices.
- The cost of entry is relatively affordable for a paperback novel, about the same as for a movie ticket. Hardbacks not so much.
- Novel readers tend to be collectors and so there is additional attraction to having something permanent to return to in the future. The impact of digital distribution and mobile presentation on this aspect isn't yet known.
- The increase in the use of e-readers and software cannot be underestimated as it increases the opportunities for digital or direct distribution and reduces the price point. See the next section on Mobile Apps for additional possibilities.

For more on traditional novels, see Chapter 6 of this book.

Mobile Apps

Separate from games are a whole category of applications (programs) for mobile platforms that can be created in support of your transmedia storytelling property. We're already talked about second-screen support for Blu-ray/DVD releases or for television series accomplished through mobile apps and there are scores of other opportunities. For example, there is a popular iOS app for the Apple iPhone and iPad called the *Game of Thrones Companion*, which acts as a reference work to the characters, places and events of the George R. R. Martin novel series *A Song of Ice and Fire* (Bantam Books, 1996–present), upon which the HBO television series *Game of Thrones* is based. The fan-produced app is not an official or licensed release from either the novel series publisher or HBO, and at the time of this writing remains for sale in the iTunes store. (There are other similar apps also available in the iTunes store.) It is fan-produced, much like many popular websites produced in support of motion picture, television or video game franchises. Interestingly, again at the time of this writing, HBO has not elected to produce a stand-alone app in support of *Game of Thrones*, presumably relying on the content and experience provided by their own second-screen capabilities built into their *HBOGO* app, but there is no reason they could not produce an app that is synchronously tied to a television episode that provides similar, but not identical, functionality.

Interactive novels, which are not technically games though often grouped with them, are another avenue for providing transmedia storytelling support for your franchise. There are a large number of apps that are nearly identical structurally to the tried-and-true "Choose Your Own Adventure" format books, as well as many others with significantly enhanced audio-visual components. (Check out Her Interactive's 2011 *Nancy Drew: Shadow Ranch HD* for the Apple iPad for one example.) Additionally, there is no reason the wonderful "viral" videos produced for the summer 2012 motion picture release of Ridley Scott's *Prometheus* couldn't easily have been assembled with other discoveries into an engaging piece of transmedia storytelling disguised as an app from the Weyland Corporation. (See our interview with Phil Hay later in the book for some thoughts on this.) There's no question that many of these opportunities overlap with marketing initiatives, but it's very easy to slip some real transmedia storytelling into these products.

The Internet

This is a big subject with bigger opportunities. The most important thing to understand about the Internet is that it's just a delivery and interaction mechanism for nearly anything that you can think of to support your transmedia storytelling project. Instead of trying to address the Internet as one big thing, let's break down some things that it can do:

Content distribution: the Internet can deliver audio-video content in a variety of forms and styles. We'll talk about it in Chapter 4, but the web presence built for the NBC television series *Heroes* (2006–2010) with its co-complimentary assortment of video, graphic novel and other methodologies did a great job of pulling fans of the series to the website to give them more of what they wanted and equally pushed those who discovered and were intrigued by the website independently toward the television series. We already mentioned the character-driven video teasers for the motion picture *Prometheus* that appeared scattered across a variety of sources prior to the film's release. (We'll get to audience communication in a moment, but a quick trip to http://www.prometheus-movie.com shows how they blended the motion-picture marketing support site with the fan engagement/discussion site. We're not fans of blackmailing fans by making them sign up to remove the annoying external ad content, however. It's important to create and maintain a direct channel (in this case, email) to your property's fan base, but we're not sure that annoying them to get them to sign up is the best way to do it.)

YouTube and similar services are well known for video content delivery, but exclusive use also means surrendering branding and presentation control of your content. Fortunately, many of these services allow you to make use of their delivery infrastructure while keeping the content (primarily) on websites under your direct control. Other content distribution services, such as Akamai, are also available but aren't free. There can also be issues of content ownership when material is placed on sites like YouTube, Facebook, Google+ or similar services with complex end-user license agreements.

Audience communication: Audience participation and engagement is critical to the success of a transmedia storytelling property. We talk about exactly that in its own section, but these days the Internet (and we're going to include social media like Facebook and Twitter under that umbrella) is the primary channel for communication to and from your audience. Name a popular genre motion picture, television series, video game, novel or graphic novel series and you are more than likely to find more than one official and/or fan-driven website out there. Some of them are more, shall we say, professional and polished than others, and for that reason it is often wise to create a home for your property on the Internet and try and direct traffic and interest to that site, while at the same time encouraging and supporting fan-based sites. (Fans, bless 'em, 'cause we include ourselves in with them, aren't always able to match their enthusiasm with web design and content management skills.)

If you are lucky, your audience is going to want to talk about your property and it is better they do it where you can see what is being said and can respond to it. Yes, respond to it. We're not saying your showrunners or lead writers should be constantly responding to audience chatter, but there's real value in having some form of community manager who can answer questions, guide discussions and generally act as a liaison between the audience and the franchise. The more an audience feels part of the process, even superficially, the more engaged they are and the more loyal.

Overt and viral marketing: Hopefully it is obvious that the Internet is a great way of directing relatively low-cost impact at very specific demographic groups. This isn't just through buying ads on relevant websites, but through maintaining solid promotional relationships with existing blogs and media sites. When the Paramount/Bad Robot J. J. Abrams *Star Trek* revival was underway in 2007–2009, its makers understood that they had to not only broaden the appeal of the franchise in order to re-ignite it, but they had to reach out to the existing hardcore fan base who was more than a little nervous about what was being produced. In 2006 *Star Trek* fan Anthony Pascale started a fan blog at www.trekmovie.com dedicated to following events of the movie as it entered preproduction, production and beyond. The site quickly became one of the "go-to" sites on the Internet for information and discussion about the upcoming film, so much so that *Star Trek* executive producer and co-writer Roberto Orci started regularly visiting the site and posting in its discussion threads under the not-so-pseudonym "boborci." While television showrunners like Ron Moore (*Battlestar Galactica* Sci-Fi, 2004–2009) and J. Michael Straczynski (*Babylon 5* Warner Brothers Television, 1994–1998) are well-known for their frequent direct communication with their fan base, it was pretty unheard of for feature films of the magnitude of the *Star Trek* film. To many, however, Orci's presence and willingness to discuss his thoughts and views on *Star Trek* in general and discuss the current production (within reason) proved a major public relations boon for the production with the hardcore fan base. This level of communication with fans has become typical for most Bad Robot productions since then. We would argue that this approach came naturally to Bad Robot writers/producers like Roberto Orci, Alex Kurtzman and *LOST's* Damon Lindelof, who also see themselves as fans and understand exactly what a franchise needs to interest them and keep them engaged and so are willing to provide exactly that to the fans of their own work (within reason).

All of the above is pretty overt, and there's an entire sub-genre of marketing known as "viral" marketing where video clips, images, entire websites, fictitious web accounts, web-based games, social media messaging and a variety of other techniques are used to lure potential fans to more directly branded franchise sites. Sometimes the marketing campaign has an overt component that connects to vaguer viral elements that reflect back to the main campaign. Sometimes the viral campaign has only tangential connections to the property being supported, as was the case with 42 Entertainment's *I Love Bees* 2004 alternate reality game (ARG) masterminded by company founder and veteran game design Jordan Weisman and built to promote the Microsoft/Bungie Xbox game *Halo 2*. (We'll talk more about alternate reality games in the next section and elsewhere, and you'll find an interview with Weisman later in this book.)

One of the interesting things about *I Love Bees* was that it was only loosely related to the *Halo 2* and *Halo* franchise storyline. Later, some of the elements present in the alternate reality game were formally added to the *Halo* Universe in supplemental material. What *I Love Bees* did, however, was get *Halo's* potential audience wound up and talking about the game's story and universe. In a very real way it generated a buzz that simple advertising and marketing may not have been able to.

Alternate Reality Games

Alternate reality games use real-world technology, devices, locations and sometimes people to create an engaging story-driven experience for its players. There are always one or more mysteries to be solved and a long, involved chain of clues scattered around the real world (or real world accessible) that as unveiled tell the game's story. ARGs aren't video games in the traditional sense even though computers, cell phones and other mobile devices are often used as part of the discovery process. Alternate reality games may also rely on actors playing key character roles and real world events and interactions to help tell the story.

A key element of an alternate reality game is that the players of the game often act cooperatively to solve the mystery with fan-produced websites and discussion forums appearing specifically to compare notes and exchange clues, because a key component is that no single player can discover all of the clues and solve the mysteries on their own. This led to early ARGs, like *The Beast* created by Microsoft (and Jordan Weisman again) in support of Steven Spielberg's 2001 motion picture *A.I. Artificial Intelligence* or Electronic Art's 2001 Windows game *Majestic*, having to scramble to keep up with content production as collaborative groups of users found and solved mysteries at a staggering pace.

Alternate reality games are inherently transmedia and in fact the ARG community (perhaps rightly) takes a great deal of ownership in the term. All forms of media are routinely used in an ARG, often simultaneously and synchronously, to propel the story. The fact that alternate reality games exist in so many shapes and forms, from the aforementioned *I Love Bees*, to the Audi car promotion *The Art of the Heist*, to the puzzle-card driven *Perplex City*, to *Why So Serious ...* for *The Dark Knight* motion picture, to ABC TV's *Push Nevada* television series, to *The LOST Experience* for that same network's series *LOST*, to ... well, you get the idea, makes them very difficult to categorize or quickly explain.

There are so many types of ARGs and so many possibilities to how alternate reality games can be used to support a transmedia storytelling project that there's no way we can cover it in sufficient depth in this book. We'll try and do it justice in a later chapter, but we're clearly giving short-shrift to such a potentially powerful platform.

Transmedia for Creatives

Transmedia storytelling creatives, or those who develop and make transmedia content, have a unique set of responsibilities to satisfy an inquisitive and insatiable audience. The rising generation of media savvy consumers are adept at using social media tools to find information. They are "seekers" who do not want to be given all of their content in one place, but are willing to be hooked by the primary platform and then asked to seek or search for ever deepening levels of story and character served up via multiple creative and distribution platforms. ABC's *LOST* was a tremendous television success, but creators give some of the credit to their savvy transmedia approach, seeding the series online with leaked clips and continuing the online fan relationship with specially designed web based content to deepen the audience's relationship to the story, the world and the characters.

Seekers want to interact with their content, to comment and "play" within the worlds of their characters. They are active members of what Henry Jenkins has termed "participatory culture," a culture that does not only want to view media but participate in the media, to have an effect on the story and even to utilize fan fiction to tell their own versions of popular narratives. (Henry Jenkins, *Convergence Culture: Where Old and New Media Collides*, NYU Press, 2006). The transmedia creative is not making for one audience, i.e. a film audience, but for many audiences over multiple platforms, often times simultaneously.

A Story for All Screens

Because of the need to create across media platforms, the transmedia creative must see their core narrative or story as not being tied to one media platform, i.e. a motion picture, video game or television show, but rather developed to have multiple lives on multiple screens.

As an example, characters developed as the main, or even minor characters of a movie must have deep enough back stories to provide a year's worth (24 episodes distributed bi-weekly) of a 2–3 minute web series that focuses only on the minor characters and their past, unseen in the film. So it is a deeper way of thinking about character, that you must be able to extend their narrative across multiple creative and distribution platforms.

The need to explore a single segment of a core narrative on multiple media platforms can be determined by an audience's desire to see more of a character, or to explore a riddle or a mystery within the core narrative. A good example of this was the fan fervor associated with knowing more about *LOST's* Dharma Initiative, a strange cult-like scientific faction that occupied the island before the plane crash. These inhabitants, the so-called "Others," took on something of a life of their own online, generating fan fiction, creator-based web content, as well as merchandising opportunities. Was that a planned relationship? Did J. J. Abrahams and the Bad Robot production team seed the story with the Dharma Initiative to start a transmedia strand? Or did fans connect to this part of the narrative first and then Bad Robot fed the excitement? We will explore this more closely in Chapter 5.

One World, Many Stories

What is a world? Well, in terms of storytelling, a storyworld is a fictional or constructed setting that may differ dramatically from the real world or may be historically accurate or consistent with the real world except that there are certain elements and/or characters that, being fictional, differ from the real world.

An imagined or constructed fictional world is the context within which stories are told. It provides an all-encompassing backstory without which the story would not make sense. It sets up the history of the world, the geography, the physical rules that govern the natural and elemental aspects, and creates or defines the usually sentient beings, whether human or other, that populate and interact within the world. Within these defined populations exists the cultural, political and intercultural relationships of the world. This includes government, politics and commerce as well as the level of technology and whether or not magic and the supernatural are at play. It establishes the hierarchical rules that allow for the understanding of power differentials amongst individuals and cultures as well as any mythological or religious elements. It will also establish existing conflicts, alliances and important pre-existing personal relationships. The world must contain all that is needed for the story to begin … and to be believable.

The process of crafting worlds is called world building and will be discussed in detail in the next chapter. For now it is sufficient to say that world building is the act of designing and constructing believable fictional universes. The backstory contained in this world will give a context to the story and aid in the creation of a "suspension of disbelief." The concept most likely comes from the poet William Taylor Coleridge who is quoted as saying in 1817 in his *Bibliographia Literia* with regard to poetry, "That willing suspension of disbelief for the moment, which constitutes poetic faith" and refers to a reader's (or audience's) willingness to accept the author's vision of a time, place, world, or characters that, were they not in a work of fiction, would be unbelievable. The audience has to be willing to put aside the fantastical, the incongruous, the unlikely and even excuse narrative shortcuts or streamlining in order to accept and be engaged by the story.

The author or creator must literally "play God," in that he or she must create a "world" and the lives of those who dwell there, whether that world be a story-specific set of characters and situations that exist within our world or that live in a world much like Earth or that function in a world completely different from Earth with its own physical rules geography, ecology, history, cultures and mythologies. From the fertile world crafted by the author, many stories, many lives and their struggles must be able to flow forth.

In the genre of transmedia, a world would be defined as a single intellectual property or concept that extends into multiple creative and distribution iterations or "stories." The rule being that with each iteration, story and/or characters must change. We see this idea of "one world, many stories" as the pillar of transmedia storytelling. An originally conceived transmedia world must be spacious and detailed, rich and fertile enough to allow for growth over time with the ability to be slightly different in each medium. The world must either be based in our real world with elements and/or characters that differ, or if an entirely fictional world and characters are presented, there must be universal human elements or themes that allow us to connect to and believe the constructed world and allow the audience to be willing receivers of the intended story.

Adaptation vs. Extension vs. Expansion

When working with story material from one medium to another, there are several different strategies, each with its own strengths and challenges. Sometimes people talk about these different strategies as if they were equivalent, but in fact they are quite different. Applying processes of translation, interpolation and inspiration to the same story material results in very different results.

Adaptation

Adaptation retells the story told in one medium in another, with applicable changes depending on the requirements of the new medium. At its core, this is a translation process, much like we might try to translate an English phrase into another language. This is a process of adapting the material to a new form, remaining as faithful to the source material or original story elements as possible. We want to retain the meaning of the original phrase as closely as possible, but each language has its own syntax.

Adaptation transfers the story elements to another medium, creating a derivative work. Many if not most of the films made in Hollywood are based on story material that originated in another medium, whether that was prose (*Fahrenheit 451*, 1953), radio (*The 39 Steps*, 1935), plays (*Wait Until Dark*, 1966), games (*Silent Hill*, 1999) or graphic novels (*From Hell*, 1991).

The attraction to adapting material is that there is already a built-in audience, people who already love the intellectual property and are eager to experience it in new ways. The challenge is to somehow be both familiar (so the fans feel that the fidelity of the original material has been kept) and new (so the fans feel there's a value in seeing the adaptation by discovering new aspects to the original story) at the same time, a tough line to walk. Just think about controversies surrounding the casting or costumes of certain films.

In general, we do not think of adaptation as a transmedia process because it implies that we're simply taking a story and presenting it in a different medium. The differences between the adaptation (or adapted form of the story) and the source material is solely the result of the fact that each medium has its own storytelling and aesthetic conventions, its own syntax (to extend our earlier analogy).

There may be times, however, when an adaptation contains additional information not present in the original that blurs the line. For example, the 1982 Paramount Pictures film *Star Trek: The Wrath of Khan* featured a new character named Saavik, played by Kirstie Alley. In the film, Saavik appears to be fully Vulcan, albeit with some interesting mannerisms. The novel adaptation of *Star Trek: The Wrath of Khan* was written by Vonda N. McIntyre, based on the screenplay by Jack B. Sowards, from the story by Harve Bennet and Jack B. Sowards. The novelization includes the detail that Saavik is in fact half–Vulcan and half–Romulan, which was included in the original screenplay, but cut before production. (If you are not a *Star Trek* fan, trust us when we say that it's a notable distinction.) We talk about canon (official elements of the universe) in the next chapter, but this is a case where this particular fact was originally part of the official story, but was cut, and because of its inclusion in the novelization – the official adaptation of the motion picture – is viewed by many fans as "canon."

With that said, there may be times when adapting material may involve just one story within a larger intellectual property universe, so we cannot say that adaptation is never a part of transmedia, just that it cannot be the only approach. If it is, then it does not meet the accepted definition of transmedia storytelling.

Extension

Extension draws from the narrative elements of the original source story. At first glance, it may seem that we're telling the same story, but unlike adaptation, we do not need to remain as faithful to the original material as possible. An extension includes new narrative elements that build directly on the pre-existing material, but does not extensively introduce new story elements. In some ways, this is akin to interpreting the material, finding nuances and new inferences in the plot and or characters that can be further explored and developed, but in effect, it is interpolation, inserting new material into existing material. As a result, this process creates a richer and more defined text. It could be argued that the *Wrath of Khan* adaptation just discussed is in fact an extension due to the "new" material in it, but it was intended to be an adaptation.

When we extend the universe, we are deepening the storyworld and our understanding of it. This extension might provide insights into the backstory, such as the original website for *The Blair Witch Project* (http://www.blairwitch.com) which establishes a context for the film crew and events that happen to them, or help us better understand specific characters, such as the deeper portrait of Gaeta in the third web series for *Battlestar Galactica* (Sci-Fi, 2003–2009), or bridge two iterations of story, such as the *Star Trek Ongoing* comic book series that connects not just J. J. Abram's two *Star Trek* films but also links his films to the original 1966–1969 TV series universe.

Extensions can also build off of the original material's loyal fan base while making the new iteration of the story exciting because it mines the original material for deeper characterizations, mythology or events. The risk is that audiences may find that the new material contradicts their view or interpretation of the original material.

Expansion

Expansion broadens the story, introducing parallel or companion narratives that often provide new perspectives, insight or clarity to the existing story. As a process, this is developing new story material that's inspired by the original narrative or universe. We are no longer tied to the specifics of the original story as long as we follow (or at least do not contradict) the established rules of the previous versions of the intellectual property – we draw inspiration from it.

Aliens and *Alien*[3] are particularly interesting case studies of the ways in which each new writer and director expanded the story mythology of the film(s) that preceded it – not just in terms of themes but in terms of the aliens' behavior and characteristics – and built upon previous story strategies and aesthetic considerations, such as changing the genres that are hybridized, the characterizations and the visual look in each film. Even the much later Ridley Scott motion picture *Prometheus* attempts to expand the *Alien* universe without contradicting the previous films (at least the ones before Predators got involved). Some audiences already familiar with the intellectual property find these new stories exciting ways to experience the original property afresh, while others may be distressed by the fact that their favorite character doesn't appear in the expansion or events evocatively alluded to are now made more literal.

One of the counterbalances to the challenge of expanding the storyworld is that expansion is where interactive components of transmedia can be most easily introduced, allowing the audience to be more than just viewers but also co-creators, contributing narrative elements or singling out characters for further thought and development.

In all of these cases, these processes are primarily governed not by co-creation but rather licensing, where subsequent iterations of the story material remain faithful and subservient to the original narrative property. The more we want to create complex and co-created worlds, whether with our creative and production teams or with our viewers/users, the more thought we need to give to the universe from the concept's very inception in order to create a rich, complex world in which to create or facilitate meaningful narrative expressions.

Where to Start

To begin the creation of a transmedia property one must either find an existing core narrative property and extend it or develop an original core narrative rich enough to be told across multiple media platforms. It should be noted that the term transmedia is often associated with big franchise science fiction and fantasy properties like *Star Trek*, *LOST* and *Star Wars (Lucasfilm*, 1977–present) but we needn't limit transmedia to these kinds of stories. Any story set in a well-developed world with characters that have sufficient backstory and conflicts to sustain them through multiple story-strands via multiple platforms, can become transmedia. The CBS Television series *NCIS* (2003–present) and *NCIS: Los Angeles* (2009–present) tell different stories set in the same fictional universe, which seems to be shared with *Hawaii Five-0* (2010–present), based on the cross over episode with *NCIS: LA*. Is this Transmedia or shrewd marketing? We think the latter, but you get the idea. *Buffy the Vampire Slayer* (WB/UPN, 1997–2003) and its spin-off *Angel* (WB, 1999–2004) shared the same "Buffy-verse" universe and were tied closely enough in creation and production that they could be viewed as transmedia storytelling.

Finding the Starting Concept

Different creatives begin the development of a story from different starting points, but most will agree that the first big step to creating a story is to find the concept. A concept consists of characters in a setting soon to be involved in a meaningful struggle. A good question to ask at this point is "What am I trying to tell the world? What do I want to say?" "Do I want to warn the world of the dangers of developing sentient machines?" This would have been a possible jumping off point for many popular science fiction stories, including James Cameron's *Terminator*, the popular television series *Battlestar Galactica* as well as classics like the motion picture *2001: A Space Odyssey* (MGM, 1968) and the original Isaac Asimov novel *I, Robot* (Gnome Press, 1950).

Universal human themes are a great place to begin mining for stories and for the motivations and conflicts of character. These themes are at the core of most stories as well as character relationships and conflicts. They are needs, wants and desires shared by all humans regardless of who they are, where they are or even when they were born. They are needs that humans have had since the beginning of time, although as we become more complex, the addition of themes that reflect our complexity are added to the list. Examples include: the need to be loved, to be happy, to have sex, to survive, to protect that which is yours, to belong, to enact revenge, to take what isn't yours, to feel superior to others, etc. If you examine James Cameron's *Avatar* (20th Century Fox, 2009) you will find many of these both at the core of the narrative and the character's motivations.

From these universal human themes one can extract a core need to be further developed and then populated with characters that are in sympathy or conflict with the core need. For example, in *Avatar* humans had a core need to extract Unobtanium at any cost. In conflict with this core need was the core need of the natives to protect their heritage as exemplified by the "tree" that happened to be sitting smack dab on top of the largest stock pile of Unobtanium. It is the age-old story of "outsiders," usually technologically superior, invading a "tribal" society and "stealing what's not theirs" while the tribal society feels the "need to protect" what is theirs. Universal human themes create universally understood conflict.

So conflict is essential and a conflict that has its roots in universal human themes is sure to trigger an emotional response from its human audience. We are drawn to that which feels familiar, even in unfamiliar settings.

Conflict usually demands that we choose sides, that we root for one side and against the other. Thus we have the age-old terms of "antagonists and protagonists," although in a 21st century context these delineations are often blurred and even interchangeable. We tend to want "villains" who we sympathize with and even root for. And still, we decide at some point during the story that we want someone to "win," and that is usually the someone whom we have the most in common with, or who is at risk in a way that makes us feel vulnerable.

This is why so many successful transmedia properties are science fiction and fantasy. These types of stories usually have risks we easily understand and sides we can choose quickly. In short, there are bad guys and good guys … and gals. We need only look at the ongoing transmedia success of Marvel and its Marvel Universe where heroes fight villains. No guessing, no confusion, Spider-Man is the hero and Lizard is the villain, even if sometimes the villains are tinged with shades of sympathetic gray. That said, the best heroes are flawed, as we are, and the best villains, even the Joker, have aspects that we feel sympathy for.

And so after we have developed a concept and characters based on universal human themes, needs and desires we must make sure that the characters have a clear conflict that matters to the audience. If the hero does not get what he or she wants, then either we may be adversely affected or a character that we care about will be adversely affected. In order for an audience to be endeared to content, they must perceive that something is at risk that is of value to them or to a character that they care about.

Sufficient jeopardy is especially important for building a transmedia property because the audience must care enough to not only view the primary form but to seek out extended story across multiple media platforms. If there is not enough at risk, then the audience loses interest. Big science fiction and fantasy franchises tend to literally put Earth, mankind or entire species at risk or they place the main characters that we care about, in extreme jeopardy.

When we have a conflict and characters involved in that conflict, we can work outwards to construct a storyworld that will be the context or setting for the conflict to go into full swing. We will speak in depth later about top-down or bottom-up development, but suffice it to say that the characters and what is at risk for them must have a world in which to play out. That world must have geography, ecology, cultures, religions, alliances and conflicts (see Chapter 2).

Reboot and Reinvention

To look at many transmedia properties, you would think we've run out of new ideas and are recycling old ones. In fact, we don't even have to look at transmedia properties. Films, TV series, games, graphic novels – lots of singular media experiences build off of pre-existing material. This can range from remaking previous material as faithfully as possible – Gus Van Sant's 1998 near shot-for-shot duplication of Hitchcock's original film *Psycho* (Paramount Pictures, 1960) may be the extreme example of that impulse – to rebooting old TV shows like *Battlestar Galactica*, reinventing them to be relevant and/or entertaining for a modern audience. In fact, *Battlestar Galactica* is the television series known as much for popularizing the term "reimagining" as for its actual storylines.

With transmedia, our goal is not to literally adapt or simply recreate, replicate or remake pre-existing material but rather to reinterpret it, to make it reflect the interests of the present-day audience. Reboot has traditionally been used in comics to mean that we discard much, if not most of the continuity, with the source story and start afresh as if it were a new property, even if there are knowing nods to the original that can please its diehard fans. In television and now transmedia intellectual properties, the term usually means something a bit less aggressive with the source material, though we might use the terms reimagine or renovate to indicate a substantial break with previous continuity and the effort to use the source material as the barest of skeletons on which to build a new beast (or pet).

Reboots can be seen as *relatively* safe bets for producers – there's a built-in audience who already have a certain loyalty to the material and yet by treating the property as if it were new, there's the opportunity to lure new viewer/users to it. This process can invigorate franchises that are seen as stale or having backed themselves into a corner through a dense and complex recorded mythology and backstory (*Star Trek*, anyone?), bringing in new revenue.

For every success we could name – TV's *Battlestar Galactica* and *Hawaii Five-0* for example – we can also identify recent failures – *Bionic Woman* (NBC, 2007) or *The Night Stalker* (ABC, 2005–2006). All four of these projects tried to retain certain narrative traditions established by the source material while taking certain liberties with specific details (Starbuck! A man! A woman! Kolchak! Old! Young!).

All four took similar approaches toward their source material and yet the two that succeeded perhaps succeeded for different reasons – *Battlestar Galactica* took itself very seriously, reflecting contemporary cultural anxieties in much the same way that some have argued the original series did as well. *Hawaii Five-0* didn't take itself too seriously at all, embracing its sheer adrenaline-based entertainment value much like the original series did. Maybe that's the similarity in their success – their tonal similarity to the original material.

If that's the case, we can just as easily find exceptions or contradictions to that theory. The films *21 Jump Street* (Columbia Pictures, 2012) and *Dark Shadows* (Warner Brothers, 2012) not only redesign certain story elements but also change the mood and tone of the source material, taking a young adult police drama and a supernatural soap opera and turning them into (self-referential) comedies.

As we noted earlier, we owe the concept of reboot to comics, where there is a certain tradition of taking long-standing franchises and reinventing them, in effect breathing new life into them and enticing audiences who have drifted away or lost interest to come back. This process can invigorate not just the audience and the property but the creative team as well.

As with the term transmedia, many of the words used for when we base a property on pre-existing material are softly defined and a bit confusing. However, this idea of developing new intellectual properties by taking pre-existing material and expanding it into a more complex universe that can allow us to tell stories that will reach today's audiences is not that much different from some of the mashups we hear in music – we're like a DJ who's not just re-recording a song, but we're actually adding new material to it, creating something that is not quite like either element and yet harkens to both, ideally better than its individual components and greater than its sum.

Good stories are good stories, whether we thought of them today or we license them from someone who thought them up years ago.

Cornerstone Platform/Property

In masonry, the cornerstone is the starting point, the first stone set in the construction of a foundation. This cornerstone is essential because it determines the position and way in which the entire structure will be built; all other stones will be set in reference to it. We can easily see how this notion has come to be applied to the key basic indispensable element – or foundation – of anything that is constructed or developed, whether an actual building or a persuasive argument or a transmedia property.

Even with the ideal of a holistic multi-faceted approach to universe and transmedia property development, there is little question that the initial introduction of the universe occurs through one primary form or medium which is then supported by other mediums. All other media expressions depend on – or are created in reference to – this initial cornerstone platform and property.

In our conversations with Carlton Cuse (*Nash Bridges*, *Adventures of Brisco County Jr.*, *LOST*) which you can read later in this book, he used the term "mothership" to refer to *LOST* in relation to its associated transmedia expressions. We'd not heard that term in that context before (except that the original *Law and Order* television series is sometimes referred to as the "mothership" of the franchise) but it seemed a fitting one for the primary transmedia property, from which all expressions spring. You'll find us using the terms cornerstone and mothership interchangeably throughout this book. One way to think of it might be that when you are crafting the transmedia property prior to launch, the primary property is the cornerstone and once it launches, it becomes the mothership.

The transmedia cornerstone or mothership introduces the key narrative elements of the overall intellectual property, including the rules of the world as well as significant characters, conflicts, themes and aesthetic styles. The cornerstone is not necessarily the first visible expression for the intellectual property.

The cornerstone for the recent *Star Trek* re-iteration is J. J. Abram's 2009 film, but in fact, the key narrative elements of the new universe were established in the 4 IDW comic books (*Star Trek: Countdown*) released just prior to the film. These were intended to service the hardcore *Star Trek* fan's narrative concerns and to provide deeper backstory and setup for the events of the film, which allowed the movie to have a broader or more casual feel. As a result, the film was able to draw in both longstanding *Star Trek* fans and people new to the franchise.

From a narrative aspect, the IDW comic series enhances the viewer's experience of the film as well as help publicize and generate interest in the films, particularly exciting the fan base and enticing readers to see the first movie. This enticement adds a marketing aspect to the comics' release, reflecting the ways in which various expressions of an intellectual property can bring an audience to other manifestations of that intellectual property. How this differs from historical marketing techniques is that the primary goal in these transmedia expressions is to provide first and foremost meaningful narrative experiences within the intellectual property universe. Each platform or property becomes a potential entry point that will lead or encourage the audience member to embrace other components of the larger narrative.

Story and Medium

Choosing which should be our first block or cornerstone of the universe requires an understanding of the various advantages and disadvantages to starting the intellectual property's expression in a particular medium. In the following chapters, we will discuss in more detail the unique (and shared) characteristics of storytelling in film, television, game, novels and comics. Having an understanding of these will help us better decide which property should be our cornerstone and how to build out the intellectual property from there. In addition, we need to consider not just the storytelling aspects of each medium, but the audiences that medium is most likely to reach and the production timeline each medium requires.

Television, comics and webisodes each provide a medium for serialized storytelling, building a longer story arc that is presented to the audience in installments. Much like the chapters in a novel, each episode can cover a specific portion of the narrative without requiring a seamless, continuous or uninterrupted connection to the surrounding chapters. The scale of the longer story or the amount of material that needs to be covered in each episode will be one of the factors determining which of these you might choose. For example, *Battlestar Galactica* provides several interesting examples how a 42-minute television episode develops narrative elements in comparison to a 3-minute webisode installment.

Each of *Battlestar Galactica*'s three series of webisodes is structured and placed within the intellectual property's timeline differently. Just looking at the first series that bridges seasons 1 and 2 of the broadcast series, we see that the webisodes introduce or follow several secondary characters from the television show. However the time constraint of a webisode does not allow for full character development and the strength of these webisodes lies in their ideas and provocative concepts. It is in these webisodes that the cultural relevance of *Battlestar Galactica* came into full focus, drawing from the audience's anxieties about terrorism and the Iraq War and inverting those with the events on New Caprica. Thus, webisodes may be a great way to parse out conceptual ideas within the universe or a broad (and therefore less personal) overview of the conflicts or certain events while TV episodes allow for a deeper exploration of the impact of narrative events on the characters.

Films offer a more streamlined and focused story that takes place over a relatively limited time span in the narrative but engages the audience only 90 to 180 minutes (with the average being around the 2-hour mark). In a sense, within a transmedia property we could consider our film similar to an episode, though we usually consider it more complex and on a larger cinematic scale than a TV episode. Films also tend to have much higher budgets than a single television episode, so they often feature special effects or spectacle that a web series or TV series cannot. The challenge for the transmedia producer is that if the film seems too much like an episode rather than a full cinematic experience, such as the last *The X-Files* movie, *The X-Files: I Want to Believe* (20th Century Fox, 2008), the audience can be disappointed. We expect the story in film, while streamlined, to be on a grander scale than can be captured in a single TV episode or webisode.

Generally, all of these media discussed so far are considered one-way interactions with the audience, the producer and creative team the primary shapers of the content and pushing it out to the viewers/users.

Video games require a much more active viewer/user than films, television or webisodes and interestingly, there is a sort of inverted relationship between audience and protagonist in terms of activeness and passiveness. Ignoring interactive programming such as social television, we can generalize that films, television and webisodes usually feature an active protagonist and require a (happily) passive audience; games require a passive (controllable) protagonist and necessitate an active audience.

Web content can run the gambit between these two extremes, ranging from the one-way passive audience response to highly interactive or social content in which audiences are active not just in controlling a limited avatar but become fully engaged co-creators in the intellectual property universe, contributing to or shaping the narrative experience for themselves and even sometimes for others.

Audience and Medium

Audience demographics are shifting in all media and as a transmedia producer, it is important to look at the current data and trends. As an example, in the 2011 Nielsen State of the Media Cross Platform Report, analysis found that age, gender and ethnicity are significant factors in how an audience accesses media. Each age group dominates a specific platform: the largest segment of the traditional television audience in the first quarter of 2011 was made up of adults 50–64 (25%); the largest segment Internet video audience was adults 35–49 (27%) – though 12–17 year-old Americans, who were a smaller percentage of audience, actually spent a higher percentage or one third of their Internet time watching streaming video; and the largest segment of the Mobile video audience was adults 25–34 years old (30%). In terms of gender, women watched TV programming more than men, though men consistently spent more time watching streaming video. African Americans watched more traditional TV programming, Asians spent more time watching video on the Internet and Caucasians watched the most time-shifted (DVR) TV.

During roughly the same period, the Motion Picture Association reported that most moviegoers were 25–45 (over 20%), that women went to more movies than men and more Caucasians (over 60%) went to movies than any other ethnicity – though a higher percentage of the total Latino population went to movies more than the percentage of any other ethnicity.

The demographics of who plays video games is changing as well, though the Entertainment Software Association reported in 2012 that the average game player was 30 years old and had been playing games for 12 years; 47% of all game players were women (ESA, 2012, http://www.theesa.com/facts/pdfs/ESA_EF_2012.pdf). In 2011, Nielsen found that African Americans spent more time playing games than Caucasians in the 18-to-49 age group.

Likewise, the audience for graphic novels and comics is broadening, though a poll by Harris in 2010 indicated that readership still skews young and male. At that time, 18% of 18–33 year olds had read a graphic novel while only 4% of people over 65 had; 15% of males had read a graphic novel, but only 8% of females had.

Development, Production and Medium

Once we determine the strategy for dispersing our story content, which platforms we will be using and which will be our cornerstone, we have to consider the time it will take to develop and produce that content in each medium. We will talk more about this later. For now, what's important is to remember that each medium has its own timeline and process for implementation. This means that while your cornerstone property will be the first property released to the public, it may not be the first property you need to develop and produce. This is where having a thoroughly conceived intellectual property bible/transmedia bible can be invaluable, especially one that considers or anticipates production issues.

Once we consider the larger overall narrative, the strengths of various platforms for conveying specific story material and the timeframe each medium requires for development and production, we are ready to identify our cornerstone property. Don't take anything for granted. Always work from the latest data and update your intellectual property strategy periodically so that you are always anticipating, responding to and maybe even shaping the trends. This will help assure that your cornerstone and overall intellectual property are as dynamic and as engaging as possible.

Engagement and Participation

The toughest aspect of getting transmedia right is that you have to build two-way communication into the apparatus of your narrative.

—Jeff Gomez, CEO, Starlight Runner Entertainment[6]

One of the most exciting aspects of transmedia is the ways in which storytelling can become a more dynamic relationship between the creator(s) and the viewer/user(s). Old notions of "writer" and "reader" are giving way to the idea of "co-creator" or "collaborator." Not all transmedia properties are created equal in this regard and some have more potential than others. Certainly too, there can be a marketing imperative at play here – the more engaged a potential audience member is, the more likely they are to consume other iterations of the intellectual property. But those enticements designed purely from marketing considerations provide pretty limited engagement, simply channeling the audience to another medium. The challenge for a transmedia producer is to identify and plan for the parts of the narrative that can be best experienced as a collaboration or dialogue with the audience.

With careful thinking about and planning of the story universe, and integrating into those earliest stages of development additional avenues for audience engagement and participation, we can maximize impact. For example, as successful as *The LOST Experience* was in teasing audience expectations and assumptions about the ABC Television series *LOST*, it ultimately only provided superficial connectivity with the program itself since it was crafted after the primary creation of the series, rather than alongside it. *The LOST Experience* was treated as a marketing extension, rather than a narrative extension and so contained very little content that really affected how the viewer experienced the television program. Similarly, *Eagle Eye Free Fall* and *The Beast* were in effect simply promotional tools for the feature films *Eagle Eye* (Dreamworks Pictures, 2008) and *AI: Artificial Intelligence* respectively.

Ideally, engagement is a type of relationship. It is an active courtship. A continuous wooing and responding. An unrequited coupling. Interactivity has been the gateway to audience participation, with technology innovations that allow users/viewers to interact with content, alter it and even the ability to vote during live events or on posted videos, see the results and get feedback from the content makers. This kind of intellectual property expression breaks the fourth wall, the sense of being shown or observing a story rather than being an active participant in the intellectual property Universe or even co-creating the narrative. Sean Stewart describes this as making the audience part of the play:

you can make works of art that feel intensely personal in ways other artforms are hard-pressed to match. When I read about Lucy going to Narnia or Harry Potter entering Hogwarts, I have a wonderful second-hand experience of exploring a mysterious new world. If I can use my browser and my phone to enter a fiction, however, that experience isn't second-hand any more. I am not imagining what it would be like to explore that world, I am actually exploring it.

—Sean Stewart[7]

A complex transmedia property can be more than one individual can reasonably explore, encouraging interaction not just with the property but with other viewer/users. Henry Jenkins has compared this aspect of audience engagement and participation to Pierre Levy's concept of collective intelligence, where participants pool information as they work together, citing the map flashed in a second-season episode of *LOST* that fans then captured as

[6] interviewed in www.dmwmedia.com/news/2011/04/11

[7] "Interactive Fiction," accessed June 22, 2012, http://www.seanstewart.org/interactive/

a freeze-frame and put it on the web where together they extrapolated about what it might reveal regarding the Hanso Corporation and its activities on the island. The viewers/users rely on the insights of each other to actively build a larger view of the *LOST* universe ("Collective Intelligence vs. The Wisdom of Crowd," accessed June 22, 2012, http://henryjenkins.org/2006/11/collective_intelligence_vs_the.html).

By having story elements span a variety of mediums, viewer/users have to rely on each other to construct a complete (or as complete as possible) understanding of the intellectual property. But simply spreading story information across multiple platforms will not accomplish this. We have to spark the viewer/user's curiosity, his imagination.

A complex and well-designed transmedia universe is big enough to sustain multiple interrelated characters and stories, more than even we as transmedia producers can imagine. There is an element of "happy accidents" that viewer/users can pick up on and run with. We want to plan as thoroughly as possible but also be open to the surprises or alternative interpretations of events viewer/users might bring to our intellectual property expressions.

Small details may spark a viewer/user's imagination, compelling him or her to discuss, explore and elaborate on those in such a way that expands the world and its stories. This might be expressed in unofficial venues such as fan fiction or playing with action figures or donning costumes and "becoming" fictional characters within that universe.

Clearly, this desire to know more about the universe, to speculate on other aspects of that world, its characters and stories, provides its own pleasure. Our goal is to find ways to bring these compulsions, impulses and sense of pleasure into official interactions with the universe.

Feeling a part of the narrative or story content seals the audience's relationship with the transmedia property. A successful property has enough room for a viewer/user to keep coming back into the material and discover new things, keeping that curiosity alive. Rather than a work of fiction that means one thing to many people, we are creating a property that means many things to one person, rewarding multiple engagements and re-engagements.

In order to accomplish this, we need to know who our audience is and which forms of expression they are currently following. Right now, a lot of the more active viewer/users are insatiable early adopters who seek out their content and enjoy the chase. They tend to be comic book fans, super hero fans, science fiction fans, though this may just be an expression of the newness of transmedia and that as it becomes more established, the audience base will reflect different traits. Either way, transmedia that actively engages its audience assumes that viewer/users are part of a growing participatory culture that does not desire just to watch but to interact, comment, help shape the course of the content and look for (hidden) answers. Curiosity is their creed. They want to see and play with what they find. They want to participate and they like mysteries, puzzles, codes and believe in the unknown. As transmedia producers who want to actively engage our audiences, we must speak their language: the language of social media, apps and alternate reality games.

Marvel Entertainment has been one of the most successful in engaging their audience, the result of a long-term, consistent and dependable strategy. Marvel meets its audience everywhere their audience plays and then creates spaces and places for the audience and the brand to play together, whether that be conventions, events, multiple websites or a constant transmedia barrage of connected but innovative communications from wallpaper to movies, stickers to coloring books.

Examples of early attempts to actively engage viewer/users include newspaper-initiated *Dreadnot* (sfgate.com, 1996), the television show *Freakylinks* (Fox, 2000–2001), the game *Majestic* and film *The Blair Witch Project* (Artisan

Entertainment, 1999). As notions of transmedia have become more complex and producers gain more experience, we're seeing projects like *Dirty Work* (http://rides.tv/dirty-work/) that embraces mobile device viewing with its text messages, phone calls, emails and additional video content *ReGenesis* (The Movie Network/Movie Central, 2004–2008), a Canadian TV series with a real-time alternate reality game in sync with episodes as they aired and Australia's coming of age TV series *Slide* (Fox8, 2011) which encourages viewers to view extra online content via apps, social networks and YouTube webisodes. Sean Stewart and Jordan Weisman's *Cathy's Book: If Found Call (650) 266-8233* (Running Press Kids, 2006) is a young adult novel with alternate reality game elements that includes an evidence packet and encourages online discussion of reader/players' theories about what has happened to the characters and narrative events. Jeff Gomez has argued that *Glee* is one of the best examples of audience engagement, with its incorporation of iTunes, live theatrical events, YouTube and Twitter, though one could argue that many of its methods for engaging are less about expanding the narrative world and more about advertising or guiding the audience back to the main TV series ("Talking about Transmedia with Jeff Gomez," accessed June 5, 2012, http://mobilizedtv.com/talking-about-transmedia-with-jeff-gomez).

A final consideration with engagement has to do with the investment of viewer/user time each medium requires or encourages. A video game may require 40 to 50 hours of play to fully explore, where as a film is approximately a two-hour experience (though some viewers might watch the film multiple times) and serialized storytelling in TV series, webseries and comics is designed to be experienced in segments divided by intervals of time ranging from a week to a month or more – though DVDs and DVRs have changed the ways in which we watch TV series and graphic novels that bind together multiple issues of a comic series provide a comparable experience.

These are just some of the factors that will affect our choices as a producer and/or creator when we strategize how we will break narrative elements across platforms and build an audience.

Chapter 2
Worldbuilding and Key Story Elements

Most often, transmedia stories are based not on individual characters or specific plots but rather complex fictional worlds which can sustain multiple interrelated characters and their stories. This process of world building encourages an encyclopedic impulse in both readers and writers. We are drawn to master what can be known about a world, which always expands beyond our grasp. This is a very different pleasure from what we associate with the closure found in most classically constructed narratives, where we expect to leave the theatre knowing everything that is required to make sense of a particular story.

—Henry Jenkins[1]

Let's imagine for a moment we're crafting a transmedia property that revolves around the final voyage of the Starship *Gigantic*. Our key storytelling elements are going to revolve around the lives of the passengers, who come from a variety of cultures and social classes, as well those who built it. We're going to create a television series that follows the life of one young man from Prime City, Mars — a structural metal worker named James who helps build the great liner and then, having saved up enough money, intends to journey on her maiden voyage to a new life on Earth. We're also going to create a novel series that deals with the lives of different members of the crew of the *Gigantic* (who are based on Earth) and their lives leading up to that maiden voyage. Additionally, there will be a website and mobile app that allows you to explore the starship and speak with our established characters, as well as others, as the ship prepares to head to Earth. Lastly, if all goes well, we're going to end with a big-budget motion picture of the Starship *Gigantic*'s collision with an uncharted asteroid and learn the fate of the characters we've been following.

This is the story (or set of stories) we want to tell.

So, where do we start?

It is reflexive to say "at the beginning," but the reality is we have to start before the beginning:

We need to build a world.

Or more accurately, a universe. And then a world. Or several worlds. And then tell some stories. We're probably going to need more than six days.

[1] "Transmedia Storytelling 101," accessed July 25, 2012, http://www.henryjenkins.org/2007/03/transmedia_storytelling_101.html

That's why in all forms of storytelling, there is a development period, whether we explicitly call it that or not. The idea for the story occurs to its author who then thinks about it, makes up some things and researches others, thinks some more, puts a version of the story on paper (or screen), thinks about it some more, revises it, maybe has someone else look at it, listens to that person's feedback, decides that person doesn't know what they're talking about, thinks about it even more, gets accused of doing nothing, revises it again, has someone else look at it, gets more feedback, revises it again. For a novelist, this process might be fairly solitary and all take place at home or sitting at a desk. For media makers, this process might involve lots of others (producers, writers, and later, actors and crew).

Stories take a lot of work, even the simple and small ones.

Here, though, we're talking about creating something on an exponentially larger scale: transmedia storytelling can be a sprawling endeavor that covers many different media platforms and if successful, might span years or decades.

The Challenge of Transmedia Development

This process of *worldbuilding* (or building a fictional universe for our stories) is hard enough when dealing with a single property that will only ever be a single property. When building a transmedia world, an awareness of the fact that the elements of this world will be used in multiple incarnations across many different media is necessary. This means that the world has to be rich and deep enough to support all of this exploration and elaboration. For example, characters created for your transmedia property may need to have the immediate impact required for motion pictures, the slow burn necessary for television or the perspective demanded for video games. Can the same character support all this different shading? Or is it better if the primary elements that cross over between stories and platforms are more story-, plot-, or setting-oriented rather than character-oriented? (The major source of dramatic conflict still has to be character-driven, that's not what we mean — we're referring to the primary elements shared by the different manifestations of your property.) Captain Kirk, while an expansive character, does not exist in all of the myriad *Star Trek* worlds. The basic universe elements, rules, style and tone, however, are evident in all iterations. The fundamental core franchise narrative remains consistent. How does this awareness affect your decisions when building your transmedia world?

As we alluded to earlier, when we're talking about building a world, we're really talking about building a fictional universe. The scope of that creation could be limited to a single planet, continent, city, block or even room, but by defining the rules of that world we're defining the rules for the universe that surrounds it. Or the scope could literally be an entire universe … or multiple universes. It is limitless.

There are numerous examples of transmedia properties that sort of stumbled into existence, maybe initially as a single film that had a sequel, and then that sequel had a sequel, and pretty soon it was a film series with lots of films. But then someone suggested there be a related video game or a tie-in novel or a television series (*Terminator*, perhaps?). Suddenly the original creator is looking at a full-blown transmedia project, one they didn't plan for. And before they go further, they may feel a pressing need to go back and figure out the larger story, the larger universe and the larger potentials for their property. They have to think through their story retroactively, trying to make the pieces of previous versions fit together into a consistent picture of a larger story universe so that they can create more stories. This is why we sometimes hear of studios or companies hiring someone to go back and compile all the story information already presented, to create a bible or guiding reference document for future producers and writers to use. (The *Halo* video games and the *Jason Bourne* motion pictures are just two examples of this retroactive bible-making that we'll look at when we talk about transmedia bibles later in this book.)

Planning a transmedia property is one of the hardest things to do. There aren't many models for how it's done, and few have much experience in planning story elements so far ahead of when they're needed. Most conventional narrative development occurs in-process, which is to say once we've started developing the property. For example, screenwriters and film producers learn a lot about their storyworld, characters and plot as they look at subsequent drafts of the project. The entire development process brings that world into focus. Sure, there might be some initial basic assumptions, rules and character bios before writing the first draft of the script, but a lot of the "breathing life into the project" happens during development.

Transmedia requires a new way of thinking about development. We can't afford to wait till the screenwriter is five drafts into the screenplay to discover a key plot point or character development. For example, "It wasn't until the fifth draft that Shyamalan finally realized the real hook that made his movie so special: the trick ending in which the main character realized he was dead" (Jacob Krueger about *The Sixth Sense*, accessed June 30, 2012, www.scriptmag.com/features/is-your-idea-good-enough). In a case like that, our game developers may already be so far into programming the game and creating its content that they can't incorporate any new discoveries about the property's universe.

Because we're often so familiar with (and have to manage) the individual development processes and timetable for each medium, we sometimes forget that there has to be an entire development period before we even begin to consider specific platforms. The temptation is to not allow enough time for that process.

Transmedia development requires a great deal of upfront thinking, planning, and decision-making. Developing an idea isn't just a matter of sitting down and writing a bible. It takes thinking. It also takes not thinking, in other words not thinking explicitly about the story but letting it sit there in the back of our mind, growing just below our consciousness.

The risk of course is that we might discover way down the road some possibility that would make the story much richer, but we've already locked in details about the universe that won't allow that possibility. Then we're faced with a question of whether to break continuity (and some properties have chosen to do so, though usually try not to.)

Sadly, we can't wait for the individual platform development processes to figure out "good stuff." We've got to find most of that good stuff before that point. And we will miss a lot of good stuff if we shortchange the development process of the property's universe before we hand material over to specific platform developers.

Our best advice is to learn (and understand) as much about your intellectual property as you can before you begin platform development. This learning is going to happen in at least three major areas: story, platforms and goals. This learning does not happen in discrete stages or even as self-contained topics – these three areas all overlap and are often simultaneous. Did we already say that creating transmedia stories can sometimes be messy?

Story: *Learning about our property's story possibilities is going to look a lot like the development process for any narrative – we just have to do it before we know exactly what script format we'll need to use because we don't know which platform the story will work best in yet. Think about how long a novelist or a filmmaker or a series creator thinks about and develops their story before it gets presented to an audience. Their development process for one singular story may take months or even years. You're trying to create a universe complex enough to sustain not just one story but many. It stands to reason that the development time for a transmedia property – before it's handed off to the development teams of specific platforms – could take just as long if not longer.*

Platforms: *In addition, you will want to acquaint yourself with all the possibilities for transmedia narrative. A lot of us are coming to transmedia from one (or maybe two) area of expertise and we're very familiar with the storytelling conventions used in that medium. But story is influenced and shaped by the medium it's told in, so if we simply rely on "how it's done in the medium I* *have most experience in," we may make disastrous mistakes when we try to create a story for another platform. You don't have to be an expert in all the different possibilities of expression for your intellectual property, just know enough to be able to make some initial decisions and talk to the various creative teams and to understand each medium's strengths and challenges.*

Goals*: Interwoven with all of these is learning why you want to make this property and what you want to accomplish with it. These are probably both financial and creative goals. Setting goals for the overall property that can anticipate and guide you through different platforms and different stories over the next few years and the few decades will keep you focused. Goal setting can take as much thinking/non-thinking time as story development.*

One of our major goals in this book is to give you ways of thinking about (and learning about) your property in the big three areas (and a few others as well).

Development takes time. But the rewards are great. The more you think through the universe, the stories you want to tell, how you want to tell them and your goals for the intellectual property, the easier your job will be.

With that said, you don't want to be closed to happy accidents or unexpected discoveries later. You're not trying to make every decision you will ever have to make about the property now; you're laying a foundation that can serve as a reference point. This in turn helps form a strategy for assessing new ideas, collaborating with your creative and production teams, and making future decisions.

One of our high school guidance counselors once mangled a fairly famous quote, saying "if you don't know where you're going, you'll probably end up nowhere, but if you know where you want to go, you may not end up there, but you'll end up somewhere." Transmedia planning is a bit like that. Have a plan, but be flexible. Be prepared but be open to new insights and new ideas. Don't be afraid of "in–flight adjustments" to your goals or the universe. You will grow and change in the coming years; it's natural that your ideas about your intellectual property will as well. The market's responses to your property could inspire changes as well. If you have a good foundation, a well-considered initial plan, you will be able to let the property take on a life of its own while remaining true to its intent.

Development Processes

At this time, there are two primary processes that producers and creatives talk about in relationship to developing transmedia properties.

The first is a sequential development process, sometimes referred to as "bottom-up": the transmedia property builds on and expands what started as a single standalone story, developing its elements (more on those in the last half of this chapter) into a more complex set of stories existing within a larger world or universe.

The second process is thought of as more of a simultaneous development process, wherein the larger world or universe and the multiple story possibilities are developed at the same time, even though they probably won't reach their audiences all at the same time. This is called "top-down" development.

Let's take a moment and look at each of these processes more fully.

Bottom-Up Creation

Transmedia properties, created from the "bottom-up" start with the conceptualization of a property in a single medium, which is then expanded to multiple media. It is, in very many ways, after-the-fact transmedia development. Bottom-up properties are very often limited by the original medium and by the scope and depth of the original concept, which may not have been ever been thought of beyond that original medium. Motion pictures, television and video games each have unique storytelling, production, and distribution characteristics and therefore come with certain strengths, as well as a certain weakness that must be considered as the material is expanded into a broader transmedia property.

What film brings to the table (besides a historic place in the culture and cutting edge of media production techniques and technologies) is the ability for the big launch and grand cultural statement. The phrase "hit movie" is appropriate, because a successful film can quickly embed itself in mainstream culture. The news/entertainment media typically embrace film at a greater level than any other medium and that coverage fuels the property. What that means is that trying to expand a film into a full-fledged transmedia property (despite varied success of transmedia marketing pieces) can be challenging because of this impact of the initial expression. Films tend to be definitive and specific story statements with only so much room for additional expression of the kind of multiple story threads that are an essential part of many transmedia intellectual properties. Much of the time when the film is the originating mothership, the other pieces can often feel like inauthentic add-ons. Film is great at creating the window to launch a transmedia intellectual property but doesn't always have the universe to back it up.

What television brings is a timeframe and medium that allow for development of both the big arc and as well as a variety of story strands that can be developed over a season (or multiple seasons). While the limitations are money and audience viewing habits, the dynamic of a successful television show can establish both the world and the connection to the fans that can serve the creating of the transmedia story. There have been some real successes for television properties (*LOST* and *The X-Files*) that have generated a large universe beyond the launch property. The challenge is often that the television property can sometimes be a bit of a niche property with a limited audience and limited cultural exposure. Turning that into a widely accepted intellectual property has proven a stumbling block. Since *LOST* there has been a long list of series with intentions to launch a major intellectual property. While *Heroes* achieved some traction, *The Event* (NBC, 2010–2011), *V* (ABC, 2009–2011) and *Flash Forward* (ABC, 2009–2010) all failed to achieve traction in the market and the culture, failing as the launch point for a bigger universe. While a television series has many elements that provide excellent material for a large story, the problem is often moving that intellectual property into the wider culture.

Video games bring a cultural impact like film, but with a different set of characteristics: a sense of immediate engagement that neither film nor television matches. What the challenges are for a bottom-up attempt using games as a starting point is that only certain people play games (we have yet to see a *Words with Friends* feature film, but you never know) and generally only certain types of games become big hits. There are always exceptions, such as the ongoing success of *Angry Birds* (Chillingo, 2009 – present) as it morphs into a variety of expressions. Even more traditional blockbuster video games still often have a "story deficit," or in some cases a story overload, that poorly translates into multiple media. While this has improved immensely over the last ten years as game-makers have worked to improve the stories beyond the "kill the zombies" scenario, the fact is there always seems to be a limit to how well a video game story translates. Story-driven games tend to be very good at universe, but not so good at uncomplicated plotting or accessible characterization, and it will be interesting over the next few years to see how each medium's strengths and weaknesses begin to influence how the others tell stories and contribute to the development of a true transmedia story universe.

The process of bottom-up creation tends to be an on-the-fly process with the variables changing all the time. What makes it so challenging is that the right answer one time might not be the right answer next time. Each circumstance has unique variables; our goal is to understand these in order to maximize the chance for success. That means looking critically at the property from the very start, remembering what the mothership is, and to not let success in the short term blind you in the need to develop a long-term strategy, if the commitment really is to do transmedia storytelling.

Top-Down Crafting

The notion of top-down crafting has become increasingly the focus of the media industry over the past few years. We see more and more companies looking at intellectual properties with the intention of developing them into true transmedia properties. Even with a very short history and marginal success (who played the *Avatar* game?), the push for top-down crafting is becoming common, often using a range of property sources (such as comics, among others) as a starting point. A transmedia property requires many moving parts and in a top-down imagining we must see the big picture from the start (or at least early on).

The first step of the process is crafting the "big picture," which given the challenges of creating a large scale property is not a simple process. A producer (and subsequently any creative brought onboard) needs to think about a property in a manner that allows the development of multiple points of access and styles of audience engagement. Having a big picture perspective requires the producer to not focus on a single great character or story; but rather on the possibilities and potentials of the transmedia property, and spending time to think about what makes sense, realistically, and what does not. The perspective and vision required is grander and more complex than with any single medium.

When looking for examples of top-down crafting of properties originating in motion pictures, television or video games, the pool is unfortunately not very rich. Few transmedia properties starting in those media have been created and executed in this manner, even though this type of process is now considered the ideal. Most of the transmedia examples we think of as coming from film, television or video games were developed bottom-up, and the few top-down properties that do exist are not viable examples for our purposes, because none have reached sufficient maturity or complexity of expression to really warrant close analysis.

Crafting a transmedia property involves building the universe of the intellectual property and the worlds that each expression of the property inhabits within the universe. It also involves determining how and when the audience is going to first experience the new property, and what their subsequent exposure will be, and on what timetable. And it involves pre-thinking what aspects of the universe story are revealed in which expression or platform, and how the various key elements of the transmedia property interact across those expressions. We'll deal with each of those thoughts at the appropriate time.

The challenge is creating a universe that is both defined enough to build upon and broad enough to engage an audience over an extended period across multiple platforms. This reinforces the fact that top-down crafting is really universe building in the guise of property development. We're going to spend a great deal of time talking about universe and world building in subsequent sections and chapters, but suffice it to say this is the most critical aspect of top-down transmedia property development. It can also be the most cost-effective development dollars spent since it involves the input of a small team of producers and creatives (primarily writers) and does not involve full-blown production budgets, but can allow for the creation of cross-platform creative and development synergies that enhance each, and may even lead to more efficient and effective time in production.

Weaving the Universe

Weaving the universe relates to the fact that any successful transmedia intellectual property is like a tapestry – many threads that are well-woven to create a beautiful pattern. This points to the concept that really successful intellectual properties tell many stories that weave into a larger picture or larger understanding of the story.

The biggest challenge is that no matter how much planning things rarely go as planned. The "big picture" vision we just touched on is typically impacted by both financial and cultural factors. Even building the master plan is a huge undertaking with many factors to sort out. Whether it is a universe from scratch (top-down) or a universe adapted from one that already exists (bottom-up), each has different pressures and different advantages and those need to be taken into account.

Economic Issues

This isn't about production costs, *per se*, since we're talking about raw universe and world building, but the reality is that anyone who is building a universe for a transmedia property has to think about how expensive any of it is to produce. The more alien, or more fantastical the environments the stories play out in, the more it's going to cost.

How much can you afford to develop? When you look at all the possibilities, the inclination is to think that a complete development process is critical and very expensive. That is of course true to some degree. However, how much of this needs to be done is really a question of how much you need to develop to be able to conceptualize the world.

How much you can afford to make translates into "what do you need to actually make the world work?" Choosing which elements are crucial to weaving a story is a story-based decision as well as a pragmatic one. Where will the first success be? Is that the most important expression that defines the universe?

The economic considerations have a huge impact on how the elements are brought together because they define what elements are in the mix. Few properties and therefore few creators have unlimited resources, so virtually all need to go through a process of prioritization based solely on a sound financial model for the property. This is where creativity meets a pragmatic business approach, and subsequent chapters can help you anticipate some of these issues.

Cultural Impact

The cultural issue is present through the weaving process. Intellectual properties often have a long arc in terms of development and execution. The world we live in always provides a background; properties come in and out of focus, look different than they did ten years ago, for better and worse. Times change, so the setting and even the context and the meaning of the content changes, which can affect how the universe is shaped and structured. In addition, other properties emerge that change the culture's perspective on certain topics. *Harry Potter* set the table for supernatural topics, but discouraged another big property about wizards. *The Hunger Games* is a smorgasbord of teen-on-teen violence, which may have opened the doors on a long delayed property with a similar element, a motion picture version of Orson Scott Card's *Ender's Game* novel (Tor Books, 1985).

Intellectual properties establish what is topical and appropriate on a regular basis. Part of weaving an intellectual property universe is weaving in the culture around us. This is partly why one intellectual property universe makes a connection and becomes a hit while another disappears. The thread of "now" increases the chance of that connection. We're not striving for "timeless," but rather what is often referred to as "universal stories" – the irony is that partly what makes stories universal is their specificity. How an intellectual property places itself in the moment using what is available is incredibly important.

Cast of Characters

A distinguishing characteristic of properties is whether they are a single thread or a multithread character arc. Examples of each are *Harry Potter* and *Game of Thrones*. *Harry Potter*, while a rich universe of people, places and events is always clear whose story it is and who is the center of that universe. While Harry might not be present, Harry is always a presence – ultimately he is the thread all the other threads connect to. *Game of Thrones* is at the other end of the spectrum, a multithread universe where the Stark family is presented as the core of the narrative, with Ned Stark as head of the family and easy to interpret as the protagonist, until his head is chopped off at the end of Season One. (Oh, sorry :::SPOILER ALERT:::)

Outside it being a great plot twist, it is also proof that the story, be it in novel or television form, is the story of the universe that the audience gets to see from multiple perspectives. A multithread universe has more moving parts, so to speak, but on the other hand a misstep with one character could be quickly forgotten if you can effectively move on to the next and the next. Managing a single thread arc, while more challenging from a simple storytelling point of view, is less complex from a transmedia standpoint because we never wonder whose story it is. That is always clear. Keeping a large complex universe together requires that the grand vision is clear and being maintained by a producer with a handle on all the elements of the story. Not an easy task.

Platform Implications

How the media differences impact the weaving is another issue that has to be delineated. Each medium has its own strengths and weaknesses that accentuate different qualities in the universe. It goes back to the same question of what to start with. This time the question is not one of entry point, but instead how a given medium lays the groundwork for the introduction of the next element and the next and the next. Motion pictures provide the big splash, television the big picture and games the profound connection with the audience. Then the question becomes, what next and why? Is the point to focus on character or on universe or on pulling in a new audience or cementing the core? How do you use the unique traits of different media to strengthen the property as a whole? Is it a simple additive process or is it some synergistic process that is challenging to quantify? Add to that, what constitutes a timeline for success? The reality is that when and what order elements are introduced matters greatly. How do they amplify the expectations of the audience without killing momentum? People are used to waiting, but at what point does waiting damage the long-term position of the property? This is why the weaving of the universe is the greatest challenge of the process.

The past has already shown that you can have all the pieces in play and still manage to screw it up. An example of success and failure, and the circumstances surrounding each respective property, will illuminate the challenges of weaving and how they have been dealt with in the past.

Two Weaving Examples

The Matrix is a property ahead of its time and conceptually original. In fact we could argue that it is one of the first intentional transmedia properties. The initial film introduced the story's universe and because of its huge success, the creators were able to implement their original intentions to create the grand vision they had imagined, telling the story of that universe in animation, video games, web comics and feature films.

What we as an audience experienced, however, was not a grand vision, but instead, pieces that sort of fit together, interrelated, but without real synergy. In hindsight, the issues have to do with the loss of focus by the filmmakers, perhaps caused by trying to do too much, which led to a lack of crispness in the continuation of the mothership in the subsequent features.

In addition, their original vision was stymied by the video game's development in particular. The vision of a game that truly functioned as part of the transmedia storytelling process was hindered both by the technology of games and maturity of the form, an issue that is only now seemingly to the point where those challenges can be overcome. It was also the first real effort to extend the narrative from a motion picture into a video game, and in a way back again. A major character departs during one sequence and heads off to take care of something, the events of which are depicted in the video game. The character returns later in the motion picture, with minimal explanation as to where she was or what happened. The connections are tenuous, and frankly it creates a significant gap in the movie's plotting as it seems odd that she was off doing something important, but we don't (in the film) know what it is. That said, the weaving of *The Matrix* universe, well executed or not, is an important step in the maturation of the process of transmedia storytelling.

Launched in 1963, *Doctor Who* is an example of a property where there is a single entity in charge for many years – the BBC – with multiple media expressions and a very popular mothership, the television series. However, the BBC decided abruptly in 1989 that enough was enough (a clear example of how not to bring a property to conclusion) and put the property on "hiatus."

After that, the image that comes to mind is of a mom leaving her child on the doorstep of an orphanage. In this case an orphanage run by the fans … What occurred (and it is rare) was essentially that the weaving was turned over to the fans, some through more traditional channels like the *Doctor Who Magazine* and the novels, but eventually through less traditional methods, such as fan generated videos that kept the tapestry going. The fans maintained story momentum when the holders of the intellectual property refused and since the rebirth in 2005, the parents (or BBC) have done as excellent job of doing what they refused to do two decades earlier: weave a rich story universe with multiple successful expressions. The reemergence of this property has been an astonishing turn of events.

These two examples amplify how hard this process of weaving is. While not really helpful, the underlying truth is that how the elements are woven together is truly unique to each property. There are too many factors in play to come up with a simple formula or a single path. These examples make you wonder how *The Matrix* would look if launched today. *Doctor Who* in some ways is an example of how you learn from the past and redefine a property for its era. If you look at how the elements are now woven, it speaks to a modern audience and in fact a wider audience than it had in its previous runs.

Weaving the property through multiple expressions is how you establish it in the culture and establish the connections that make one property succeed and another slip into oblivion.

Ready to dive in? Let's build a universe … or is that *world*?

Story Universe vs. The Storyworld

Tomato, tomato. Oh, wait. On the page, there's no difference. And in most cases, your storyworld and story universe is the same thing as well. In those cases we say just call it the storyworld, 'cause that's much less intimidating than "universe." The term story universe comes into play when your property has multiple storyworlds all springing from the same core property concept. How can that happen? Very easily with transmedia.

Let's look at a pretty popular example right now, the Marvel Universe. The term "Marvel Universe" refers to all of the stories, all of the properties, from comic books to television shows to motion pictures – you name it – that initially sprang from the pages of Marvel Comics. The summer of 2012 saw the blockbuster release of *Marvel's The Avengers* (Marvel Studios) that put the super-hero characters of Iron Man, Thor, Captain America, the Black Widow, Hawkeye, and the Hulk together in the same motion picture for the first time. The character of Iron Man/Tony Stark had appeared in three motion pictures – 2008's *Iron Man* and 2010's *Iron Man 2* (which also featured the Black Widow) and a brief appearance in 2008's *The Incredible Hulk*. Thor appeared in 2011's *Thor*, which featured an extended cameo by Hawkeye. Captain America appeared in 2011's *Captain America: The First Avenger*. The character of the Hulk appeared in 2003's *Hulk* as well as the 2008 film (though everyone is pretty much ignoring his first movie appearance.)

So, here's where it gets complicated.

Each of those characters exists within the Marvel Universe, but each also exists within different storyworlds within that universe. Iron Man, for example, has his movie series (*Iron Man 3* releases in May 2013), as well as *Marvel's The Avengers* and the inevitable sequel. He's also the main character in *The Invincible Iron Man* comic book series, the 12-part *Iron Man: Animated Series* (a joint-production between Marvel Entertainment and Japan's Madhouse animation studio), and one of the main characters in the animated series *The Avengers: Earth's Mightiest Heroes*. So, Iron Man appears in all these properties … that's great, right? It is, except he's not exactly the same character in each incarnation.

He's really really close, but there are subtle differences. His personality is very similar across all the versions, but the relationship he has with other characters varies. His backstory, what the Iron Man armor itself can and cannot do varies as well. What's more important, and indicative of the differences in Iron Man himself, is that each of those incarnations listed above exists in a slightly different storyworld that is a sub-set of the Marvel Universe. Also, his storyworld is different from Captain America's – they encounter different villains, allies and conflicts and yet both exist in the larger universe.

The Marvel Studios motion pictures seem to all exist within the same storyworld, though we've seen the term "Marvel Cinematic Universe" used to refer to them … in fact Marvel packaged all the Marvel movies (except 2003's *Hulk*) in a special edition that was released in Fall 2012 called *Marvel Cinematic Universe: Phase One – Avengers Assembled*.

Categorizing abstract things like storyworlds and universes is a pain in the butt and has only limited practical use, but a fairly significant conceptual purpose. Ignoring the fact that the Marvel Cinematic Universe must therefore exist within the greater Marvel Universe … or perhaps alongside … that must be it… what's really going on is that each of the super-hero film series like *Iron Man* or *Thor* are built around a particular set of key story elements that distinguish them from each other, elements such as their own variations on story/theme, plot, characters, setting, and style or tone. One of the biggest challenges for *Marvel's The Avengers* was how they were going to make all these characters, from inter-related, but different storylines come together in one cohesive film. The Marvel Cinematic Universe thus far is doing a pretty good job of keeping everything working together and behaving as if it were one unified whole, but the second you wander outside, all bets are off. Fox's *The X-Men* motion picture series, for example, is part of the Marvel Universe, but not the Marvel Cinematic Universe.

Because the processes and considerations for building a story universe and a storyworld are similar, we are going to refer to this process as *worldbuilding* (as it was dubbed by science fiction writers even before transmedia) and use world and universe interchangeably except in those cases where there is a significant distinguishing difference between the two.

Building Blocks

As we have been talking about, the storyworld is a created or constructed world that acts as a setting for the story, or stories, of a transmedia property. It is literally the birthplace of all possible characters and conflicts and therefore must be well thought out, developed, and documented since multiple creatives will probably work within the property. Worlds have their own set of physical and metaphysical rules and mythologies that govern the characters and the environment. Some may mirror or actually be on Earth (as in, the one you and I live on) while others, especially in the transmedia-ripe areas of science fiction and fantasy, may be altogether different. The "rules" of the world however must be stated or dramatized early in the story (and the creation process) and remain consistent for the audience to believe the story. A complex World must be built.

This is a relatively straightforward process for a single media property, such as a stand-alone motion picture, television series, video game, novel or novel series, comic book series, and so on (at least if we ignore the amount of creative and organizational effort expended). When Gene Roddenberry created *Star Trek* in the late 1960s, he had no idea the level of cultural impact his television series would have, nor any conception of the breadth and depth of the narrative elements that make up all the myriad versions of *Star Trek* today, nearly 50 years later, but we're creating transmedia storytelling properties, so our perspective is from a higher perch, where we can see (or at least pretend we can see) all the possible expressions, and start making decisions about them from the very beginning.

We *know* we're creating an expansive world that is going to drive multiple manifestations of the property across a variety of media. Some opportunities will spin up naturally, mimicking the development course of nearly all intellectual properties that have become transmedia properties to date, but we're looking at the bigger picture. We can see motion pictures, television series, video games, comic books, novels, toys, websites, and a whole lot more in the future of a property, and we know we have to build our world to allow for these evolutions, from the start.

When building the storyworld itself it is vital to keep in mind that every choice has to enable storytelling in some manner. Every decision should open another door as much as possible – the more possibilities, the better, in transmedia storytelling.

The level of detail you need to develop for your world varies from creative to creative and story to story. However, one of the foremost authorities on world building for fantasy storytellers, Patricia C. Wrede, developed an intricate list of questions for fantasy world builders to ask themselves that can be currently be found on the Science Fiction Writers of America website at http://www.sfwa.org/2009/08/fantasy-worldbuilding-questions/. The list is primarily designed for a creator of a fantasy world, but it is easy to see how her questions can apply to, or be extrapolated for any kind of worldbuilding.

Let's look more specifically at some of the aspects to consider when building a viable transmedia world.

Physical Geography

Physical geography usually refers to the appearance of the outside world and how it has changed over time. A world may be mountainous and dry now, but millions of years ago may have been flat and covered by water. It is important to understand the geographical history of a world so that one may create from a place of knowing. You may want to tell the story of a creature that has been hiding beneath a small lake that has survived since the time that this world was under water. The knowledge of the geographic history of the world serves as context for the story to be told.

Additionally, the ecology of a world defines the pattern of relationship between all organisms of a world and their environment. This is not limited to the "human" or sentient beings, but to all life forms in a given world: the flora and fauna, the elements and non-sentient beings. So we do not limit ecology to what we consider to be nature or plant life, but extend it to all life. In James Cameron's *Avatar* the local Na'Vi tribe has an intimate relationship to the ecology of the planet. The relationship is adversarial with some plant and animal species and almost familial with others. This ecological relationship is at the heart of the story's central conflict, to defend their ancestral home and ecology from the invading and hostile human intruders.

In the case of science fiction or fantasy stories, how the geography came to be the way it is may be part of the story. Also, don't limit yourself to thinking that geography is all about mountains, and fields, and the course of rivers, and so on. Cities have geography as well … think about Seattle compared to Miami or Tokyo. The physical layout of the city as well as more general contexts affect your storytelling. For example, you would probably tell your story differently if it were set in an old, sprawling city that sprung up over decades in the middle of the agriculture belt, versus an extremely dense, modern city that was constructed in a very short span to support industrial growth. You could tell very similar stories in each of these places, but the nature of the place itself has to affect the story. Otherwise, why bother to set it there?

Culture

Why and how the people live in our stories should affect how they act. And so as we build transmedia worlds we must create cultural history for the various populations or cultures within this world. We must dig deep enough into the backstory of these cultures to understand their mythology, religious and spiritual beliefs, values, alliances and enemies and how they have developed over time and across the physical geography of the world.

The cultural history of our own planet provides plenty of starting points for building new cultures, but it also means that there's research to be done if we're setting our story within an existent one.

History

The history of a world is the construction of the complete world backstory. We must construct a world from the "beginning of time" until the present moment, when the story begins. This includes the geographical history, cultural history as well as the mythological, spiritual and religious histories of the cultures that populate the world. Any wars or conflicts, alliances or betrayals of trust are important aspects of the world history.

There can be too much history, however. It is impractical to document a timeline reaching back thousands of years, but you do need to think of what major historic events occurred that directly impact your story, or stories, or that have some bearing on the culture or even geography woven through your stories. History, to some extent, can be discovered as needed, but the high points, or foundations, need to be there from the start.

Mythology and Cosmology

World mythology refers to the "real" history of the world and its cultures, combined with the fantastical or story-world-created parables or religions for various cultures within that world. It is important that you understand how the world you've built really works … even if you're not letting the audience in on the secret. If the odd powers your characters have are really magic, you have to figure out the "rules" behind it, and maybe what the real source of that power is, which will be different if their strange abilities are due to genetic mutations or psychic powers. Similarly, you have to know if there is a god, or gods, or if that fact is important to your storytelling. If it doesn't have an impact, you can leave it as an unanswered question or narrative gap.

A Caveat

You probably already sense that many of these kinds of details form our backstory and may not even overtly become a part of the narrative. And certainly these aspects above point to some of the ways where the word *world* might fail us unless we fully embrace the idea of *storyworld*, such as:

1. If we were developing a transmedia property on the scale of something like Frank Herbert's *Dune* series, where we would need to consider whole planetary systems or galaxies as part of the storyworld. In that case, the above examples are only the first smallest worldbuilding step in our property's development.
2. If our story does not take place on a literal planet; in terms of storyworld, we may need to think of physical geography more broadly as environment, such as when the story takes place in an enclosed spaceship (say, CTV's 1973–74 series *The Starlost* or Universal Pictures' 1972 film *Silent Running*).

So far, we've been talking about the tangible aspects of the world, whether physical or sociological, but we also need to give consideration to less tangible aspects – the psychological and the existential. Which leads us to …

Mysteries or Secrets Hidden and Revealed

Everyone loves a good mystery, and mysteries – or mysterious elements – seem to be something that transmedia storytelling properties thrive on. In fact, we argue that it is one of the fundamental necessities of engaging transmedia storytelling. Without the mystery, the unanswered questions, the sense of discovery, there is little to drive the audience to other experiences related to the property.

Your audience, whatever demographic they might be, needs to be encouraged to seek out the other channels of the transmedia narrative. Putting aside whether (or how) they come to know about the other channels, when they do become aware of them, the audience members have to feel compelled to seek out those other channels or be open to them if they just happen across them. The audience must believe that without these other experiences their initial experiences (maybe the mothership, maybe not) is somehow lacking.

We just used *lacking* for emphasis, but it's a poor choice of wording, ultimately. If an experience feels lacking, the audience isn't going to want to hunt for more of it. That initial experience has to feel utterly complete and satisfying unto itself. Even if there is nothing more than that experience, the audience has to be satisfied, but transmedia storytelling works if there's also a sense that there's more out there waiting to be discovered, both in terms of additional transmedia storytelling experiences, and the mysteries in the story itself. The audience has to want more.

It is, however, a difficult tightrope to traverse. There has to be enough mystery, and the right kind of mystery, to compel the audience to seek out additional experiences, but at the same time there cannot be too many mysteries, too many unanswered questions. Likewise the mysteries that the audience sees have to be engaging, and there has to be faith that when the truth behind the mystery is discovered, it will be as engaging as the mystery itself was.

At a TED conference in March of 2007, writer/producer/director J. J. Abrams (*LOST, Fringe, Super 8, Alias, Star Trek*, etc. etc.) talked about his literal "mystery box," which is a plain brown box (taped shut) with a giant question mark on the side that was bought at Lou Tannen's Magic Shop in New York City years before. Abrams has never opened the box and claims he never will, because to him the mystery of what could be inside the box is more interesting than what might actually be in there. He said, "It represents infinite possibility; it represents hope; it represents potential. Mystery is the catalyst for imagination. maybe there are times where mystery is more important than knowledge." To him, that is the essence of storytelling.

Fans of the television series *LOST* understand the mystery box well, since that program was built from many mystery boxes, some of them nested like Russian Matryoshka dolls. Critics of the program argue that there were too many boxes and not enough pay-off to those mysteries. From Abram's TED quote above, it is clear that he personally believes the mystery to be more important than the secret behind it, so it shouldn't come as any surprise that *LOST* ended with many boxes unopened. To get a peek in those boxes, however, *LOST* fans devoured websites, video games, and novels … all in an effort to figure out what was inside. They were driven to follow the trail of breadcrumbs, and some of those trails led to answers (sort of), but more often than not they just led to more mystery boxes. Our interview with Carlton Cuse, executive producer and co-showrunner of *LOST* with Damon Lindelof, later in this book, looks at those boxes and breadcrumb trails and how some of them came to be and ended, or didn't …

As a result, the series ending left many perplexed, confused, and in some cases angry with its ambiguity. Again referencing Abram's TED quote the nature of the final scenes in *LOST* should come as no surprise … but surprise or not, it caused quite a good deal of controversy that persists to this day. (Cuse and Lindelof refuse interviews or interview questions that involve the *LOST* finale.) With that said, *LOST* dared to walk this tightrope, and the bottom line seems to be that there need to be enough mystery boxes to keep the audience interested, but there also need to be enough answers to keep them satisfied.

There is a real danger to this approach that we also touch on in other chapters: the audience of the mothership property (or any of the transmedia storytelling expressions) cannot feel that they are missing out if they don't also partake or participate in the other transmedia elements. The only way to discover the deeper truth that is a primary focus in one expression cannot be solely answerable in a different expression. Whatever content is in those other expressions can reinforce or enhance the mystery, but it cannot be the sole source for solving that mystery. That said, additional mysteries present in the mothership can be solved or revealed in supplemental media. So, for example, if a major thematic mystery in the mothership is whether human beings can find redemption by their own actions alone … that has to be answerable in the mothership. A possible secondary thematic mystery present in the mothership (say, "Must we pay for our sins?") could become a major thematic mystery in a companion expression, and possibly answered there. The audience for the mothership can then be led to solving the primary mystery, and left to ponder the second, or explore it further in the other expression.

The reason we like mysteries is because we love to solve them. That "ah-hah!" moment, and then being right makes us feel powerful and successful. Detective fiction is so popular in all forms of media because we enjoy pitting ourselves against the detective in an effort to be smarter than they are. Sometimes we can be, and sometimes we cannot, such as in the *Sherlock Holmes* stories, movies, television series, and video games … especially in the original stories where the author, Arthur Conan Doyle, denies the reader the same information that Holmes is using when he "deduces" the solution. The Holmes stories really aren't about solving the mystery, since the reader can't, but rather marveling at how Holmes can.

The video games are an interesting problem since Holmes is supposed to be the superior intellect and, well, most of the rest of us really aren't. Often in the *Sherlock Holmes* video games, a good part of the game play is gathering evidence and then presenting it to Holmes, who then confirms or refutes the player's hypothesis, since he's already figured it out. Rarely in the video games does the player get to control Holmes while in full deduction mode since we're just not smart enough …

The term *deus ex machina* (Latin for "god from the machine") is used to describe a plot device that resolves a seemingly unresolvable problem through the introduction of a new character, plot element, object or situation that wasn't present before. Many mysteries have *deus ex machina* solutions of a sort in that the final clue the detective uses to solve the mystery shows up at nearly the last moment and is kept from the audience. The detective reveals the final clue and solves the mystery all in one grand swoop, which takes away some of the magic. The famous rabbit-out-of-the-hat magic trick works because the audience sees a mundane hat – and mundane hats don't have rabbits in them … and see that this particular hat is empty and has no rabbit, so when the rabbit is pulled out, it's magic. Revealing the final clue and the solution to the mystery at the same time is like magically creating the hat and pulling the rabbit out at the same time. An amazing trick certainly, but if the trick was supposed to be the rabbit coming out of an empty hat, that result is lost since the rabbit could have been in the hat all along. If the trick was conjuring both at the same time, it's all good, but if it wasn't …

What does all that lead us to? We like to experience mysteries, especially when we could have solved them ourselves. A perfect example that caused at least one authors of this book to slap his forehead when it happened occurs in the 1986 motion picture *Manhunter*, by Michael Mann, based on the novel *Red Dragon* by Thomas Harris. (:::SPOILER ALERT!:::) In the film (as in the novel) the serial killer known as "The Tooth Fairy" has murdered multiple families in multiple states. The FBI, led by chief investigator Jack Crawford, has been unable to get anywhere in their investigation and brings in former profiler Will Graham to aid in the investigation. The mystery of how the Tooth Fairy is picking his victim families haunts the investigators and a good chunk of the film before the solution is revealed, and we discover that it has literally been in front of us the whole time. Throughout the film the investigators, and the audience, are shown home movies of the murdered families. It's the narrative device the film uses to show us the dead families and build sympathy for them. (In many ways it's a diegetic flashback technique, if you want to get all film geek about it.) We see clips from these films over and over … until in the revelatory scene Will Graham is talking himself through the murders, out loud, and realizes that the Tooth Fairy has to have seen the same home movies he (and us) are looking at all along. The scene is brilliantly played, and structured: as Graham verbalizes his thought process in figuring out the solution, there's a momentary pause built in when all the pieces come together, but before Graham blurts out the answer. That moment allows the audience to put the final pieces in place themselves and come to the answer seemingly before Graham does. It's a synergistic moment where the audience feels brilliant for having figured it out, is amazed that Graham did, and boggles that the solution has been there the whole time.

Is it possible to structure every revelation in this way? Probably not, but it is important to write mysteries that can be solved with the information at hand, even if retroactively. What we mean by this is that after the solution to the mystery is revealed, if the audience didn't get there first they have to be able to back-figure the clues presented and see how they could have, or should have, put the pieces together. Think of how many people went back to watch *The Sixth Sense* again (and again) to see how they missed (and could have figured out) the crucial fact about Malcolm.

So how many mysteries are too many?

At the risk of laying out the wussy answer "However many are appropriate to your story," we're going to point you at a fascinating piece of cognitive psychology called Miller's Law. In 1956 George Miller published a piece in the *Psychological Review* called "The Magical Number Seven, Plus or Minus Two: Some Limits on Our Capacity for Processing Information" that posited that human beings can manage five or six different stimuli with relative ease, but as that number rises performance rapidly decreases. We won't detail everything that Miller goes into in his paper (you can find it easily on the Internet), but will proudly stand beside Dr. Miller and note that his findings seem as worthwhile a starting point as any for "how many is too much?" We think, though, that this isn't the total number of mysteries present, but rather the most important ones, or the ones carrying the most emphasis. We'll leave it to the curious storyteller to decide if this 7+/−2 formula might apply to the number of characters in an ensemble cast as well.

Key Story Elements

When speaking of key story elements that make up our story universe and Worlds, it is important to understand that these elements are the contextual aspects of storytelling that all stories stem from. These are the basic tenets, rules and emotional tonality of the defined universe. Unlike many single standalone narratives, the transmedia story universe is the catalyst for the storytelling, and so we speak of story/theme, plot, character, setting, and style/tone as not just the fundamental tenets of good storytelling, but also within the context of an expansive transmedia story universe.

Story/Theme

The story emotionally endears an audience to content. It stems from the needs, wants, desires and challenges important to the main characters, their struggles and what they are willing to do to get what they want. What comes first, story or characters? Depends whom you ask, but either way, the two are intertwined in a thing called motivation.

Motivation is usually a term associated with character, but for our purposes we must understand character motivation as stemming from circumstance or context. Indeed, if a Terminator had not come back to kill Sarah Conner in the original *Terminator* film (20th Century Fox, 1984), she would not have been motivated to run and eventually to fight back. And so story also generates cause for action.

But where does story come from? The answer is premise, concept, and central question(s) of the intellectual property. These three terms refer to the same one or two line pitch that tells us the innate mystery of a story, what will keep fans watching and ultimately what will remain unanswered for the duration of the content, over all media, until the concept is done. In the example of *Terminator* the premise or central question becomes "Will Sarah Conner and later John Conner survive long enough to put an end to Cyberdyne and prevent the Terminators from exterminating the human race?" In the case of *Transformers* it becomes "Will the Autobots and human helpers be able to defeat the Decepticons and save the world?" In *Sherlock Holmes* it is more episodic in nature, but what we need to know boils down to "Is Sherlock Holmes smart enough to foil even the most dastardly of villains?" In *LOST* it is "Will the survivors live long enough to get off of the mysterious island?" The stories that drive these properties across all of their expressions always stem from these basic central questions. These are the franchise engines, the places where endless stories are generated and countless characters will live and struggle toward the same ends.

For the most part transmedia successes in mass media have been science fiction, fantasy and action based. This will change as transmedia becomes more prevalent, but the need to have a fertile enough storyworld or universe to generate content over time and across multiple media, changing slightly with each iteration, will remain a necessity to sustain the audience's interest.

We also find that the stories we most often see in transmedia are hero or many-hero based, and we define hero as either underdogs who must find something extraordinary within themselves in order to face sizable villain(s) or those who already have super or fantastical qualities within themselves that they then must mortgage to defeat villains. These premises stem from our archetypal need to see people, or personified beings, confront undefeatable foes, rise to the occasion, struggle and ultimately defeat the foe. We also desire to see these heroes then bring back the spoils of their victory, to us, to society, to human kind. This may simply fulfill in us some sense of observing and knowing that now, thanks to our collective hero or heroes – all is well; we are safe – until the next time.

The themes associated with successful transmedia content are universal human themes, the larger archetypal needs, wants and values shared by us all regardless of ethnicity, socio-economic background or religious belief … we all want good to triumph over evil; we all desire to survive; we all desire for wrong to be avenged. These are the types of giant themes that, so far, transmedia has addressed and successfully generated stories for over time and across multiple media.

These types of stories also tend to be about quests; they tend to be about a search for something or about running from something or a combination of both. Whether it is a search for the unknown in space as evidenced in *Star Trek's* catchphrase and property-driving statement "To boldly go where no one has gone before" or whether it be about *Heroes*' (NBC Television, 2006–2010) first season arc hook "Save the cheerleader, save the world," there is urgency in transmedia stories. Something is at risk … there is sufficient jeopardy.

Jeopardy refers to the danger inherent in the story itself. Audiences of transmedia stories crave jeopardy; in fact, they want to participate in the jeopardy of a fictional universe. They want to be at risk along with the characters.

There also needs to be a unifying emotional or sub-textual through line running through the property, regardless of the expression. In big transmedia worlds it is possible to tell all kinds of stories, but all kinds of stories may not be appropriate for your property. Whatever story it is that you tell, be it in a motion picture, television series, video game, novel, comic book, webisode or alternate reality game, it has to feel as if it's part of the property. If it feels disconnected from the core ideas or themes of the property, disconnected from brand identity, you risk losing the audience's connection to the property, or even alienating them. We've seen this problem with many television series reboots (*Bionic Woman* NBC, 2007 or *Night Stalker* ABC, 2005) where the update or modernization just didn't feel like the intellectual property that we were familiar with. That said, it is always important to remember that doing something really well lets you break the rules. Case in point, the 2004 reimagining of *Battlestar Galactica* which turned the original 1978 property upside down, shook out core elements, and reconstructed it as something familiar yet very different. Some fans of the original incarnation couldn't get past the changes, while others embraced it.

Building mystery into the theme and story of the transmedia property can be tricky, but it can be ultimately rewarding. This is the least concrete of the types of mysteries that can be a part of each key story element in that mysteries of theme and story are probably most subject to interpretation. A great deal of discussion about *LOST* focused on perceptions of what the story really was about – was it just, as it seemed on the surface, a survival story about plane crash victims, or something much deeper, like a journey of redemption. The not-so-simply answered question "What the hell is this show really about?" became a huge driving force for its fan base.

The thematic elements of a story can sometimes be painfully obvious, and that's often a turn-off, though the failure of *LOST*-like television programs such as NBC's *The Event* or ABC's *Alcatraz* could signal that audiences are looking for more obvious signposts. Because thematic mysteries are so subject to interpretation, they can easily and quickly become the most frustrating. The subtlety involved in thematic storytelling is significant, but it becomes difficult to signal the answers to those questions in a way that enough of the audience "gets it" without having a character almost literally hold up a placard that reads, "It's all a metaphor for grief, dummy."

Thematic mysteries have to have layers. There needs to be the upper-most or surface layer that provides one answer that is completely acceptable. Deeper down, for those who want to make that journey, is the real answer that has to be investigated in order to be discovered and understood. This is not really any different from what any good, deep, story should be doing, but with transmedia storytelling the clues to what lies deeper need not be limited to one medium or expression.

Plot

Plot differs from story in that plot reflects the mechanics or actions needed to traverse a story sequentially and to get to the desired story goal. Plot is a tool of story and is the way in which we structure the story (which we'll talk about more in the next chapter). If the story needs a character to fall in love with a woman that he cannot have, then the plot takes him, beat by beat and step by step, through the paces needed to have him fall in love, have the love unrequited and the story unfold as needed.

As part of the plot of the story universe you should also define any over-arching or master storylines that are present and exist in all possible platform and media expressions. For example, in the *Terminator* property all stories revolve around the "Rise of the Machines," their subsequent domination of humanity and humanity's battle to overthrow them. In order to assure consistency, it is wise to define key parts of that narrative as part of the story universe so that the stories created (regardless of platform or medium) have the same reference points. For the story universe what is most important about defining the plot is identifying the kinds of stories that can be told. For example, *Star Trek* is always about exploration, be it of physical space or questions of the human condition. For the *X-Files* it involves uncovering secrets and solving mysteries that only serve to reveal deeper questions or conspiracies.

The term *mythology* has come to refer to those mysteries within a story that tend to remain unanswered for long periods of time. In *LOST* the mythology is seemingly endless, beginning with the island itself and extending with the smoke monster, the Others, the Dharma Initiative, Hanso Corporation, and so forth. It is these very elements that are ripe for transmedia extension and indeed the alternative reality games of *LOST* dealt heavily with the mythology. Mythology keeps interest and sparks "seeker" exploration or participation in the universe. Fans want to know more, and transmedia extension, aided by narrative gaps, gives them new and exciting places to look.

By *narrative gaps*, we are referring to purposely unanswered "pieces" of story arcs. A series introduces an interesting or mysterious storyline and then allows it to disappear from the series, making some reference to it, but not continuing the storyline for a period of time. Fans then desire to know more about the storyline, and transmedia extensions can provide "pieces" that have been left out of the primary narrative in the primary media platform.

Plots in transmedia narrative properties, especially those that bridge across multiple expressions or platforms, are inherently full of surprises, red herrings, misleads and mysteries within mysteries. These plot twists serve the story. If we indeed are going where no man has gone before, then it had best be a mysterious journey to get there … but of course … we never quite arrive … there. As a result, our plot makes use of what is in effect an unanswered mystery, and plotting a story has to take into consideration at what point (if ever) we will answer any or all of the mysteries, but this isn't as simple a decision as it might seem.

Chris Carter's *The X-Files* (FOX television, 1993–2001) is viewed by many as the father of complex, inter-woven mystery-driven television storytelling by virtue of its complex mythology, which is really just a framework of mysteries. In many ways the show was driven by its slogan "The Truth Is Out There," which made a promise in some ways that there was a real truth, a real set of answers to the mysteries the show presented. The ongoing, serialized, no-end-in-sight nature of television programming meant that more and more mysteries needed to be produced with each passing season, but the primary mysteries could not be solved as that would mean the end of the show. *The X-Files* had many episodes that maybe, possibly, presented what the "truth" was, but these "truths" were often contradictory to the other "truths" presented in different episodes, but yet each of them seemed to be the real "truth." (Take a breath …) The truth became so convolved, and so many of those truths debunked in prior episodes, that it became harder and harder, some would say all but impossible, to bring the series to a satisfying conclusion. Production realities brought *The X-Files* series to a close in 2002 with mixed critical and fan reception. By the time the series ended, some fans found it difficult to believe there was a real "Truth" out there and that they weren't just being strung along endlessly. *LOST*, with its equally complex storytelling, faced similar criticism.

As we discussed earlier, any plot mystery that is presented as being a key or pivotal mystery in the mothership property has to be answerable in that property. There can, and should, be multiple plot mysteries that aren't fully revealed in the mothership, but can be addressed in companion expressions. Plot mysteries are often structured in such a way that the revelation of the truth behind the mystery solves it, but also launches another mystery or provides some additional clues into solving a different mystery in the story. This "chain of mysteries" can be a very effective storytelling tool in that it provides closure and satisfaction related to one mystery, while keeping the audience engaged by revealing another. The audience, however, has to feel as if there is an ultimate end to the chain and that they're not just going to be strung along forever. They also have to feel that there is a real solution out there, and not just more questions.

In many ways plot is the standard mystery component: What happened? Who are those people? Did Betty somehow survive the truck explosion? Who framed Roger Rabbit? Mysteries are inherent questions, and there are any number of approaches to building in plot-related mysteries based around who, what, where, when, how, and why… though the last is better answered in terms of character.

Characters

It is important not to just think about storyworld building as creating the physical place. Proper worldbuilding requires placing the seeds for your stories in all of its forms, and we know that stories require drama, which is conflict, whether external or internal, physical or emotional.

Conflict, the inherent incompatibility of two opposing forces, is the foundation of all stories. There must be a need or a want expressed by one or more characters (or forces in the world) that comes into direct opposition with the needs and wants of another character or character(s). However, in some stories, characters are up against non-sentient obstacles like nature, the supernatural and/or technology. For there to be "story," there must be conflict, and within the idea of conflict there inherently must be a winner and a loser. By the end of the story, the character either gets what she wants or is denied. The story takes place from the moment we know what is desired until the object of desire is either gotten or denied.

Universal conflict can best be defined as conflict between "good" and "evil." Traditionally, this has been expressed as between protagonist or hero and antagonist or villain. In the types of big franchise films and television series Hollywood has chosen for its transmedia blockbusters, there are, for the most part, clear good guys and bad guys, and we are meant to root for the good guys. However, in the world of video games, well, sometimes you play the bad guy … who is still the hero of the story in many ways.

In video game stories of the last few years, there has been a trend toward giving the player the option of playing a protagonist or hero who is defined not by a universal sense of good and evil, but rather by how the player chooses to play. Gamers are given the choice to play the clear "bad guy" in a game like *God of War II* (Sony Computer Entertainment, 2007), a reformed bad man in *Red Dead Redemption* (Rockstar Games, 2010), or a character whose moral compass is determined solely by the player's actions, as in *Fallout 3* (Bethesda Game Studios, 2008). And there is certainly no "good guy" in the *Grand Theft Auto* game series (Rockstar Games); you play a criminal, committing crimes. You not only cheer for the bad guy … you are the bad guy.

By the same illustration, we see a movement in television to blur the lines between good and evil. The *Dexter* television series (Showtime, 2006–present) is the best example of this in which Dexter, at once a serial killer and a detective who hunts serial killers, is the hero. He is a garden variety, used to kill animals in the back yard, serial killer except that he kills … serial killers. And so we root for a serial killer, and not from the place where you secretly "like" the villain or the monster, but from the overt stance of this is the main character that I want to win.

And in film we need only look at the works of Quentin Tarantino to see that heroes can be "bad." One is hard pressed to find a good "hero" in his works, but rather a collection of villains where you root for the villain that you have the most in common with, or the villain with flaws that humanize him enough to place him as "less evil" than those he opposes.

The transmedia character, whether good or bad, must be well developed in order to extend across multiple media, to be compelling not just in one form, but through many story strands. In order to maintain consistency across multiple media and platforms, it is imperative that the characters in each feel as if they are part of the same story-world or universe or "cut from the same cloth." It is therefore important to lay out what common or defining characteristics the various primary characters in the storyworld must have in order to be identified as part of that world. In a way we are again dealing with archetypical expressions of characters in order to assure that no matter what medium or platform, there is a consistency to the kind of characters we find. Additionally, if there are going to be central characters that appear or are referenced across multiple platforms or expressions, it is important that they be defined up-front to insure that they meet the needs of the property, not just the platform of their first appearance.

The good news is that the same basic components that make great characters in traditional storytelling also make great characters in transmedia storytelling … with a few considerations.

Characters are "people": Are character's real? Well, to the creator they must be real or the audience will not engage with or become endeared to them. You are creating "people"…even if you aren't. In short, the things that attract us to Yoda in the *Star Wars* universe – wisdom, kindness, patience and the ability to kick major ass – are the same qualities that attract us to Gandalf the Grey in *The Lord of The Rings* and Professor Xavier in *The X-Men* series and Morpheus in *The Matrix*.

Characters have lives: In order for characters to be believable and compelling they must have "lives" or intricate backstory strands. They need to have a backstory beginning from birth or even earlier, from their parent's situation at conception. This backstory must include the good and bad of a life lived, with all of the anxieties, fears, abuses, accomplishments, loves and celebrations that you and I may have. This "life" follows them right up to the start of your story and then is the partial motivation for how they act, think and speak.

Mystery: All good characters have some sort of enigma behind them. Good questions about who and what they are should circle those characters constantly. Every character needs some degree of uncertainty, something unclear about them, that presents a mystery to be solved. Characters that are not carrying those questions are either archetypes or stereotypes, but they're not full-bodied characters. Dimensional or lifelike characters have their own mythologies. Motivation and backstory are aspects that the audience will discover through the story and that add depth to the character, but the surface character presented to the audience has to be interesting enough that we care about those mysteries. Each medium has particular necessities of character construction that we'll address in later chapters, but whether it's a character in a motion picture who's only in our lives for 90 minutes of screen time, on a television show where their character arc has to bridge dozens of hours and hopefully multiple seasons, or in a video game where in some ways we are that character and that character is us, it's the mystery or enigma behind the character that keeps us engaged.

Relationships: Characters need to have other compelling characters to bounce their personalities off of character is best illustrated through relationships. It is also important to understand that a great deal of what a viewer comes to understand about a character comes from how other characters in the story treat them.

Subplots: Many characters seem to charge toward their goals without any other aspects of life colliding with the main plot. Subplots are smaller stories within the large story that allow the character to show aspects of character not seen in the main plot. Love is the most common subplot. An action hero that has a soft spot for an innocent child for instance reveals that the otherwise callous hero is actually sentimental and we like him or her even more.

Sufficient jeopardy: In order for a character's true colors to be shown they must be in some type of jeopardy or danger or someone that they love or value must be. This is part of the test. The hero is taken out of his normal element of status quo everyday life and thrown into a situation of dire jeopardy. Then we see what he or she is truly made of.

Villain: For a character, especially a hero, to be fully developed they must face off against a worthy foe. Usually the villain is especially dangerous to the hero; in some way they are opposites. What one wants, the other wants more.

Characters flow out of the storyworld's premise and are the personified "doers" or "seekers" of the answer to the central question. In *LOST* we ask ourselves from the very first scenes, "Will they survive long enough to be rescued?" Characters that either help fulfill that premise or stand in opposition are required by the property. Much of the premise of *LOST* circles around questions related to science vs. faith. Jack, a surgeon with clear leadership skills, wakes up and immediately begins to help them "survive." He is the rational thinker, the man of science. Locke, a doubter who was crippled, finds he can now walk on this strange island and is transformed into a true believer, the man of faith, but neither stands fully in the right, so the conflict of the premise manifests through them and their actions.

When looking at transmedia narrative characters we must see them as having a different set of responsibilities from characters limited to one media form. They must have "media-endurance" or character traits, charm and ability to rise to face challenges on many screens and devices and through multiple creative forms. A transmedia character must be as compelling on screen as in a comic book, alone in a webcam confessional or at play in a video game. For this reason, so far, most transmedia success stories are science fiction, fantasy, supernatural and action. (Perhaps because they have more depth, or perhaps for the exact opposite reason.) Maybe these transmedia heroes are successful because they are larger than life characters up against larger than life odds. We root for the hero who can face down villains that we would run from instantly. The transmedia hero is bigger than us … but he or she stands for what we want to be. The transmedia hero is aspirational in nature … we want to be him … we choose to play him (sometimes) … he is the best of us without the worst … the courage without the fear … the life that cannot truly die … but has multiple "lives."

Setting

If story talks about the emotional stakes, plot about the kinds of things that happen, and character about the kinds of heroes and villains present, setting defines the physical environment all of these exist within. Setting gives context to story, gives it a sense of place, and a history and geography upon which story organically stems. In terms of transmedia universes, they tend to be of three general types:

1. The "real world" with fictional elements, such as *The X-Files*, *Heroes* and *Terminator*.
2. A slightly different world that mirrors ours in many ways and in which our physical rules still apply, as in *LOST*.
3. Or a completely fictional world with different rules and beings as in *Star Trek*, *Avatar* and *Prometheus*, but even in the latter, trackers or real world elements by which to juxtapose the other worlds are given. As in *The Lord of The Rings* trilogy, we experience a strange world, but humanoids are the main characters/heroes.

Again, consistency is important across platforms and mediums, especially in the areas of environment, culture and technology (and/or magic), which are the key elements of setting. Looking at *Star Trek*, the setting includes not only what the inside of a Federation starship (like the USS *Enterprise*) looks and feels like, and how its technology operates, but what the Klingon or Vulcan cultures are like and what elements are required for them to consistently feel like different cultures.

Stories should be inexorably linked to the time and place of their setting. If they're not, there's no reason for that story to be set in that place, at that time. Fantastical and unusual settings inherently spark curiosity in the audience since so much of the world is unfamiliar. If the property is connected to another expression (like the television series *Game of Thrones* is connected to George R. R. Martin's fantasy novel series *A Song of Ice and Fire*), then some of the audience are already familiar with the setting, but many may not be. The world, however, ultimately has to be rooted in something familiar, or something that can be extrapolated into something familiar, or audiences spend too much time trying to make sense of every little thing and become distracted from the story.

The more familiar and mundane the setting, the harder it is to build curiosity or mystery about the setting, unless perhaps you are *Twin Peaks* …

Actually, *Twin Peaks* (ABC, 1990–1991) demonstrates how what could have been a familiar and mundane setting was transformed by not only the production design, but the storytelling as well. The secret, however, was that setting (somewhere in the state of Washington) became someplace uncertain. Familiar and mundane settings can be transformed by the introduction of disconnected or inexplicable elements: Where does that odd red door go? Who painted that giant mural five stories up the side of that building? As storytellers, we have to be sure that mysteries in familiar places tie into the story being told and don't distract from them.

Style/Tone

Though we list it last, this is an equally important key story element. While *Star Wars* and *Terminator* are both ostensibly about rebellion against an overbearing force, those two properties feel very different in terms of tone and execution. *Star Wars* has a heroic, pulp-action, larger-than-life, "space-opera" feel to it, whereas *Terminator* is dark and dirty, with its "heroes" only barely managing to survive and fight another day, and the specter of ultimate defeat is very real and present. In the same way, the style and feel of the universe presented in the Tom Clancy movie adaptations – *The Hunt for Red October* (Paramount Pictures, 1990), *Patriot Games* (Paramount Pictures, 1992), *Clear and Present Danger* (Paramount Pictures, 1994), *The Sum of All Fears* (Paramount Pictures, 2002) – while about politics, espionage, and international action, feel very different from the *Mission: Impossible* films or the *James Bond* motion pictures, even though Bond has moved more toward Clancy and away from *Mission: Impossible* with its latest incarnation.

Tone speaks to the emotional takeaway of the content, while style speaks to the way the story is told utilizing visual, sound and written techniques. *The X-Files* and *Millennium* (Fox, 1996–1999), the second Chris Carter TV vehicle, were both investigative procedurals dealing with mystery and the unknown, except *Millennium* dealt with graphic depictions of serial killer violence; it was dark and scary ... and canceled. *The X-Files* dealt with subject matter in a more PG-13 manner, more about the mystery than the graphic details of violence and torture. It survived for multiple seasons and many transmedia offshoots. Tone and style can make or break content.

Style and tone also help to create a brand identity and must remain consistent in each story world. However, some brands, like *James Bond*, may change in tone as, over time, audience expectations change, but Bond remains Bond and his martinis remain shaken and not stirred ... although Heineken seems to have made its way to his lips of late.

Visual style, writing style and marketing all must serve and be consistent with the story universe. If a director chooses a visual style that is out of harmony with the universe style elements, then fans will complain and fan forums will be full of negative chat. Fans live and breathe the inherent style, tone and texture of their content, and so must the makers.

More to Explore

Now that we've got our story universe and storyworlds built – what? You don't have yours done yet? That's OK. As we said at the start of this chapter, development takes time. And the media chapters in Part Two will be considering these key story elements from the unique perspective of each medium, so there's more to consider, but once we have a good sense of the universe and world that we're building, we will be ready to start considering the question of how we will shape, structure and present the stories that our world has sparked.

Chapter 3
Storytelling and Narrative Continuity

Stories are cognitively linear so they can describe a path of events with a goal, a conflict, and the promise of resolution. This doesn't mean that stories can't be constructed in a nonlinear environment. They can; that's part of the excitement about using the tools of a transmedia world to assemble the story. But the linear link is what provides coherency so that the parts fit together, whether it's backstory or clues to unravel mysteries in the main story arc.

—Pamela Brown Rutledge[1]

We've built a Universe. We've developed its world(s) and key story elements. Time to rest? Not yet. Now we need to begin telling our stories, building story experiences for the audience. The term *storytelling* gives equal importance to *story* and *telling*, because the story only comes alive in its telling.

The temptation is to jump right to which medium we will use. After all, each platform does tell stories differently (more on that in the chapters on different media in Part Two), so we will need to understand the strengths and limitations of each to tell a story. But rather than let the medium dictate the story, we feel it's better to work the other way around, to let the story dictate the medium. In other words, how do we know which medium will be best if we haven't worked out the types of stories we want or need to tell or that best reveal our Universe? Stories don't just exist, they are constructed, and as transmedia producers and creatives, we need to understand the possible ways we can structure story.

We can describe story structure in a variety ways, some more general and some more nuanced: high concept or low concept, three-act structure; plot; genre. As transmedia storytellers, we can present stories as a series of events in chronological order. Or our stories can reveal small moments that are based on association rather than arranged by chronology. Transmedia stories can exhibit a tight logic of cause and effect (one action clearly leads to another) or be episodic (jumping from event to event in the characters' lives or the storyworld). Stories can move forward like an arrow in flight, come full circle or even be told in reverse chronology. Before we can talk about the various ways of approaching story structure, it might help to review the distinction between story and plot.

[1] "Transmedia Storytelling: It's the Story, Stupid," Positively Media, Psychology Today, published October 21, 2011 and accessed September 1, 2012, http://www.psychologytoday.com/blog/positively-media/201110/transmedia-storytelling-it-s-the-story-stupid-0

The *story* is all the raw material having to do with the characters, their actions, the conflict, and the situations which fill in a full world, both seen and unseen by the viewer or audience. The story draws from, expresses and is inspired by the entire fictional universe that we have created in the previous chapter. In some ways it is the *why* of what happens.

The *plot* is how we organize, sequence, edit and present that raw material in a specific medium so that it has the most dramatic impact, by showing the audience which of those elements we have decided are important to understand in order to make sense — and feel the emotional pull — of the story. Plot is the structure we use to tell the story. It is the *how* to the story's *why*.

Driving the Story

While at one level we could (rightly) consider transmedia storytelling as *world driven*, when we begin to parse out and formulate the individual stories we are going to tell from the story universe, we need to take into consideration the ways in which individual platforms have developed their own take on the key story elements we discussed in Chapter 2.

Stories are often classified as either *character driven* or *plot driven*. Of course, all stories have plots (or structures) and characters, but many stories tip the balance more toward one or the other.

Character-driven stories are sometimes referred to as *low concept*, and the story's events grow out of the unique traits of the character. We watch the repercussions of the decisions the character makes, and character-driven stories often include some sort of epiphany, insight or recognition on the part of the protagonist. This might be seeing whom he really is or gaining a better understanding of the situation in which he finds himself. Most importantly, this recognition usually provides the character with an opportunity to change, whether he takes that opportunity or not. *Garden State* (Fox Searchlight Pictures, 2004) is an example of a character-driven film as Large begins to see his life for what it really is, but so is *My Best Friend's Wedding* (TriStar Pictures, 1997), where Julianne has to realize the error of her ways and try to set her personal world right again. Memoirs tend to be character driven.

Plot-driven stories are those where the situation or the concept is more important and enticing for the audience than the individual characters. Sometimes referred to as *high concept*, these stories are built around a premise that can often be described in terms of the action: "terrorists hijack the President's plane", *Air Force One* (Columbia Pictures, 1997) is not about a president taking stock of his life and becoming a better person (which might be how a character-driven film would develop); it's about a situation that requires action. The pleasure is watching that action (or more precisely, the President kicking ass). High concept stories are usually easy to describe as a one-sentence concept that expresses a certain thrill or curiosity factor; *Snakes on a Plane* (New Line Cinema, 2006) puts its high concept right in the title. People heard that and wanted to see the film, though it may also be a cautionary tale that films ultimately have to be more than just a concept; they have to have a story that deepens and fleshes it out. Video games and most television series are high concept.

Genres are an example of plot-driven stories, and the term *genre* simply refers to specific narrative structures or story conventions that have been used so much that they have become standardized. For example, the detective genre often starts with the arrival of the protagonist at the crime scene, and it's only through the course of the story that eventually the protagonist meets the antagonist and finally figures out that the antagonist is responsible for the crime.

But this kind of structure wouldn't work for a romantic comedy, which generally requires that the two main characters meet early on, are clearly fated to be together but either are unable to recognize that fact or are confronted with a series of obstacles that keep them apart until the end. Just from your own reading and viewing experiences, you know that comedies tell their stories differently from dramas, and that romantic storylines are presented differently from mystery or detective storylines. With that said, there are some commonalities, similarities or elements that connect them all as expressions of storytelling.

Most transmedia properties to date have been classified as high concept (or plot-driven), though the film and TV components may have strong character development, balancing the character-driven and plot-driven elements much like the first *Die Hard* film (20th Century Fox, 1988), where the protagonist goes through internal growth and recognizes what's important to him personally (low concept) even as he has to fight the terrorists who have taken over a skyscraper (high concept) or like the television series *LOST*, which intertwined elements of high and low concept storytelling in startling ways. Though video games are a prime platform for high concept storytelling, Quantic Dream's *Heavy Rain* and BioWare's *Mass Effect 2* are critically acclaimed efforts to imbue video games with more character development resulting in deeper, more engaging stories. With all of these, though, you can see the heavy presence of genre.

Genre Types

As we noted a moment ago, genre is a term used to classify stories by their recurring use of certain specific elements, such as the femme fatale in film noir, the wild and untamed landscape of Westerns or the gradual piecing together of "whodunit" in a mystery. Stories within a specific genre (regardless of platform) share formal characteristics; the way in which the story is told draws upon specific conventions that the audience has become familiar with and expects. These are standardized formulas built around the idea that a certain content or type of story requires a particular form or structure. In some cases, these conventions may be about the type of protagonist, the type of conflict, the way in which the story is plotted, the story's mood/tone or its style. Some of these are related to the narrative events of the story and some are related to the aesthetic elements of the story. Most of the mass media properties we see these days fall within or include aspects of genre.

Classifying a story by genre can seem pretty easy until we start to realize that the exact definition of what constitutes a genre and what constitutes a subgenre is often debated. Websites like IMDB or Wikipedia might classify genres differently from not just each other but from a film critic, a marketing team or vendor as well. Some lists do not differentiate between genres and subgenres, treating them all the same. For example, within the genre of drama, we could have subgenres such as the coming-of-age drama or the family drama or the romantic drama. Or we might list coming of age as a genre in and of itself (as we will in a moment).

Here are the most common genres for our purposes (acknowledging that some readers might disagree and feel some of these are subgenres or not genres at all):

Action: *like the name implies, focuses more on actions than emotions, featuring a relatively simplistic (or one-dimensional) protagonist or protagonists whose conflicts require active and visceral engagement through fights, chases, explosions and impressive feats of physical prowess to succeed.*

Adventure: *often set in exotic locales and features a heroic journey through the unknown.*

Comedy: *designed to elicit laughter and entertain the audience through humorous exaggeration, often resulting in a happy ending.*

Coming-of-age: *focuses on the emotional and psychological growth of the character, either literally or metaphorically from youth to adulthood.*

Crime: *glorifies criminal acts and/or the lives of people who live outside the law, whether based on real-life figures or characters created by the writer.*

Documentary: *often assumed to be "true" or depicting real life events and therefore synonymous with "non-fiction"; however, with the advent of mockumentaries and fiction films that are shot to look like documentaries (such as* Cloverfield *or* The Blair Witch Project*), as a genre definition we are looking at specific stylistic and formal elements such as handheld camera, talking heads, multiple characters, subtle performance, etc.*

Drama: *realistic or psychologically recognizable characters who struggle with an external obstacle that comes at a crucial point in their lives, affecting their understanding of themselves and the world they live in, building around emotional themes.*

Epic: *an ambitious and sweeping panorama of events that change the world, often focusing on a single heroic character (whether historic, mythological or created solely for the story).*

Family: *often featuring animals, children or family as protagonists, these are stories that can be enjoyed by a wide range of ages and demographics, in other words, all members of an extended family (children, parents, grandparents); though it can be argued that the family genre is defined by the intended audience and not really a genre at all, there are certain story conventions regarding subject matter and protagonists that lead some people to include it in a list like this one.*

Fantasy: *often involves superhuman forces (whether magical, mythological or simply super-powerful) and wildly imaginative worlds wherein the protagonist undergoes some kind of a mystical transformation with the assistance of these powerful, superhuman forces; though Joseph Campbell's* Hero's Journey *can be applied to several different genres such as epic and adventure, its structure most closely resembles the elements we often find in fantasy.*

Film noir: *sometimes considered a subgenre of crime films or a classification of stories from a specific historic/cultural moment (post-World War II USA), in terms of aesthetic or storytelling conventions, film noir usually features low-key monochromatic visuals paired with sexual politics and cynicism; more recent films in this genre are sometimes referred to as neo-noir.*

Historical: *based on real historical events or famous people.*

Horror: *often exploits personal or psychological universal fears of the unknown or unease about family or body, wherein the protagonist is a victim (or intended victim) of monstrous forces which are often supernatural or in contradiction of our understanding of the natural world.*

Musical: *incorporates songs as a form of character expression, often revealing interior thoughts or feelings, that are interwoven with more traditional narrative elements.*

Mystery: *sometimes considered a subgenre of the crime film or the thriller, a film that is built around a puzzle and usually focuses on the protagonist trying to solve a crime or unexplained occurrence through investigation and deduction.*

Romance: *a love story that focuses on the emotional and physical attraction and subsequent relationship between characters.*

Science fiction: *hinges on changes to the world as we know it, changes which have a rational explanation or are extrapolations of what we currently know; science fiction stories may explore philosophical implications or express apprehensions about the future or technology; our protagonist is often a bystander or witness who then has to take action.*

Sport: *features an individual or a team who prevail through faith in their abilities and learning to work together at a specific sport despite overwhelming difficulties or obstacles.*

Thriller (suspense): *keeps the audience at the edge of its seats by creating a story that maximizes anxiety and surprise as the antagonist presents increasingly stressful obstacles that the protagonist must overcome.*

War: *depicts warfare including battles or daily non-combative life in wartime; if this depiction questions the value of war or depicts it negatively, it may be considered an anti-war story; the protagonist may be an individual or a team.*

Western: *embodies the spirit of the new frontier where the landscape or environment is so prominent as to become another character in the story, expressing tensions between wilderness and civilization, freedom and settling down, danger and security; the protagonist is often an idealized expression of masculinity (alone, self-reliant and with a personal but honorable sense of justice).*

YA or young adult: *even more than family films, the YA classification is more about the demographic or audience these properties are marketed to than identifiable storytelling (or even aesthetic) conventions used; the primary defining factor at this point may simply be that the protagonist is roughly the same age or (more likely) just slightly older than the intended audience.*

In recent years, we have seen much more experimentation with combining genres – such as *Firefly* (Fox, 2002–2003)/*Serenity* (Universal Pictures, 2005) which mixes Western generic elements with science fiction elements – but we can find examples in older properties like films from the *Alien* franchise as well. *Alien* (20th Century Fox, 1979) is a hybrid of the horror genre and the science fiction genre. *Aliens* (20th Century Fox, 1986) is both a science fiction film and a war film. *Alien*[3] (20th Century Fox, 1992) is a combination of science fiction and prison drama (or even religious drama). In some ways, this notion of combining genres is what led to the historical view of genre and subgenre. As we combine genres in new or unexpected ways, the genres may be in more of an equal tension, hence the currently favored use of the term *hybrid genre*: subgenre implies that one genre is subservient to the other; hybrid genres imply a more equal relationship of the elements from each.

Regardless, classifying material by genre is a strategy used in comics, graphic novels, video games, TV series, novels, poetry and just about any medium that tells stories.

Plotting Points and Curves

Once we have a general strategy for the type of story we're going to tell, we then have to figure out the individual story events and how these events relate to each other. Most fiction stories – and many nonfiction ones – follow a dramatic curve or arc that incorporates exposition, rising action, climax, falling action, and resolution, and these five components are the key to building transmedia stories.

Exposition *usually refers to information you present at the very beginning so that the audience can get to know the character and storyworld before disaster – or drama – strikes. A common mistake is to believe that exposition needs to be all laid out at the beginning. Truthfully, the entire story is exposition – it exposes the characters and situation, creating a sense of discovery for the audience. This means you don't have to wait for exposition; you can just dive right into the story.*

One way of thinking about this is that the first 10% of the story should reveal the main character, the main conflict, a basic introduction to the world and a general sense of the narrative, its tone and even in some ways, its structure. For a 500-page novel, this would mean 50 pages or so; for a 22-episode serialized television season, this might mean two or three episodes. For a video game, maybe four or five hours of initial gameplay. For a feature film, ten script pages. (If you think this doesn't sound like much, consider the fact that the Sundance Screenwriters Lab makes its initial round of eliminations based only on the first five script pages.)

Rising action *simply means that as your protagonist surmounts one obstacle, another one takes its place, and each successive obstacle requires more determination or is harder to get around. The conflict becomes more complex, escalated and accelerated.*

The **climax** *is the point where the protagonist engages the conflict in one last confrontation, usually with a conclusive success or failure.*

Falling action *contains the immediate effects of the climax's outcome and anything that happens before the final resolution; this is sometimes referred to as the denouement.*

The **resolution** *is the long-term effects, usually only hinted at in a film, such as the clichéd image in many westerns of our protagonist riding off into the sunset or in dramas, a sun breaking through the clouds. Each of these images implies a general sense of the emotional state of the characters or the larger story. Think of the classic fairytale ending sentence, "and they lived happily ever after." In the resolution, the protagonist's situation can be one of three possibilities: better than it was at the start of the film, worse or about the same.*

These five elements are often diagrammed like this:

This traditional diagram of a narrative plot curve helps reveal the proportion of the elements to each other – you'll notice that it's not

Figure 3.1 *Plot points.*

an equilateral triangle, rather the left angle is very shallow and long, and the right angle is very steep and short. This means that the falling action is much shorter than the rising action or events that built up to the climax. The slope of the left angle represents the idea of escalation, that events get more complicated (or risky) and the consequences of each action get greater; there's a literal build toward the climax.

Within this plot curve, there are smaller moments or events that help make up the story. These are sometimes called Plot Points or Turning Points or Beats and are a way to designate specific shifts in the action or direction of the story. "Plot Points" is probably most common, because turning points and (especially) beats can also refer to tools that a director and actor might use to build a performance. But we're not ready for actors yet – we're still working on our story! We'll talk about plot points more in Part Two's media chapters, but generally, we think of each act ending with a major turning point even though only one appears on our plot curve: the climax.

Though *acts* as a structural element is borrowed from theatre, there's no set number for how many best tell a story. Regardless of how many acts the story has, the story's plot curve will usually look quite a bit like our diagram. We see stories in many forms that could be considered one-act, two-act, three-act, four-act, five-act or seven-act. Not all stories are literally three acts even though many if not most are described as adhering to that kind of structure. So what makes three-act structure so popular as a concept? And is three-act structure different depending on the platform (film, television, webisode, play or video game)?

Three-act structure has become a bit of a generic term to simply mean the way in which we sequence story material, particularly media storytelling, regardless of how many acts we really use. Some of this may be because three-act structure is often conflated to mean "beginning, middle, end" – three words would seem to equal three acts. But these words do not really tell us about *how* to structure the story (all stories have a beginning, middle and end, whether they're one act or 12). More importantly, they provide no clue as to the *proportion* of each part in relationship to the others.

The proportion of story will vary from platform to platform. Films are often described as conforming to three-act structure but arguably have four acts. Television episodes might be divided into five acts. A single webisode is probably not even a full act but rather a single plot point, and video games use the term to refer to a general progression through the storyworld by way of the player's interactive experience through the game. We will talk more about how each of these platforms structure story in Part Two. However, regardless of platform, every story has a starting point and an ending point.

World Out of Balance

Notice that our diagram of a plot curve doesn't continue off the paper in both directions. There is a definite point where the line starts and where it ends. Stories are the same way. Seems obvious, but figuring out exactly where a story should start and end can sometimes require a lot of thought (and even a few drafts) and can still be hard to get right. Just look at the controversy surrounding the ending of the video game *Mass Effect 3*, which required BioWare to appease unhappy fans by creating a downloadable "extended cut" to supplement the ending presented in the original game, clarifying events and resolving plot holes. Hollywood regularly has test screenings to try to figure out the most audience-pleasing ending before releasing a film theatrically.

In simple terms, most stories are structured around crisis – they start when the world or the protagonist's circumstances are tipped out of balance or changed (sometimes referred to as the inciting incident), which causes the protagonist to struggle to right these changes or adapt to them, and the story ends when the protagonist either succeeds or fails (climax and resolution). The hero's journey (which we talked about briefly in Chapter 1) is a variation on this model, but there are numerous other ways of thinking about story structure, and a quick look at any books on writing (whether screenplays, novels, comics, television series or games) will provide you with myriad examples. One of our favorites is Orson Scott Card's M.I.C.E. Quotient.

Besides creating the *Ender's Game* series (affectionately referred to as the Enderverse and including the *Shadow* Saga), Card has written a couple of books and numerous articles for people who want to be better storytellers. In these books and articles, he has proposed that there are four primary elements in any story, but that one will dominate and provide the basic structure to the story.

M.I.C.E. stands for *Milieu* (or a story structured around the exploration of a world), *Idea* (or a story about seeking and discovering new information), *Character* (or a story about the transformation of a character's role) and *Event* (or a story about something that puts the world out of order). Again, all stories have a setting (or world), ideas, characters and events. But determining which one will dominate our story will provide us with a way to understand where the story should begin and end.

For example, a story structured around Milieu would begin with the character arriving in the new world (think *Stranger in a Strange Land*, literally) and ends when the character leaves or decides to stay. A story built around an idea would start as close to possible where a question if first raised, such as in a mystery to be solved, and ends when the question is answered. Character-based stories have a long tradition in theatre, film, prose and even comics, and there are many different ways to think about them, but Card describes a story organized around character as beginning at the point when the protagonist is so miserable in his present role that he tries to change it; the story ends when he either succeeds in changing his role and settles into a new role or decides to give up and remains in his old role. The event story begins when the protagonist becomes involved with the struggle to combat some element that has disrupted the normal course of events and ends when the protagonist has helped forge a new world order or the world is restored to its former order (or the protagonist fails and the world descends into chaos).

(For a more in depth summary of his ideas, see his post "The 4 Structures that Dominate Novels," http://www.writersdigest.com/writing-articles/by-writing-goal/write-first-chapter-get-started/4-story-structures-that-dominate-novels, or his books *Character and Viewpoint* and *How to Write Science Fiction and Fantasy*, Writer's Digest Books, 2011 and 2001, respectively).

Our universe can be expressed through all different types of stories and plots, depending on the platform. Going back to our transmedia idea about the final voyage of the Starship *Gigantic* (Chapter 2), each of our stories might not just be on a different platform but might also use a different one of Card's plot organizing strategies. For example, our TV series about our Martian shipbuilder might be a Milieu story, our novels about the various crew might be more about character and our feature film about the collision and survival could be an event story. Maybe we'd create a game that would be about seeking out specific information (idea).

Though each individual medium will address three-act structure, plot points, genres, types of story and beginnings and endings slightly differently, all stories use this terminology to describe the way in which they're told.

The Beginning and End of Our Universe

As we just talked about, a major consideration for our individual story plots is where to begin and end. But we also need to think about them in terms of the entire transmedia property. Beginnings and endings really deal with what can be translated into entry points and exit points from a universe. At what point do you introduce your story, and if it's under your control, where do you choose to end it?

Beginnings are easier but challenging to deal with, because when we're talking about the mothership or cornerstone, they are the very first entry point into the story and the first glimpse into that universe. There are considerations as to where, narratively, to start the story, and questions as to which platform, or platforms, to launch the introduction on. In addition, each extension will create its own entry point into the story universe, being that first glimpse for audiences who come to the property through the extension.

These are holistic decisions and will be governed by many considerations that are particular to the narrative realities of your property, as well as your budget and production realities, but we can look at some generalities.

Entry Points

Where did you start when you got hooked on *Harry Potter*? For some it was the novels. For some it was the feature films, and it is likely there are even some whose moment of getting hooked was over an extended session of playing the *Harry Potter* Lego game. So the question of entry points is a simple question with multiple answers. Do you want to lead with a single entry point, and then follow-up with others, or open with multiple entry points that either complement each other or provide contrasting views of the property? Do you want a high price point on the first entry to your property, such as a mass-market video game, or something inexpensive (for the audience) like a television show, novel or comic book?

Entry points shape the audience's perspective and give them an introduction that is inevitably attached to the experience of the medium that was their initial entry point. This consideration is not just about the property; it is also about the audience, in that audiences are different depending on the medium and their self-perception and expectations. The entry point can make a huge difference in the nature and intensity of the connection the audience has to a property. This first taste will set the audience's perception for your property, and you have to be careful to not misrepresent it. Your audience will think they understand your property based on that first taste. If that initial exposure is different from what comes afterward, you could be setting the property up for failure. As one example, it means you shouldn't probably kill off the most compelling character who seems to be the protagonist in your first story (though George R. R. Martin would disagree …), unless it is basically the inciting incident for the property (now he would agree). Don't panic. The challenges you face here are the same challenges any storyteller faces: how to get their story a foothold in the culture and the market.

We live in a world that is in a state of constant change. Producers confront the changing nature of the audience, the large palette of possibilities and an industry that sees continually evolving technology. Besides the obvious issue of how the fans connect to the intellectual property, we need to consider the connection between the entry point and other expressions. Does starting with the book put you off the films or does the game make you want to watch the television series more? These questions reveal the challenge of how to evaluate the property and calculate a strategy. All we're really saying is, choose your entry point(s) wisely.

You start with the mothership or cornerstone because it is typically, but not always, the first property launched and the first entry point for the audience. Examples of successful mothership entry points that have had very different results are *LOST* and *Avatar*.

Entry Into LOST

LOST is often identified as one of the greatest television pilots ever and launched what was a very successful run on network television. That alone was an achievement, but what makes *LOST* important is the universe that grew up around the show. This story universe contained elements that were both producer-created and fan-influenced, and the producers willingly wove both into a universe that captivated a huge chunk of the culture during its run. The question is whether the alternate reality game (*The LOST Experience*) brought in a significant number of new viewers. Did the video game bring in some people who don't watch television, or did it turn them off? (Did anyone who was unfamiliar with the television series really play the game?)

While the ability to really analyze what happened has passed (unless the ABC marketing folks have data squirreled away somewhere), what is obvious is that disparate elements in the *LOST* property all worked together to inform the *LOST* universe. Was it marketing or was it something more? *LOST* is an important transmedia landmark because many of the tools normally associated only with marketing were appropriated by the creators to enhance their storytelling. As a result, the various entry points stayed connected to the core narrative and were integrated into the larger experience, ensuring that the other entry points would bring the audience back to the center of the universe, in this case, the television series.

Entry Into Avatar

The release of *Avatar* was the event of the holiday season, 2009. It was hugely popular and subsequently has led James Cameron to state that "he is in the *Avatar* business" exclusively ("James Cameron on Chinese Filmmakers, Censorship and Potential Co-Productions," accessed July 1, 2012, http://mediadecoder.blogs.nytimes.com/2012/05/05/james-cameron-on-chinese-filmmakers-censorship-and-potential-co-productions/). While designed as a transmedia property with the video game launch preceding the premiere of the film, what has evolved is a property with a limited number of entry points. The video game got mixed reviews and proved to be a lackluster companion to the film. What else is there? Action figures and lunch boxes, but in reality there have been a limited number of entry points into the story-world, which in turn limited the audience. This is ironic given the success of the film, but when compared to other properties that achieved such success in their mothership expressions, *Avatar* has a smaller footprint. Yes, the motion picture was a monstrous success, but from our transmedia storytelling perspective we have to wonder what happened to everything else. Why were there no novels or graphic novels? Why did a video game have such limited narrative content? It may be a control issue, but what has evolved is a property that has become dependent on the impact of a single media iteration without other expressions to contribute to ongoing success. Does this signal that the implied narrative depth in the *Avatar* universe just isn't really there? With multiple sequels promised (someday), time will ultimately tell.

Managing Multiple Entry Points

Instinct tells you that a varied approach to entry points would make sense. In launching multiple points, you maximize the opportunity to make that foothold in the culture that at least gives the property the opportunity to succeed. Multiple entry points in different media also allow for a niche appeal strategy. Different audiences find the style of storytelling that best connects to them, and this introduces them to the larger world and the other aspects of the property. The challenge is maintaining a coherent universe while the multiple entry points more often than not pull in the other direction. The demands of each medium and its audience can sometimes transform that piece of universe into something different and disconnected.

How does the universe survive multiple entry points? Various factors contribute to maintaining universe coherence in this model. The first is consistency of character. Given the similarities in the language of motion pictures and television, consistency is relatively easy to maintain. Video games are a different matter. As soon as you introduce an "agent" into the universe that has free will, things can get a wee bit off track. Does the gamer play the main character, or is he a new character, and where does that character belong in the overall story? Game dynamics raise many questions, including whether restricting game play based on character considerations makes it problematic for games to be a viable transmedia property entry point. This is an issue Hollywood is still struggling with. The issue of transformation by media choice is really one of language. Translation of one language to another is interesting because idiom and culture make for an uneasy and imprecise translation from one to the other. The same is true for the challenge of multiple media entry points. Separating out the "language" of the medium and the narrative expression of the universe in that medium is not easy. The mothership's platform can't help but have an effect on the overall storytelling and therefore each of the other expressions.

On the other side of the equation, the major issue is that of audience expectations. The challenge is to express the intellectual property in a way that translates perfectly from medium to medium. When the audience is added to the mix, more issues come to life. People have a dominant media interest, which can be as specific as those who only surf the web and watch YouTube. We are creating audiences who share one simple declaration: "I want what I want when I want on what I want." The industries now chase the audience at every opportunity and make them capable of articulating demands in a way that wasn't possible ten years ago. A strategy for multiple entry points has to take into account that if you don't put it directly in front of the audience, they might not see it.

Multiple entry points speak consistently to the tension between the specific and the universal. Multiple entry points increase the chance for audience engagement and audience disappointment. What always has to be balanced is finding those universals that exist in all successful properties and then finding a way to focus the message for a specific medium and each medium's specific audience. When this has occurred successfully in the past, it has been more of an organic process rather than a constructed strategy, but are still challenges for transmedia. This won't change as producers and creatives become more savvy and more experienced in transmedia storytelling.

Endings

Ends are a different matter. The end of a successful transmedia property can happen for a variety of reasons: the creators want to move on; the story has reached a natural resolution or the property is no longer fiscally viable. Sometimes the ending is planned, or at least anticipated, but too often the end comes somewhat abruptly, leaving its creative forces to scramble to set up a proper exit point for its audience.

Whatever the reason, reaching the end means someone will not be happy. No matter what the reason, the hardcore fans are not happy because you killed their favorite people and brought the apocalypse to their favorite place. Part of the inevitable outcome of a successful transmedia property is that sense of ownership among fans, making it hard to please them when the property reaches its conclusion. Just ask the creators of *LOST* or *Mass Effect 3*.

Even with the understanding that you can't please everyone, some large properties have been brought to a reasonable conclusion. Probably the most noteworthy is the *Harry Potter* series, which as a series of novels was designed from the beginning to have a conclusion. George R. R. Martin's *A Song of Ice and Fire* novel series (and so presumably HBO's *Game of Thrones*) will resolve similarly. The pressures are different in other media, however, especially television series where the networks tend to want the series to stay successful for as long as possible. Too often in the past, television series with long arcs, that may or may not have had a transmedia component, were canceled with little notice. Ideally, you would know how the story will conclude when it begins, but that seems a remote possibility as most media properties are subject to a variety of pressures as they run. Budget cuts, casting changes or world events can all have an effect on the course of a story being told. Even with the best laid plans, you can end up in a different place from where you imagined.

Lately, networks have been more willing to work with showrunners and production companies to provide some lead time to the end of a show. That notice, however, doesn't always guarantee an ending that everyone likes. Perceptions and expectations are difficult to overcome in the fan base, especially for shows with a solid mythology built around many mysteries and narrative gaps. We've mentioned *LOST* repeatedly, but the ending of *Battlestar Galactica* was in some ways just as controversial, and its showrunner (Ronald D. Moore) built the final season to lead into that finale. Both *LOST* and *Battlestar Galactica*, however, chose to end with a degree of narrative uncertainty and questions unanswered. Par for the course, perhaps, for properties built around mythology and mystery, but that didn't prevent a faction of each's fandom from clamoring for complete closure and all questions answered.

Given you can't please everyone, the reality is that there is no good ending. Even the *Harry Potter* series' conclusion begs the question of "what next?" with its tipoff of the main characters' future, knowing that fans are waiting for more, demanding more. A successful ending seems to be tied most clearly to a definitive large arc that can be resolved with the world going on in a fashion that the hard-core fans can continue to buy into.

It becomes a battle between satisfying fan expectation and the creative/narrative impulse of the creators. Too much fan unrest could poison the well for future projects, but at the same time – though they'll fervently tell you otherwise – fans don't really know what they want. When they're unhappy, they'll let you know… and they'll tell you what they think they wanted. Our advice is finish the story you were telling. The fans will be there with you or they won't.

And even ends aren't always ends. Sometimes properties have unexpected continued life – just ask Arthur Conan Doyle about *Sherlock Holmes*. Some properties, like *Doctor Who* in the years after the series' "cancelation" in 1989, are carried by what we'd normally consider support, extension or secondary platforms like novels, audio plays and comic books, until they can spectacularly re-emerge over 15 years later.

Some fans in Nebraska will get together and translate scripts into plays for a fan convention, and others will create a website specifically for sharing fan-generated stories based in your storyworld. Some will even pool their resources and produce surprisingly sophisticated and professional video projects.

What history has shown, and the last 20 years in particular have demonstrated, is no property ever really has an end. All that happens is that a resting point is reached and the possibility of a restarted franchise exists forever in the hands of fans.

Narrative Coherence

In many ways, the audience's most basic want is the simple desire for their story to remain coherent. While there are times when confusion or a lack of clarity adds to the telling of a story, it still needs to, at the end of the day, make some sense. In a story set within a universe this is even more complex because while the story itself must make sense, it also must be in sync with the universe, and there's the rub.

The obvious assumption would be that confusion and obfuscation would be a challenge when the key story elements are not under a central control but are being licensed out to a variety of creators to generate the different pieces. While this is often true, it is not the only reason that problems along these lines occur. There are always tensions at work in a transmedia property as it expands and gets more complicated, and the notion of a keeper of the flame or gatekeeper for the universe seems simplistic. In fact the question is whether tightly held control leads to clarity or confusion over the long haul. Does control always lead to the best storytelling? How much do you let current culture impact the story and contradict canon? The lists of questions are both interesting and endless.

In order to sort out these issues, it is first important to define what is meant by coherence. Narrative coherence really equates to the over-arching commitment to canon. The question is less about who defines canon and more whether a majority of the audience can be in some agreement of what defines the universe. In order to understand its importance, it is helpful to look at properties that have achieved a strong level of coherence. Two good examples of coherence are *Star Trek* and *Naruto*.

Star Trek is a property that (while having a long history and many, many expressions in virtually every medium you can imagine) has maintained a discernible identity with understandable rules and characters. In fact part of what has attracted and maintained *Star Trek* as a successful intellectual property are the values consistent to all its iterations. While the characters may change, Starfleet and the values attached to that fictitious organization stayed consistent, providing a set of rules that helped define the people and the actions those people took. (In a strange way, it's kind of like a canon within the canon.)

For those not familiar with *Naruto*, it is a hugely successful manga/anime series in Japan that follows the life of Naruto Uzimake as he journeys from outcast to hero of his village. What is noteworthy is the extraordinary attention to detail and level of agreement among the wide array of expressions. We see this most in the dynamic between the manga and the anime. The manga is the mothership property but due to the nature of the medium is often skeletal in its storytelling and ability to depict action. The anime is capable of going into depth with characters that would be challenging or hugely page consuming in the manga. *Naruto* creators take full advantage of the differences by using the anime to reveal and deepen our understanding of the characters without the anime contradicting the manga. The result is two different pleasures as the story arcs are in two different places, the magna blazes (and moves along) the story while the anime follows, enriching our understanding and often amplifying the emotions that go along with the epic nature of the tale. Coherence can strengthen the intellectual property with each step.

This evaluation implies that coherence and continuity are good things. That may or may not be true, but they do reward the audience in certain clear ways. What coherence gives you is a clear connection to the audience. When people understand the rules or know what to expect, they know what kind of story they will be getting and feel connected to it because of that trust. This coherence forms a foundation to build on as the intellectual property universe is expanded. The rules are clear and the stories being told fit together in some version of a master plan, and all this allows the creator to envision a path forward. A recognizable product (or brand) is also the result of this kind of attention to coherence. Fans of *Star Trek* can recognize a story as part of the *Star Trek* universe because of a wide variety of things: iconography, technology, conflict and even history and supporting characters. The same is true of *Naruto* because of the unique world they live in and the headbands they wear. This is much like returning to a town you know well; familiar pieces fall into place and are reminders that you are returning to someplace that you know and love. As you can see, there are clearly many advantages to coherence.

Issues with confusion and obfuscation make the world a very unpredictable place. Contradiction and internal logic issues are part of the process by which a property can unravel. Producers who try to redefine a property ignoring what already exits can get themselves into the situation where the fan base begins to wonder "just what universe am I in?" *Terminator* has suffered from this where a feature film and television series existed side by side with no real comprehensible connection. Granted, *Terminator* exists in a world with time travel, and things can get a little complicated as a result, but in a case where there is a discernible universe established and there is some continuity, the audience expects more coherence. Reboots of *Batman* and *Sherlock Holmes* can have their own distinct worlds in a larger universe because the expectation is not coherence but rather, what you are doing that's interesting with the property. One thing that these properties have is longevity and multiple generations of fans, which can trump coherence in terms of importance. When a property has a short timeline and begins to contradict itself, fans naturally disengage. Contradictions offend that desire we all have for narrative logic. The audience perceives the storyteller as having failed in some way: "This doesn't make sense anymore," and they are off looking for something new to engage with. In many ways, a large universe can become a house of cards, the core story can be lost by the addition of stories that are obscure or confuse the audience. When stories don't seem to fit or send the property in an irrelevant direction, we can lose the sense of (and focus of) the core story. It is easy for confusion to set in and make the audience wonder, "What am I buying?" A large transmedia property is a brand, like James Bond. We understand who he is fundamentally and hope each time they get it right, but any connection to those books has long been unimportant because the property has taken on a larger life than its source material. When a property (or brand) doesn't deliver what is expected and becomes meaningless, the fans look for new things. If the quality or kind of storytelling is so far from expectation, the importance of the universe is greatly diminished.

The *Star Trek* property has been a constant struggle against these issues. While the reins of the property have essentially been in one set of hands, Paramount Pictures, with the presence of Gene Roddenberry having an impact on the property until his death (and some would say after), the attitude toward the universe has varied at times, which is normal given the corporate ownership. The size of the property and seriousness with which Trekkers take their canon are significant factors in any iterations of its universe. The fan base is extraordinarily committed and in many ways is the prototype of modern fandom. But *Star Trek* is a property that got so locked by canon that it became a difficult story-tell. Add to that, canon is often hard to define. Are stories told in the short-lived animation series part of canon? Some details that grew to be a part of the larger universe were established there but argument of canon continues. What about the novels? Fan videos? The balance *Star Trek* achieved among the various factors was relatively coherent until *Enterprise* came to television.

Star Trek: Enterprise is the only Trek series that did not run its expected seven-year cycle. In was different from the start — dramatically different is what the producers promised — because it went back into the past of what is a very clear and established timeline. *Star Trek: Enterprise* is a true mixed bag for Trekkers and more importantly never really caught on with a larger audience. The storytelling struggled to be inventive in a universe with so many mile makers. It is an example of, "damned if you do and damned if you don't." In trying to be something different, it offended *Trek* fans and in trying to please *Trek* fans, it got too caught up in canon. In retrospect we've learned that the right uniforms and changing the name from *Enterprise* to *Star Trek: Enterprise* doesn't make a *Star Trek* series. What is really interesting is what followed. As the series was canceled, a feature film was announced. The following question arose: Where do you take a feature film, and what series will it be based on? When the word slipped out that the film would address the early days of Kirk and Spock, there was much concern. Didn't a series just fail that attempted to go back into the timeline? How do you deal with mothership characters that are cultural icons and their stories as close to undisputed canon as you can get? How doesn't this suck? The answer was they did the only thing they could: start over. Reboot the series (thank you time travel) in a manner that wouldn't upset the hard-core fans but make it possible to tell new stories accessible to casual fans and not be so encumbered by canon. The *Star Trek* universe is familiar, but the new path allows for new stories unencumbered by too many defined points in time and space (and canon). The pivot of the franchise and its success really is a reminder of how much an audience likes clarity and coherence. What the producers did was find the balance of something old and something new supplied by a deft plot twist.

Does narrative incoherence ever benefit you? Of course, chaos can be a good thing. It can create energy and open new doors and create a dynamic where a property can redefine itself, but the reality is that the majority of the time confusion and obfuscation are an expression of a property in trouble. A property that doesn't seem to understand its own universe is a property prone to mistakes and losing its audience. While in some of the long-term intellectual properties this doesn't matter, loss of focus and confusion is typically how a property unravels and becomes less a transmedia story than a simple brand.

Continuity, Canon, and Consistency

When dealing with sprawling transmedia storytelling properties, continuity, canon, and consistency are all vitally important, and failure to acknowledge and respect each of them can lead to disaster, or at the very least the slings and arrows of an outraged fanbase. And given how important the care and feeding of that fanbase is, it may be wise to take an almost religious view of the three "C"s …

Continuity

Readers familiar with motion picture and television production are probably used to hearing the term "continuity" in association with the script supervisor. Given that a particular scene could be shot across multiple days (and sometimes out of order), a script supervisor is responsible for maintaining a record of the physical continuity of the production, with regard to wardrobe, makeup, hair, objects on the set, and so on – anything that needs to be consistent within a scene and from scene-to-scene. The script supervisor also logs exactly what scenes were shot, and various other production details that are then shared with the various production departments. The script supervisor also acts, in effect, as an agent on the set for the editor and helps insure that the film can be properly edited and continuity from shot-to-shot and scene-to-scene is maintained.

In storytelling of any form, continuity simply refers to internal consistency with regard to people, places, things, and events that occur in the story. So, if Sir John is described as having red hair, or being left handed, and then later is blond and/or right handed, that is a break in continuity. This seems fairly logical, and one would think easy to maintain, especially in a single property, but even then continuity errors do occur. For example, in a novel, it is the author's responsibility to track continuity, and then the book's editor's responsibility to watch out for any missed mistakes. Author Stephen King, who is known for his epic, sprawling plotlines has his research assistant Robin Furth maintain a record of the details in his *Dark Tower* series of novels in order to help avoid continuity errors from book to book. Furth's work was eventually published in a two-volume set called Stephen King's *The Dark Tower: A Concordance* when King realized the encyclopedia-style work would be of interest.

Cross-Property Continuity

The Dark Tower series is an important touchstone for us because it is a transmedia storytelling property, with the story told across the eight novels (1982–2012), multiple prequel and sequel comic books, and an online video game – *Discordia* – playable through King's official website. Plans are afoot for a combination of motion pictures and multiple seasons of a television series, but these would be an adaptation of the *Dark Tower* stories in some form, not a transmedia storytelling extension.

With the exception of the comic books, King has been the sole author of the *Dark Tower* stories (he oversaw the comic books), and he needed a work on the scale of the *Concordance* to keep everything straight. Of course, having a research assistant who can compile all the information is a great help. The television show *LOST* realized after season one that they needed someone to keep track of everything that was going on, and named Gregg Nations the "continuity czar" for the program. We'll get back to the need for continuity support like this when we deal with the practicalities of transmedia management in a later chapter, but for now let's continue on with straight-up continuity and its importance.

We'll be talking about the BioWare/Electronic Arts video game franchise *Mass Effect* in at various points throughout this book, but for the moment let's look at a problem that its makers had with cross-property continuity. The novel, *Mass Effect: Deception* by William C. Dietz, was released in January 2012, prior to the video game *Mass Effect 3* which hit store shelves in March of that same year. The book was immediately ripped apart by *Mass Effect* fans for it significant continuity errors in the areas of alien biology, technology, history, culture, and history… so, pretty much everything. The uproar among fans was pretty significant to the point that a group of them created a 16-page Google Docs document listing all of the errors (viewable at https://docs.google.com/a/kotaku.com/document/d/1XBpMF3ONlI308D9IGG8KICBHfWKU0sXh0ntukv-_cmo/preview?pli=1). Bioware (the creators of the game series) and Del Rey (the novel's publisher) eventually apologized for the mistakes in the novel and indicated that changes would be made in future editions of the novel.

How so many errors had crept into the *Mass Effect: Deception* novel is hard to understand. This was the first *Mass Effect* novel from Dietz (the previous ones were written by Drew Karpyshyn, one of the games' writers) so it might be understandable that he may not have had his head fully wrapped around a universe as vast and complex as *Mass Effect*'s. The Del Rey contract for the tie-in *Mass Effect* novels, however, should have contained an approval process by which someone at BioWare – presumably from the *Mass Effect* team – reviewed and signed off on the novel. With *Mass Effect 3* deep in production at the time the novel was being prepped for publication, we can only assume that the details were not reviewed as tightly as they should have been, to put it mildly. The uproar was embarrassing to BioWare, especially since they positioned themselves in the video game market as a company all about storytelling.

Fans thirst for ancillary material about their favorite worlds and universes, but they can quickly lose faith when it seems that the producers of the material aren't taking continuity seriously, as that implies a lack of respect for the property. Continuity maintenance is mandatory for a transmedia storytelling property, and sometimes requires going to great efforts to ensure. Sometimes, however, the fans themselves help things along …

Fan-Driven Continuity Websites

If you are looking for some degree of proof that continuity and complex transmedia storytelling properties go hand-in-hand we present Memory Alpha (http://en.memory-alpha.org) and *LOST*pedia (http://lostpedia.wikia.com). The former was created in 2003, and the latter in 2005.

Both of these sites were created by fans in order to record continuity-related information for the *Star Trek* and *LOST* franchises respectively. Both sites contain detailed entries about the episodes (and/or movies), characters, locations, plot, technology, culture, and so on from each franchise. The sites are edited and maintained by fans of the show who use it not only to document the fictional elements of the franchises, but some of the behind-the-scenes elements as well, such as actors, writers, filming locations, and others. Both evolved into deep and complex sites (Memory Alpha has over 34,000 entries and *LOST*pedia over 7,200) and became center points for fan discussion about the programs and speculation about their mysteries. The writers of the 2009 *Star Trek* motion picture, Roberto Orci and Alex Kurtzman, have talked about using Memory Alpha as a reference when working on that film's script ("More Fan Q&A With Roberto Orci," accessed July 22, 2012, http://trekmovie.com/2008/01/28/

more-fan-qa-with-roberto-orci/), and the creators of *LOST* have spoken of using *LOST*pedia when their in-house continuity czar Gregg Nations was unavailable ("The LOSTpedia Interaview: Carlton Cuse and Damon Lindelof, accessed July 22, 2012, http://lostpedia.wikia.com/wiki/The_Lostpedia_Interview:Carlton_Cuse_%26_Damon_Lindelof).

Interestingly, there is a *Dark Tower* site similar to Memory Alpha and *LOST*pedia called the Dark Tower Wiki (we'll talk about what a wiki is in a later chapter) which has only about 700 articles (http://darktower.wikia.com). Is this an indication that *Dark Tower* fans are less passionate about the novel series than the fans of *Star Trek* or *LOST*, or just that there are fewer of them? What impact did the release of Stephen King's *The Dark Tower: A Concordance* have on contributions to the site? We don't know, but it begs some interesting questions about allowing fan passion to drive support for a franchise (an idea we'll come back to again and again …) versus brand managing it.

We strongly believe that fueling fan passion is required for the success of a transmedia storytelling property, and the existence of Memory Alpha, *LOST*pedia, the Dark Tower Wiki, or the Wiki of Ice and Fire for George R. R. Martin's *A Song of Ice and Fire* novels and HBO's *Game of Thrones* series (with over 4,800 articles), are very clear indicators of a property's success in engaging fans, and keeping them (http:// http://awoiaf.westeros.org/).

Pause for a moment and consider the amount of time and effort fans are willing to put into any of the continuity sites we just mentioned. Some rights-holders, and perhaps some readers of this book, may see such fan-driven efforts as damaging to the intellectual property involved, but we believe that perspective to be outdated and exclusionary. Modern transmedia storytellers should tap into fan power rather than fear it.

Comic Books and Continuity Chaos

Holy crap, Batman … we're going to talk at length about comic books and graphic novels in a later chapter, but we wanted to touch on comic book continuity briefly here. Anyone who follows comic books, especially the big two publishers Marvel Comics and DC Comics, knows how crazy continuity is in the world of comic books. Two titles, each focused on the same characters, can have different continuities (different storyworlds) even though they co-exist within the same story universe. Other titles that also exist in that universe could reference the continuity of the one, and then the continuity of the other at another time. Writers change, and continuity self-destructs as new backstory is fabricated and long-standing "facts" of the character's origins are ignored. Madness reigns … and comic book fans take it all in stride.

Continuity chaos is assumed in comic books, and the kind of mayhem that would drive them mad somewhere else is barely even worth a note in comics. This seems to be a conditioned response, meaning that it's just the way things are in comics. It also seems to imply that with the right groundwork any group of fans can handle multiple continuities of their favorite properties simultaneously.

This shift is evident in the current state of the *Star Trek* franchise, where the 2009 motion picture launched a new continuity, while the old continuities persist in novels, comics and video games. (We'll get more into the specifics of this in the section about canon coming up.) Initially, *Star Trek* fans were up in arms over the "reboot" of the franchise, but ended up embracing it once they saw it. (We suspect strongly that there would have been a very different reaction if the movie had sucked.) While some pockets of resistance remain, most fans contentedly accept the multiple continuities in the franchise.

The television series *Terminator: The Sarah Conner Chronicles* (Fox television, 2008–2009) occurred ostensibly between the motion pictures *Terminator 2: Judgment Day* and *Terminator 3: Rise of the Machines*, and did not shy away from engaging the implications of time-travel altering the events of the franchise' timeline. By the end of the second season, it was clear the *Terminator: The Sarah Conner Chronicles* was off in its own continuity and that some of the events in the series perhaps nullified, or at least should have greatly altered, the events leading up to *Terminator 3*. It seems clear that *Terminator: The Sarah Conner Chronicles* existed within its own continuity, separate from the *Terminator* film franchise.

Retroactive Continuity

The term retroactive continuity, or retcon for short, refers to after-the-fact alteration of previously established continuity, usually to revise history to allow additional story elements, or to fix or explain what would otherwise be a continuity error. One of the most famous retcons in literary history is the "death" of Sherlock Holmes. Tired of his creation, Arthur Conan Doyle killed off Holmes at the end of the novel, *The Final Problem* (Strand Magazine, 1893). Years later Doyle wrote a short story entitled *The Adventure of the Empty House* (*The Return of Sherlock Holmes*, 1903) where it is explained that Holmes' death was only a ruse and that he'd gone into hiding. This is retroactive continuity since Holmes' death in *The Final Problem* was intended to be permanent, but needed to be retroactively altered to allow him to return in later stories.

Retroactive continuity can be a powerful tool for a storyteller, but it can also lead to a breach of faith with the fans who view this sometimes as "cheating" because it changes their established understanding of the story. It is important to note that retroactive continuity can only apply to plot elements that have objectively occurred to the audience. So, if a character dies on screen unequivocally, but then returns later with an explanation of how they survived, that's retcon. If a character only speaks about another character dying, but it doesn't happen on-screen (or the appropriate reference for the medium) it's not retroactive continuity.

Fanwanking

About fanwanking, it's not what you think. (Well, maybe – more on that in a moment.) Fanwanking is a practice performed by fans to explain away continuity gaffes. For example, if in a scene a character suddenly reveals knowledge of an event or piece of information that they're never seen learning, fans will "fanwank" an explanation of how and when the character could have, based on the known continuity. Yes, this is basically the unofficial version of retroactive continuity, but it can involve or explain plot elements both large and small. A great deal of fanwanking occurs during the process of story speculation and discussion as fans discuss how things might have or could have occurred.

The term fankwanking has a different definition in the United Kingdom, where is evolved in relation to the long-running television series *Doctor Who*. In that context it refers to excessive use of continuity references designed explicitly to get fanboys and fangirls overly excited. So, in that context, it is probably what you were thinking it is …

Canon

The term "canon" (and yes, it does derive its usage from references to religious texts) refers to which material in a property's continuity – or perhaps more properly which continuity – is the official one. With the increasing presence of ancillary media expressions, and fan-fiction, it is important to differentiate, for creatives, producers, and fans alike which story elements are official/canon and which are not.

To understand the complexity of canon, let's look at the *Star Trek* franchise. From its broadcast in the late 1960s, *Star Trek* has sparked fan interest and speculation like no other property, save perhaps *Star Wars*. In the early to mid-1970s, while the *Star Trek* franchise was cold though still popular among fans, a book called *The Star Trek Starfleet Technical Manual*, written by Franz Joseph Schnaubelt, was published by Ballantine Books, and reached number one on the New York Times trade paperback bestseller list. (Not bad for a cold property, eh?) The book was presented as a document written in the future *Star Trek* universe and sent back to the past (our time) and as such represents a true transmedia storytelling expression, albeit a fan-produced one. It is interesting that the *Technical Manual* is fan-produced in that it represented Franz Joseph's take on the *Star Trek* universe and his attempt to define and explain the technology and organizations in the show, rather than specifically duplicate what had been seen on the show. There are discrepancies between what the *Technical Manual* described and what appeared in the show, but since the property was considered dead by its creator Gene Roddenberry and the rights-holders, there was no insistence that it had to match the show completely, or accurately. Interestingly, the book so ignited fan engagement that parts of it became canon for the *Star Trek* franchise in later years, when those involved in production of movies and television episodes of the show incorporated information from it. Additionally, within a year of the publication of the *Technical Manual*, Gene Roddenberry was in talks to revise *Star Trek*, which would result in *Star Trek: The Motion Picture* released in 1979.

When it comes to continuity and canon, some interesting circumstances and problems arise with *Star Trek*. First, let's state that the official canon of *Star Trek*, according to the rights-holder (which is CBS Studios) includes only the television series *Star Trek*, *Star Trek: The Next Generation*, *Star Trek: Deep Space Nine*, *Star Trek: Voyager*, *Star Trek: Enterprise*, and the *Star Trek* motion pictures. Anything from *Star Trek: the Animated Series*, novels, comics and video games are specifically not canon, though some elements of them could be, if they appeared in the list of television series and motion pictures above.

We're going to look at three areas: *Star Trek* novels, the *Star Trek* animated series and the 2009 *Star Trek* movie revival. (And yes, we're cherry-picking which *Star Trek* tie-ins we're looking at. An entire book could be written just looking at the history of *Star Trek*, its tie-ins, and continuity.)

Star Trek Novels

Adaptations of *Star Trek* episodes were published by Bantam Books (and written by James Blish until his death in 1975) initially while the show was still on the air. Blish wrote the novels based on early screenplays of the episodes and never saw the episode before they aired. These adaptations were close to the episodes, but contained many inaccuracies, but since they were adaptations were not viewed as canon. Blish wrote the first original Trek novel aimed at adults in 1970, *Spock Must Die!*, which was a sequel to the episode "Errand of Mercy" in the original series. Blish viewed his work on the novelizations as a collaborative endeavor between himself and the script writers and he fully embellished various elements and added in his own that seemed to logically fit. *Spock Must Die!* continues the continuity of Blish's novels, so it could be said that the continuity of *Spock Must Die!* includes the television series and the novelizations, but that the continuity of the television series does not include the Blish stories. So, the original series is viewed as canon, the Blish novels are not.

To date, there are over 500 *Star Trek* novels.

Think about that.

The novels remain non-canonical, but an interesting thing occurred a few years back. With multiple novel series in production, each with their own continuity, there was chaos in the *Star Trek* novel world, and fans were beginning to decry the contradictions across the different series. For example, a big event that occurred in Peter

David's *Star Trek: New Frontier* series of novels was not acknowledged in the *Starfleet Corps of Engineers* stories, even though both occur contemporaneously with the events of the *Star Trek: The Next Generation* television series. It was decided that the writers and editors of the various novel series would start working together to maintain some semblance of continuity between the novels. So, now each novel series has its own continuity (its own storyworld), which is in turn tied into the continuity of the entire *Star Trek* novel-verse (the *Star Trek* novel universe). Additionally, there are novel series that tell stories set after the end of each of the canon television series. Lastly, William Shatner − the actor who portrayed James T. Kirk, Captain of the *USS Enterprise* in the original television series and some of the motion pictures, co-authored a series of novels (with Judith and Garfield Reeves-Stevens) that are outside even the continuity of the novels and are often referred to as occurring in the "Shatnerverse" continuity.

By allowing the novels to set outside the continuity of *Star Trek* canon, CBS Studios (as the rights-holder) removes from itself a huge burden of having to fact-check and approve for continuity the dozens of novels publisher every year. Undoubtedly the novels are still reviewed to insure they do not deviate too greatly from *Star Trek* and contain nothing that would damage the brand or embarrass CBS Studios, and the monster that is *Star Trek* canon and continuity is tamed somewhat.

Star Trek: The Animated Series

The *Star Trek* animated series (NBC, 1973–1974) initially extended the continuity of the *Star Trek* original series directly and originally aired solely under the name *Star Trek*. Some of the episodes were direct sequels to original series episodes, and many episodes were written by notable science fiction and *Star Trek* original series episode writers, such as Larry Niven, Samuel A. Peeples, D. C. Fontana, and David Gerrold. The series was originally considered to be canon, but Gene Roddenberry requested that it be removed as a canonical source around 1988 due to the inconsistencies in the series.

Though the series is not considered to be part of the official canon, numerous elements from the animated series appeared in later television series episodes and motion pictures. Perhaps the most famous is the identification of the middle name of James T. Kirk as Tiberius.

Star Trek 2009 Movie

Elsewhere we talk about how the continuity in *Star Trek* had become so deep and so convoluted. Creative teams working on the series were having problems coming up with ideas that didn't somehow violate established continuity. To remedy that, in part, and to re-set *Star Trek* for the current movie-going generation, the writers of the 2009 *Star Trek* motion picture created a time-travel story that changed the fictional history of *Star Trek* prior to the start of the original series' timeline. In doing so they became able to cherry pick which existing elements they wanted to focus on, and which they wanted to be able to ignore, or be able to re-invent, moving forward. Fans of *Star Trek* were significantly concerned that this was the death-knell for the series, but the success of the film shows that this was an unnecessary concern.

Though the makers of the 2009 *Star Trek* wanted to expand the appeal of the franchise beyond hardcore fans, they knew that they could not ignore those fans or the continuity they cared so deeply about. The script for the motion picture was written to appeal to a broader audience, but with enough acknowledgment of existing continuity to engage the hardcore fanbase. The writers, Roberto Orci and Alex Kurtzman, knew though that in order to really engage the hardcore or long-time *Star Trek* fan, they needed to do something that appealed specifically to them.

The avenue they chose was transmedia storytelling and the creation of a multiple-part comic book prequel to the motion picture.

That comic book series, *Star Trek: Countdown*, links the 2009 motion picture and the *Star Trek: The Next Generation* continuity directly and explains how the characters of Spock and Nero traveled back in time to the 23rd century. It included other connections between the new film and the existing continuity and, in fact, served to make the 2009 film part of the official continuity and therefore *Star Trek* canon. That said, the contents of the comic book series are not they themselves officially canon. Still confused? This means that the comic book series is part of the main continuity, but it is not part of the canon.

So, in the official *Star Trek* continuity the time has changed and the events of the 2009 motion picture, its 2013 sequel, a comic book series that occurs between the two films, and a video game that occurs between the two films are all part of the main *Star Trek* continuity. Even so, there is still some confusion, with some properties – including the *Star Trek Online* massively multiplayer game – continuing their storyline post *Star Trek: The Next Generation* and beyond, and referring to that timeline as the "*Star Trek* prime" timeline, and viewing the timeline created by the 2009 motion picture as an offshoot or parallel continuity. This is even though the 2009 motion picture has been marked as *Star Trek* canon.

Why the confusion? Well, it's not really confusion, but rather a testament to the vast number of fans who still feel there is life in the post-*Star Trek: The Next Generation* continuity and don't want to give it up, and there's no reason for them to. *Star Trek* has existed for a long time with multiple continuities and there's no reason at all that it cannot continue to do so. What will be an issue is which continuity any future *Star Trek* television series would recognize. Logically, it would be the main continuity, which includes the 2009 motion picture, but it doesn't have to. Time will tell.

Maintaining Continuity

We've mentioned Memory Alpha and *LOST*pedia, among others, as massive fan-driven continuity websites, and we also named Gregg Nations, who was the continuity czar on *LOST*. We haven't mentioned Leland Chee whose official title is continuity database administrator, but he's basically the continuity go-to guy for Lucas Licensing and therefore everything *Star Wars*, from movies, to television, to novels, to comics, to video games and reference books. Chee maintains a database of more than 30,000 entries that tracks all of the who, what, where, when, why and how of the *Star Wars* universe. Is this necessary?

Absolutely yes.

Part Three of this book is all about managing transmedia storytelling properties, and we'll talk about the specific technology behind Memory Alpha and *LOST*pedia, as well as what Leland Chee uses for his database tracking. This may be something that feels as if it can be held off until the property becomes "hot," but that's exactly when it's needed most, and it's absolutely the wrong time to start going back and compiling it.

Maybe you'll be fortunate enough to have dedicated fans who will build an awesome online database for you, but even that only contains information that has been made public. The secrets and mysteries yet to be revealed aren't part of those sites, and those are critical for your writers and creatives. Also in Part Three we'll talk about who to let in on these secrets, and how.

Part 2

Many Media

Chapter 4

Motion Pictures and Visual Storytelling

Film as dream, film as music. No art passes our conscience in the way film does, and goes directly to our feelings, deep down into the dark rooms of our souls.

—Ingmar Bergman, director, quoted in John Berger[1]

The term "motion pictures" is most commonly applied to film or the cinema: movies projected to audiences of relative strangers in a theatre setting. Our daily lives are now so immersed in moving images, it's hard to believe there was a time they didn't exist. Few of us can remember a world without television, movies or video games. The oldest of these three – the medium of film – is still extremely young in the broader history of storytelling and yet is a primary influence and consideration in developing transmedia properties.

Years ago, people were very careful to distinguish between film and video, but nowadays, you'll hear the term "film" applied to any moving image, whether it was created using a light-sensitive emulsion or with a series of 0s and 1s in a digital environment, whether it's a feature-length movie or the cut-scene in a video game, whether it's delivered to its audience via an iPhone screen or a smart TV. With computer graphic imagery (CGI) and the ability to compose pictures digitally, we no longer even need a physical camera to create the images or physical film stock to record those images. What matters is not how these pictures are created or even how they're delivered but how the audience perceives them, as an illusion of movement through space and time.

The underlying concepts that grew out of filmmaking still inform the ways in which we talk about stories conveyed in moving images and the way in which those images are presented or perceived, whether in a movie, television show, video game, webisode, mobisode or installation. Regardless of the term we use – moving images, motion pictures, film, video, cinema, cinematics, animation, animatics, cut-scenes, TV – we are referring to a series of still photographs or frozen moments in time. Each of these individual photographs is called a *frame* and taken together, they are not that different from the sequential panel art you might find in a graphic novel or comics – except that they are recorded and then presented to the viewer at speeds fast enough to create the illusion of movement, based on the same principles that make flip books so fascinating for kids.

[1] "Ev'ry Time We Say Goodbye," *Sight and Sound*, London, June 1991, accessed September 1, 2012, http://quotes.dictionary.com/Film_as_dream_film_as_music_No_art

The brain ignores the missing information "between" these still photographs and instead synthesizes the recorded information into a fairly seamless sense of continuous movement. Of course, the actual images are not moving; they are, as we have already noted, simply a series of still photographs or frames shot and projected in a succession so rapid that when flashed before our eyes, the images or the content within the frames appear to move.

Edward Muybridge was a 19th century photographer who was commissioned to prove once and for all, through a rapidly taken series of photographs, whether there was a moment when all four of a horse's feet were off the ground when trotting and when galloping. When viewed in rapid succession, the images from this study create the illusion of the horse moving and inspired the possibility moving images.

How Fast? Speed

The speed of presentation is usually measured in terms of "frames per second," or how many frames flash before the audience in a single second – fps. The ideal number has evolved over time, but at the start of the 21st century, the long-standing tradition has been 24 fps for movies and effectively 30 fps for video and television. You may have heard of some films, such as *The Hobbit: An Unexpected Journey, The Hobbit: The Desolation of Smaug, The Hobbit: There and Back Again* (New Line Cinema, 2012, 2013, 2014) or *Brainstorm* (MGM, 1983), that were shot (or shown/projected) at an increased speed – the most recent at 48 fps – in an effort to make the illusion of continuous movement even stronger, and there is much speculation that a new standard for frames per second will be established in the coming decade or so.

Regardless of the actual fps rate, the primary distinction here is that cinema controls the speed at which the audience experiences the story. Unlike a graphic novel, where we can linger on a single panel as long as we want or flip back to a previous page, and home viewing systems like DVRs and DVDs where we can fast forward or reverse, jump ahead or jump back at our discretion, the projection experience cannot be interrupted or changed by the audience. This may be why people sometimes talk about "the power of cinema" and the need, as an audience member, to give oneself over to the experience. It is also part of the reason why cinema is often compared to dreaming – the experience is bigger than us and we have to relinquish control in order to fully enjoy it. We are pulled (or perhaps pushed) through a film story by the director (and editor).

Film is sometimes compared to a rollercoaster. That analogy is actually pretty accurate. Both are a ride – the rider does not "drive" but rather is "driven." The track or path is already laid down and the rider is taken where the designer planned. The enjoyment is that the thrills are (more or less) safe; we experience the emotions and events from a comfortable and safe position, knowing that there is indeed a plan, a design, and that all will come to an end within a certain amount of time.

Those aspects would be catastrophic for a narrative game where the player (not a rider, but a *player*) expects her actions to have an impact on what happens next and moves through the landscape at her own pace and skill level. Likewise, a film story cannot be as complex as one might find in a TV series.

How Much? Duration

Imagine being at the carnival and the tilt-a-whirl guy thinks he is doing you a favor by leaving us on the ride until the next group of customers came up. Problem is the park is pretty empty that day. You get the equivalent of four or five rides with no stopping. By the time you get off, you're so sick you can't stand or move around for hours. The rest of your day at the park is ruined. (One of our authors can vouch for this ...)

Rides are designed to have a fairly consistent duration. If they go shorter we feel gipped; if they go longer, what was pleasurable can become un-pleasurable.

Film stories are the same way. More so than television (which is influenced by the amount of advertising needed) or gaming (which assumes both multiple plays and more duration per play because of the player's active involvement), the amount of story for film is based on a sense of what an audience can tolerate or what the limits are to their enjoyment in a single sitting.

Films are meant to be seen in one sitting; therefore, the story has to be big enough to engage the audience fully for the time they're watching but be small enough to be contained in a comfortable single viewing duration. Beliefs about the ideal comfortable film viewing experience have varied from era to era, at times considered two hours or more and at others closer to 85 minutes, but a film's ideal running time is currently considered to be roughly 100 minutes, though you'll find some notable exceptions, both shorter and longer.

The film's story genre is often a factor in comfortable duration. This is why dramas and comedies tend to be shorter than blockbuster special effects-laden films – we are generally willing to spend more time watching a film like *Avatar* or *Transformers* because there is so much to see (literally). A quiet drama may start feeling long at 80 minutes depending on how compelling we find the actors or the scenario.

Besides the duration of time an audience can comfortably give to a particular story experience, we can also talk about the "size" of the story content itself – how much time is needed to tell this particular story well. You have probably heard that feature films are like novels, and short films are like short stories. But in fact, the scale of story in a feature film is more akin to the scale of a short story (and short films are more like flash fiction or short stories). Television's limited series, miniseries or a standard series' single season are a more accurate comparison to novels. A major consideration when choosing film as a story medium is whether the amount of story we have is comparable to the amount of time we have to present it on the screen.

There's nothing worse than watching a film that feels "padded," like it would have made a great short film but the producers must have stretched a thin story as far as it would go just to hit that magic running time that makes a film a "feature" rather than a "short" – *Vibes* (Columbia Pictures, 1988) feels a bit like this.

Likewise, watching a film that has tried to squeeze too much story into its running time can be confusing or feel incoherent with gaps or inconsistencies in the logic. Though some find it powerful, *Brokeback Mountain* (Focus Features, 2005) takes place over decades in the characters' lives, making huge leaps in time which can feel disruptive to the emotional arcs of the characters and choppy for the audience. This is why film narratives often deal with a very specific and small time frame. For example, *Ghost World* (United Artists, 2001) takes place in the summer between graduation – where Enid finds out she has to take a make-up class in order to get her diploma – and when she finishes the class at the end of the summer. We're only following three months of her life.

Sometimes, the compression of story time is even more severe. There are fiction films that essentially take place in a single day or 24-hour period, like *Last Night* (Alliance Atlantis, 1998), *Ferris Bueller's Day Off* (Paramount, 1986) and *Dazed and Confused* (Gramercy Pictures, 1993), and there are others where the screen time (or the roughly 100 minutes the audience is sitting in the theatre) matches the time the characters experience (or 100 minutes in "real time" for the story), such as *Rope* (Warner Bros. Pictures, 1948), *Phone Booth* (Fox 2000 Pictures, 2002), *High Noon* (United Artists, 1952), *Cleo from 5 to 7* (Cine Tamaris, 1962) or *Nick of Time* (Paramount Pictures, 1995).

How Big? Shot Size

Projected cinema images are many feet high and wide (usually at least 30 × 70 feet, allowing for a variety of screen presentation formats). Experiencing a movie on this size of screen allows for a grander scale of image composition within the frame. Before television and small screen distribution possibilities, cinema was much more likely to include extreme long or wide shots because small details in the landscape would be rendered large on the giant screens. As screens have become smaller, extreme long shots are no longer always considered the most effective or artistic way to communicate visual information, because filmmakers know that a substantial part of their audience will see the material on a smaller screen. As a result, modern films often incorporate smaller shot sizes, such as close-ups or even extreme close-ups.

Besides the size of objects in the image and therefore visible to the audience, TV Safe Lines are another consideration for material that was originally designed for theatrical projection and then shown on smaller screens — some of the edges of the image get "lost" or are not visible on a TV, computer monitor or mobile phone. This is partly why letterboxing became preferred for watching films on tradition television screens which had an aspect ratio (or relationship of the width to the height of image) of 1.33:1. As viewers have wanted a more cinematic-like experience in their homes, television screens have been resized/reshaped in recent years from something closer to a square to a horizontal rectangle which is closer to a theatrical widescreen presentation (a 1.85:1 or even 2.35:1 aspect ratio).

Why Film?

When we're looking at intellectual properties for transmedia storytelling, we need concepts that can make for viable expressions in games, TV, webisodes, graphic novels as well as films. As you read the next few chapters, you'll better understand the strengths and limitations of each of those platforms, and it's these considerations that may be why genres and high concept properties are more easily realized (or created) in transmedia.

Aspects of a transmedia intellectual property that are meant to be experienced in a single sitting and require a scale of wonder and complexity to the image may work best in film. In addition, cinema benefits from stories that encourage a certain passivity in the audience, a desire to experience but not participate (except at an emotional level). In other words, as a viewer my own impulses or interests have to be quelled as I give myself over to the film. This is why films and filmmaking are sometimes derided as manipulative. The cinema experience *is* manipulative — you are guiding the audience through a story and a series of emotions in a fixed and limited amount of time. Let's look at some of the storytelling techniques that shape the audience's film experience.

Basics of Film Storytelling and Structure

Hollywood has had a huge impact on storytelling in cinema, partly because of its long history making feature-length films and the sheer number of movies Hollywood has flooded the world with. In fact, when we talk about Hollywood film, we no longer necessarily mean where the film was made as much as the way in which it tells it story. For example, in the 1990s some of the best Hollywood films were coming out of Australia — filmmakers there had taken to heart the storytelling conventions developed in Hollywood and used them as well as, if not better than, the films being made in Hollywood at the time.

Hollywood feature-film storytelling is also sometimes referred to as "traditional narrative" or "western narrative," and though there are some variations from film to film, its touchstones include:

Psychologically defined characters *who struggle to solve a clear-cut problem or to attain specific goals – characters come into conflict with others or external circumstances as they work toward these goals. The protagonist must want something and want it so badly that he cannot help but fight to get it.*

Character (and the protagonist specifically) as the **primary causal agent** *in the story – his actions drive the story forward as he takes actions that are attempts to achieve his goal or solve the problem he is faced with. Each action has a consequence, creating a series of cause and effect events.*

Cause and effect events structured so that their order, frequency, pace and duration on the screen bring out the salient causal relationships (sometimes referred to as the **causal chain***).*

A **double plot line** *with a primary plot that features a conflict with the larger world (work, society, technology, nature, supernature) and a secondary conflict of an emotional nature that takes place in the protagonist's personal world, often romantic.*

A **deadline** *or timeframe in which the conflict has to be resolved, creating pressure on the character to "do something now" and heightening tension for the audience. This is sometimes referred to as "the ticking clock" or "the ticking bomb" – if the protagonist procrastinates, bad things will happen.*

An ending that provides a **decisive victory or defeat** *for the protagonist or a clear achievement or failure to achieve his goals. In other words, there is a resolution to the problem, and this resolution is a direct result of the protagonist's actions.*

The basic story structure or plot could be described as world at rest, world at war, world at rest. There is an undisturbed stage in the protagonist's world, then a disturbance, a struggle to "right" the disturbance, elimination of (or total succumbing to) the disturbance and resolution (a restored or a new world order).

Story Structures

There are a number of strategies that can be employed in creating a film story that build from or serve as alternative considerations to those discussed in Chapter 3. One approach is to build the material around a *central question*. In *Sleeping with the Enemy* (20th Century Fox, 1991) the central question is whether Laura will escape her abusive husband. The story is then configured around scenes that either pose that question or seem to answer it, alternating "yes she will" and "no she won't" until there is a final climax, a point where the question is asked one last time and answered decisively: yes she will, because she's killed him. Any scene or story material that does not either imply, ask or answer the question would be cut. But this is just one strategy.

Films can also be built around a *central theme or truth*, finding situations and interactions that will metaphorically illustrate that theme, such as *Pleasantville* (New Line Cinema, 1998). Director Gary Ross is quoted in *Reel Diversity: A Teacher's Sourcebook* (Peter Lang Publishing, New York, 2008) that *Pleasantville* is

> *about the fact that personal repression gives rise to larger political oppression; that when we're afraid of certain things in ourselves or we're afraid of change, we project those fears on to other things, and a lot of very ugly social situations can develop.*

A film structured around a theme might begin when the thematic material is first introduced or implied in a scene and then end when the theme has become unmistakably illustrated.

Another option is to build the story around a specific *event*, like *Home for the Holidays* (Paramount Pictures, 1995), beginning and ending within the timeframe of the actual event, in this case a family holiday gathering. Or we learn that an asteroid is about to hit the earth and we only have so much time to deal with it, like *Armageddon* (Touchstone Pictures, 1998) and *Deep Impact* (Paramount Pictures, 1998), one of which ends with the asteroid being destroyed/diverted and the other ends with the asteroid hitting the earth – either way, the film ends when the dilemma with the approaching asteroid concludes.

As you can see, there are multiple ways of thinking about story structure in film, and there are more than the few we've just mentioned. However, the above examples demonstrate that structurally, film stories usually start when the main conflict is set into motion or the protagonist becomes aware of it. When do things start going wrong for the protagonist? When does the world become endangered? In these kinds of story structures, the film would end when your character's conflict is resolved once and for all or when things start going better for your protagonist or when the world is clearly out of danger or has been destroyed.

Structure also requires thinking about the sequence or order in which you show the story. Some stories are most effective when told in chronological order, telling the narrative events in a straight line. *In America* (Fox Searchlight, 2002) begins with the narrator telling us she has three wishes and ends when the third one has been granted. The story can also be told as a circle: *The House of Sand and Fog* (DreamWorks SKG, 2003) begins and ends with the same scene, (sometimes referred to as "bookending" or "coming full circle"). All of the story material between that first and last scene is presented as extended flashback and told in chronological order. In recent years, we've seen more movies experimenting with what we might call a spiral structure: *In My Sleep* (Morning Star Pictures, 2010) starts with Marcus trying to clean off the blood covering him as the police pound on his apartment door. The film then flashes back weeks earlier and tells past events in chronological order until we catch back up to the police pounding on his door – at the end of Act 1 (more on acts in the next section) – and moving forward through the story from there. *The Invasion* (Warner Bros. Pictures, 2007) does a wider spiral, starting with Carol tearing apart a pharmacy and then flashing back to the space shuttle fragments hitting the earth (our inciting incident), telling us the story events in chronology until we reach the pharmacy scene again; in this film, the pharmacy scene is the event at the end of Act 2, and the story moves forward through the third act from there.

A more traditional approach to flashbacks is to interweave them within a "present day" sequence of events, much like *Sophie's Choice* (Universal Pictures, 1982) does. The film shifts back and forth in time in order to delay the exposition of her choice until near the end of the film – even though she made the choice very early in her chronological story. What she had to choose is withheld from the audience until it will have the most dramatic impact. In *The Grey* (Open Road Films, 2012), the recurring flashbacks are more evocative than literal, revealing and gradually (slightly) expanding a single moment until we understand its meaning and significance to John and the next few moments of the film.

The use of delayed exposition whether interwoven or more akin to spiral, circular or even in chronological structures can create a sense of discovery, a feeling that there's more going on than we know (at first), hooking us and pulling us in with a sense that there's something mysterious underneath the story or a puzzle to be solved. Curiosity and anticipation can be powerful enticements to stay involved with the story until we figure out why the characters are saying and doing what they are.

Turning the Plot Curve Upside Down

Regardless of how we sequence the story events, the plot curve (or how the plot builds from the story's start to finish) will pretty much match the diagram we saw in Chapter 3.

This inverted checkmark reflects the intensity of the plot, with the rising action (or conflict and complications) actually angling higher as the

Figure 4.1 *Plot curve, again.*

Figure 4.2 *Main character discomfort.*

stakes and consequences increase and escalate for the protagonist. As such, this diagram is a pretty good representation of a film's plot. But in most films, though to varying degrees depending upon the genre, the character's inner journey is important as well.

We can flip this plot curve on its back and see the same elements in terms of the discomfort for the main character – the ways in which we can diagram things getting worse and worse till they reach the breaking point.

This second diagram actually helps us better understand the notion that movies are about things going wrong – especially for the protagonist. Before the film starts, there has been some sort of equilibrium. The world was in in balance and going along fairly well. This would be our backstory (remember Chapter 2?) – "the way the world has been." Then something disrupts that balance and makes things get worse for the protagonist. Ideally, this disruption happens near the beginning of the film – either just before or soon after the first image – and is often referred to as the *inciting incident* or sometimes the *catalyst*. In those cases where the inciting incident has happened off screen (or earlier in the story's timeline), then the story starts when the protagonist learns of or realizes he will have to deal with the repercussions of the incident.

After the inciting incident, the protagonist makes decisions and takes actions that she hopes will make things better and restore the world (or at least her personal world) to balance. Each of these decisions and actions has consequences, and it is this combination of action and consequence as she continues to react to and engage with the conflict that creates the rising action.

This rising action escalates in terms of speed (events begin to happen more quickly) and risk (the consequences become greater) until things are so bad that the protagonist may feel hopeless – this is sometimes referred to as the "all is lost" or "oh, shit" moment. As a result, the protagonist may see (or be forced to see) either herself or the situation in a new way, a way that wouldn't have been possible for her to see before seeming to lose everything. This *recognition scene* can result in a new insight, a new way of thinking about the conflict that allows the protagonist to see a course of action she had missed before. With renewed commitment, she gears up to battle her obstacles one last time.

The protagonist's re-commitment to her goals leads to a final confrontation between protagonist and obstacle, a final (usually decisive) moment of conflict. At this point, the protagonist will either succeed or fail.

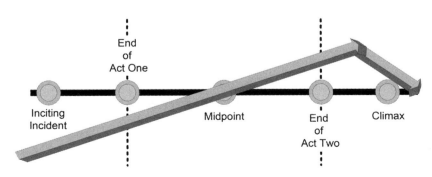

Figure 4.3 *More plot points.*

Moments in the script such as the "all is lost" or "recognition" scenes are sometimes referred to as *plot points* or *turning points*. There are a variety of ways to think about these, but let's look at a simple diagram of the primary plot points of a film story overlaid on our initial plot curve diagram.

These five plot points help define three-act structure. For example, the second plot point above equates to the end of Act 1, turning the story into a new direction – sometimes this might be the protagonist's call to action or it might be the protagonist making a decision that seems right at the time but ultimately makes things worse for him. The midpoint is halfway through Act 2 and may be the point of no return or the point where a surprise

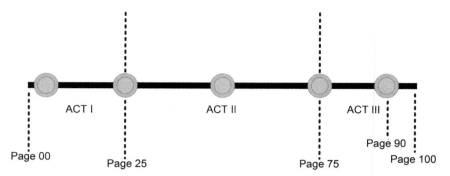

Figure 4.4 *Three-act structure.*

happens that shifts the direction of the story or it may be a symbolic scene that serves to reveal a theme or subtext. The all-is-lost moment defines the end of Act 2 and is usually in proximity of the recognition scene. The climax occurs near the end of Act 3. We might add more plot points between the ones diagrammed above to more fully diagram the action or story events of the plot, but these five form the basic spine of film stories.

To help us better understand the relationship of these acts to each other in terms of scale and proportion, let's add the page number where we'd typically expect each of these five main plot points to occur in a 100-page script.

We can see from this diagram that Act 2 is much longer than Acts 1 or 3. In fact, it's about the same length as the two of them combined. This is why some writers and producers describe this traditional kind of film structure as more accurately four acts than three acts. Ultimately, what we call it isn't as important as understanding the structure itself, so for our purposes in this book and to be consistent with the way act structure is usually described in film stories, we will refer to this general approach of organizing story material as three-act structure.

In traditional film narratives, the characters are actively engaged in the conflict, driving the story forward. As a result, they are significantly responsible for their own fates by the choices they make, and the conflicts and obstacles get worse for the main character. This is because the protagonist will make choices that will seem like they'd make his situation better, but they have (unforeseen) consequences which complicate his life more. The more he is out of touch with a true understanding of himself or the world around him, the more likely he is to make the wrong choice. Now you see why that recognition scene in character-driven narrative is so important – it sets up the third act (recommitment to the goal with new insights and a final reckoning with the primary obstacle or source of the conflict in the climax).

What becomes apparent from this is that most narrative film structures are a series of causes and effects, sometimes called a "causal chain." One thing leads to another. Every action has a reaction (to paraphrase Newtonian physics). This becomes a chain because each effect causes something else. And so on and so on. Another way of thinking about cause and effect is that every cause's effect is the cause of something else, so every link in the chain is both a cause and an effect.

Therefore, it's perhaps more accurate to diagram our plot curve as not a set of smooth lines but rather a series of highs

Figure 4.5 *Another plot curve.*

and lows, peaks and valleys, much like the sawtooth pattern of handsaw blade. After every action there is a small lull where the consequences come into focus, requiring a new action from the protagonist.

At first glance, each of these diagrams makes it seem like all films have one plotline, but from all the movies you've seen, you know that this isn't true. What we've really diagrammed is the main plotline, sometimes referred to in film as the *Action Line* or the *A Story* or *A Plot* ("A" meaning first or primary, as in the first letter in the alphabet).

As we mentioned at the very beginning of this section, most movies that we see have a double plot line, or an Action Line and at least 1 subplot or *B Story*. In most of the genres we've listed, this second plot line is a heterosexual romance involving the main character. In *Die Hard*, this is McClane's estranged relationship with his wife that impacts his decisions on how to deal with the terrorists.

Each plotline possesses its own goal(s), obstacle(s) and climax. In most cases, each plotline is distinct and interdependent but usually converges at significant points within the narrative. *Se7en* (New Line Cinema, 1995) is probably one of the most disturbing examples of this, when Doe kills Mills' wife, forcing the inevitable climax and resolution of the action line.

Three-Act Structure in Film

In broad strokes, and building off the concepts and approaches we've just examined and from Chapter 3, a film story's structure has to accomplish the following:

- Beginning (Act I, though the basics have to be set up within the first ten minutes of the film):
  - introduce your main characters
    - show the protagonist
    - show the antagonist
  - foreshadow the ending
  - show characters under stress
    - establish the conflict
    - establish what the hero wants
    - show what's at stake
    - establish the setting
    - set the tone of the story
    - set the style of the story
- Middle (Act II):
  - use scenes to tell your story (more on that in the next subsection)
  - develop your characters through action and dialogue
  - include all the elements needed for the conclusion
  - give your characters believable psychological motivation
  - develop the plot as a series of increasingly serious problems
  - create suspense
  - show your characters changing
  - shows the emotional toll on the protagonist and raise doubts of his success
- End (Act III):
  - present a final, crucial conflict

- Throughout the story:
  - ensure everything has a reason
  - use images, metaphors and symbols deliberately
  - know the genre conventions and utilize them effectively

Finally, good cinema storytelling is sometimes described as starting *in medias res* ("into the middle of things"). Though you'll find other interpretations for this Latin phrase's application to storytelling, filmmakers usually mean that films are most effective when you start in the middle of the story. Another way this concept is presented, both in terms of writing story and particularly with individual dramatic scenes, is the admonition, "come in late, leave early."

Key Transmedia Elements and Motion Pictures

Earlier in this book, we talked about a set of key elements of transmedia storytelling property: *theme/story*, *plot*, *character*, *setting*, and *style/tone*. These elements are as important in feature-film development as any other media, but manifest in different ways. Let's take a brief look at each of them in the context of films.

Theme/Story

Inexperienced storytellers can easily confuse theme with premise, subject matter and even story. Each of these is a different concept. Though film has borrowed these concepts from theatre and literature, it has put its own spin on them, and so it's important to realize that other media might use these terms differently.

In broad strokes, our story will have a topic ("love") or basic subject matter that we can talk about, a theme ("love conquers all") or a subtext that expresses a position, opinion or viewpoint about the subject matter, a premise ("boy meets boy, boy loses boy, boy gets boy back") which lays out in one sentence a simple plot or narrative arc. Thinking about the larger story in these terms can help us see if the story is in fact consistent, cohesive and coherent. Let's look at each more closely.

In the best films, there are larger story implications that create (at least) two levels to the film.

The immediately apparent level is the one that overtly communicates information by literally showing us events and character actions; film theorists might refer to this as text. We should be able to identify the film's topic or subject matter from this overt material presented, and identifying this material as a topic provides a concise label for thinking about the larger story material that we're working with, in terms of the physical, psychological, sociological and emotional context of the events we will portray.

The other level communicates covert or hidden information, allowing us to consider that the story's literal events (or text) have broader implications. This second level is what we call subtext, and it is the underlying or hidden meaning of the script or film. Whenever you hear yourself saying, "the film is really about …" you're more than likely talking about its subtext. You're providing an interpretation of the film, getting at this idea that there is a meaning beyond the simple events portrayed on the screen, some central truth or insight about the real (audience's) world or being human.

When a storyteller has deliberately constructed a particular subtext, we call this a theme. Like the moral tag at the end of a fable, some films (particularly older ones) clearly state their themes through dialogue (like *The Wizard of Oz*'s "there's no place like home"). Other films might overtly state their theme in a written quote either at the beginning or ending of the film (*Gattica*, Columbia Pictures, 1997). And there are films that disclose their theme in the title of the film itself (*Life is Beautiful*, Cecchi Gor Pictures, 1997).

The trend these days is for films to never explicitly state the theme. The filmmaker may still be working with a central statement of truth but leaves it to the audience to uncover it or figure it out. Another approach is to raise moral or ethical questions that are left unanswered within the narrative, provoking the audience to weigh (and debate) the actions of the characters or the events of the story, forcing them to examine their own values. Regardless of whether themes are conclusive opinions presented as truth or unanswered moral questions, we generally expect to infer the themes from the situations, characters and stories presented on the screen.

Plot

In an earlier section (Basics of Film Storytelling), we talked quite a bit about structure, or the way in which we shape and present story material. As you can see from that earlier discussion, storytelling in film is highly formalized; film stories — especially those from major film industries like Hollywood or Bollywood — tend to have very specific ways of presenting their stories on the screen. Much of this owes to the characteristics of the film medium itself. To state the obvious, stories for moving image media have to be visual.

Even though we've all heard that a picture is worth a thousand words, words can sometimes do things that visuals can't. Novels and short stories allow for deeply subjective and internal stories, able to explore and present complex psychological motivations to the reader. While films can have a subjective point of view, as a medium, they're not particularly conducive to deeply internal stories or extremely contemplative characters (more on characters in the next section). The film's plot reveals story through an observational method, and we can't observe thoughts. We can observe actions and behavior, and in film storytelling these have to be discernible enough to imply what the characters are feeling or thinking.

In addition, films are designed to be experienced in a single sitting, requiring consideration of how much story can effectively be told, and once that's figured out, how much (or how little) of that story to show on the screen. This is why film stories often take place in a fairly compressed amount of time — they are about people in crisis who need to act, and act now! And they have to tell their stories quickly, which makes dense, complex or multiple plotlines a challenge to do well in the medium. Hence, we usually only have an A Story and a B Story or main plot (action line) and subplot.

Finally, most film plots operate along a strong line of cause and effect. There are consequences to every choice the protagonist makes or action he takes, and the audience can see these even if the character can't.

Character

We mentioned earlier that the characters in films generally have to be active in order for us to have something to see on the screen. Any internal struggles (or what William Faulkner once described as "the human heart in conflict with itself") have to be externalized in a way that is visible to the audience.

This doesn't mean that film characters aren't angst-ridden, just that their angst is expressed through their actions. There's a temptation for novice screenwriters to want to have the characters describe all these internal thoughts and feelings in dialogue, but film storytelling puts a premium on showing, not telling, in terms of both character and story. We sometimes call this "trusting the audience" (to figure out what's going on and why). *Lars and the Real Girl* (MGM, 2007) and *The Invisible* (Hollywood Pictures, 2007) are each effective in showing their stories and using dialogue as an example of character behavior rather than a way to tell the audience story information (as many plays and even some types of television programs do). In each case, the characters want something and take action, even if sometimes misguided or misunderstood (by others in the story), to fulfill that want.

The test for this is not what the filmmaker intended but what actually gets on the screen – what an audience unfamiliar with the original story or characters sees and understands about the characters and story. This need for observable behavior and action may be why so many films are high concept – high concept films have very clear external conflicts for the character to engage with (such as human against human, human against technology, human against society, human against nature, human against supernature, just to name the most common ways of classifying the types of story conflict).

Setting

Unlike theatre which has to find a way to portray (or more accurately, evoke) all of the story's settings in a small confined space, a film camera can go anywhere (on and within a fairly close range of Earth). In digital image production done entirely on a computer or in traditional animation, the audience can be taken *anywhere* filmmakers can imagine. Setting then is another choice we make in telling our story, and the common wisdom is that a story should be set in that location or environment that intensifies the conflict or helps reveal textual and subtextual information about the character or story.

Of course, because the camera can go anywhere, there can be some blurring of the distinction between setting (where the story is set) and location (where the story is filmed) – but most audiences these days are savvy enough to know (and accepting of the fact) that a film where the action takes place in New York may have actually been shot in Vancouver. Los Angeles has traditionally stood in for other settings in television shows and movies all the time.

Traditionally, films were edited in such a way as to make sure the audience always knew where that moment of the story was taking place. Often any scene would start with a long shot or wide shot that would reveal the environment surrounding the characters (sometimes referred to as the establishing shot) and then cut to a series of closer shots where we could see the characters' expressions and behavior (breakdown) and then cut back out to a wider shot of the characters in their environment (re-establishing shot). Re-establishment shots fell out of use quite a while ago, but more recent films may start scenes right in close to the characters, in effect reducing the importance of (or delaying the exposition of) the environment or setting.

Style/Tone

There are all kinds of films and film stories. The style and tone is influenced by the genre of the story being told as well as the audience it's intended for. The story's style and tone is alluded to in the script but it is ultimately communicated to the audience visually, which brings in factors such as the production design (or the way the setting is presented), the sound design (which can create a sense of the larger storyworld as well as create its own emotional responses in the audience), and the actors' performance (or the way the characters are portrayed in terms of mannerisms, dialects, expressions and actions big and small).

Our goal with all of these, whether we're making an individual film or creating a larger transmedia story, is to make decisions about our story based on an understanding of how all of these elements build together to create a unified (or consistent) experience for the audience. And to realize that audiences have been conditioned through years of watching films to have a certain set of expectations of how a film story unspools – how characters will be presented and story material will be revealed. Most of these filmmaking decisions happen long before we start filming. We work out these choices and possibilities on paper, using words on a computer screen like an artist might use a pencil and sketch paper. Let's turn our attention at some of the ways in which film stories are presented before the cameras roll.

Presenting a Visual Story with Words

Some producers, screenwriters and/or directors like to figure out their story while actually writing script pages, while others like to plan out the entire story as much as possible before they begin writing. There are a number of ways to develop story, but all require some format of text on the page. Besides a script, common methods of presenting film stories in the development stage are to create a logline, a synopsis or a treatment, a scene outline or a beat sheet (sometimes considered synonymous with a step outline). All written documents created in relationship to a film story are considered as something like blueprints – an intermediate step and not the finished work.

Though each of these have different formats, there are several common stylistic devices or approaches in all writing about film story: all are written in third person, present tense and in terms of observable externalized behavior (reflecting the fact that we ultimately have to be able to see the story on the screen). In all but the logline, the first time a character appears in the script, his or her name is in ALL CAPS. (Please note that this is different from how character names and some other elements are handled in television scripts.) These documents do not have to be created in any particular order, but all can be helpful in keeping the story focused as you develop and present it to others. With all of these, you will probably rewrite them multiple times before you feel they best represent and communicate the story.

Loglines

The logline serves as a thumbnail sketch of the film's essential conflict and scenario, a concise summary of your story's plot (not theme). It should be a single sentence from which the reader is able to identify the main character (not by name but by type) and the main conflict. A good logline may even include a hint as to the resolution. Loglines are a quick way to remind someone what the story is about in one or two sentences. A possible logline for *The Wizard of Oz* (MGM, 1939) would be, "An unhappy farm girl, who doesn't appreciate what she has, is swept away to a dreamlike land only to discover that there's no place like home." No two people will come up with exactly the same logline for any one project; the only "right" logline is the one that most accurately represents the story you plan to tell.

Outlines

A *scene outline* generally creates one paragraph for every scene you envision in the final film. These are written in third person, present tense, and briefly describe what we could expect to see in that particular scene. Outlines usually do not include specific dialogue unless the specific phrasing of that line of dialogue is critical to the story or character.

Scenes break the film story down into smaller segments of dramatic action that move the story forward by showing us:

- new aspects of the conflict
- the protagonist taking action against the conflict
- new obstacles
- important information to help the audience better understand the circumstances of the conflict or the characters' motivations

Though individual scenes may vary, the average duration for a single scene is about three minutes of screen time, and scenes are usually defined by events taking place in one continuous time and space. In other words, if your action moves to another space, then it's usually considered to be a new scene. Likewise, if there's been a gap or jump in time, you usually consider it a new scene even if your characters are still in the same space.

Each scene has a clear relationship to the scenes (or story material) that has preceded it and the scenes that follow, helping the audience construct a coherent and consistent sense of time, space and relationship of story events to each other in terms of cause and effect.

Scenes are different from sequences and montages, which may show a series of activities that occur in different times and spaces to advance the story in a fairly rapid manner. Sequences and montages tend to show us only actions and events. Scenes show us the underlying emotional currents of a particular moment or of the characters. Scenes are about more than the behavior and action we can see. They are about the emotional toll behind them.

A *step outline* or *beat sheet* uses brief paragraphs or statements to summarize the major action of the story. Some of these actions might take place over several scenes, so this type of outline is less concerned about what might happen in an individual scene and instead emphasizes the general arc of the story through key narrative actions that will be portrayed.

For example, we may have a block of story action that could be written as "the criminals case the joint" and yet require several scenes (different locations and/or different times of day) to portray this story action – maybe in one scene they observe the place they're going to rob from the outside at a distance where they can take in the entire street, and in another scene one of them goes inside and pretends to be a customer, and in a third scene they watch to see if there's a pattern in how the employees lock up and leave.

Though it doesn't happen as often, there can also be stories where multiple story events are expressed within a single scene.

We call these step outlines or beat sheets because filmmakers refer to these external plot developments or story events as steps or beats. (It's important to note that we're using the term beats here differently from how actors and directors might use the same word to describe their method of identifying the internal shifts within a character to build psychologically complex or emotionally nuanced performances.)

Either of these techniques – a scene outline or a step outline – can help you see your story in a manageable scale (just a few pages as opposed to a script which can be 100 or more). This makes it much easier see the whole story at once, analyze whether the story makes sense in terms of cause and effect, determine if there are accidental gaps or redundancies of story material, and make changes to the plot if necessary.

Story Summaries

There are two major types of story summaries for film stories: a synopsis and a treatment. Both are written in third person, present tense.

Synopsis

A film synopsis is a concise overview of the narrative that does not include dialogue and paints the story in broad strokes. It's usually just one page long, typed in four single-spaced paragraphs with a double space between each:

> **First paragraph**: *a brief but precise description of the protagonist, his or her name in ALL CAPS the first time it appears. This description should focus on his or her psychological characteristics: key personality traits that help explain why the character does what he or she does. This is one of the only times you as a filmmaker will write internal information about your characters for others*

to read. The goal is to succinctly describe the character in a few precise terms that make him or her vivid in the reader's mind. You may include basic demographic information (age, gender), but any physical information (appearance, physicality) should only be noted if it's important to the narrative or will be part of the story. You might write a brief description of your antagonist as well in this paragraph.

Second paragraph: *a brief but precise description of the protagonist's basic desires or objectives, and the obstacles or opposition he or she faces in realizing those objectives. This is the premise of the story. Include the inciting incident (or the events that set the story, protagonist and conflict into motion). In a feature-length film, this would be the story material set up in the first act.*

Third paragraph: *a general or broad summary of what ensues – the development or progression of the conflict toward the climax. In a feature-length film, this would be primarily a summary of the second act. Because Act 2 in a feature film usually includes an "all is lost" moment and a recognition or realization on the part of the protagonist, include those moments in this paragraph if appropriate to your story.*

Fourth paragraph: *a brief statement that identifies the outcome of the conflict and its resolution, or how the plot is resolved in regards to the original premise and conflict. In a feature-length film, this would be the part of the story that would be contained in the third act, including the climax.*

Treatments

There are two types of treatments that filmmakers use – a narrative treatment (or an expanded version of the story's synopsis) and an aesthetic treatment (a summary of the elements that will reflect or affect the style and tone of the finished film). While each can give you perspective on your story material, people asking to see your treatment usually mean the narrative treatment. Depending upon the length of your project and what you find most helpful, your narrative treatment could be as short as two pages or as long as 40 or 50. However, the general trend over the years has been for narrative treatments to get shorter, usually under ten pages.

Unlike a synopsis, the narrative treatment should begin with the first image or scene that will appear on the screen and conclude with the last image or scene the audience will see. The material between these two scenes summarizes the entire arc of the story, closely following your story outline and told in the order it will be presented on the screen.

As you write your treatment, you want to evoke the characters, situations, settings, and tone of your story. You're not trying to describe everything, just enough so that the reader can imagine it. Nor is a narrative treatment really like a short story (though it should be engaging to read), because it concentrates on telling us what the characters do, not their internal state. Just like the viewer has to do with the finished film, the reader has to infer what the characters are thinking or feeling from their behavior and actions.

We usually recommend not using any "film language" such as "we see" or "close up on" or "cut to" in a treatment (or synopsis for that matter) – the descriptions alone should convey what the viewer will see.

Scripts/Screenplays

There is a variety of formats for screenplays or scripts, but all of them have several elements in common.

A script is a scene-by-scene description of the dramatic action of your story. Because scripts are treated as a guide for telling the story on the screen rather than literary works in and of themselves, they are continually being revised and reconsidered. Scripts are a sketch of what the final film will look like, not the film itself, in the way an artist might make a preliminary drawing before painting. They help those working on the film to see its overall design.

Script formats have become standardized over the years to help make filmmaking more efficient and economical. As long as you're familiar with the specific format, any and all scripts in that format are quick and easy to read, allowing you to get to the issues you need to consider for making the film. To this end, scripts are formatted to have lots of white space. Descriptions and dialogue are short and spaced on the page in such a way that the page looks more white (lots of space) than black (lots of text). The goal is to evoke the action in a handful of words, not to describe it in painstaking detail. A bonus is that lots of white space allows room for handwritten notes in the margins. The specifics for script format are quite precise and standardized; scripts that deviate from standard format are generally perceived as unprofessional.

Scripts need to be as clear as possible about what is happening in the story. Scripts are written for the producing team, the director, crew members and actors, not your audience. This means that you have to give information in your script that your audience might not yet know if they were watching the finished film, such as a character's name or the fact that the scene is a dream sequence. These need to be clearly and consistently identified in your script. As we tell our students, you wouldn't expect a carpenter to build your house based on a blueprint in which you've hidden certain design details because you want to surprise your guests when they walk in. Such a house might fall down. The same holds true for scripts and films.

There are primarily two specific script formats you are most likely to use: a master scene script and, as you go into production, a shooting script.

The primary purpose of the master scene script is to present the story scene by scene; a shooting script will present the story in ways that make it easier to plan each shot. There are lots of books and software programs on script format if you're unsure how to do it.

Proposals

If your film project is being produced independent of a film industry like Hollywood, you may need to seek investors and/or granting foundations, and they will probably want to see a brief description of your planned project or a description of your concept. The specifics of such a proposal may vary depending upon whom you approach for funding, but there are some basic elements that are usually common to all: what the film is about, who the film is for, and why you're the person to make it. Proposals can be standalone or be a part of the business plan. If the people you're approaching ask for the material to be presented according to a particular template, always be sure to use this. If they do not provide a specific format, then you can create your own. At a minimum, your proposal should include a description of the film's:

> **Prime theme**: *the underlying meaning you have deliberately chosen and developed within the story; theme statements may be as long as a short paragraph, but ideally you should state your theme in a single sentence. Either way, the theme statement is different from the logline (which is more about plot) or a tagline (which is more about marketing) and serves as a quick summary of the film's focus and therefore comes first in the proposal.*

> **Prime goal**: *like theme, your goal statement should be clearly identified and brief, in this case no more than three paragraphs. These paragraphs provide an overview of your rationale for developing your identified theme.*

> *You might begin by referring to the specific context of your proposed film's setting and conflict. Depending on the project, you might include personal anecdotal information to demonstrate your familiarity or experience with the subject matter or you might summarize common knowledge or researched factual information that is relevant to the topic. Either way, you are demonstrating that you have something authentic to say.*

> *Any information that is important for your reader to know in order to understand why this film needs to be made and why you're the person to do it is valid information to include — as long as you can say it in three paragraphs or fewer.*

You generally want to conclude with a sense of how your particular story and approach will address, work with or reveal your theme and goals. This allows you to emphasize in a different way what the film is about.

Prime audience: *in one or two sentences, describe the ideal audience member or the demographics of those who are most likely to pay to see this film. Hollywood films generally have very specific demographic definitions for their ideal audience, which they sometimes call a target audience or intended audience. Many of the Hollywood films made in the late 20th and early 21st centuries were targeted towards what is sometimes referred to as the "adolescent male market," which means upper-middle class Caucasian heterosexual males with an age range from early teens to early thirties.*

If you're not sure who your audience is, a good clue is to look at your protagonist, because your protagonist is often whom the audience is supposed to identify or empathize with.

An added benefit to having a written proposal is that it can serve as a reminder of your original intentions. Because making a film or developing a transmedia property can take months or years, it's easy to get halfway done and lose sight of why you started the project in the first place. The proposal can keep you focused in the long haul by reminding you of your original theme, goals, and audience.

Film Production Realities

Let's just get to the bad news first. The biggest production reality facing filmmakers is cost. Film is an expensive medium, partly because it is time and labor intensive and partly because the technology used to make films, while becoming cheaper at the consumer end, is still quite costly if one is looking to produce a feature film. Other factors (such as name talent, which is just a fancy way of saying "famous actor," location shooting, the number of shooting days and other factors) can drive the costs up even more.

Filmmaking in the United States is usually talked about as one of two extremes, Hollywood studio projects and independent film projects. The assumption is that one is expensive and the other is cheap, but you can find very low-budget studio films as well as independent films that cost as much to make as the average studio film. Production models (studio vs. independent) are not the sole determining factor, though they can be a general indicator.

On average, studio films cost hundreds of millions of dollars to make, and therefore have to attract large audiences in order to make back their money. *The Hobbit* films were originally estimated as costing $270 million each, putting them among – but not at the top of the list of – the most expensive films produced so far, though that initial estimate was based on their being two rather than three films. By comparison, the last two Harry Potter films (*Deathly Hallows: Part I and II*, Warner Bros. Pictures, 2010, 2011) were each budged at $125 million. Either way, though, Hollywood films are often expensive to make.

Independent films can range from microbudgets (less than $50,000, like the first *Paranormal Activity*, Paramount, 2009) to low budget ($50,000 or $100,000 to 3 to 5 million dollars, such as the first *Saw*, Lion's Gate, 2004) to moderate budgets (3 million to 80 million, such as *Reign of Fire*, Buena Vista, 2002). Sadly, even though their budgets are smaller, independent films are no less dependent upon audience and box office. (All budget information from www.the-numbers.com, accessed July 4, 2012.)

This need to recoup the negative costs (or all those costs associated with producing and shooting the film) has a huge impact on how films are made, the kinds of stories chosen to go into production, the way films are marketed and distributed, and the ways in which they're thought of as either failures or successes. Add in the costs related to distribution and promotion, and filmmaking is clearly an expensive venture.

A Film's Life Cycle

The average length of time it takes a film story in Hollywood to go from being optioned to being on the screen is five to seven years, accruing costs through all five of its primary production phases or stages. Most film projects never make it all the way through the process, but even films that are never released may have cost (someone) a lot of money. A film project's process from concept to screen is usually talked about as specific phases that are not that different from the phases we might see a video game or a television series go through, but what occurs in those stages, the amount of time each averages, and the costs associated with them do differ between film and other platforms.

In terms of film, before any these stages can start, someone has to have an idea. A concept. It might be a producer. It might be a screenwriter. They might have come up with the idea completely on their own or someone might have suggested it. Regardless, the person with the concept will often be thinking about it for quite a while before deciding it's time to find someone to help make that concept into a film. It's at this point that development begins.

Development

Development refers to that period when the story is being crafted and refined. There are a couple of ways in which films go into development. The producer with a concept hires a writer to turn the concept into a scripted story. Or the writer with a concept might write a treatment for the story and pitch it to a producer; or the writer might go ahead and write a draft of the script on his own (sometimes referred to as a "spec script") and then shop it around to studios, production companies or producers. Whichever way it happens, the writer and producer begin working together to shape the story. In Hollywood, this is sometimes called the *notes* process because the producer (or in a studio, development execs) will read drafts and provide some combination of verbal and written feedback to the writer.

Please note that we are assuming the writer and producer are two different people; in short films or ultra-independent labors of love, they might be one in the same (usually with the role of director thrown in for good measure … or nervous breakdown, perhaps). If they are, it becomes even more important to find outside readers knowledgeable about film story to critique the script in an effort to have the best screenplay possible before cameras start rolling.

At its best, development is a conversation and a collaboration. Discussions about the story are not about who's right or who's wrong, but what works best for the story, what will make it a better film. This conversation can make the story stronger as the writer and producer examine and ponder every aspect of the story that they can, making decisions about the shape of the story that have a clear rationale and that can be articulated. The script may go through a number of drafts during this period, and with studio films, the screenwriter is paid for writing these.

At its worst, development can go on so long or lead to so many different people trying to steer the story that the narrative loses focus or becomes inconsistent in terms of character development and/or the cause and effect linkage of the narrative events. This is when people refer to the process as "development hell."

If you're lucky, the script gets to the point that you feel it's ready to set a date for production to begin. This is sometimes referred to as greenlighting the project (like a traffic light telling you to go, go, go). Even though the script will continue to be revised during subsequent phases, at the point the production date is set, development has officially ended and preproduction has officially begun.

Preproduction

During preproduction, a director is brought to the project if she hasn't already been attached during development. Under the producer's watchful eye, the director casts the film and assembles her department heads, or the crew members who will be in charge of the major areas of the production, such as a cinematographer and production designer. These department heads will then begin to develop the visual look of the film in consultation with the director. For cinematographers, this might include the creation of storyboards, especially for complicated scenes that require a lot of camera placements or movement, or test shoots to determine the best way to achieve the look the director wants. For production designers, this could include the development of a production design bible to guide the art direction of the film and three-dimensional models to represent any sets that will need to be constructed or the types of interior locations that would be ideal.

Directors are also responsible for casting the film. Films are more likely to secure funding or get a distributor if they attach a star or an actor with some degree of name recognition. Of course, stars and known actors come with a price, literally. Attaching a star can radically inflate the budget, and the producer is constantly balancing the future benefits to marketing with the financial realities of shooting the film today.

Production

Production officially commences when cameras roll and principal photography begins. Though people unfamiliar with filmmaking often assume that it's the director who guides all the stages, production is often the only time in the process that the director is pretty much completely in charge – at least on set. It is her responsibility to get the film in the can (or shot). As much as possible, the producer tries to step back and not interfere, staying behind the scenes. As in all the stages we're discussing, the producer still keeps an eye on the logistics of the production because these directly impact the budget. For example, if the director falls behind and the film takes longer to shoot than planned, this film goes over budget, and that might affect other stages down the road.

Postproduction

Postproduction as a specific stage of a film's life cycle is often described as officially beginning when principal photography ends, but that flies in the face of the realities of production. Even before the advent of digital postproduction technologies, it was not uncommon for an editor to begin assembling the footage during production, so the starting point for this stage is somewhat arbitrary.

Postproduction includes picture editing and sound design, with key milestones including picture lock (or the point when picture editing is done, allowing final sound design, music scoring and digital effects to be finished) and at the end of the process, a final print – or a completed version of the film ready to distribute.

Along the way, there is usually a series of test screenings to gauge audience reaction and interest as a predictor of the film's possible success. These audience surveys tend to get a lot of attention when they result in major re-editing of the film, especially if the ending is changed. The studio and producer's goal is to have a film that will make back the money it cost to produce plus some. If that means changing the ending to potentially bring in more viewers, then that will usually supersede any concerns about story logic (or the ending's consistency with the story up to that point).

Marketing/Exhibition/Distribution

The film's ability to reach an audience is one of the first questions a producer considers, all the way back at the concept stage. So while we might think that marketing concerns come at the end of the postproduction process, the reality is that a great deal of thought has been given through the film's life cycle on who will want to see the film and how to let them know it exists, factors that affect whether the film will make a profit or not.

Marketing budgets for big Hollywood films are now regularly reported to be as high as $40 million, and a lot of that budget goes to promoting the film before its release. *The Hunger Games* (Lionsgate, 2012) – which is an adaptation, not a transmedia property at this point – had a marketing budget of $45 million, and the film was aggressively promoted via the web, including a game on Facebook, various YouTube videos and a Tumbler blog (www.reuters.com/article/2012/03/25/entertainment-us-boxoffice-idUSBRE82O0AS20120325 accessed July 3, 2012).

Massive pre-release advertising is a somewhat new strategy that has been largely influenced by the advent of mobile devices and social media, such as Twitter. Opening weekend has become critical for the financial success or failure of a film. Word of mouth about films no longer requires several days or weeks or months to reach a critical mass; audiences' responses to a film can be shared with millions while the audience is still sitting in the theatre watching the film. This means that if people start tweeting during the screening that the film sucks, its chance of making a decent box office is greatly diminished. The solution has been to try to get as many people as possible into the theatre that first weekend so that a huge volume of tickets have been sold before anyone hears the bad reviews. This might also explain why studios are increasingly making movie tickets available for presell before the film is released.

Theatrical distribution is not our only option for film. While it is still considered the most prestigious distribution avenue for motion pictures, the home market has become a financial savior for many films in recent years because of the income generated by DVD sales, streaming the film on rental services like Netflix, cable broadcast of the film including second screens like HBOGO, and other opportunities for making a film story available to audiences. Our marketing strategy may need to consider ways to promote the film in these various forms as well.

The other factor that has shifted in recent years is that the box office revenue for a particular film can vary widely between its release in the United States and in other countries. Sometimes the domestic box office for a film can be disappointing, and based on those numbers, we would consider the film a failure, costing significantly more than it brought in. But that same film might have impressive box office in Europe, and when domestic and international sales are tallied together, we might consider it a success.

All of these considerations go into determining a marketing and distribution strategy for the film, and these become even more important to weigh when the film is part of a transmedia story. Of course, one of the benefits of being part of transmedia property is that the film can benefit from cross promotion or the fact that there are audiences of the property on other platforms who will be interested in seeing the complementary film, in effect drawing a built in audience.

Here are two final caveats about a film's life cycle or the stages of production:

1. Even though we've just laid these different phases out in nice neat paragraphs, the reality of the process is much messier. These are not discrete stages that are each wrapped up and finished before moving on to the next one. Especially as filmmaking technologies have become digital, members of the postproduction team might be on set editing or laying in effects while the production crew is shooting. During postproduction, you may decide that you need to add or reshoot a scene, and suddenly the director and a production crew are back in action. Throughout the entire process, the story is continually being rethought or rewritten in an effort to make it the best possible film with the resources available.
2. Whether studio or independent, all films go through these five stages or something similar. The big difference between the two, besides cost, is that studio films usually have a much more rigid hierarchy and division of labor. In independent filmmaking, specific roles might overlap or be combined.

Film Franchises and Sequels

We've talked earlier about how many current transmedia properties began accidentally because a successful film spawned sequels, which were originally seen as a way to draw upon a pre-existing audience who wanted to see "more of the same" – but bigger and better. As the vision for these films moved past a simple shortsighted one-at-a-time sequel strategy into a broader longer view of how to make multiple story-related films and how those future films would relate to each other and could extend the property's life, we began to refer to these kinds of film series as franchises. These are of course different from trilogies like *Lord of the Rings* or *The Hobbit* which are in effect telling one story over three feature films. Film franchises are made up of individual films each with their own stories but those films share common elements, most often the same characters.

Thinking in terms of film franchises opens up the possibility of developing stories much in the way serialized television does, but the danger is that one bad box office could make studios wary of investing money in the future installments. That may be why most film franchises treat their component films as more episodic in nature with a little development of character arcs from film to film but nothing like a franchise-long story arc comparable to what we might find in a television series' season arc.

The bottom line is that films have a complicated journey from concept to screen, and any transmedia property that incorporates films into its overall narrative will need to navigate these challenges and find ways to counterbalance the various factors that can stall a film. To date, *X-Files* is probably the best example of a film (well, the first one) integrated into a larger story told across different media, partly because its cast was in place and the television series had already been working with long story arcs, planning certain narrative developments long in advance, as well as having established a large universe and mythology complex enough to support feature film iterations.

Film and Transmedia

Now that we understand more about the storytelling elements used in film stories, let's consider them in relationship to other platforms and media expressions of our intellectual property.

Like any moving image medium, whether television, videogames, webisodes and others we can think of, film tells stories visually. That becomes a primary consideration for the type of story we can tell in film (or really, any of the moving image media).

Visual Storytelling

Before deciding whether our property is appropriate for moving images, we need to analyze its visual potential. For example, if the story is better told through words than visual images (maybe because it relies heavily on the protagonist's internal thoughts to shape the story or its pleasure will draw heavily from its use of language), then it should be a book.

Stories that work best in moving image formats use cinematic techniques to guide the audience's attention to story information that is crucial for them to see or understand in order to make sense of the story or the character's actions. Cinematic considerations include:

Mise-en-scène

Mise-en-scène is a French term that is used to refer to everything in the frame or the image, including lighting, action, composition and art direction (props and set), all of which combine to create a singular effect. The issues of mise-en-scène can be summed up by the simple question: What do you show on the screen?

You can think of it as standing at a window; depending on where I stand, I see something different. What I see is the mise-en-scène, and in film, most if not all of this material is determined by the filmmakers. This leads us the concept of point of view and how we shape POV specifically through different aspects of the mise-en-scène, staring with framing.

Framing *equals the elements of a scene, environment or action which will be visible on the screen. Of course, the frame was originally a result of the photographic process which was required to create the image. Now, even in media where cameras are not required to create the images, we still talk in terms of camera placement to describe the choices related to image composition in telling our story. Framing can be determined by a number of different techniques including angle, height, level, shot scale and mobile framing. We're not going to go into a great deal of detail — there are plenty of books on cinematography and production design that can help you if you want to know more — but here is a brief rundown of these various factors.*

High angle (or down) shots have the camera located above and aimed down toward the subject; straight-on (or eye level) is when the camera is located at normal eye level in relation to the subject; low angle means the camera is positioned below the subject and shoots up at it.

Camera height is very similar to camera angle, though angle determines the direction in which the camera is pointing and height determines where the camera is positioned in vertical space. A camera can be positioned straight on to a subject or high or low regardless of the angle, and this is one of the aesthetic choices we have when we put the story on film.

Finally, the camera can be level, meaning that the horizontal edges of the frame are parallel to the environment's horizon, or the camera can be canted, which means that the camera is tilted sideways to make the environment's horizon a diagonal line in the frame.

Shot scale *refers to the distance that seems to exist between the camera and the subject. The larger the subject appears on the screen, the closer the camera is assumed to be, regardless of the actual distance during shooting. We saw illustrations of the most common scales for shots in the earlier section, "How Big? Shot Size."*

The mobile frame *refers to any movement perceivable by the audience, which they will usually attribute to moving the camera, whether the effect was achieved that way or not. The most common types of mobile frames are pans, tilts and zooms. More elaborate types of mobile frames include handheld, steadicam, dolly, tracking and crane shots. All of these will affect the mood and tone of the story and are choices that are made when considering the visual design of the motion picture.*

There is an assumption (and some evidence to suggest) that all of these affect the audience's understanding of what's happening on the screen or their emotions while watching. For example, canted angles are described in film studies as creating suspense or anxiety for the audience.

Regardless, all of these considerations — as well as story structures and decisions about what parts of the story we actually show — shape and are shaped by the point of view (POV) we want to create for the audience, the viewpoint from which they see (or experience) the story. The fable of the blind men and the elephant is a good analogy. All of the men encounter an elephant, but each "sees" something different because of where they are positioned in relationship to the animal. As a transmedia maker using moving images, we are in effect telling the men where to stand so that they see the elephant we want them to see.

Film and Other Media

As we talked about earlier in this chapter, films usually work best for stories that are compressed in terms of the time frame experienced by the characters –- stories that take place in hours, days, weeks or months rather than years or centuries.

The director of the film controls how much story the audience sees, in what order, and how quickly. The audience is not an active participant in a tangible way, though we are usually hoping to engage their imaginations and emotions.

Many of the properties that people currently point to as transmedia started as accidental expansions of a singular film's storyworld, often initially through film sequels. At the point that someone realized that there was a built-in audience or fan base that could be "transferred" to other storytelling platforms that could create new complementary content, we started moving past the idea of transmedia as a marketing tool with simple adaptations like tie-in novels and towards actively embracing the notion of transmedia storytelling.

The *Terminator* stories are a good example of an original film (Orion Pictures, 1984) that spawned a sequel (then another), eventually expanding its storyworld with new stories in other platforms, such as the television series *The Sarah Connor Chronicles* (Warner Bros. Television, 2008–2009).

There are also examples of television series or games that expanded their intellectual properties into film (such as *The X-Files* or *Mortal Kombat*, both of which are talked about more in future chapters).

Many of these efforts have met with limited success … so far. This is why a good understanding of the individual storytelling nuances with each platform can help a transmedia-maker more accurately plan and develop material. For example, many failures (or less than stellar successes) are the result of their creators not taking into account considerations such as the fact that video games require a very different kind of protagonist than film or television does or that television needs a different level of development of character or world development to sustain a multi-episode story arc.

One of the most exciting and ambitious transmedia efforts attempted in the past couple of years has been *The Dark Tower*, adapted from Stephen King's books but using multiple platforms for that adaptation, such as interweaving feature films in between a multi-season serialized television show, some of which will be influenced by a prequel comic book series. In 2011, it seemed the project had stalled but then seemed to breathe new life in 2012. The challenges of a project of this scale may have to do more with the production realties inherent with each medium than with difficulties with the storytelling aspects of the individual platforms, though when we're developing a transmedia production, we have to consider all of these issues.

As you read the other chapters, you can compare film to the various other platforms and better understand the challenges of incorporating any of these platforms into a larger transmedia story.

Interview: Phil Hay

Phil Hay is a writer/producer/director living in Los Angeles, and with partner Matt Manfredi has written films ranging from the acclaimed intimate romantic drama *Crazy/Beautiful* (Touchstone Pictures, 2001, starring Kirsten Dunst) to *Aeon Flux* (Paramount, 2005), a live action film based on the animated series and starring Charlize Theron.

Their 2010 remake of *Clash of the Titans* (Warner Brothers), starring Sam Worthington, Liam Neeson, and Ralph Fiennes, was one of the year's biggest hits, grossing nearly half a billion dollars worldwide. At the time of this interview, *R.I.P.D.* (Universal Pictures, 2013) was in postproduction. The film stars Ryan Reynolds, Jeff Bridges, Kevin Bacon and Mary-Louise Parker.

In addition, the pair directed the 2002 independent comedy *Bug* (2002) and produced the 2008 D&D (*Dungeons and Dragons*) documentary *The Dungeon Masters*.

Phil Hay was interviewed by the authors in late spring 2012 specifically for this book.

Figure 4.1.1 *Phil Hay.*

Interviewer(s): We were picking people based on certain projects they've worked on that were interesting from the standpoint we're taking. So what initially sparked for me was *Aeon Flux*.

Phil Hay: Can you reframe for me your definition of what you call transmedia storytelling?

Interviewer(s): What we've realized working on the book is, no one is quite sure what it is, and everyone has some ideas about it.

Phil Hay: I know it when I see it.

Interviewer(s): Right. And the term gets thrown around a lot. I think the main distinction we've been trying to make, and it's a hard one to keep track of sometimes, is that we're really looking at transmedia in terms of storytelling. There are a lot of things that get labeled as transmedia that are more marketing. They're tie-ins or things really designed to generate interest in the original property. Our focus is whether within a larger core universe, there are particular aspects of stories that work best as transmedia and if so, how can you coordinate that kind of storytelling.

Phil Hay: That's the ambitious side of it. It's like a touch of *Rosencrantz and Guildenstern*, the Russian style.

Interviewer(s): The Producers Guild (of America) transmedia producer's credit defines a transmedia property as three different stories that exist within the same fictional universe. They don't necessarily argue that they have to cross paths or even exist in different media platforms, but for this book, we're talking about it ideally doing both. It could be webisodes; it could be graphic novels; it could be television series. Does that help?

Phil Hay: Yes, totally. When we did *Aeon Flux*, there was also a comic book series that they put out as a tie-in to the movie. It was the same characters but also some prequel stuff, like the origin of the Handler and how that all happened. There were bits and pieces that tied directly into the film's story, and there were interesting snapshots of what that world was, what that culture was like, and I thought it was pretty well done. It was interesting because we're working from the animated series, and the writers of the comic book are working from our script, though in a way, the people who wrote the comic books were adapting both our movie script and the animated series, weaving in and out of those things, giving this extra level of interpretation of these characters.

Interviewer(s): Did you have any input at all on what was going on with the comics?

Phil Hay: Not really. I know we were given some outlines, and we would check on things, and they were very open to suggestions; they were very cool about it. They said where they thought they were going, and we maybe had a few notes, I can't remember now, but it was really their job to come up with a property that wasn't just a comic book version of the movie. It wasn't a comic book version at all. It was very much something that went along side it and went deeper into certain characters and kind of set up certain events in the movie. One of the first times when this kind of simultaneous divergent narrative came to my consciousness was when I was in college. It dates me because of the terminology, but I was in a hyper-text fiction workshop in the days when none of us had personal computers. Some had little Macs but the Internet was just not something that anyone except for the computer geeks even knew anything about. We basically worked on this storytelling idea where we had a shared narrative world called "Hotel." The professor had written a basic text describing the lobby, and each of us students were to write a room for the hotel. They would literally have the rudimentary links you would click on to go that room, and you'd click on a character within that room. And then someone else might use that character, so that a character that was an incidental background character in one of the stories becomes the center of another story, and his perspective reframes everything. I became really interested in that kind of thing. You know, having a master narrative and having sub-narratives. Someone actually wrote a song as if written by a character in another story, but it existed only as a song and the guy actually went and got a guitar and recorded it. So there does seem to be some continuity to that stuff. Something operating within a world. In that case it was different media because in the case of this song; it was just a great song. If you read the thing, you would have realized it had been written in character by the voice of the character that someone had created in this larger project that was contributed to by 22 people.

Interviewer(s): One of the aspects that some people feel is really vital to transmedia is active engagement with the audience and interactivity, allowing for the possibility of co-creation. Stories can be co-created with the audience or with other creators which sounds similar to your college experience. You were co-creating that hotel.

Phil Hay: Exactly. You had a measure of control about your own room, your own area, but someone could take your characters and do something quite different with them if they wanted to. Suddenly they're doing something you hadn't intended. So there is that sense of collaboration and co-creation. And I think people are also really respectful of each other's creations in that environment. They weren't really trying to mess with your character. So it was interesting. I found it really fun and exciting. And also, it weirdly relates to *Aeon Flux*. One of the things that originally drew me to the animated series which I feel is truly loved, was the fact that it was so anti-narrative. There's no conventional narrative continuity; the main character dies at the end of every episode. Which makes it an incredible challenge to adapt *Aeon Flux* into a Hollywood movie.

Interviewer(s): And a lot of people confuse transmedia with adaptation.

Phil Hay: Adaptations as a screenwriter are always interesting. We've done adaptations that were extremely close in some ways [but not in all ways], adaptations that were very faithful and some that were not very faithful at all. Something like *Aeon Flux* is something that's incredibly faithful on some levels and incredibly unfaithful on other levels. So it's more of a real combination in that case.

Interviewer(s): How did *Aeon Flux* come about as a project, I mean, how did you start making a story for that?

Phil Hay: What happened was my partner Matt [Manfredi] and I had written a couple scripts and our first movie came out, called *Crazy/Beautiful*, which is extremely unrelated in tone, style, everything else to *Aeon Flux*. But we got a movie made and we started to talk to someone at MTV Films who we knew from college actually. She was in charge of this project, and at the time it was the adaptation of the series into a movie, which was kind of dead. It's interesting; we tried it once before and came out with a script that really just had the name of the character Aeon Flux, you know, and for what it's worth, it was structured in an extremely conventional action movie style. It was, take the name and turn it into an action movie that didn't have to be Aeon Flux, just the name of the character in this thing. But that just didn't click for whatever reason and so we kind of, with nothing to lose, just said look, what if we could try to find a way to take the narrative bits and pieces and our interpretations of them from the episodes, and from our elaborations on those kind of come up with a more traditional narrative but that still maintains some of the hallucinatory weirdness of the show. We pitched that and figured out how to have enough of a sense of action in there that was interesting, and we were able to show them what the characters would be in this other form in a way that got them excited, and we wrote the script. The interesting thing that happened along the way is that the war of the movie was always between the art side and the action movie side. In the end the action movie side won a devastating victory. But that was always the discussion. Each draft there was a different level of weirdness and bizarreness and certainly our original takes would really try to bring that bizarre sense of experimentation within the character and kind of a "stay true to the spirit of the original" in that way. And the battle always was, as it often is in movies, about how much explanation is being demanded, how much you have to make everything literal or be understood literally, and that sometimes fights against the nature of a think like *Aeon Flux*. Its very nature is not that, you know.

Interviewer(s): I didn't realize there had been a script before and so it's really interesting to think that that earlier script and you're going back to the source material in a different way.

Phil Hay: For something like *Aeon Flux*, the best way to honor the original material is to kind of leave it alone and to allow your thing to exist in parallel. Refer to it and be connected to it in some way but to create a different experience of it, which I think does go to this transmedia thing you are talking about. An experience that goes alongside the other experience without invalidating the other one or erasing it or rewriting it on some grand level. I think, our idea was this, and we had all kinds of crazy interesting ways for ourselves to frame it that were really just for ourselves. We'd joke sometimes that the relationship between the movie and the series is that for the characters in the movie, the series is their dreams, and for the characters in the series, the movie is their dreams. People who live in this crazily non-linear world, and they go to sleep at night and dream in linear fashion. And people who live in a more realistic linear world, when they go to sleep, they dream of, you know this crazy world of bizarre imagery where you could die and come back to life and all that stuff.

Interviewer(s): So do you think of the film as existing in that same universe? Is it just a different story within that universe?

Phil Hay: I think that, in that case, I would say it exists in its own universe. It took a lot of cues from specific stuff, whether imagery or story beats or relationships from that animated series. The animated series had two kinds of stages. One, the episodes and shorts that had no dialogue. And the next generation had dialogue which was delivered in a certain way, in a sort of style which was very ironic and very kind of witty and dark, and that was kind of the same vibe that we used for some of the dialogue in our movie, so it's closer to that. I mean if I were to categorize it, I would say it's like; it's funny. It's hard to say. It does exist; we use the same terminology in some ways, the same place, the country and the rebel group within it, the same identities, but they are so different in style that it's almost like parallel universes, I would say.

Interviewer(s): How does that compare to *R.I.P.D.* which is based on a novel, right?

Phil Hay: It's based on a graphic novel, but in that case we diverged pretty wildly from what was there while keeping the original premise.

Interviewer(s): How would you compare the two?

Phil Hay: I would say it's a very different animal in terms of that type of adaptation because the comic book of *R.I.P.D.* takes place in the same type of world as the world created for the movie. It's much more traditional, not in a bad way. It's much more within the language of comics and movies that we have a more collective understanding of than *Aeon Flux*, which comes from a whole different place, not just in terms of what happens but where even cause and effect is in question. For *R.I.P.D.*, we just kind of decided to tell a different story about the characters that were introduced by that comic book.

Interviewer(s): So in a way it can be like another issue of the comic?

Phil Hay: We took the characters and gave them personalities and a way of speaking that were kind of unique to us in a way but could also co-exist with some of the mythology creatures, other things that were introduced in the comic book. We've actually had a lot of contact with the creator of the comic book [Peter M. Lenkov]. He's been incredibly supportive of everything we've done, and I think he sees the continuity. He's a really good writer in his own right, so he's been just nothing but supportive. It's a really nice extension of what he started.

Interviewer(s): Peter Chung was kind of unhappy with *Aeon Flux*. Am I remembering that correctly?

Phil Hay: Yes, except for the word "kind of." Actually we had a good exchange online. There was this message board, and I don't know if it's still active, but very devoted fans of *Aeon Flux* congregated on, and it was extremely intelligent discussion. You could tell, very knowledgeable and intellectual people. There was a back and forth that we had there because that was a place where people go. He kind of made it clear, his disappointment and unhappiness with the movie and the way it turned out. Then I kind of illuminated some of our stance on some of those things and explained the process a little bit. It was actually kind of a fruitful and interesting exchange where all these types of things come into play of an individual and a corporation and an artist who's created something, people who are in charge of interpreting that. How you can make your best effort to do that, and it still may not please the creator. There can be all these other factors that come into play. Anyway we did have an online, respectful back-and-forth about that stuff. It was definitely part of the discussion after the movie came out.

Interviewer(s): One of the challenges of transmedia is you're telling multiple stories as they're spanning out, who is the keeper of the continuity? Who is the person who say's like, "I don't think that's what the characters would do."

Phil Hay: And who owns it, you know. And I definitely feel there is a very strong claim of ownership that Peter Chung can make over *Aeon Flux*, because he certainly was that keeper, and for us, we share some of his frustrations with what came out and in other cases don't share those. We saw some things we saw as successful about the movie. It's interesting for something like that which has a very dedicated fan base, but small by real number terms when compared to *Twilight* or anything of a true mass market phenomenon. But those fans are very devoted. It's different with something like *R.I.P.D.* which is a really great comic book, but it never reached a very big audience in its original incarnation. Hopefully with the movie, it will bring some attention back to that. But there is definitely a different responsibility and a different freedom that you feel when you're working on adapting something like that than if, for example, you're adapting *Harry Potter*. It would boggle the mind for me to have someone really try to interpret *Harry Potter* in a way that went against what the books were, because that's just critical to the whole enterprise, I think, putting those books on the screen.

Interviewer(s): It's interesting because *Harry Potter* was one of the places that we've had some discussion internally among us co-writing the book, because when we were thinking about transmedia franchises and properties, we just sort of brainstormed a whole bunch of titles initially, and that one showed up on it. Then in our discussions, we were going, wait a minute, that's just an adaptation. It's a different medium than the source material, but it's not really adding to the story or reshaping the story in a significant way other than the limits of adapting a huge novel to a time limited, huge theatrical …

Phil Hay: It's a different expression of the same thing. Of the same material. Obviously movies are very different than a book, and that's not a bad thing. That is exactly what is called for and what should be in that case. Which is not to say it's easy to do that. It's very incredibly hard. You can argue that it's harder because obviously a lot of work has to go into adapting it, which as a series was really brilliantly adapted. So anyway, in a way it doesn't make it any easier. You know, it may make it harder.

Interviewer(s): You do have that challenge of you've got to tell the story, and it's got to have the same emotional impact and same drive.

Phil Hay: And you have to understand what the true core of it is because you're not going to be able to put every single thing on the screen.

Interviewer(s): Do you have a sense from either *R.I.P.D.* or any of your upcoming projects whether transmedia is something that people in Hollywood are thinking about in terms of storytelling or is it still more this idea of adaptation? Like finding really great source material and finding a way to translate it to the screen.

Phil Hay: I think that the latter. Traditional adaptation is by far the more dominant thing. I think that as you said at the beginning, right now a lot of the stuff that is transmedia is in the realm of marketing, but can start to cross over with narratives. The kind of viral marketing stuff, like for *Prometheus*, I think is very interesting because it does tell you a very different area of that story. I'm fascinated by that stuff; I love that stuff. I love that a lot of the material they put out for *Prometheus* takes place not within the confines of the timeline of the film even. We're talking about the company that has invented the Android and that's eventually going to send the ship on a mission. Where they come from, so that's getting closer to this idea of transmedia story development, and I definitely think with a couple of our things, we've talked about it would be great to shoot a couple of short films, little web things that are just what's happening in this little side room of headquarters while the real stuff is going on. So that would be kind of fun. I do think there are examples of that. There are things where people are seeing that it can be interesting and fun, but of course because it costs money; it's like the first question is, "well, how can this help us make money on the project?" as opposed to just doing it in its own right. But it's interesting. I remember when I was a kid I liked novelizations, which is a form that has completely disappeared as far as I know, replaced by the Internet and all the information you can get there. But I remember poring through my favorite movies and then the novelization came out, and yes they generally were just the plots of the movies, but there would occasionally be different scenes or there would be an insight to a character that you couldn't have weaned from the movie that was a different thing. It was not that the book came first; it was this adaptation into a different form from the movie, but it had value and what always intrigued me were these little sides. Like I was the person trying to read, in *Aliens* when they were having the inquest into what happened in the first movie, and they have slides of all the characters that were deceased from the first movie, and they've got information about where they were born and everything. I'm trying to peer and see all that information. I really was curious and so like, I'm that guy. When I was growing up especially, I was so interested especially in the movies that really tend to this stuff like science fiction movies and fantasy movies and comic book movies. They are really kind of tended to, and they work really well with expanded stories and exploring nooks and crannies of that storyworld and things. I was definitely a voracious consumer of all that, wanting to know more about the characters and the world and not being satisfied with just what was on the screen.

Interviewer(s): I was always really fascinated with the novelists, and again it tended to be science fiction and fantasy, like Larry Niven, who I think said in some interview that he had generated hundreds and hundreds of pages of material just so he would understand the world and the characters that never even made it into the novel. It might have been around the time of *Ringworld* ...

Phil Hay: It sounds like that would be something he might do from what I've read of his stuff. It's so complete. I'd love to read that stuff. Sometimes the closest we get to that in our screen writing stuff is we will sometimes, either for just ourselves or for a director or for an actor, write a character bio of a character, for example, and create an entire history in great specificity of where they grew up – what happened to them, what their family was like. Even if that stuff was never even close to being revealed in the movie, it's text for the director and the actor to think about. In the case of another movie that we co-wrote, which is the remake of *Clash of the Titans*, when we were trying to get Ralph Fiennes to play Hades, he really wanted to get more about the character, and he asked us to write this kind of, well, not a bio. We were joking, Hades went to Glendale Community College, and he graduated … But it was more about his relationship with his brothers and sisters, or his brothers and relatives, and how he felt and things like that. So there is sort of an extension there. None of that stuff really comes out, but some of it turned into plot. It's about who this person is and what has happened to them to make them feel this way, their perspective. Because their perspective is different than the story's perspective. In the story, he is villainous, and in his mind, he is not.

Interviewer(s): Do you ever find that when you're generating material like that or when you're in the thick of writing, that sometimes there are these, say, stray narratives? I don't know if that's exactly the right word but these things where you go, "Wow, this could be a really interesting short film" or "This could be an interesting parallel story" where you can tell it in another way.

Phil Hay: I think I'm always looking for that, I think that does happen fairly often. I'm always really interested in the minor characters in movies. I kind of always want to know more about them or know how they relate. We tend to tell these stories about the best of the best, the hero, and I'm interested in the people that surround them. Something that is obviously probably the greatest example of this world is the *Star Wars* universe, which is has expanded across I think every kind of media you can imagine with so many iterations and so many in the discussion of what's canon and not canon, you know. Anyway, I think that's a great example. Take someone who is a very small character but who I love in *Star Wars*, Wedge. If you go to the expanded universe, he's got an entire insanely large resume that's built over time. And that stuff is really interesting to me. It always has been. So when we are writing stuff, there are definitely times where it would be really interesting to tell this little side story of what happens between, like they sent these guys off to get some information, and we learn later that they were killed. I wonder how that happened or I wonder what they were thinking about when that happened, what their feelings were about the guy who sent them off to do that.

Interviewer(s): Back to *Rosencrantz and Guildenstern*.

Phil Hay: Exactly. Hugely influential. I think people are really into that. I do think in the modern world, the Internet especially is a perfect enabler of all this stuff. All those viral videos from *Prometheus* or all those things that, they were never meant to be in the continuity of the movies. They weren't clipped from the movie; it's not a trailer; it was invented to tell its own little story about that same character and illuminate something about the process. That I find truly fascinating because it shows the character details of the world. I argue one of the greatest things about Ridley Scott is that it's all incredibly detailed. You can look in the corner, and it makes sense. You don't get this set that when the set ends the world ends. Things like that just underline that feeling, you know, that you can go into those little corners and find an interesting story, and its two-and-a-half minutes long; it's on your computer, and it teaches something to you about one of the characters.

Interviewer(s): Most of the examples that we've been able to come up with while writing the book for expanding the story and the storyworld have been genre, particularly science fiction and fantasy and even horror to some degree. And we've been trying to figure out like whether there are other possibilities. One of our co-writers every once in a while will pose the argument that soap operas are a logical place for there to be these kind of extensions. Except, I think, they are all gone now.

Phil Hay: Yeah, those things kind of zonked out, but that's interesting in the way that they're following an immense number of characters, and people might find they are more interested in this pair or that pair, and if they could have more time with them, they would choose that over time with other characters, and you could still tell the story.

Interviewer(s): It might be a way to regenerate this interest in that type of storytelling.

Phil Hay: Yeah. Well it's interesting because I always think of how people talk about soap operas, like the way that my grandmother and I think probably tons of people refer to them as "my stories." And that was fascinating because I remember growing up and my grandmother would be like, "Well you guys are going to have to take a break," or "you guys are going to have to go into the other room because my stories are coming on." So obviously that sense of ownership was pretty high.

Interviewer(s): Well it definitely does seem like transmedia. One of the elements of transmedia is that sort of ownership by fans and their desire to dive in, and you're right, I think the Internet has become a platform for that.

Phil Hay: And fan fiction. By nature, that whole world is kind of interesting in terms of how far you can go with somebody's characters before someone says, "Uh no." And the answers seem to be pretty far.

Interviewer(s): There is a part of me that always worries a little bit about the person who created the characters or the actors who played them. I'm always like, "Do you read your fan fiction?" And I sure hope not.

Phil Hay: Yeah, it would not be healthy in most cases to be in there. You're going to see some things that you can't un-see. But it's interesting because that actual level of ownership, which is to write. Well what's also interesting about fan fiction is that you're writing it purely for pleasure because you can't own it; you can't sell it to anybody. So in a way it's a very pure act of connecting with those characters, because you're doing it because you want to step into the creation of them, and you know there's not going to be any reward at the end except for people maybe liking it, saying hey, that was great.

Interviewer(s): Do you ever find yourself wanting to tell stories in a different medium than film or is film pretty much it?

Phil Hay: Actually it's definitely, mostly doing film. I started out writing fiction, and I went to UC Irvine in the MFA Fiction Writing program. I wrote a novel, and I started writing short stories and things. I do want to keep doing that, and I have done it recently after a little gap, so I am definitely interested in narrative fiction. But films have definitely become the prime thing and without any real contender. So it's definitely how I spend my time and now how I think of things, how I, when I come up with a new idea, it's in the language of movies generally. But that wasn't always true. There was a time I came up with more ideas that felt they were in the world of fiction, and some of them I thought, well I could make this a movie, and I prefer to make it a movie for whatever reason. Now I have ideas that go directly to novel, but even those I feel like I'm envisioning them as a movie. I tend to that naturally.

Interviewer(s): I think one of the questions transmedia sparks is how to decide where stories start or when an audience will first encounter them. And also, because of the inherent strengths and challenges with each medium, it requires now a more conscious kind of thinking about. What kinds of stories are best for film? What kinds of stories are best for novels? Or webisodes? TV series?

Phil Hay: A narrative rule that we really tend to follow to the tee, especially when it comes to large scale films, is the "why now?" question. Why does this story start right now? Can it start a moment later? Can it start a moment earlier? Ideally, the answer is no. It has to start right now. This is exactly why this story begins here, and this is why it ends. It's usually clearer where it ends in some ways, but in your universe if you're thinking of a story universe, things can become less clear as the story expands. The whole *Star Wars* saga is such a great example of how something gets reframed as a story, as a whole story, over the course of many movies. I was talking to a film executive that I know, and we were talking about *Star Wars* movies. We both have young sons who are just discovering the *Star Wars* world, which is extremely fun for me, and we were talking about it to those kids, and you know, it's not the story of Luke Skywalker; it's the story of Anakin. And you realize that if you look at all those movies as a whole, it's a story about a guy who starts off good, becomes tempted and becomes evil and redeems himself at the end. And Luke comes in in the middle, and it's kind of the way Anakin redeems himself ultimately, but it's kind of mind blowing because it's like, to me of course, growing up, *Star Wars* is about Luke, Han, Leia and what they do. Yes, Darth Vader is revealed to be Luke's father, but that's the plot twist, and it's a character thing, and he redeems himself in the end but then when you see it all in context, you realize that it's really a story about Darth Vader, you know? So that's another way of thinking about how the start point changes with the core narrative in some ways.

Interviewer(s): Personally, what's the most intriguing thing about the idea of transmedia or the possibility of creating expanded stories?

Phil Hay: For a screenwriter, I think what's really attractive are those side-stories, those "other" stories, those kinds of smaller bits within the world of characters that you created for a massive movie release. By their very nature of being smaller, it seems like you could do them, you're more likely to be left alone than do them, letting them be a more pure direct expression of something you'd like to get across. So in that way, it's a great. A huge movie belongs to so many people, and it kind of belongs to everybody and you, the screenwriter, are trying to preserve what you think is important, and you're trying to help people understand, using those terms. But there is so much by the sheer scope of the story and spectacle that you want to do, that there are little moments that tend to get left out or things that could be really interesting to people who are interested in the movie. And so to me, we always volunteer to do little things and do them ourselves. A great example of this is *Aeon Flux* that fell under the purview of marketing but was actually one of the most interesting and fun things we wrote. For all of their movies at that time, MTV did all these interstitials that served as commercials but were really interesting. You could do a little tone poem for like 30 seconds, and they'd shoot their own dedicated imagery on the sets of the movies; they'd get the actors, and it would be very kind of, almost experimental film with voiceover. It was extremely satisfying to write some of that voiceover and stuff because you really weren't bound by any of the stuff that you need to be bound by when you're working on a big movie. No one is giving you notes. You're just trying to stretch out, and it's interesting in its own right. So Matt and I always talk about and jump at the chance to help do those subsidiary things. Having a chance to just sit down with these characters and come up with another weird little beat. Because it's beyond the pale, it's not something that's going to be monitored and scrutinized nearly as much than what the actual film will be. So you have a little bit more of a sense of exploration or freedom if you get them to put up enough money to make these little side stories, these little bits of narrative. Obviously, a great thing would be to be able to create across different platforms whether it's video games and film and TV and books and comic books. I feel like one of the attractions of writing movies is the singular experience, you know, that you're writing a film, and it's between an hour-and-a half and two hours long. It's not an infinite thing and it's not a TV show where you're going to pick up at the this episode's end in the beginning of next week, so in a way there is an attraction in the finiteness of it. But in a world like the kind of science fiction and fantasy fun type of things we do, I'd love to write a comic book about these characters, or maybe get some of the moments back that didn't in the movie or create new moments that just kind of allow us to live in the world of the characters more.

Interviewer(s): That makes total sense to me.

Phil Hay: Because that's definitely fun to do in its own right. When you're a screenwriter, you do get very used to the idea that your job is very much to communicate the vision not only of yourself but also of a lot of other people. To embrace all that and make it cohere together, all those different visions and opportunities that support these extra things, these "other" things; I think it can help people appreciate the central movie more. On a personal level, I'm curious to see how people continue to use these mediums. Obviously, it's developing. The Writers Guild regularly talks about how do people get paid doing work on the internet. What are the new paradigms of how stuff is distributed? Is that going to affect the way we do business? I think it's just scratching the surface now about how people can use this technology in terms of the expansiveness of these stories. How many tools you now have to explore these bigger stories in smaller chunks or parallel ways or however that is. So yeah, in Hollywood generally, people are interested. A lot of people are very interested, but I think we are still very focused on the singular entity – as a movie, as a TV show which is a singular entity in a series of episodes. I think that the paradigm is still that. But people are curious. And a lot of writers, directors and actors are really interested in imagining all these characters and stories over a lot of different media. In Hollywood, it seems that the impetus for transmedia is mostly coming either from marketing departments or from the individual writers, directors or actors themselves who are like, "this is fun, this is interesting, I'm just going to do it."

Chapter 5

Television and Serialized Storytelling

America seemingly went from no television to television everywhere overnight. The industrial base of post-World War II was ready to go, and that manufacturing prowess began cranking out television sets at an astonishing rate. What happened next was the result of an unexpected confluence of cultural and market pressures. Former B and C movie stars moved to television and went from relative obscurity to household names overnight. A furry coonskin cap pops up on a kids' show and sells millions in a matter of weeks and a handful of viewers watching experimental stations scattered around the country suddenly become millions of Americans waiting with bated breath for Lucy to have her baby. Little Ricky was everybody's kid because, well, that was the effect television had on the American audience.

Television was different from the movies because it was in your living room, like a member of the family. Radio had been there too, but while it inspired your imagination, television gave you pictures and let you see just what the wrestlers looked like – and yes, Gorgeous George really did wear makeup.

Of course, the most important thing was that television could sell stuff, really sell stuff. Advertising became the engine that drove television programming, because advertisers needed some way to attract audiences to see what they had to sell. Despite this pressure to be a vehicle for selling, some saw the potential of television as a storytelling medium right from the start: writers like Rod Serling, Reginald Rose and Paddy Chayefski told stories that couldn't be told anyplace else. From them, television as a medium for powerful stories has grown and matured over the last 50 years, to the point now where more stories are told with greater impact in television than in any other medium. What was once just quantity now has become quality – dynamic and groundbreaking storytelling.

Early on, the networks weren't sure what kind of programming would work, so they tried everything, limited only by technology and cost. And at first, that was quite a limit – there were lots of inexpensive live studio-based programs. But that changed over time, as each decade added or overlaid something new: more film production, better sound, color, a greater number of channels, and so on.

Television has always been a smorgasbord with new dishes regularly added to the buffet. Different types of shows attract different types of audiences, and some of the most common formats are scripted fiction, such as the sitcom, the hour drama and the movie-of-the-week (MOW). Unscripted shows, television's term for nonfiction programming, include reality shows, news, entertainment news and sports; documentary prevail as well. All these different forms of storytelling live side by side and are consumed with gusto, originally by an American audience and eventually audiences around the world. The demands of the networks have driven relentless innovation and allowed for experimentation in ways that seem unimaginable. Just remember that *Cosby* (1984–1992) and *Twin Peaks* (1990–1991) were both on network television at the same time.

Looking back, it is important to understand that television created the first mass audience that had simultaneous viewing of picture and sound. Life and world events were tied to television in a way no other medium could do. Lists of the events that "everyone" shares include the Kennedy assassination, the moon landing, Nixon's resignation, Reagan being shot, the Berlin Wall being torn down, OJ and the White Bronco … the list while not endless is robust. In addition, personal events are tied to television as well – when your kids are born, a parent passes or you get the good news about a job, television is present in your house and therefore a mile-marker in your life. In addition, television memories – the shows we watch – almost become a substitute for actual events.

Looking ahead, what is important to understand is that the medium of television has rolled with the punches, adapting to technology and culture changes in surprising and sometimes unexpected ways. The exponential growth of available channels needing programming has created more room around the edges for niche programming, and our definition of mass audience has been scaled down. Who is watching has become just as important as how many are watching, creating the opportunity for much more idiosyncratic storytelling; it is hard to imagine *Mad Men* (AMC, 2007–present) as a success a decade earlier, no matter how wonderful the storytelling.

The industry is also figuring out how best to adapt to multiple screens, coming to grips with the cultural shift of ubiquitous computers and handheld devices. Watching television shows while you have your iPad in your lap is not some figment of a marketer's imagination, but what happens in homes all around the world on a regular basis.

This brings us to television and transmedia. Even in a short time, many aspects of television have proven to be comparable and compatible to the issues, elements and goals of transmedia narrative, both on network TV and cable, with large audiences and niche as well. In this chapter, we will look at the dynamics of engagement, longevity and universe building as they relate to television and potentially come into play or even become models as you plan a transmedia story.

Basics of Television Storytelling

The basics of television storytelling are really a tale of two dynamics. In one, television shares many storytelling elements, concepts and techniques with cinema, because much of the language of television was initially adapted from film. The other dynamic is one of a gradual evolution over time, with television storytelling being slowly reshaped by strong forces tied directly to a medium that is dictated by broadcast networks and their financial model. Traditional television storytelling and development is derived from the harsh demands of a weekly broadcast distribution schedule.

Television, unlike film or video games, is fundamentally a sponsor-driven medium, paid for by advertisers that buy commercial space during a particular show based on ratings information gathered by services like Nielsen which electronically track who is watching what, when and for how long. Sponsors identify those shows with the most potential for reaching customers for their products. Shows with higher ratings allow the network to demand more money per minute from these advertisers, who are now often competing with each other to buy commercial time on a hit show. Conversely, shows that receive low ratings are usually canceled – they are not generating enough revenue for the network by not reaching a large enough audience (or the type of audience) to interest advertisers.

Though the sponsor-driven revenue model of television dominates, it has some competition of late from the subscriber-driven revenue model used by premium cable networks like HBO, Showtime, and others. Under this model, the cable network uses its total subscriber value, the aggregate of the ratings of all of its programs, to dictate its licensing fees to the cable providers, like Comcast, DISH, or Direct TV. Subscriber-driven networks don't show commercials (other than for their own programs, which are promos), so programs produced for the network don't have commercial breaks. The majority of this chapter deals with the more complex issues of television creation and production that involve commercial breaks.

Due to the sponsor-driven revenue model of television, advertising has become an integral part of the way television stories are organized and presented. Every episode needs to be structured in such a way as to keep audiences from changing the channel during the commercial breaks. This is why you sometimes hear derisive comments that television stories are simply a method for delivering advertisements, but writers and producers in television have worked this seeming limitation to their advantage, creatively adapting traditional storytelling techniques into new forms that are unique to television but dynamic and creative in ways that have begun influencing the ways other media think about storytelling as well.

Structured Acts

Television shows can be characterized both by their format, which is the length of a standard episode, and by larger narrative issues including genre conventions (though duration and genre have become so interlocked in some types of shows that they are sometimes talked about almost interchangeably). Regardless of format or genre, the basic building blocks of a television story are *acts*, or the ways in which the narrative is broken into parts that, unlike film, do not flow immediately from one to the other but rather are separated by commercial breaks.

These breaks occur at regular intervals – interrupting the story, arbitrarily and artificially creating narrative chunks that do not immediately or easily line up with the three acts described previously. As a result, television storytelling has had to rethink the way that stories are told, borrowing or developing additional storytelling elements, such as the recap, prologue, teaser, tag, cliffhanger and previews (more on these later) as well as rethink three-act structure.

Though there are some television shows – like *The Simpsons* (1989–present) – that have tried to anchor their stories in a three-act structure, we've seen more and more examples in recent years of these basic constraints of broadcast television and sponsorship being the impetus to creatively redefine the way acts are defined and what each has to accomplish. These constraints have been around for a long time and explain why television has always had examples of storytelling structures like the two-act and four-act show in addition to three-act approaches. But in recent years, we have begun seeing more and more shows that are considered four-act, five-act, six-act and seven-act structures.

Though the number of acts and what has to happen in each are somewhat dependent upon a show's format and genre, in all of them, Act 1 establishes a character (or in some cases, characters) who has an important need, want or desire. This need is the result of something being out of balance, and the character *needs* to take action, to do something, to get things back to normal. This need is sometimes referred to as a goal, and the rest of the show is about the character trying to get what he needs.

This first act establishes not just the need but also the conflict, or those things that make it difficult for the protagonist to have what they want. Whether drama or comedy, there must be conflict. Conflict occurs when obstacles are placed between the character and the attainment of his goal. The more challenging the obstacle, the harder the character must struggle against it, and the more compelling the story.

Just like in film, the obstacles must become increasingly more difficult to overcome as the story progresses. Obstacles in Act 2 are harder than in Act 1, and each subsequent obstacle within Act 2 is more difficult than the one before it.

The character will either get what they want or be denied what they want during the climax, which in film traditionally occurs in what's labeled Act 3, but in television generally occurs in the last full act of the show, whether that's called Act 3, 4, 5 or 6. In both comedies and dramas, the climax is the highest point of action, where everything is on the line. After the climax, the central problem is solved one way or the other, and we move on to resolution, which tells us how the characters are doing after the climax.

Simple, huh? Not so fast … this is just the primary story for the show; we've got several more to go.

A Story … and a B Story, C Story, D and Sometimes E!

Television shows tell multiple stories simultaneously during one episode. This crosscutting or moving back and forth among alternating stories can help maintain the audience's attention as well as hide narrative leaps, such as having moved significantly ahead in each storyline's chronology when we come back to it. For example, if we're following one character continually, any jumps forward in time are much more noticeable. By alternating stories and the characters we're focusing on, we are less likely to notice these leaps, much in the way that novelists will sometimes alternate point of view from chapter to chapter.

Our *primary story* is called the *A Story*. In terms of scale and proportion, this story usually involves a problem or conflict big enough to require the most time in the episode to resolve. This story centers on the main character(s) and provides a narrative thread that we keep coming back to.

The *B Story* is smaller, focusing on a different character and requiring less screen time than the A Story. In some series, the B Story merges with the A Story at a key moment to aid in the resolving of the A Story, much like the A and B stories in film often intersect at key moments.

C Stories in television tend to be even smaller stories that sometimes are simply a *runner* or a running theme or joke that is repeated three times during an episode.

The exception to this traditional model of telling multiple stories in a single episode is hour-long shows that feature ensemble casts. In these types of series, the audience is endeared equally to all of the principal characters. These shows may have C, D and even E stories that are meaningful, a story for each character, as in NBC's *Heroes* (2006–2010.) In a serialized series like *Heroes*, the A through E stories may not be resolved by the end of the episode but may instead last the entire season or series.

Act Breaks and Bridging the Gaps

Act breaks occur directly before commercial breaks and traditionally have posed an important question or put a main character in jeopardy right before cutting to an advertisement. The goal is to make audiences want to see what will happen next so badly that they will remain glued to the screen in order to find out – after watching the commercials. Of course, in a post TiVo world governed by DVRs and video-on-demand, where people don't watch commercials in the same way if at all, the structural device of act breaks now serves more as a technique to keep up momentum and to enhance the feelings of suspense and mystery. Act breaks also serve to shake things up by adding new information, characters and/or jeopardy. As a result, when we return to the story after the commercial break, we may have a slightly different or revised view of the central conflict that then plays out in the next act.

The desire to keep audiences interested during those intervals when the story is interrupted by commercials or credits is the primary reason that act breaks are designed the way they are, and this same motivation has driven the development of those other television storytelling elements we alluded to earlier:

A *recap* is a series of short highlights from previous episodes that are especially pertinent to the current episode about to start. These are most common in television series that have story elements that span multiple episodes or even seasons (see the Arcs section later in this chapter). Think of *Supernatural*'s (Warner Brothers Television, 2005–present) "Then" and "Now" recaps that are shown right before most new episodes. This allows viewers who may have missed or forgotten previous episodes to understand where tonight's episode fits in that larger overall story, making it more likely that audiences will come back to a series even if they have missed an episode or two.

A *prologue* is typically used to set in motion story elements for the episode that don't yet involve the main character. A good example is the discovery of the body or the crime that begins most episodes of the various *Law and Order* series. While at the very beginning of the episode, the prologue is different from a teaser because it sets up and gives essential information for the episode's main story.

A *teaser* or tease, also referred to as a *cold open*, operates as a hook to immediately draw the viewer in, enticing him to continue watching. The teaser could be simply the first few scenes of act 1 but usually is an independent short scene or series of short scenes that occur right at the front of the episode, often before the show's opening credits. Teasers are consistent with the tone of the overall show, funny in comedy and dramatic, thrilling or scary in dramas. On some drama you can recognize the end of the tease by the pithy line delivered by the main character, usually after dramatically removing his sunglasses.

A *tag* is sometimes used in sitcoms as a kind of abbreviated final act, bringing the episode's core conflict to some clear resolution. The shortened resolution works well for sitcoms because the humor of these shows is typically in the journey, in the events the character has to deal with. A complex or drawn out emotional resolution is unnecessary for series where the characters do not change from episode to episode. The tag then allows a quick resolution of the conflict and the affirmation that the world has reset and can start all over again next time.

A *cliffhanger* (or cliff) refers to the idea of posing a question or putting a main character in jeopardy right at the end of an episode. Audiences return for the next episode to see what happens – how the character gets out of the danger or problem presented.

Previews are used at the end of the show, now typically in tandem with the credit roll to give the viewer a taste what is coming in upcoming episodes, thereby encouraging the viewer to tune in again next week.

Not all of these techniques are used in every show or even every episode of a series; producers choose the ones that are most relevant to the format, genre, style of story and type of series they're creating. But like act breaks, all of these devices are designed to keep an audience intrigued and watching, wanting to see more of the show in order to find out what happens next.

Episodic vs. Serialized Storytelling

When we mentioned *Heroes* earlier, we alluded to the fact that some television shows are told in standalone episodes where you could in theory watch the individual installments of the story out of order without affecting your enjoyment of the show. You can imagine why this might be advantageous when shows go into syndication. But audiences also like shows where the story events in one episode might have an impact on future episodes – stories that feel more interconnected because the events that happen to the characters change them, even if just incrementally, or their situations develop in (albeit, slow) ways that seem more true to life. The first type of series is usually called *episodic*, and the second type of show is referred to as *serialized*.

Episodic Storytelling

Episodic refers to television series that have the same characters and situation each week but a different problem, crime or mystery to solve. By the end of each episode, the problem is solved and everything is back to normal. Story arcs and character arcs do not generally continue from one episode to the next, and each episode feels self-contained and complete in terms of story.

Episodic content is dependent upon the audience's endearment to the same characters, locations and innate situation weekly – for the life of the series. Most sitcoms are episodic, with the characters, locations and innate core conflicts and relationships changing very little over the run of the series. The exception to this is shows that run for a decade or more like *Friends* (NBC, 1994–2004), *Cheers* (NBC, 1982–1993) and *Married with Children* (Fox, 1987–1997), where small changes occurred over extremely long periods of time, as actors grew older and relationships had to mature. The advantage to animated episodic series like *The Simpsons, Futurama* (Fox, 1999–present) and *Family Guy* (Fox, 1998–present) is that animated characters need not age, making the shows prime for long episodic runs – *The Simpsons* is the longest running series in television history, beginning in 1989; as of the writing of this book, it has been on air for 23 years.

Sitcoms are the leaders in episodic storytelling. The rule in sitcom has been to start a story problem in the first act, escalate it in second act, and solve it in the third act, getting things back to the way they were at the start of the first act. Repeat this 22 times a year for multiple years.

While it is difficult to find a purely episodic hour drama, certain shows like the various *Law and Order* series for the most part steer away from the personal lives of the central characters or series regulars and concentrate solely on the elements of that week's crime or mystery instead.

Serialized Storytelling

Serialized storytelling allows for story, plot and character arcs to occur over entire seasons rather than being contained within one episode, as is required in episodic storytelling. Establishing a season goal and then individual episode goals allows us to play with the ways that the arcs are expressed within the show. Once we know where the season is going, we can begin to structure the ebb and flow of a larger story across multiple episodes in order to get us closer and closer to the season goal. There may even be multiple season goals depending on how many stories are opened at the start of the season. Major A, B, C and D stories that begin the season's first episode may continue, always escalating the central conflict of those individual storylines and the larger overall story as they progress.

These story arcs must work in tandem, and serve any character arcs, which are influenced by the experiences that each character needs to go through during individual episodes as well as throughout the season. If a character arc is determined first, then the story and story arcs must work in conjunction with it to make sure that the necessary experiences occur at the exact right time, to bring about the changes needed for the desired character arc to manifest.

Serialized television series characters must have deep backstories and personal mythology. The pilot episode, the first episode of a series, introduces an audience to the main characters of a show. It begins the unfolding of the characters' backstory by alluding to certain things from their past that have an effect on the present story. But this is just the beginning. The entire rest of the series will be a continuous expansion of our understanding of who the character is, who they were, who they are becoming.

It is also a continuous line of lies, misleads, deceit and withholding of important information by the character and by the writers and producers. This withholding forces the audience to fill in the blanks, to make up reasons why, and to suppose and anticipate the answer to questions posed by gaps in character information. In this way the audience never really knows for sure everything about the characters, keeping their interest in the characters over long periods of narrative storytelling. Even if certain characters seem to be archetypes, tapping into our preconceived notions about what they will and will not do in a given situation, modern day storytellers often add twists to these universally known character types, enhancing our sense of mystery and suspense.

Besides gaps in our knowledge of the characters, narrative gaps are often created in serialized shows to leave the audience wanting or even needing answers within the larger story of the show. Locke's discovery of the mysterious hatch in the first season of *LOST* is a perfect example of a narrative gap. The hatch was discovered, but not opened until the next season, leaving fans to speculate about what the hatch was, why the hatch was there and how – or even if – it could be opened. Story extensions flow from narrative gaps like this one, and many a forum and *LOST* dedicated chat space were filled with hatch speculation.

Serial storytelling relies heavily on mystery and curiosity generated by mythology, or the show's unknown elements that require the audience to figure out the mysteries as the show runs. Supernatural elements, alternative universes and dimensions, space, aliens, lost civilizations, time travel and similar scenarios are elements that amaze or intrigue most of us in real life and so when they are included in television storytelling, they make for ideal show mythologies. The trick is to not explain these mysteries too quickly, to always leave something to the (audience's) imagination. Curiosity is piqued when the full nature of the story is hidden, and the audience's sense of discovery is enhanced when narrative clues of that mythology are distributed little by little, episode by episode, so that viewers keep tuning in to learn more. This is the magic of serialized television storytelling: the mystery magnetizes viewers to the show, allowing for a rich participatory life where they will be inspired to seek more and more information about the characters and the storyworld.

One of the more interesting examples of serialized storytelling is *24* (Fox, 2001–2010) mainly because of its conceit: each hour of screen time equated to an hour of story time (or the time experienced by the characters), following the characters through one day. Twenty-four hours meant 24 episodes, each deeply connected by a literal chronology. More than most serialized series, each episode was completely and totally dependent on the episode before it. Fox utilized the Internet to allow audiences to watch previous episodes on their website, and recaps were used to update the audience on events in previous episodes; audiences watched the show religiously. The idea of experiencing an actual day-in-the life of an antiterrorist agent not only entranced America, but the world.

Arcs: The Long and Short of It

Arcs are what make serialized stories … well … serials. They are the basic building blocks we use to guide the development of characters and story over multiple episodes, a season or even multiple seasons of a television show. Arcs are long-term questions or mysteries posed in one episode that will require many episodes to answer. When shows successfully employ character and story arcs, audiences become actively engaged with the show, interested in finding out the answers or speculating what they might be. The Internet has become a major component in this quest to learn more about and discuss with others these show's larger stories and mythology, and fueling this curiosity can help assure that the audience will keep watching the show.

As in all drama, the most engaging stories tend to be about conflict, and all *story arcs* involve struggle. The main character needs, wants or desires something but soon finds out that there are sizable obstacles in the way. As the story progresses, the obstacles increase in difficulty, forcing the character to struggle harder. The difference with serialized storytelling that builds a long arc is that the resolution of the larger struggle, the final attainment or the final denial of the long-reaching goal, won't usually occur until the end of the series (assuming the show is able to plan its finale ahead of cancelation). These conflicts express universal themes and insights into what it means to be human, and the most effective story arcs grow organically out of the show's story engine, consistent with the tone and characters of the show.

A story arc can begin in as many different ways as there are stories to tell, but in general a mystery introduced into the series takes longer than one episode to answer. This mystery comes in the form of an implied question posed to the audience in the form of an action or event at the beginning of the series or episode. That action or event forces the audience to ask themselves a literal question. In *LOST* there is a plane crash at the very beginning of the pilot. Survivors of this crash are stranded on a mysterious island. The implied question is, "Will they survive long enough to ever get off of this island?" And instantly a series long arc is established.

Initially, audiences watched *LOST* because of this very story arc, to see if the characters would indeed survive and be rescued. Of course the series was about many more threats and mysteries than whether or not they would escape the island, but that was the initial hook, the mystery that began to draw the audience into the show's expansive mythology.

With *The X-Files*, audiences watched to see if Mulder could prove to Scully that we are not alone and to see if the romantic attraction would pay off. *The X-Files*, however, used a combination approach to storytelling that involved the long arc, but also the monster-of-the-week style of episode arcs. *Buffy The Vampire Slayer* (WB and UPN, 1997–2003), *Babylon 5*, and *Star Trek: Deep Space Nine* (Paramount Television, 1993–1999) also experimented with having more long-running storylines even as individual episodes usually told a standalone story, sometimes called an episode arc. Crime of the week, monster of the week, medical emergency of the week – all allow for a story arc to be introduced, escalated and resolved within an hour.

Story arcs can occur over sequential episodes, but that is not a requirement. Some story arcs flow freely episode to episode and then disappear for a number of episodes while the character involved enters into another story arc,

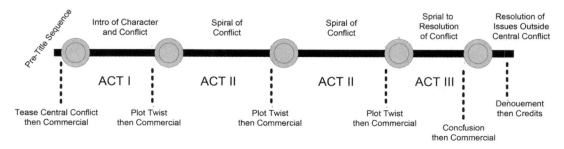

Figure 5.1 *Hour Long Arc.*

which could be his own or that of another character. The audience hopefully still wonders about the absent story arc even as it embraces episodes that do not include it, waiting expectantly, returning week after week to see if the answer is given, if the arc will escalate in jeopardy or if it will even continue. And in the mean time they become hooked by other story arcs in the series, some with the same character and some using other characters.

Often, in an ensemble piece, like *Heroes*, *LOST* or *Battlestar Galactica* there are as many story arcs as there are main characters, each a standalone storyline and also intertwining over the course of the series. At first, they may seem independent of each other and only slowly come together, encouraging the audience to guess if and when they will intersect and allowing for common elements to be introduced into both arcs that foreshadow their coming together.

Season arcs, like those used in *Heroes*, are story arcs designed to last one season of the series, with a new arc established with each new season. Set up refers to the moment when the audience is introduced to the arc-question, and pay off refers to the moment when the story-arc question or problem is resolved. Writers and producers track the main story arc, meant to last the entire season, through each episode, making sure that the larger arc keeps progressing but that it is scarce enough not to crowd the other story lines. They are also checking to make sure that the season arc remains mysterious and unanswered until the season finale. The goal in long story arcs is to keep the audience excited, endeared and full of anxiety about what will happen next, tuning in each week.

Figure 5.2 *Season Arcs.*

Besides story arcs that have to parse out specific narrative information, serialized stories also have *character arcs*, character-specific story-lines that encourage characters to change over time. Character arcs usually express a more personal and even internal struggle of some sort, be it mental, romantic, emotional or physical that forces characters to do things and think differently than they have in the past. Usually character arcs put the characters into situations that are not easy for them to deal with, often involving something or someone meaningful to the character and to the audience. Character arc and story arcs have to work in tandem to get to the desired story goal and desired character change.

In *Battlestar Galactica*, Lee Adama's decision to leave the fleet and work for the President served two purposes: it moved along the story arc of the military versus the presidency, and it moved along the character arc of both Lee and his father (Commander Adama) having to perform their duties alone, without the support of the other. This particular development of their character arcs could also be considered a relationship arc.

Relationship arcs refer to how a relationship between two characters evolves over the course of an episode, a season or the entire run of the show. In serialized series, characters are designed to have escalating conflicts, like the conflict between Jack and Sawyer in *LOST* or Commander Adama and Lee Adama in *Battlestar Galactica*. These arcs help to reveal aspects of character not seen in the normal course of the story. Characters faced with relationship conflicts are forced to act differently than when relationships are at status quo, adding aspects of conflict that yield drama.

The planning of story arcs occurs during the development of the season. In the case of a new series this occurs before the pitch so that the creators can demonstrate that the series has viable arcs that move the story forward, create a sense of mystery and mythology and engage the target audience. Outlines that track arcs across episodes, seasons and the length of the entire series would be developed. Each episode has a beginning, middle and end as do seasons and multiple seasons. Arcs must be woven through being careful about the pacing of information. Pacing of information refers to the deliberate withholding of important arc information and disseminating it or sprinkling it over the course of the arc run.

The challenge with serialized content is that what happens and what is learned in one episode is not only carried onto to the next episode, but usually key to understanding what is happening in the entire season or series. If you joined *LOST* in season 3 without going back and viewing seasons 1 and 2 you would be … well … lost. For this reason, network executives have been pushing for fewer serialized pilots and more episodic pilots. However, fans have pushed back, demanding the richer storyworlds, story arcs and character arcs generated by serialized content.

Procedurals and the Best of Both Worlds

While television series are usually talked about in terms of being one or the other, episodic or serialized, shows are not always an either/or proposition. In the past ten years, we have seen the evolution of a combined form of episodic and serialized storytelling: the procedural. This group of modern procedurals are an important development in the way that television stories are told, because they have dominated the ratings and programing of several networks (yes, we mean you CBS) and have become a significant storytelling form.

The idea of the procedural is nothing really new; we've had investigative procedural series, or detective shows, since the earliest days of TV with *Dragnet* (NBC, 1951–1959 and 1967–1970) leading the way. We have also had legal process shows, *Perry Mason* (CBS, 1957–1966); and medical procedurals like *Ben Casey* (ABC, 1961–1966) have been around since the 1950s and 1960s. What is new, however, is that these procedurals, while episodic, also employ elements of serialized storytelling, in effect becoming a combination of the two. With that said, though, these procedurals tend to be more episodic in nature, featuring a "monster, murder, illness or crime of the week" main storyline that is solved by the end of the standalone episode. However, personal storylines and larger thematic storylines tend to extend from episode to episode, allowing for richer character development and character arcs.

Whether episodic or serialized, longevity is a core principle of show development. Television series are designed to generate multiple stories from one core narrative property, and in that sense television development is a microcosm of many of the issues we face in transmedia storytelling. Story comes directly out of worldbuilding, although the term "development" is used for this process in most television series. Regardless of the label we put on it, we must construct a storyworld that will sustain the series. This world needs a physical geography, ecology, human geography and backstory, political or hierarchal character relationships, mythology ripe with unanswered mystery, continuous threats or jeopardy as well as consistent physical rules of the world. This approach gives priority to properties that have a strong story engine or premise that will serve as an endless source of narrative material, generating a potentially limitless number of stories.

Formats and How Long It Takes

As we talked about at the beginning of this chapter, we can talk about television shows in a variety of ways, many of which overlap and even sometimes obscure others. Format (or duration for the viewer) and genre (or type of story) are intricately tied together in some types of television storytelling, but we're going to pull them apart for a moment to better understand how all the elements we've been discussing work. Seeing the dynamics of story and commercial breaks is key to understanding how television developed its forms.

Television stories are generally developed in half-hour or hour-long formats, correlating with the standard way television time slots are scheduled (acknowledging of course that we are writing this book in the United States, and that other countries have their own scheduling and format conventions). Each has its own specific timeframe or amount of story material that can be presented (screen story), taking into account that some of that half-hour or hour is devoted to commercials.

Half-hour shows traditionally feature 22 minutes of story, and hour programs are traditionally 48 minutes of content. These traditions come from a time before cable, when show length and scheduling was very regimented to fit broadcast network standards. In recent years, the placement of commercial breaks can vary from network to network, depending on whether the show is made for broadcast or cable, and whether it's airing as first runs to reruns. In addition, some creators have started to mess with the form in some rather extreme ways (four-, five-, or six-act structures), but we will use the example of this traditional approach (22 minutes/48 minutes) to provide a sense of the basic strategy for how formats address story material.

In a half-hour show, which is typically a comedy (already we're encountering the linking of genre with format), a classic structure would be a tease, Act 1, Act 2 and tag, each separated by a commercial break. The tease lasts no more than two minutes, though it can be much shorter. This is followed by the show's opening credits and commercials, which take us to the first act. Act 1 lasts until the middle of the half hour where there's another commercial break, which then launches us into a second act which is followed by the tag. A final set of commercials and the show's closing credits round out the half-hour.

Half-hour comedies can also have a three-act structure that places the main commercial break in the middle of act 2. This break typically shifts our focus from the A story to the B Story – in *The Simpsons*, the first part of Act 2 might follow Bart's storyline and after the commercial break, the second half of Act 2 would switch to Homer's storyline.

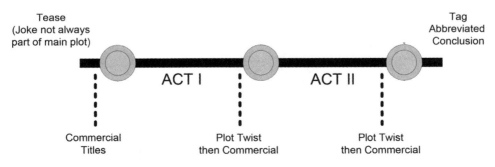

Figure 5.3 *Sitcom Arcs.*

An hour-long show traditionally uses a three-act structure that breaks Act 2 into two parts as well, but rather than using that midpoint commercial break to switch from the A Story to the B Story (like in sitcoms), the two parts of Act 2 operate as their own spirals of conflict.

Spirals of Conflict

We use the term spirals of conflict to refer to a smaller progression of conflict within one of the acts of a television program, particularly Act 2 of hour long dramas. Conflicts within a conflict are just an example of the ways in which multiple approaches to structure have gradually overlapped in television storytelling and affected each other.

This smaller progression follows its own mini three-act structure, internal to the bigger second act it is placed in. These tiny three acts introduce what seems to be a relatively minor or small problem, raising the stakes building to its own mini-resolution before the commercial break. In that smaller resolution, however, a new more serious issue arises. Why we call this a "spiral" is because we are ultimately referring to the fact this mini three-act structure has spiraled up and raised the stakes for the larger conflict of the overall story in the show.

As a result, spirals of conflict continue building momentum by creating a problem for the audience to have to worry about (what, now?), provide the viewer with a sense of immediate reward (one problem solved!) and then move the show's larger story along by making the central conflict even more important (oh, no!). This storytelling technique is often most apparent in those two parts of Act 2 that fall on either side of the midpoint of the hour show (or Acts 2 and 3 if you call this four-act structure). In two back-to-back mini-three act sequences, the hero solves an issue only to learn that solution makes the larger story's conflict more serious. Of course, we know that the real resolution won't happen till the final act of the show, but our protagonist doesn't.

It's All About the Timing

In terms of proportion, Act 1 is the first quarter hour minus commercials, introducing the main character and conflict. This is easier for television shows than films because the ongoing characters need no introduction, having been a part of the ongoing series. This means Act 1 in television has a stronger focus on conflict and comes to a close with the first plot twist and commercial. At this point viewers rush out and back for snacks, assuming that the plot twist has done what it should: asking a question that needs to be answered or posing a problem the audience wants to see solved.

If we're talking in terms of three-act structure, Act 2 is broken into two parts that occupy the next half hour, with a commercial break occurring in the middle. Each of these quarter-hour segments form their own spiral of conflict – those smaller three-act structures we just discussed – taking the viewers through a specific problem or threat that is resolved but only causes more problems in the larger story. Each spiral of conflict should continue to raise stakes for the larger conflict that is then resolved in the final act.

The final act is the final quarter hour of the show that brings us to the climax and resolution of the large conflict and a denouement that brings resolution to issues outside the main conflict, for example, *Magnum P.I.* (CBS, 1980–1988) and the boys sitting having a beer after they have solved the big problem. Closing show credits follow, and then as always there are more commercials.

This structure in its most pure form is seen less today than 20 years ago and has been evolving in recent years to allow for more layers of complexity to the story.

Hour dramas now have multiple structures. The most common structure is four-act structure plus a teaser at the top, much like the mode. This structure is also called five-act structure, using the teaser as Act 1. Act breaks come after Acts 1, 2, 3, and in four-act structure the climax occurs near the end of Act 4, with a cliffhanger at the very end. In a five-act structure an act break occurs after Act 4, the climax toward the end of Act 5 and a cliffhanger at the end of Act 5. Six-act structure follows the same basic act-to-act structure with the climax and cliff in Act 6. As the structures evolved, audiences initially became used to the 15/30/15-minute time structures for hour-long programs but as the format has moved on to five- and six-act structures, the time frame of each act has also had to be adjusted.

Why Television Loves Genres

Genres, in many ways, allow storytellers a wonderfully complex shorthand to connect quickly with the audience. Genres often have a deep codified language the viewers familiar with — and loyal to — that genre understand and connect with. The relationship of television storytelling and genre goes to the very start of the medium, because early programing was often adapted from film or radio, whose own programs were based on the successful genres in the culture. As a result, early television saw lots of Westerns, detective, and medical series. Success breeds imitation, and adaptations were soon replaced by original stories created and developed specifically for television, but these still copied the genres that were most popular. We now have decades of genres going in and out of favor, with any success being replicated by multiple shows, resulting in that saturation point where the audience votes with their remote control and tries to find something new. Television loves genres. That's a given. The real question is why television has doubled down on genres going as far as having individual cable channels dedicated to a particular genre.

The demands of television storytelling make any sort of shorthand attractive. Getting across complex information is much easier and faster when we work in a genre the audience already understands. Sci-fi people aren't thrown by alien technology. Supernatural folk don't mind ghosts, and people who love medical shows enjoy the long explanation of a diagnosis. The elements of genre provide a foundation that television series can build upon, with clear designators of the good guys and bad, of dangerous places and safe, or goals to be attained.

Genre is both a way of attracting audience as well as speeding the storyteller's ability to move through plot and story, especially when a complete story has to be told in a very limited amount of time, like in television. Year upon year of programing has built a fairly extensive common language and understanding of a variety of genres that regular television viewers can decipher, which enables the audience's ability both to choose which program to watch and which program to commit to over the long haul.

Television viewers can be a fickle bunch, some looking for narrowly defined genres while others enjoy things a lot messier. The latter have encouraged one of the most interesting aspects of genre stories told on television: mixing genres. Television audiences have been confronted with all sorts of interesting combinations of genres: medical/detective (*House* Fox, 2004–2012), crime/family drama (*The Sopranos* HBO, 1999–2007), spy/comedy (*Chuck* NBC, 2007–2012). These and countless others take from and mix multiple genres, trying to find the magic combination that attracts a wide audience. In fact, television has on occasion generated new forms like dramedy, a combination of traditional television drama with strong comedy elements, often with another genre thrown in for good measure (law or medical, for example) — all in an hour format. Of course, there have been both good and bad results from all this genre-mixing, but television has become a place where this kind of experimentation can occur, especially as cable networks have begun creating more and more original programming.

Key Transmedia Elements and Television

Earlier in this book, we talked about a set of key elements of transmedia storytelling property: *theme/story*, *plot*, *character*, *setting*, and *style/tone*. These elements are as important in a television development as any other media, but manifest in different ways. Let's take a brief look at each of them in the context of dramatic television series.

Key, though, in understanding these elements in the context of television is that television series are always playing the long game. They want to engage you from the first moment of the first episode, but at the same time there has to be an awareness and understanding that this same show, with this same core characters and conflict(s) could be running for three, five, seven years or longer. There has to be periodic payoff, and a great deal of television is a "slow burn" building to that payoff, revealing mysteries and creating new ones along the way.

Theme/Story

To a large extent, theme in combination with story is the backbone of television storytelling. Theme, to a large extent, tells us what the television series is about, and story (told through characters) is what brings it home. Unlike motion pictures and most video games, theme and story isn't as locked to a single focus as it is in those mediums.

Television tells stories over time. Its characters, stories, situations and settings are developed to maintain audience interest season after season, year after year. Because of that long view, television series can and should be constructed to evolve over time. The shift has to be organic, however. Ultimately, for example, *Battlestar Galactica* was a show about surviving the decisions of the past, both on a personal and civilization level, and learning not to repeat them. The series also explores questions of the nature of sentient life, determinism vs. free will, utilitarianism, and justice. The emphasis on these various themes ebbs and flows throughout the series and often follows various thematic "arcs" through and across seasons. The transitions, however, never felt overly abrupt or forced as the exploration of these themes was properly focused on the actions, or inactions, of the characters. *Buffy the Vampire Slayer*, as another example, maintained the same basic narrative spine throughout the series, but allowed the dominant themes to mature as the main character matured, and her concerns (in addition to killing vampires) shifted from teenage concerns to more adult concerns of responsibility and family.

Thematic shifts have to be supported by story, which means that all of the pieces have to be in place for the story to manifest the theme episode after episode, season after season. The pieces come into existence in the storyworld as part of the worldbuilding process. It is always possible to make things up as you go along, and there are things that you will discover or come to understand as the series matures and evolves, but the more possibilities built into the initial story framework, the better, even casually. Even if you don't entirely know the specifics about a particular story element beyond that you know you're going to need it, you can still weave it in.

For example, if you think that the heroes of your global conspiracy-driven television series are going to run afoul of sinister forces in the US government in the second, or maybe the third season, you can create a list of names of senators or congressmen that can be offhandedly (or more concretely) referred to in your first season. Then in the second season, when it turns out that Senator Strong is the antagonist astute fans will remember the references to the senator last season. And if you make the references to the senator and never use him or her, it doesn't matter. Who that person is or was remains a mystery.

The important thing is that you build your world, and the possibilities for your stories and themes, in from the beginning. The series will evolve, episode to episode, introducing new information, adding to the stories, revealing more and more and to do so it must be able to extend the core mythology. If the television series is the mothership platform, then it must be considered that it is from here that most, if not all, stories will flow throughout the transmedia narrative property.

Plot

Stories play out over arcs of single to multiple episodes to even multiple seasons. The plot is the sequence of events that play out to tell the story. On a television series, the process of figuring out that sequence of events and how they flow is called "breaking" the story. Any given episode will have an "A" plot, which is the primary plot the episode spends the most amount of time on, and then may have "B," or "C" plots that are interwoven with the events of the "A" plot.

This format of a primary plot and one or more secondary plots can also stretch out over episodes and seasons. Again, we talk about arcs elsewhere, but here's an important point to remember – this is a transmedia property, so your plots don't have to be confined to just the television series. For example, the NBC television series *Heroes* did a great job of weaving in "B" and "C" plots related to new characters into a particular episode's "A" story in order to push the viewers toward other media expressions. The character of Hana Gitelman, also known as "Wireless," first appeared in a series of online graphic novels released through the NBC *Heroes* website (http://www.nbc.com/heroes/novels/) that were focused on her. Her first appearance was on in December of 2006 in the graphic novel *Wireless, Part 1*, and she appeared for the first time in the television series in the episode "Unexpected" that aired in February of 2007, where she was played by actress Stana Katic. Gitelman's story arc was primarily through the graphic novels, where she was the "A" plot, but when she appeared in the television series she only contributed to the "A" plot of that episode, and the mystery of who this new hero was a "B" or "C" plot at best. The character of Gitelman, however, though only appearing in one episode of the mothership, featured prominently in the *Heroes 360* and *Heroes Evolution* alternate reality game where she was the player's primary contact. (For the character's in-story case file, go to the website http://www.primatechpaper.com/AT_2.0/assignmentTracker.php, which is ostensibly the front end used in the storyworld to track Primatech's agents. Select file _C001 in the left column and when prompted enter the password "HGghx11a.")

Character

Characters in television series really come in two flavors; those that evolve and those that never change. This has nothing to do with the quality of the storytelling, the acting, or the production. Television, in fact, because of its long view, has many opportunities to both reveal and evolve a character. If a character changes, or not, is based solely on the need of the story and the desire of the writers. If Bart Simpson changes, for example, *The Simpsons* is screwed. On the other side *Battlestar Galactica* needed some characters to change following their discovery that they weren't human, but were actually Cylons, mankind's enemy. And they needed to be able to react to that revelation and responding accordingly within the story and change if the drama was to move ahead.

Also, static secondary characters, who may have more life and breadth in one of the other transmedia expressions, allow the writers to clearly show any evolution or change in the main characters. There's a potential stumbling block here, however, with regard to the synchronization of the stories in the different media. If a secondary character is an asshole in the mothership, but becomes more kind-hearted in one of the graphic novels, there will be an assumption among fans that chronologically the graphic novel occurs after the relevant television episodes. If, however, other plot elements contradict that and seem to place the graphic novel before the television episodes, there is narrative confusion and a subsequent weakening of the property.

Setting

Setting stems from the demands of the story. The setting(s) chosen or constructed depends on the type of story and characters, and the needs of the plot. It is one of the earliest decisions made for a realistic or real-world television series since the time and place chosen will dictate to a large extent the type of characters in the story. The characters in *The Wire* (HBO, 2002–2008) are dramatically impacted by the socio-economic, political and historical elements of the harsh Baltimore ghetto. Characters born and raised there, for the most part, are innately under pressure, sometimes living without real hope, and often times prone to lives of crime and violence. So the struggle for them does not begin with a weekly crime or with the action that begins each episode, but rather with their daily struggle against their environment, regardless of that week's plot.

By contrast in *Desperate Housewives* (ABC, 2004–2012), the same applies but from a different angle entirely. The wealthy wives of this affluent neighborhood are confronted with the obstacles, many self-created or married into, that force them to be in a constant state of struggle as well. Their dramatic conflicts, however, will be innately different from those confronted by characters in *The Wire*, though at times some of the plot elements (drugs, violence, etc.) may be similar.

Television series set in fantasy, science fiction, or non-realistic worlds can take a slightly different approach. While we advocate building in as many plot elements as possible from the very beginning, certain things can be decided as needed. For example, in a space-faring television series if a new character needs to come from a dystopian matriarchy, it is easy enough to fabricate that part of the world, as needed. Still, it is better if the origin of that character ties into something already established, or at least mentioned, previously rather than just poofing into existence when first mentioned.

Setting also has important realistic components in that you have to be able to depict it on screen, episode after episode. If your show is set in modern-day Chicago, then you have the choice of shooting in Chicago or shooting on the back-lot or using another city as a stand-in and "faking it," as is often the case. (We wonder how many cities Vancouver has pretended to be…) If your setting is on alien worlds, or spends time in the prehistoric past, you have to be able to show that setting effectively. Visual effects are nearly seamless these days, but they're not cheap. That said, if your transmedia storytelling extensions on other similar platforms use the same setting, you may be able to leverage some of the visual effects assets from one production into the other.

Style/Tone

Style and tone are more subtle aspects of story and must be consistent for the entire run of a series. A show's style speaks to how the story is told and takes into account writing style, visual storytelling style, art direction and the "look" of the show and characters, as well as the thematic palette to some extent.

Tone can be seen as the emotional undercurrent of the story. Tone is more abstract than style, and consists of varying degrees and type of emotional triggers contained within the storytelling. In general terms, tone can be the overall feel of a piece of content. A situation comedy, for instance, can be said to have a "funny" or comedic tone and that would be accurate. But then if we compare the teen-friendly comedic tone of *Community* (NBC, 2009–present), a sitcom about a lawyer who faked his legal degree and now has to attend community college, with that of the mature *It's Always Sunny in Philadelphia* (FX, 2005–present), the story of bar owners who do not hesitate to stoop to any level to make money, we find that these two situation comedies, while both funny, have extremely different tones.

Tone is also related to thematic and story elements. For example, two superhero properties could have very different tones. *Smallville* (WB/CW, 2001–2011) told the story of the early years of Clark Kent/Superman and had very bold, or distinct thematic and story elements regarding good, evil, and justice. *Alphas* (SyFy, 2011–present), on the other hand, portrays the dark side of superherodom where heroes and villains often share the same life issues and dysfunction.

Tone becomes a voice through which the creators can comment on both the state of the character's world, and their own. Some shows are suspenseful and audiences feel a sense of anxiety or dread. Other series may be uplifting and the audience feels inspired each week.

Television Production Realities

Television series have various development models, but the basic process is the same. Shows start first as a concept. A show's creators are usually a core group of television writers and producers who create the show's concept or premise, including the principal cast of characters, the innate situation, the central problem or driving dramatic conflict of the show, and the storyworld the show will inhabit. This primary development process will generate a show or series bible (more on bibles is included in the appendices). In general terms, the bible will have a clearly stated premise that defines the show concept and why it's intriguing, character descriptions with key relationships and conflicts, a pilot treatment, casting ideas, and loglines for a full season of episodes. Loglines are the simplest form of storytelling, and these initial loglines encapsulate each entire episode in one or two lines. They usually state, in simplest form, the A and B story. This is the material that is pitched to the networks.

Networks will, after a pitch, decide whether or not to buy a pilot. If the pilot is purchased, it does not mean that the show will be greenlit to go to series. Networks buy upwards of 20 pilots per year, and of those 20, they greenlight only five to ten to go into pilot production, and only a few of those will ultimately make it onto television.

Showrunners are attached to a pilot after it has been commissioned, if they are not already a part of the creator pool. Showrunners are high-level writing producers who are responsible for all creative decisions on a series; they sit at the writer's table but their duties flow to all areas of production, working with the writers, producers, cast and crew as well as the network to insure that every episode delivers. They are in charge from idea pitches at table for future episodes to postproduction to final cut before network.

While the pilot is being written, producers will go ahead and cast it. Notes are given and rewrites made before the pilot goes into production or shot. Pilots are usually viewed by focus groups consisting of the show's target audience, as well as network and marketing executives. Advertisers are allowed to view pilots and decide whether the series is right for their brand or product, and advertisers have been known to give notes on pilots, requiring adjustments be made to them before they air, in order to get sponsored. The concept of target audience is an important consideration in the creation of television stories, because networks make their money from advertisers, and those sponsors maximize the value of their advertising dollars by only buying commercial time on shows that are most likely to reach their preferred customers. The study of target audiences or consumers, sometimes referred to as demographics, has made a science out of identifying what specific audiences (those presumed to have lots of disposable cash – 14–35 year old males, for example) like to watch and buy.

Rewrites, reshoots, re-edits and even re-casting takes place between the pilot and the premiere. Sometimes the entire writing staff is changed or main characters cut. The pilot you pitch is rarely the pilot that goes to air.

Development continues throughout the series run. Audience response and comments as well as ratings are a major factor in determining the flow of the show; however, its showrunner is responsible for charting the season and making sure the series stays consistent episode to episode and season to season.

A Season at a Time

Season planning changes depending on the showrunners and network demands. Some showrunners will plan their season out over hiatus, coming to the first day of the writer's table with a detailed episode-to-episode breakdown. (Hiatus refers to the breaks that shows take either during the season which are usually of a week's duration, and after a season is finished filming. Summer hiatus usually begins in late March and lasts till August for production staff and cast; writers and producers, however, return at the end of May or beginning of June.) Other showrunners will only have a vague idea of where they'd like to see the season go and pitch these ideas to the writing staff. The season will then be developed, at the writer's table, with showrunners and writers working hand in hand.

Seasons are planned once a season goal is decided by the showrunners, articulating where they would like to see the story finish up by the end of the season. After the first season, writers and showrunners start each season where the previous season left off (the end-of-season cliffhanger) and develop episodes in sequence that will take the show where they want it to go. Just like an individual episode, seasons too should have a beginning middle and end. Looking at the entire season and determining an arc is as important as the individual show arcs. Think of it as building a structure where the smaller arcs form the structure of the larger season arcs.

The writing staff of a television show have a hierarchical structure beginning, from the bottom up, with staff writer, story editor, executive story editor, co-producer, supervising co-producer, co-executive producer and executive producer. The showrunners are usually the executive producer and co-executive producer. All of these are writers. "Staff" are writers and producers hired to work at the writer's table of a show. In addition there are freelance writers. They are non-staff writers hired during a season to write one or two episodes. The Writers Guild of America West (WGAw) requires that all signatory shows, or shows required to hire WGAw writers, must allocate a certain number of scripts per season to freelance writers. As you can see, television is a collaborative effort. From a writing staff of 14 to the vast numbers of crew to cast and network, one show requires the efforts of many to make it a success.

In serialized television, everything begins with the show premise. The premise or concept in turn generates the show's story and theme. The series needs to have a premise or story engine at its heart that can generate not only a good story but a hundred or more good stories.

The premise is the kernel of the story, its engine that if properly designed will power the series for years to come. In many respects it is the first and most important element to define. It is the one piece of the show's story that will be communicated to all the interested parties and carry the day as decisions are made to make one show over another. The premise of the show should be clear, articulate and easy to communicate even if it doesn't get at all the subtleties that will be a part of the ongoing series. When they listen to pitches, networks are trying to find the story or concept that will have longevity. The concept or idea must have at its core a storyworld with characters in a situation so fertile that it has endless stories flowing from it.

Writing styles vary from series to series. The way the story is told and indeed the storytelling devices, like flashbacks or narration, help to dictate the overall style of the series. Writers on the staff of a particular series have to develop a common voice for the series. This common voice, established in the pilot, will then be synonymous with the show. Multiple writers, each with their own individual narrative voices, must find a way to transform their individual voices into the common voice. In this way, a script written by one writer will not greatly differ from a script written by another writer on the same show. Tabling each script after a single writer or writing team turns in an initial writer's draft allows for the entire staff to rewrite the script, making sure that the style fits the common voice of the series.

The director is responsible for creating the visual storytelling style of a show. Often times a series will attempt to retain the same director who shot the pilot for as many consecutive episodes as possible in order to establish a replicable visual palette for other directors to follow. When a director changes the visual style of a series, fans often complain, and that director will be released or fired. Visual storytelling styles and how a director manipulates the visual aspects of a story, even among shows within the same genre, differ greatly and serve as signature aspects that differentiate one series from another.

Single-camera television directing has liberated dramatic series from having to be shot mostly inside the studio, as are most multi-camera shows. Single-camera directing, like film directing, allows for more intricate shot designs and camera movements and indeed allows for television series to move from location to location and to use cinematographers and directors of photography, which in turn gives them the cinematic feel of "little movies." However, multi-camera is still favored for certain comedy series in part for the cost but also for the live performance quality that only a multi-camera shooting scenario brings.

The world of television production is chaotic, at best. To write a definitive schedule to illuminate how television is accomplished would require a book all by itself. It resembles film production in the most basic shape of development, preproduction, production, postproduction and distribution (or in the case of television, broadcast). However, the reality is that episodes of a show are often being written, in pre-production, being shot, posted and airing all at the same time. This is simply a function of the amount of material being produced tied to the typical schedule where by a network decides on its programming. It is a condensed timeframe, and even with television's fast production schedules this translates to everything happening at once.

Television Adapts

While the tools that are available to television producers share much in common with filmmakers, what does vary a great deal is the ability of television to evolve these elements over time. This evolution is sometimes a simple issue of production getting its legs under it and/or notes from the network. A show can look very different at the end of a season than it did at the beginning. What this means is often the best storytelling we see from a series is not in season 1 (yes, we mean you, *Buffy the Vampire Slayer* and *Star Trek: The Next Generation*) but down the line, if the series has a chance refine the elements and therefore its ability to tell its stories.

The other aspect is that the circumstances surrounding a series change. Feature films are released at a fixed moment in time. Series television has an arc in the real world as well, as the actors, writers, networks and the world around them continue to change, no doubt affecting both what is communicated and how it is perceived. Circumstance always affects the perceived meaning, but, in television, circumstance can directly shape a story from year to year.

Franchises

To this point we have discussed the concept of premise in television as the heart of a television series, the well-wrought concept that acts as a story engine, generating countless stories over the run of a series. From a creative standpoint, this definition is correct; from a marketing standpoint, however, a franchise refers to the idea of one intellectual property that extends itself into multiple properties both within the same medium and evolving onto other media platforms, marketed accordingly.

The more formal definition of a franchise must include licensing a property of an original work of media, in this case a television show, to other entities besides the original owners. This licensing involves a trademarked story, characters and settings, and has become very commonplace in the world of reality television where we see the successful franchise put into production in various countries around the world. Television narrative franchises, however, usually refer to those situations where one series spawns spin-offs, revivals, remakes and reboots. License refers to the original owners of a television franchise selling specific rights to other entities. These rights are limited and grant the ability for licensees to use certain aspects of the intellectual property. Usually these licenses involve the production and distribution of auxiliary content in another media platform as well as merchandising.

The successful science fiction property *Stargate* (MGM) is one such mega-successful television franchise. The successful feature film was translated accordingly to television and successfully ran for ten seasons, and was accompanied by three other series. The *Stargate* franchise is yet another example of why science fiction, with its expansive storyworlds, deeply developed characters and immersive mythology is perfect for transmedia. The *Stargate* universe contains all the content over all media platforms that stem from this one core narrative property. Each of the iterations of the franchise, including the original theatrical film *Stargate* (1994) and the television series and movies-of-the-week *Stargate SG-1* (1997), *Stargate: The Ark of Truth* (2008), *Continuuim* (2008), *Stargate: Infinity* (2002) all exist within the *Stargate SG-1* storyworld. *Stargate Atlantis* (2004) and *Stargate Universe* (2009) are both separate *Stargate* storyworlds that dwell within the *Stargate* universe.

Science fiction is not the only television genre prime for franchise status. As demonstrated by the tremendous success of the investigative process or procedural franchise *CSI*, America has a fascination with crime, and never has an audience gotten a more in-depth and realistic view of the process of investigating a crime, week after week, than in a *CSI* series. Innovations in visual effects and the advanced technology used in forensic evidence collection have allowed *CSI: Crime Scene Investigation* to deliver a realistic graphic portrayal of how murders are investigated.

The franchise *CSI* has not only spawned spin-offs in the media of television but also has been successful as transmedia in the areas of books, video games and live events and installations. Whereas the *CSI* shows are episodic in nature, they employ the combination style of most procedurals by being a "crime of the week" show in which each crime is introduced at the beginning of the episode and solved by the end, and yet also allow for longer story and character arcs.

Spin-Offs

When a show is a hit, the audience develops an attachment to not just the world and the main characters but also to many of the secondary characters. A spinoff usually refers to the act making an entirely new show based on one or more of the secondary characters from a current hit. Spinoffs often run simultaneously with their parent series, as in the case of Seth McFarlane's highly successful animated series *Family Guy* which gave birth to the spinoff, *The Cleveland Show* (Fox, 2009–present). As in many spinoffs, references to the parent series, *Family Guy*, happen often in the new series, and cameos by *Family Guy* characters, mainly Peter Griffin, show up multiple times per season.

Referencing the parent content and having cameos serve to introduce new fans to the parent content with the goal of wooing them into becoming fans of that series as well. In addition, references and cameos connect fans of the parent content to the new series. In this way, spin-offs and their parent series enjoy a shared life and shared fans, boosting the ratings of both shows. Spinoffs of spinoffs are a testament to the strength of a franchise's core narrative, premise or concept. *Star Trek*, perhaps the mother of all television franchises, is a good example of spinoffs that spawn spinoffs. *Star Trek: Deep Space Nine* and *Star Trek: Voyager* (Paramount Television, 1995–2001) both come from the world of *Star Trek: The Next Generation*, and are all part of the *Star Trek* Universe. *CSI* has produced two spin-offs, *CSI: Miami* (CBS, 2002–2012) and *CSI: NY* (CBS, 2004–present). The *CSI* franchise is also famous for doing *crossovers*. A crossover occurs when one storyworld crosses over into another story world, all in one episode. In this case, characters from *CSI: New York* and characters from *CSI: Miami* were in one episode, which then spawned the new spinoff.

Revival

Revivals in television are not common but are typically packaged as reunion shows. Typically allowing for the passage of time, the show takes us back to see how the Captain and Gilligan are since they left the island. Most of the time, this requires gathering all (or most) of the original cast, giving the audience a chance to see what their characters are up to now. While most examples of this are nostalgia based and fairly straightforward, the revival has had some interesting turns. *AfterMash* (CBS, 1983–1984), though it can been seen as a spinoff, has the feeling of the revival in its catching up to several characters who are working at a hospital after the war. An even stranger example was the use of *Curb Your Enthusiasm* (HBO, 2000–present) to create what was in effect a *Seinfeld* reunion show.

The Remake/Reboot

The definition of reboot and remake in television tend to blend into one idea. The television remake is an updated version of the original series that stays true to the world, series continuity and canon. These shows draw heavily on the original concept, mythology and canon but tell the stories using new actors and often are set in the present.

Hawaii Five-0 (CBS, 2010–present) is an example of an old show currently being remade. While elements have been changed, the changes take more of the shape of an update to the original material. It looks to retain essential elements relatively unchanged from the original including one of television's finest theme songs.

Battlestar Galactica on the other hand, can be thought of as being a reboot. Though the difference can seem minimal, if we were to differentiate between reboot and remake, the distinction would be made that a reboot is less attached to series continuity, concept or canon, and therefore a reboot can entirely reimagine a series. *Battlestar Galactica* uses the same character names and core relationships but changes or updates the series in many ways, including the fact that Starbuck, a man in the original, was cast as a woman in the remake. Most importantly, the main theme and tone bear little resemblance to the original series.

It has been said the best place to get a new idea for a series is to steal it from the past. Executives don't know for the most part their television history (yes, there are exceptions), and when you pitch the series about a wacky redhead who is married to the leader of a salsa band, they will think you are a comedy genius. But seriously, whether it is a spin-off, revival, remake or reboot or pulling from a well-established franchise, the show or premise that has survived on television for any length of time has done so because it has a rich enough core narrative concept to support auxiliary content. When these shows extend to other media platforms they become strong transmedia properties. With a long tradition of intellectual properties conceived of for longevity and storytelling over time, television can be an ideal birthplace for transmedia and its extensions.

Television and Transmedia

When you think about why television and transmedia are a natural fit, you might first think of television's strong marketing platform, its intimacy with the audience and the longevity of its properties, but what may be most important is television's ability, and in fact its inclination, to tell the big story. Shows that stay on television for a while must by necessity develop a large universe in order to keep the series going. While historically there has not always been a deep universe – shows like *Bonanza* (NBC, 1959–1973) didn't worry much about how and when the universe changed, outside explaining why a brother disappeared or who that new kid was living at the Ponderosa – the potential for a deeper exploration and development of storyworlds has always been there. Because these elements are part of the DNA of television, some of its intellectual properties quite naturally have become the center of a transmedia universe, partly because there were enough stories to support it but also because there was enough audience interest in extending the world. The mother of all modern transmedia, *Star Trek*, went quite accidentally and easily from television to video games to animation to feature films to novels back to television and so on. Television has proven over time to be both a fertile starting point for transmedia as well as a natural partner for other properties.

The History

In the beginning, television needed content. Early properties like *The Lone Ranger* (ABC, 1949– 1957) and Sherlock Holmes originated in stage plays, novels, "the funny papers," vaudeville, minstrel shows and radio; this versatility made them ideal seed-content to feed into the early television development mills. *The Lone Ranger*, while beginning as a radio show in the 1930s, became a household name because of 1950s television. From there the concept went on to become novels and movies. Sherlock Holmes began as a series of serialized stories written by Sir Arthur Conan Doyle beginning in the late 1800s and moving quickly into novel form. Various radio versions of the franchise appear over the years and Sherlock Holmes breaks into the 20th century via the big screen with 14 films produced between 1939 and 1946, not to mention the ones since. Sherlock Holmes has a hesitant start on television, only appearing in broadcast stage plays and guest spots until 1954, but when a 39-episode series hit the airwaves and the Sherlock Holmes brand was broadcast directly into American homes, a pop-culture icon was born. Likewise, *The Lone Ranger* did not fully become a part of the American pop culture tapestry until it reached television. *The Lone Ranger* television series, aired between 1949 and 1957, released 221 episodes over five years. That's one episode a week, 52 episodes per year, 52 different stories per year. No medium had that kind of relentless personal impact before.

The reality of the early television successes made one thing abundantly clear: as television shows arrived in our homes as a consistent visitor, joining us for meals or filling our time as the evening wore on, it was truly the ultimate marketing tool. The relationship and intimacy that television had with its audience outstripped radio because of the inclusion of images. The example of Walt Disney's *Davey Crocket* hat and the millions sold after the show aired clearly makes the point. The ability of television to transform narrative into content and commercials into financial rewards made it an obvious choice to engage audiences. The other aspect of this was the ability of the medium to establish long-term relationships. A prime example of this was the now almost ubiquitous form, the soap opera, whose name literally came from its ability to market to women. While the changing market has caused the reinvention of most of these shows, the reality that television can reach an audience through commercials, through product placement or through the actual narrative still makes it the strongest choice for someone wanting to find a mass audience, though technology like DVRs and alternative screens is disrupting what has been a very successful model. While the industry is trying to adapt, forecasting the next ten years is difficult.

The question then becomes how television can extend a property and what does television do differently from other media – what can television bring to a transmedia property?

First of all, it's important to remember that television is not a monolithic form. The medium contains both multiple formats and a wide variety of genres similar to those seen in film, novels and comics. Sometimes there is a direct relationship between television stories and other media, like the one that connects manga and anime or like *Heroes* which chooses to mimic a comic book volume while using comics for its story extensions. Television can also translate large-scale stories derived from a series of novels like *A Song of Ice and Fire* (George R. R. Martin, Bantam Books, 1996–present) and turn it into a multi-season event like *Game of Thrones* (HBO, 2011–present). Television is an excellent choice for story extension because of the variety of formats and genres that already exist as well as its innate nature to respond to audience and transform accordingly. It has gone through incredible changes particularly in the last 15 years, with an explosion of both content and technology that makes it an obvious partner in building a transmedia universe. Elements of transmedia storytelling and a wide variety of story extensions have been on television for a long time. Walt Disney saw this even as the industry was in its infancy.

One medium that has always had a close relationship with television is cinema. The feature film *Voyage to the Bottom of the Sea* (20th Century Fox, 1961) spawned a television series that in turn spawned novels, board games and toys (though obviously some of these are more transmedia marketing than transmedia storytelling). Sometimes the story's move from feature film to television has been quite direct like *M*A*S*H* (20th Century Fox, 1970) but other times it's been more indirect, such as shows inspired by another medium's property, like the *James Bond* films inspiring *Danger Man* (1960–1968, AKA *Secret Agent Man* in America).

As time has gone by, properties haven't just been pulled from film into television; some have gone the other direction, with television shows like *The Brady Bunch* (Paramount Pictures, 1995), *Dark Shadows* (Warner Brothers Pictures, 2012) or of course *Star Trek* becoming movies. There has always been a strong back and forth dynamic between film and television because of all the storytelling and production commonalities.

Games have had a different relationship. While we have such translations like bringing the *Mario Brothers* to a television variety show (the film was really no better) or making *Mortal Combat* into a weekly series, they have not yielded memorable results. Children-focused properties, typically animated, have however had a strong presence. Properties like *Yu-Gi-Oh* (various from 1998) and *Sonic the Hedgehog* (ABC, 1994–1995) have had extended and profitable runs on television, adding to both the story universe of the creators as well as to their pocketbook.

And television is where *Transformers* toys began telling stories, and it has since become a very financially successful property with multiple television series, films, games and many other elements.

Another relationship that should be noted is the relationship between the novel and what was once called miniseries but is now just thought of as short-form series. In the 1980s, *The Winds of War* (ABC, 1983), a blockbuster novel from the 1970s, came to the small screen (televisions were smaller back then and were referred to that way) with much pomp and circumstance, big stars (Robert Mitchum and Ali McGraw) and a huge production scope. It among many others like *Roots* (ABC, 1977) and *North and South* (ABC, 1985, 1986 and 1994) showed the potential for television to succeed telling these kinds of large-scale stories. Going the other way, the television miniseries *Holocaust* (NBC, 1978) was later adapted into a novel by the screenwriter. In fact novelizations of television series has been a normal part of the process since the early days, though adaptations are not really transmedia storytelling as much as transmedia delivery of the same story; novels become transmedia storytelling when they create new narratives that contribute to a larger over-arching story, such as *The Walking Dead* novel, *Rise of the Governor*

(St. Martin's Press, 2011). Television has always been a content crossroads where properties have come from and gone to as a result of television's story potential and availability of a mass audience. Historically, it is easy just to view television as an intellectual property consumer because television needs content. In fact, this is now truer than ever because of the thousand cable channels available in most homes. However, *Star Trek* is the shining example of how television has always been to some degree a place where content goes to live and expand because television needs more and more content. Television and transmedia have always had a very dynamic relationship with recent history demonstrating both the pitfalls and the potential.

Case Studies

The growth of transmedia storytelling based on recent television series is at best a mixed story; one-way to describe it would be the good, the mediocre and the ugly. The three examples that follow are all real attempts to stretch and create new forms of storytelling and engagement, to create that larger narrative that is the heart of a transmedia story. Each of these properties is ambitious but met with varying levels of success. Despite the shining example of *LOST*, there are few examples of intellectual properties that have been so ambitious as these three. It is interesting that few properties have been able to learn from and/or follow their example.

LOST

In 2003, J. J. Abrams, Jeffrey Lieber and Damon Lindelof began development of a show not designed to be transmedia from the very beginning but that would ultimately extend and define the transmedia conversation. The show was called *LOST* and premiered in September 2004.

The *LOST* pilot is often mentioned in the discussion of the best pilots ever made. At the time, the premiere created a huge splash, but the phenomenon that became *LOST* is not just about the plot and characters. The *LOST* plot in many ways is a premise we have seen before. The notion of people stranded on a desert island as a plot device is in no way unique, but the show's creators were able to set in motion in the pilot a set of strong and complex storylines and characters. More importantly, the viewers were thrown into an environment that was strange and mysterious. It seemed that every time the audience thought it had a handle on what was happening, some twist or revelation would send the narrative in a new direction. Whether they were on the island, off the island or at sea, the ongoing mystery generated an energized fan base along with the mass audience that made *LOST* a cultural touchstone during its run. The success of the show allowed narrative experimentation and extension that hadn't before been conceived and implemented with such success. The series' strong mythology, intense mystery based story lines, complex paradoxical characters and expansive storyworld fit perfectly into the development process of world building, although this term was not used by the creators at the time of development.

And while the transmedia successes, and there are many, of *LOST* were not premeditated, they did not simply stem from the success model of transmedia development but rather from a combination of technological breakthroughs in social media, gutsy risk taking by the show's writers and producers and mega-funding by ABC executives. Underlying this all was a keen awareness by the showrunners of the importance of the fan base. The commitment of the core audience surprised and encouraged the showrunners at many junctures to keep pushing the envelope. The combination spelled out transmedia success.

The characters form an ensemble cast. The main character, Jack, seems to be a classic hero, the emotionally injured brilliant surgeon who, immediately upon waking up from the crash, begins to shout orders and save lives. The ongoing story revealed, as it did with many characters, that he was complex, not always as he appeared to be and at best a flawed hero.

Like the other survivors of the crash of Oceanic Flight 815, Jack is challenged by not only the formidable super-natural and natural villains on the island but also by his own past, his love and lust for Kate, and his battle with rival Sawyer. Ultimately it is the leader of the others, Ben, who will be his greatest adversary … or ally. Mystery is everywhere, misleads abound and as soon as you think you know the answer *LOST* switches up the story on you, forcing audiences into a participatory stance, forcing them to seek answers outside the series, in transmedia extensions.

LOST is also one of the only shows in network history where main characters regularly disappeared and died. The people we cared about on the show were in constant danger on the island and the danger could come from anywhere, even from other survivors. This raised the suspense for the audience as their favorite character might end up shot and buried in the sand. Other constant threats, like the island itself, the smoke monster and the Others kept the millennial audience engaged.

The showrunners used a wide variety of storytelling techniques and eventually other media to define and then redefine the narrative, keeping the audiences off balance and engaged. Flashbacks were a storytelling device *LOST* used to transform the narrative. They serve a very specific purpose and are, in most seasons, a part of every episode. They reveal to us the lives of the main characters before the crash. And we find that the survivors of the crash all have deep secrets that they have chosen to keep from each other, but we, the audience, know the truth. So within the very structural motif of the show constant dramatic irony is obvious to the audience but not the characters. Whether it was Jack's relationship with his father or Locke's inability to walk, each flashback both revealed information about the character and would in many ways redefine the actions we were seeing on screen. Innate in dramatic irony is the idea of suspense, and by the audience knowing what is kept secret from characters in the story, we are always waiting for the characters to find out, always watching how the character with the secret lies or covers up what we know to be true. Including this as a framing device was part of the strong pull *LOST* had on its audience. So concerned were the *LOST* writers and producers with maintaining mystery that they developed a new form of storytelling. The unanswered question became the *LOST* signature.

LOST creates a hierarchy of mysteries punctuated by narrative gaps in the story, questions posed but either answered in a later episode, later in the season or in the case of *LOST*, never answered at all. These purposeful gaps in the story allow for enhanced mystery and suspense forcing the audience to wait, wonder and watch baited by intricately laid mysteries, puzzles, paradoxical characters and a deep evolving mythology. The *LOST* world is purposely telescopic. It starts off in Season 1 as almost myopic in scale. Stories take place on the beach and on brief treks inland, never revealing the complete island, keeping us lost, having to watch to earn a glimpse at what is to be revealed in the next episode. This expanding world is also indicative of expansive worlds in video games like *Baldur's Gate* (BioWare, 1998) and *Champions of Norrath: Realms of Everquest* (Sony Online Entertainment, 2004) where you only see the area of the world you are playing, until you reach a new level and slowly the storyworld, its geography, additional characters, mysteries and conflicts are revealed. This is the same with *LOST*'s storyworld that literally expands as seasons go by, introducing an ever-changing geography, complete with levels both above and below ground. And characters learn in this show much as we do in real life – they make mistakes and pay the price for it.

Mysteries, unanswered codes, puzzles and paradoxical characters became *LOST*'s calling card and *LOST* became synonymous with "mystery" and unanswered questions. This endeared the show to millennial seekers, the millennial demographic born into the Internet, social networking and mobile apps, and they remained loyal to the show through six seasons and many even remain loyal today. *LOST* understood the needs and habits of their "seeker" audience and gave them what they wanted via fictional to real experiences and a series of *LOST* branded alternate reality games.

The television world of *LOST* is deepened by its various transmedia extensions. Narrative gaps in the story provide organic opportunities to begin a story extension on the web, mobile phones or in alternate reality games that purposely intertwine the real world with the world of the series and that invite fans to participate at an unprecedented level in transmedia history.

If *LOST* can claim any first arrivals onto the transmedia scene after *24* had pioneered the modern television-based transmedia model, it is in the area of virtual to real communications. *LOST* created rich alternate reality game experiences that invited fans to participate in the *LOST* storyworld both virtually and to seek artifacts and storylines, clues and glyphs in the real world. Players were rewarded with answers to long-standing story questions, codes and character backstories. In short, the only way to fully understand the *LOST* storyworld was to have participated in the transmedia extension content, as some answers to series dwelling questions were only given there.

LOST was known to write in narrative gaps in the series and to begin or extend transmedia stories from those gaps. However, *LOST* is also known for using extension content to pose more questions without answering questions left open by gaps in the narratives.

LOST *List: Transmedia Extension Platforms*

1. **Novels:** The spinoff novels, based on the show, were panned by fans and critics alike. They focused on a character not seen on the series and neither his backstory nor present story had any impact on the show nor did the novels provide any answers.

2. **Forums:** Multiple fan forums appeared for *LOST* including a site called *LOSTpedia*. Here fans chatted about *LOST* and also had the rare experience of having the forums joined by *LOST* writers and producers. Some fan comments and ideas from these forums were actually used in the series. These gave a true participatory relationship between the series and the fans. This participatory relationship would be the cornerstone of the *LOST* brand of transmedia communications.

3. **Bad Twin:** Just another novel? Yes, but *Bad Twin* was a novel read by Sawyer on the series. Its writer, Guy Troop, had perished in the crash of Oceanic flight 815. The novel would cross over the threshold from fictional to real life, being sold on Amazon.com and becoming fourteenth on the New York Times Bestseller list – the first big transmedia extension success for the show.

4. **Mobisode/Webisode:** "Missing Pieces" was a series of short-form videos starring the main characters of *LOST* that delved into the backstory and motivations of the characters that the show didn't have time to. While not essential to the storytelling, it was canon and did enrich the viewing experience of the fans committed enough to find them.

5. **Video Game:** *Lost: Via Domus* was released for a variety of platforms in the first quarter of 2008, following the third season. *Via Domus* was the story of Elliott Maslow, a survivor of the plane crash whom we never saw in the television series though main characters as well as locations did appear in the game. The real issue was that the game wasn't integrated into the narrative in any real way. Neither a great game nor an extension of the narrative, it was greeted with a very tepid response.

6. **Mobile Game App:** A game app was developed for mobile phones and iPods in 2007. The game is played as the character Jack and involves simple gameplay and reflects the first two seasons of the show.

7. **ARGS:** One example is *The LOST Experience*, a complex alternate reality game that centered around the fictional Hanso Foundation, and its origins and purpose. A new character (Rachel Blake) was created for the alternate reality game who acted as the guide and even interrupted Damon Lindelof at Comic-Con in 2006 during his presentation. That event launched her *hansoexposed.com* website (now dormant) which was the gateway to the experience. Players helped Blake by playing through a series of virtual and real clues and mini-games housed on multiple faux websites like the Hanso Foundation's official website. Players were then rewarded with answers to questions that came directly from the show such as the meaning of "the numbers" and the original purpose of the Dharma Initiative in coming to the island. It has been stated by the producers that the *LOST Experience* is considered canon.

LOST *Goes from Fictional to Real*

Releasing *Bad Twin* in the real world was just one of many ways that the *LOST* audience experienced the story sliding easily from the fictional to a real experience. The novel itself included multiple artifacts that go from fictional world to real, further blurring the lines between *LOST* and life. These artifacts further connect the hardcore fan to ever deepening levels of branded information and pose additional questions adding to the *LOST* mythology. At the center of the mystery was always the fictitious Hanso Foundation, which even went to the extent of responding to allegations through a quarter-page ad run in several real major newspapers. The ad denounces *Bad Twin* for its "attacks" and "misinformation" about the Hanso Foundation. The Hanso Foundation website also produced a press release that was equally critical of *Bad Twin*. The novel became the prototype for creating the fictional-to-real relationship between content and audience that would be later exploited via alternate reality games.

To look back at *LOST* and get a clear picture of the impact on the culture even a few years removed is still difficult. The explanation of the success can be attributed to the skill of the producers or the fine group of actors or the moment in time that allowed the Internet to implant the narrative deep into the culture. The answer is most likely all of the above, but the journey of the show and the universe that was created is by far the most successful example of transmedia storytelling in the Internet age.

Heroes

Heroes was a series created by Tim Kring that ran on NBC for four seasons starting in 2006. The series tells the stories of ordinary people who discover superhuman abilities, and how these abilities transform the characters' lives. The series reflected a comic book aesthetic often seen in superhero stories, including using both short and long arc storytelling techniques used in comics. Getting off to a strong start, the premiere made a splash and looked to be another property like *LOST* that was going to be a both a mass audience success as well as generating a devoted fan base. Right from the start Kring imagined the series as having other storytelling components including a digital-internet extension of the series, *Heroes 360 Experience*, later called *Heroes Evolution*. *Heroes Evolution* was created to explore the mythology of the characters as well as expand the universe to include new characters and storylines. As you would imagine what followed was a plethora of other elements like action figures, comics and a novel.

Heroes started with so much promise but steadily lost its mainstream audience throughout its run. Both critics and fans alike felt that the show never regained the pace and energy of the first season. The passage of time has also made it clear that a lack of focus on the mothership, on the centrality of the television series, may have helped with the show's declining popularity. New characters were introduced, brought over from the web existences and dropped into the plotline. The larger audience wondered where all this was coming from, with the hardcore fans expressing their frustration with the disappearance of the characters they cared for. This may have been a case of too many elements being pushed at once and diluting or dissipating the property rather than enriching it; potentially a simple answer of too much too soon, with the property's expansion far outstripping its foundation.

Push, Nevada

Push Nevada was short-lived ABC series from fall of 2002 that had a difference. A mystery show that followed an IRS agent's investigation, it offered layer upon layer of mysterious corporations and shady characters, but beneath it all there was a real life mystery involving the hunt for over a million dollars in prize money. Viewers were pointed toward clues through websites and hints dropped by characters in the course of the show. While clearly an interesting concept tying the fictional mystery to a real life mystery, the audience was clearly not ready. Whether it was the story itself or the use of the web at a time when a mass audience wasn't ready for that, the show never got a foothold and was canceled after seven episodes. The irony of course is the prize aspect of the series had to continue due to regulations, and the million dollars was awarded two weeks after the show last aired with a final clue given during an airing of Monday Night Football.

While failures always hold a certain interest, what is most interesting is that many of the aspects of the show should have worked. Mystery shows have always had a place on the prime time schedule and competition shows have become a fixture in primetime, so what's not to like about a show that combines the two? While it might be too easy just to criticize the show from a storytelling perspective, the more interesting point for this book is that the approach might have been too early and out of sync with the culture. Technology is always a double-edged sword, and what can engage one audience can, at a different time become an obstacle to another audience. *Push, Nevada's* failure raises many issues both about technology and how you launch a property into the culture.

Why Aren't We All LOST*?*

Since *LOST* went off the air in 2010 and even during the second half of its run, several high concept shows that could support transmedia storytelling have hit the air. While we have seen some half-hearted attempts to build a complex universe, none of those shows has really stuck around. Part of the issue has been tied to the industry's attitude toward genre storytelling, as one year you see a number of shows that are a likely candidate for the kind of world expansion we've been talking about and the next year, none. There seems to be an increased attention to small stuff, what can be characterized as the DVD extras mentality, of giving the audience the behind the scenes glimpses and character background information without really trying to expand the narrative. So what happened? The industry after some initial success and a few sharp punches in the face no longer knows where or how to begin.

The discussion really is one of chicken or egg. Do you have the big vision from the start and plan the grand rollout or do you get the opportunity through the big success? Television has up to this point really been more based on the opportunities that success gives you. As the technology improves and with it the possibility of really making money tied to a larger narrative universe, the question of return on investment could change and finally change the conversation.

Strangely enough it is possible that *LOST* arrived in a sweet spot where enough people had the interest and perhaps ironically it was easier to get made because fewer people at the network understood it. The bottom line is that there have been too many failures of shows that really afforded the opportunity for expanded storytelling and the networks didn't reach the tipping point to really commit resources. At the same time, the cable networks have experimented with a variety of add-on material like web comics and web-based gaming but these have rarely been of any scale and have been more for marketing purposes than intended as canon. While it is too easy to just declare a lack of vision by both creators and the industry, mass audience interest (or demand) and adoption of new technologies should afford some changes in the next five years. Television and transmedia should get another real go at it in the next few years. In the meantime…

A Modest Proposal … A Transmedia Network

We've talked about how transmedia storytelling properties can extend a story universe or world across multiple platforms. We've also noted that spinoff television series often seem to have a shared world, but that it's really one of narrative convenience in that the connection seems to exist only for the obligatory sweeps weeks crossover. *NCIS* and *NCIS: Los Angeles* on CBS has an interesting distinction in that the character of NCIS Director Vance (played by Rocky Carroll) appears on both programs somewhat regularly, or is at least referred to regularly. This serves to connect the two series, but other than crossovers that seems to be the extent of their shared world.

But what if you could do more than that?

Let's take the idea of transmedia storytelling in a different direction and propose something as a creative and intellectual exercise. Let's think big: What if all of the dramatic television series on a single network existed within the same story universe?

What if there was something called the CBS Dramatic Universe, and it had under its umbrella all of the dramatic television series that take place in the modern day and were on the air at the start of, or as part of CBS Television's 2012–2013 season? That list would look like this:

Blue Bloods
Criminal Minds
CSI: Crime Scene Investigation
CSI: NY
Elementary
The Good Wife
Hawaii Five-0
Made in Jersey
The Mentalist
NCIS
NCIS: Los Angeles
Person of Interest

Let's be clear about this – all of the television series listed above would co-exist within the same shared story universe. They would be unique (or semi-shared) storyworlds, but they would all effectively exist within the same universe. Is this possible?

The CBS Dramatic Universe – Possible?

If we look at the proposed CBS Dramatic Universe in terms of our key transmedia story elements we can get a sense of the possibility.

Story/Theme: This isn't really a concern, except that inclusion of all of these programs requires an adherence to stories that occur in the real world. No supernatural, paranormal, fantasy, science fiction, or any crazy stuff like that. CBS has had television series like that – *Ghost Whisperer* (2005–2010) or *A Gifted Man* (2011–2012) spring to mind – but there are none currently on the air. Each of the shows in the CBS Dramatic Universe would maintain their own story and thematic content.

Plot: Except where crossovers occur, either in terms of characters or reference to events, this area isn't a concern either. In fact, one could argue an improvement: *NCIS: Los Angeles* needs a consultation on the personality of a suspect (since they wrote out Nate Getz), bring up Dr. Spencer Reid (Matthew Gray Gubler) from *Criminal Minds* on the video conference system. Specific crossovers of characters or reference to events would obviously have to be choreographed.

Characters: We'll hit style and tone in a moment, but since those match there's really no reason any of the characters from any of the CBS dramatic series couldn't all exist in the same world. They might not all get along, but they could exist in the same world.

Setting: Done and done. Real world, or as real as it gets for television. Just in terms of narrative logistics, five series of the 12 occur in New York City (*Blue Bloods*, *CSI: NY*, *Elementary*, *Made In Jersey* and *Person of Interest*), two in the Washington DC area (*NCIS* and *Criminal Minds*, though those guys have their own jet …), two occur relatively proximate in California (*NCIS: Los Angeles* and *The Mentalist*) and the rest occur in scattered locales – *CSI* (Las Vegas), *The Good Wife* (Chicago) and *Hawaii Five-0* (Hawaii). How cool would it be if Tom Selleck was the Police Commissioner on both *Blue Bloods* and *CSI: NY*?

Style/Tone: Interestingly, dramatic shows on CBS all seem to have basically the same style and tone. We can only assume this is a conscious decision on the part of CBS Television. We haven't seen *Made In Jersey* yet, but it is supposed to be very much like *The Good Wife*, nor have we seen *Elementary*, but it seems like a tonal match for *The Mentalist*, which is to say light drama with heavy touches. So, from a style and tone standpoint all the shows seem pretty compatible. Are there differences? Of course, especially in terms of certain aspects of production design (compare the police stations in *Blue Bloods*, *CSI: NY* and *Person of Interest*, for example).

So in terms of those shared elements it seems very possible. The main problem, as it often is, would be narrative planning and logistics.

Making It All Work Together

Since all of these television shows are on the same network, and we assume the network has bought into the plan, there's no issue there. Most of these shows, however, come from different production companies working with CBS Television Studios to produce the series. Therein lies the main problem – coordinating vision, discussion, and implementation across multiple production companies with different shooting schedules and production realities.

It could still be done, however. Make all the showrunners for the programs part of the CBS Dramatic Universe Council who meet once a year prior to the start of the production season to talk about their ideas for the upcoming season and exchange ideas for possible crossovers and integration of story, plot, and characters. Each showrunner takes that information back to the writers of their own show to chew on as they break the upcoming season of their series.

As the writers for each television series generate ideas and possibilities, they communicate with the other shows through a coordinator/facilitator at CBS Television who helps track the information and maintain the lines of communication. The coordinator/facilitator can also act as a production liaison between the various production companies when it comes time to coordinating schedule and budgetary issues related to the cross-integration. Maybe CBS Television is willing to throw in a little extra money here and there to help make things possible.

Each show retains full creative control over the content of their series with full veto power, but by participating in the CBS Dramatic Universe they have the opportunity to open up new story, character, and cross-marketing/promotional opportunities.

> Think of the marketing and cross-promotional opportunities.
> Think of the storytelling possibilities …
> Hey, CBS? Think about it.

Interview: Carlton Cuse

Figure 5.1.1 *Carlton Cuse.*

Writer and executive producer Carlton Cuse grew up in Boston, Massachusetts and Orange County, California. He attended Harvard University, graduating with a degree in American History.

With Jeffrey Boam, Cuse developed the story and screenplays for *Lethal Weapon 2*, *Lethal Weapon 3* and *Indiana Jones and the Last Crusade*.

In television, Cuse began his writing career on the Michael Mann series *Crime Story*. He co-created and executive produced the critically acclaimed Fox series *The Adventures of Brisco County, Jr.* He created and executive produced all six seasons of the CBS show *Nash Bridges* starring Don Johnson. He also created and executive produced the CBS series *Martial Law*.

Cuse, along with Damon Lindelof, served as the showrunner, executive producer and head writer for all six seasons of *LOST* on ABC.

In addition to overseeing the network show, Cuse also pioneered the development of the first transmedia content for network television series.

Cuse has received ten Emmy Nominations for his work and has won two Emmys: one for Best Drama Series and the other for Outstanding Achievement in Interactive Media.

Among his other honors, Cuse has won a Peabody Award, a Golden Globe, the Jules Verne Award, four Saturn Awards, and a Writers Guild Award. In 2010, Cuse was named in *TIME* magazine's annual list of the 100 most influential people in the World.

Cuse is currently producing a reimagining of the *Psycho* franchise for NBC Universal Television and A&E Cable for 2013.

Carlton Cuse was interviewed by the authors in the spring of 2012 specifically for this book.

Interviewer(s): What was the first thing you thought of when you saw that original idea for *LOST*? What crossed your mind?

Carlton Cuse: I'm sure you know the story or read the story. I had given Damon (Lindelof) his first job on the show on *Nash Bridges*. J. J. Abrams and Damon had made the pilot and it was pretty clear that J. J. (Abrams) was going to be moving on to direct *Mission Impossible 3*. Damon had no experience showrunning, so he started calling me. We had this standing appointment at night, and I would sort of give him advice about how to keep things running. In the meantime, he sent me the rough cut of the pilot and some of the first few scripts, and I just got really activated by that. I really felt like there was something special there. It got inside my brain in a way, and I just couldn't stop thinking about it. Damon asked me if there was any way I could come and be the showrunner. I was under a deal at another studio at the time. It was just one of those moments where you make a decision based on passion and on belief. I really felt this strong connection with the material, and I found myself thinking about it all the time. I was fortunate to be able to get out of my deal with the other studio, and I came over for less money and got involved with *LOST*. At the time I think there were only two people that believed that *LOST* could be successful as an ongoing series. One was Lloyd Braun, who had been fired, and myself. Damon was exhausted and really didn't want to do the show and I said, well look it's just going to be 12 episodes; we'll just make the 12 coolest episodes for television that we can and that'll be it. Of course the pilot ratings came out and it turned out to be something else entirely. And then we started really having to cook the mythology. The first year of any show is like putting out a fire with a garden hose, so we weren't able to really deal with a lot of the mythology in great depth until we finished writing the first season of the show. And then we sat down and started contemplating it in much greater detail. The analogy that I've always used as a showrunner is that making a show is like building an iceberg. You have to construct the entire iceberg but 80% of it ends up below the water line. In the case of *LOST*, opportunities arose, for the first time in my career where we saw that there was a way to actually take some of that material that was below the waterline and put it out there for the committed fans. *LOST* came along at just the right moment in the evolution of new media, so we had opportunities to do things and pioneer things that no one had done before. And our show, with its mysteries and intentional ambiguity, was exactly the right show to engage audiences on these newly evolving platforms.

Interviewer(s): One of the phrases we toss around all the time is building a universe. That's not necessarily a TV notion; it could be a game play notion. But did you think about it that way? You've described it but did your mind go to, I'm creating this other universe that has different rules and different meaning and all the things that go into other worlds?

Carlton Cuse: I don't know that I thought about it exactly that way. I think that as you move forward in any creative endeavor, your creative vision keeps evolving and expanding. The more time I spent immersed in the world of the show, the more that world emerged with more clarity. It's not necessarily a conscious process, but it's one that occurs when you fully immerse yourself in something as a storyteller. I certainly know that I spent a good portion of my waking hours thinking about *LOST* and even some of my sleeping hours. I lived probably more in the world of *LOST* than I did in the world of my own life. In terms of hours spent in a given week, we would put in easily 60 to 80 hours a week on the show. When you're living in that world, that's the world you think about. As a result more pieces of the puzzle emerge.

Interviewer(s): Why did *LOST* turn out so uniquely? It seems many have now tried and so few have succeeded …

Carlton Cuse: It wasn't a cold calculated idea to create a brand; it just emerged naturally and organically from telling the primary story. We really benefited from the support of Mike Benson and Marla Provencio, who were the heads of marketing at ABC. They recognized that *LOST* was a unique show and therefore needed to be marketed in a unique way. The marketing had to be a reflection of the fact that the show was so different, and it gave them license to spend money on things that were non-traditional. Also, *LOST* didn't need to be marketed conventionally. They were able to divert resources to allow us to experiment and push the envelope to do things that no one had ever done before. For me, I felt like we had an incredible opportunity to be pioneers. It was fun because we didn't really know what we were getting into or where we were going. I thought a lot about the metaphor of pioneers heading out across the Great Plains and pushing out beyond civilized society, really knowing what we were going to find, whether it be a river or a mountain or a tribe of Indians. We sort of encountered the metaphoric equivalent of all those things and learned a lot of lessons along the way. Over time, we became much more sophisticated about how we approached our transmedia. It just was this incredible opportunity. We knew we had this audience that was incredibly hungry for more material, and at the same time we were always incredibly conscientious about not crushing the audience's soul with dense mythology. Now that may sound funny because people might actually think that was exactly what the show did, but it could have been much worse. For instance, we made a very conscious decision that stuff like the Valenzetti equation, or the relationship between the Dharma Initiative and the Hanso Foundation were mythological backstory items that were just way too esoteric to be in the mothership – the network show. But these other media platforms that had suddenly emerged created an opportunity for us to talk to the hardcore audience who definitely wanted to know what the relationship was between Thomas Mittelwerk and Alvar Hanso or how the Dharma initiative got financed. The first lesson we learned was that transmedia storytelling provides an opportunity to tell different types of stories than we wanted to tell on the main network show. From very early on we referred to the show as the mothership. Our primary focus was on taking care of the mothership. We also made a fundamental decision early on that proved incredibly important which was this – none of this additional content was essential to the story of the show. The only thing you had to do was watch the mothership. We just thought it was way too frustrating and demanding to make any of the additional content essential to the overall story of *LOST*. We wanted this new transmedia content to be additive but not critical. *The Matrix* made that mistake, making information in the videogame essential to your fundamental understanding of their overall story.

Interviewer(s): Talking about that exact problem, *The Matrix* had these characters on screen, and they go off to do something important, but the movie doesn't show you the important thing that they do, so suddenly it's unimportant. And there's no explanation for it unless you play the video game; you don't know who this character is.

Carlton Cuse: I think we went through a lot of struggles to try to comprehend exactly what the audience on the Internet wanted. And I think we made the right call in not forcing the main audience seek out our transmedia content to understand what was going on in the show. At first we vastly underestimated what Clay Shirky would call "cognitive surplus" of the audience. We designed our first ARG thinking that it would stretch out for many months and people would have all these clues and puzzles to solve. But the audience was so engaged and when they pooled their collective intelligence, the audience blasted through everything that we had created in hours. We quickly realized the burn rate for additional content was going to be much, much higher that we ever thought. The first ARG we did was also complicated by the fact that

Mike Benson tried to rope all these advertisers into sponsoring various parts of it, and that created all sorts of complications. Each advertiser had different requirements and criteria about how they wanted to manage their piece of it, which made it very hard to make the experience cohesive. We were operating by trial and error because we were the first guys out of the box. For example, we put an advertisement on the network show for the Hanso Foundation, this little 15-second advertisement directing people to the Hanso Foundation website. We got 34 million hits, but we didn't have anywhere to take the audience. We ran them into a pipe that was narrow and uninteresting. We channeled people into this ARG that was way too esoteric and frustrating and complex, and there wasn't a good payoff or enough interesting material. A very small percentage of people, I don't know what the exact numbers were, trickled down to the end of that experience. We learned that these ARGs needed to be managed differently in the future. While the overall ARG didn't work that well, it was extremely cool to blur the lines between fiction and reality, whether it was taking out an ad in the *New York Times* for the Hanso Foundation or putting on a character from the Hanso Foundation on the Jimmy Kimmel show, which has to be the most bizarre thing that's happened on a TV talk show ever. We had an actor playing a very obscure character from the deep mythology of the show being interviewed on ABC by Jimmy Kimmel as though he was a real guy.

Interviewer(s): In the process of prepping for this conversation that trying to find the pieces out in the world was a challenge because it's the web and a lot of the pieces are gone. You can find some of them through archive.org but a lot of the stuff is just, is disappeared. I mean it's written about but the media itself … does that make you feel *LOST* will last forever in its box-sets, and some of this other stuff … it's only been ten years ago and it's disappeared. Given that, the mobisodes, the webisodes, the conception there, what was the goal all along?

Carlton Cuse: I think ABC recognized that there was this incredible demand for additional material, so they approached us to do this really early on. We took a very hard line in that we would not do them non-union. We didn't want to get involved in making cheap, B-quality mobisodes featuring no-name characters. We said if we do this we want to do it with our A-talent meaning our A-actors, our A-writers and our A-directors and they were like, "Well there's no rules that have been written about this since it's brand new. You can do this, but we're not covering it." And we're like, "Well, we're not doing it." And we held the line. And there was about a year stalemate, and then finally Mark Pedowitz who was the head of ABC Studios was the force who broke through the log jam. At a certain point it was more valuable for them to have the mobisodes than it was to hold to this non-union line. Pedowitz went out and negotiated the first deal with the all the talent guilds to cover content for new media. So then we had to make them. We decided since they were originally designed for mobile phones that the viewing experiences were going to be very intimate. So we were thinking of the mobisodes as sort of diary entries. This was not the place to do action sequences but to do intimate moments. Then we came up with this idea that we would do scenes that were suggested by the show that we never saw, that we'd never seen. Maybe that would be fun for an audience to see those "missing" scenes. We didn't consider any of the scenes essential enough to put them in the mothership. We split the writing of them up among the writing staff, and most of our actors agreed to do them. Our main directors Jack Bender and Steven Williams directed them, and so they were made with the same quality and care as the regular show. Again, we approached this with the idea that we had additional content to give to viewers who wanted more. We thought a lot about how there's a sense of ownership that happens when you discover something first, or you know more about something than the average viewer. I remember going to an Adele show way before she was famous, and so now I feel very proprietary about Adele. I saw Springsteen early in his career.

Interviewer(s): You lived in New Jersey, though.

Carlton Cuse: No, but I saw him there. We felt, like seeing a band early, we should reward the most loyal viewers by giving them more information. This special additional content would deepen their bond with the series. We felt we were giving the really devoted audience some extra love.

Interviewer(s): How did you feel? Do you remember the first time you started seeing fan generated websites and information?

Carlton Cuse: I don't remember the exact moment. But it became apparent in the middle of the first season that the show had activated people on a level that we did not expect. When we started out' we felt that we could be bold because failure wasn't something we feared. We thought in the worst-case scenario; there would be 12 episodes of *LOST* and it would be like *The Prisoner* or *Twin Peaks*. One was 17 episodes and the other was 30 episodes. We thought it would be cool if the 12 episodes of *LOST* ended up on a DVD that people would pass around hand to hand and go, "Hey, have you ever seen this show *LOST?*" As we got deeper into the first season we realized, oh my god, fans are really getting into it. They are starting all sorts of discussion groups. Initially there was this fan site called the Fuselage that was somewhat organized by us. That was sort of the inside club. That was really the first place fans would gather. You could go on the Fuselage and see what the reaction was to episodes, and there started to be this whole social discussion. I think the first profound moment of realization came at the end of the first season when the organizers of the Fuselage had a party at the Hollywood Renaissance Hotel, inviting all these people on the Fuselage to come together and meet some of the actors and writers. I remember showing up and what was really interesting was the fans were moderately interested in meeting the actors. They were more interested in meeting the writers, which was kind of shocking, but what they were most interested in doing was meeting each other. There were these incredible reunion moments where "Jbird243" would run across the room and hug "Hurleylover12." They were so ecstatic to meet each other. The profoundness of the community that had developed around the show struck me hard for the first time.

Interviewer(s): I always thought the whole Drive Shaft thing was fabulous. Finding for example, a blog of the Scandinavian tour of Drive Shaft – it's not just fans getting together, but its fans extending the mythology, extending the story. Did that bother you? Did things have to be canon? Did things have to come from the mothership? Were you comfortable with people taking the pieces and running with it?

Carlton Cuse: We were never bothered by it. I think that we were actually flattered by it. But the Walt Disney Company had a slightly different view because they were trying to protect their copyright and had a methodology that was rooted in a different technological age. This is a huge problem that's going on right now, right? What you have is a set of laws that govern how people can treat copyrighted material, and it seems to be very much at odds with what the social culture is and what the people want to do, which is to take that material, create new things with it, then share these creations. So, for instance, in the show we wanted to have a contest where people could cut promos for *LOST.* Disney was really concerned about granting open access to their IP and letting people take it and put it together however they wanted. They didn't want to establish that precedent. Finally they agreed to release a specific number of clips and allowed the audience to assemble those. But they could not stop the torrent of fan created *LOST* material. People started creating their own *LOST* mash-ups; they started reorganizing stuff in the show to make it look like a sit-com or whatever. They would come up with funny music videos. It was really inspiring to see how people were so taken with the show that it motivated them to do something artistic. It became really a big factor for us as we started thinking about our final ARG, Dharma Wants You [.com]. At the core the idea was to engage the audience and allow them the room to form their own community. Fans on the Internet created *LOST*pedia which was an exhaustive encyclopedia of everything LOST. We didn't have anything to do with it. *LOST*pedia was an example of people working collectively for the greater good of the *LOST* community by aggregating information. So when we started doing Dharma Wants You, the idea was to set up a framework for people to engage, create, and interact, and then we kind of got out of the way. For Dharma Wants You we just allowed people to register as members of the Dharma Initiative, and we got 400,000 people to sign up. They self-selected themselves as members of the Dharma community. The lowest echelon job was to be a workman, and the highest echelon job was to be an Dharma instructor. The prized possession of the ARG was to get a Dharma Instructor T-shirt. There were literally people who were like, "I'll be a Dharma Chemist, and I'll write a test for people to be a Dharma Chemist." We also started *LOST* University. We had a physicist named Sean Carroll who teaches time travel at CalTech. He gives a course every year for 22 people on time travel. He ended up teaching this course in *LOST* University on time travel and 60,000 people took the class. This whole idea that we got everyone to join, to create virtual communities of people who participate in the world of the show – in these cases either as a member of the Dharma Initiative or as a student at *LOST* University. We won an Emmy for best achievement in Interactive media for these projects. In the future other people will do more substantial things with this, but it showed the possibilities of involving the audience in the narrative experience. It was a step on the journey, by no means an endpoint.

Interviewer(s): I ask you then, speaking of time travel, if we were launching *LOST* today, could you even imagine what you'd be cooking up? More importantly, what would you imagine out of the box if you launched *LOST* today?

Carlton Cuse: I think the primary lesson learned is you have to focus on the mothership, and you can't be too calculating about it. The mothership has got to be good or nobody gives a damn about the ancillary content. That's rule number one. In the evolution of my career, the first show I created was *The Adventures of Brisco County Jr*. I was the showrunner. I oversaw the TV show. That was it. By the time *LOST* came along I was a brand manager. Damon and I were overseeing a multiplicity of products that were sort of coming out under their *LOST* banner. Some of these we spent fairly little time on, some we spent way too much time on, but the one thing we tried to do was never lose sight of the fact that if the mothership sucked, none of this other stuff mattered. If I was starting a new show in this new media era, I'd be primarily focused on the creation of the world of the show and telling the narrative of the mothership, but I'd also be very conscious of collecting all the narrative threads that could be used to do ancillary storytelling. The problem is, as a showrunner, there is a limited number of hours in the day and there's already almost a decathlon-like level of things that you have to do in a given day, whether it's casting, editing, managing the network, overseeing production, budgets, not to mention creating the stories and scripts for the show. Then you start adding in making extra content for mobile phones or ARGs or the Internet, or a second-screen viewing experience. All of those things are interesting to do, but it takes a lot of time and thought. Traditional television is a two-dimensional art form. You're telling a narrative, but you're telling a linear narrative on one plane. With the addition of transmedia, being a storyteller and television become vastly more complicated. It's a two-way three-dimensional experience.

Interviewer(s): It's kind of an amazing thing to think about the possibilities, given how the technology has just exploded and blossomed.

Carlton Cuse: I feel like in many ways the technology is ahead of the storytelling. It's certainly ahead of the companies that produce the biggest and most expensive content. They are slow to create content. In the case of *LOST*, two showrunners who were really interested in doing this stuff plus two executives at the network who really had our backs made all the stuff happen. We were really excited about doing transmedia before the word "transmedia" was even in the lexicon. In the future, other people will pioneer different applications for new media based on personal interest. Some other showrunners maybe will decide that doing an animated graphic novel is absolutely the perfect thing for them to do. Or someone will come along and say, "I really want to produce a two-screen experience and I'm really a visual, so I want to make sure that if you're sitting and watching the show you can hold up your iPad, revolve it around the room and see other parts of the set that I'm not showing you on the main screen." There are all these cool ideas that I think you can just come up with, right? It's just a question of finding people within the company who want to give you the financial support to do them. Another lesson we learned was that you have to find good outside partners. We ended up partnering with this company called Hoodlum out of Australia just because they had done some interesting ancillary content for some British shows. Mike Benson found them, and they were really good because basically Damon and I were able to do all the creative conceptualizing, and they did the execution. That was a really huge factor, because we didn't have the resources within *LOST* to be doing that. Everyone who was working on *LOST* had a job and that job was to make the mothership. We didn't have people hired to produce transmedia. We took the time to creatively generate the content, and Hoodlum went off and actually executed it. They executed our vision for the whole ARG that led into the discovery of the Oceanic 815 at the bottom of the ocean.

Interviewer(s): What you point out is, getting it right is an aligning of all these factors. I hate to use the word random, but it feels like things just have to fall into place.

Carlton Cuse: They absolutely do. The video game is a prime example. ABC made a deal with Ubisoft to do the video game, and we never really found sufficient common ground with the video game people, and the game wasn't ideal. They had a platform, and they wanted to build it on that platform, and that platform had certain limitations about what the game could be and couldn't be. They were French-Canadian, and they would come down from Montreal and tape the meetings and sometimes it was hard to understand each other. They were smart people; they were just the wrong partners. We didn't have the same creative aesthetic about how to do the game. I remember actually taking the video game home and giving it to my kids to play. After about 20 minutes they were bored and didn't want to play it anymore; it was really frustrating. It was exactly the thing that we didn't want to happen. Damon and I were concerned about protecting the brand. We wanted to make sure that everything that came out under the *LOST* moniker met some kind of standard. We cared about the brand, and we wanted people to be able to trust the brand. We didn't feel like the video game was anywhere as good as it could have been.

Interviewer(s): Something that comes up again and again and again is the fact that the successful properties typically seem to be genre properties. You know, science fiction, detective, supernatural. Why are genre narratives seemingly more fertile ground for this material?

Carlton Cuse: That is a really good question for which I don't have a good answer. I mean genre fans just tend to be incredibly passionate about their stuff. I don't know exactly why that is, but it clearly is the case. Shows like *Battlestar* or *LOST*, the fan bases on these shows are engaged on a level that you don't get with *CSI Miami*. I mean *CSI Miami* is actually a more successful show world wide on a ratings basis and is enormously financially successful for CBS, but people are not just as passionate about it as they are about *LOST*. The one stab I can take at answering has less to do with genre and more to do with serialized storytelling. Serialized storytelling is more immersive and therefore feels more real. If you watch an episode of *CSI* and somebody puts a gun to David Caruso's head, whether you think about it or not, you instinctively know that David Caruso is going to survive. He'll be back next week to take his sunglasses off and make some quip. But in *LOST* you didn't feel that sense of security. This is one of the reasons why we killed off major characters periodically. We wanted the audience to fully believe that the jeopardy was real. I think that immersion hour after hour in a serialized show pulls the viewers into the world of the show and creates a deep association. There is something about that sustained serialized experience that is so much more immersive. As a storyteller in a traditional closed end show, like *Law and Order*, you go from A to C each episode, then you reset to A. Whereas in *LOST* you were on one big epic journey from A to Z.

Interviewer(s): What other transmedia properties do you like? Do you watch? You know now that you've got through this journey, whose stuff do you like?

Carlton Cuse: Honestly, I think that Nike is kind of king of the hill in many ways. They put out a video of LeBron when he left Cleveland to go to Miami, They made the video from his point of view of what the experience was like of being torn apart by public opinion and still wanting to play basketball that was really artful. That kind of thing is an advertisement, but it was clearly a story, and millions of people went and checked that out. Nike does an incredible job of storytelling in support of their brand. I think that Heineken is emerging as another company that is really seeing the advantage of viral storytelling. They have the ads of the guy roaming through the party having crazy Circ de Soleil-like encounters with people. It got something like 4.5 million hits on YouTube. Four-point-five million people voluntarily went to see an advertisement. Great narrative storytelling in service of a brand creates a feeling of association with that brand. I think those guys are pretty smart about what they are doing. People in advertising may be pushing the envelope more than in traditional media. I'm a fan of *The Office*, and I think that *The Office* has done a really good job of providing additional content; I think their mobisodes are really good. They do a good job of supporting an audience's interest in some of the minor characters. Don't you want to see what some of the characters are up to who don't get a lot of screen time?

Interviewer(s): So what is the future of *LOST*? You've got to think that it's got to go away for a while again before we see a reboot of some kind?

Carlton Cuse: Damon and I've talked about this. I mean look, *LOST* is a billion dollar franchise for the Walt Disney Company, so at some point they are going to want to make something under the moniker of *LOST*. Maybe it requires someone coming in and doing a Christopher Nolan-like reinterpretation of the *LOST* world. Maybe Disney will find an artist who takes whatever it is that fascinates her or him about the world we created and then turns it into something all their own.

Interviewer(s): Do you think that anyone has followed in the trail that *LOST* blazed in terms of using all the different media to tell the story?

Carlton Cuse: Not that much, no. First of all, I think we live in an environment where it's very hard to aggregate the resources to make a show on the scale that *LOST* was made, so there are fewer opportunities to do that. It doesn't seem like anyone has aligned the full array of media tools to exploit a television series across all platforms. I'm not quite sure why that is – maybe there just hasn't been the right idea. *LOST* was kind of the right idea at the right time. I don't think that all the ancillary transmedia works with every kind of show. I also think that you have to find a showrunner who is interested in doing it. Beyond that, the traditional media companies haven't made the creation of transmedia a priority. They haven't figured out how to monetize it. Things that matter to them are things they can monetize. So you really have to have a showrunner who is driven to do this kind of storytelling, who is also capable of convincing a media company that it's going to help promote the show, broaden the audience for the show and hopefully increase revenue. There are just not a lot of people that are pursuing those goals. It happens more in big movies. *Star Trek* is an example where that's also happening. I think the movie studios are further evolved in terms of understanding that to promote a movie and to build audience awareness in this age requires kind of attacking on all fronts, including all sorts of different media platforms.

Interviewer(s): In a way a television show's timeframe and cultural impact is better for this big transmedia storytelling; feature films are functionally events, right?

Carlton Cuse: Right.

Interviewer(s): So it doesn't really allow you to easily contain a lot of broad momentum for a property.

Carlton Cuse: You're right, in terms of sustaining the property or continuing its life, it's a little bit harder in movies. They are attacking it from the point of view of transmedia as promotion. I feel like we are still in the very early days of this. It hasn't been fully figured out yet.

Interviewer(s): Looking back at *LOST* and all the other stuff you did, do you have a favorite?

Carlton Cuse: In terms of favorite things, for me, I really enjoyed the whole Dharma Wants You ARG. That was a lot of fun. We had all these ideas to shoot videos and make it a lot more elaborate in terms of the content we pushed to the fans. But due to the financial crisis we were given a lot fewer resources. The simpler version was to not push a lot of content to participants, but instead allow them to organize and take control of the experience, and that turned out to be a lot better. It was an interesting learning experience. The fans started self-organizing into these various categories of Dharma types. It was a sign that pointed to the future for me. We live in a time where people don't just want to consume; they want to create and share. Clay Shirkey has done great work theorizing about this. People are looking for ways to be part of communities and will altruistically contribute to those communities. The construction of Wikipedia[.com] is the grandest sort of group collaborative effort that's come out of the Internet. In our show, *LOST*pedia is probably the greatest transmedia accomplishment because that was completely self-organized; it became an absolutely invaluable resource for anyone who wanted to know anything about *LOST*. And we didn't have anything to do with it. It was completely put together by the fans, for the fans. I think there are more than 7,000 entries. It's mindboggling. I think that my goal in transmedia is to try to come up with ideas which will allow people to participate in the creation of ancillary content. But I think that people want to do more than just passively take in content. If they are moved by your show, they want the opportunity to express themselves. The challenge is going to be to create whole new experiences that allow the people who are watching the show to themselves be part of the show's larger creative ecosphere.

Interviewer(s): And now you have the tools to do it.

Carlton Cuse: Exactly.

Interviewer(s): That's really what's happened in the seven intervening years; think of what you would have done with Tumblr[.com], Twitter[.com] and any number of technologies.

Carlton Cuse: Absolutely. There is a guy named C. J. Wilson who is a pitcher for the California Angels. He tracked me down on Twitter. He was a big fan of *LOST*, and he was Tweeting about

LOST. Then I started direct messaging him and solicited him and said, "Why don't you come up and play a whiffle ball game on the Disney lot, and if you throw the ball by us you get to ask a *LOST* question and if we get a hit, we get to ask baseball questions." And it turned into three videos we used as part of our transmedia package. Twitter actually led to content creation with a celebrity who was a *LOST* fan, so that kind of interactivity at the most basic level can lead to great things. We have some amazing fan created *LOST* artwork.

Interviewer(s): I've seen some of those.

Carlton Cuse: There's this guy named Jensen Karp who is a gallery owner, and he knows all these graphic artists, and he solicited all these artists to kind of create *LOST* inspired artwork, with Disney's permission, of course. There is this real desire to be artistically expressive within the framework of worlds that other people create. There's going to be a blurring of the line between professional content creators and amateur creators. Or to put it another way, the best amateur content creators will have the ability to participate in the world of the show alongside the profession creators. For example, having seen what people are capable of doing on the Internet, I have no doubt some guy in Ohio with access to the creative materials could probably cut a better promo than the promo department at ABC. It's entirely conceivable. I'm really interested in catalyzing the best amateur content creators and getting them involved in the creation of ancillary content for the show.

Interviewer(s): That would be a fascinating endeavor and an interesting one particularly working for a large media company.

Carlton Cuse: It's a tricky thing. They are very protective of their properties. They don't want to dilute their hold on their IP, but I think that we are living in a time that's moved way past that being a viable way of thinking about things. It was like the music business trying to ignore the reality of digital downloading. Art is evolving to take into account digital access, *Girl Talk*, for instance. Gregg Gillis is a fantastic creator of music, but he makes it out of samples of other people's music. The laws don't evolve as fast as artistic intention and invention. Art is moving faster than the speed of law. That's kind of what's happening.

Interviewer(s): I totally agree, and this is particularly a dynamic moment at that. I mean you have technology and like you say these synergies with people and all of it flying around like crazy.

Carlton Cuse: Technologically we're in a truly revolutionary moment in time. The Internet and its two way communication ability along with the ability to create perfect digital copies has created a completely different paradigm for the way in which we communicate with each other. Laws haven't evolved as fast.

Interviewer(s): So, would *LOST* really be a different show today if it was premiering on ABC?

Carlton Cuse: I don't know. Yes, it probably would. The media world in which we now live is so much more evolved than in 2004. People are much more organized based on the social fabric of the Internet. Facebook and Twitter didn't exist back then. The instant access people now have to each other and the world at large might have accelerated the awareness of the show. That could've been positive or negative. I do think that the show benefited from existing at a very specific point in time. Fundamentally the one thing that won't change is that we learn lessons as human beings by the stories we are told. Television is still the most powerful means of storytelling to large groups of people. It puts visual narrative right in your house, right into your most intimate spaces – your bedroom, your living room, your kitchen. When stories resonate strongly they create a desire in the audience to talk about those stories to share their feelings about those stories. However media changes, the power of good storytelling, of listening around the campfire, is the fundamental engine that drives everything else, and that won't change.

Interviewer(s): It's all about the mothership.

Carlton Cuse: Yes, it's all about the mothership.

Interviewer(s): I guess the last question for me was what was the big lesson you learned? It's unimaginable for me to imagine what it was like for you to suddenly have that over. Having those years, those *LOST* years as an experience. What was the big lesson learned? What was the big takeaway for you?

Carlton Cuse: I think the big takeaway was to follow your passion. All the rewards that came out of *LOST* came from not being afraid to fail. Every morning started with asking the question, "Wouldn't it be cool if we did 'x?'" and then trying to do that. There's all sorts of people who are happy to tell you why you shouldn't do something. We were lucky to have this beautiful window in time where we were able to do what we wanted to do. It was an extraordinary experience. I appreciate the specialness of it. But it also validated for me that you need to follow your heart and your passion. That's the path of greatest purity towards artistic expression that truly reflects who you are. That was the lesson that I took away. You can't second guess what somebody else wants you to do. Instead, find the path that leads you to the deepest truth about yourself, and then find a way to express those truths.

Chapter 6

Video Games and Interactive Storytelling

As technology – and as these incredible artists that work on video games – continue to push the envelope the entire video game sector will explode. It's not going to go away. If anything, it will take over.

—Shia LeBeouf, Actor[1]

Before we get into the meat of this chapter we want to take a moment to talk about video games, and video game development in general. It is very easy to view video games as a straightforward extension of the visual narrative storytelling techniques used in motion pictures and television. Frankly, this perspective is a mistake that has doomed any number of video game projects. There are similarities, yes, but there are significant differences. A great deal of this chapter is spent reviewing those differences, and to a large extent the different *mindset* that is needed when thinking about video game storytelling. There are significant differences having to do with overall structure, character depiction, camera perspective, and interactivity that have to be kept in mind from the very beginning. Writing a script, movie or TV style, and then trying to add "gameplay" will not cut it. That said, this section is not about game design *per se* though we do touch on game design concepts. This section is focused on video game storytelling and how video game development is its own thing; now let's talk about how…

The State of Video Game Development

With video game revenues at $24 billion dollars in 2010 ("NPD Sales Figures," accessed May 10, 2012, http://vgsales.wikia.com/wiki/NPD_sales_figures), there is little question that video games have evolved into the entertainment form of choice for many worldwide. According to the Entertainment Software Association (ESA) publication *Essential Facts About the Computer and Video Game Industry* (ESA, 2012, http://www.theesa.com/facts/pdfs/ESA_EF_2012.pdf), the common misconception that video games are for children is exactly that – in 2012 the average age for a game player is 30 years old. (Players under the age of 18 accounted for only 32% of the market while players over the age of 36 accounted for 37%.) Additionally, the long-perceived gender gap among video game players collapsed as 47% of all gamers are now female. Again according to the ESA, with 70% of American households owning

[1] GamePro, January 2010

a video game console and 65% a personal computer used to play games, it is easy to see how video game playing has become a cultural norm. More and more video games debut each year as blockbuster events that rival even the biggest motion picture releases. *Call of Duty: Modern Warfare 3*, when released in November of 2011, sold an estimated $750 million dollars in its first five days, and reached an estimated 1 billion dollars worldwide in 16 days of release, putting it into a position to rival the success of even James Cameron's *Avatar* ("Modern Warfare 3 hits the $1bn mark in record time," accessed May 16, 2012, http://www.guardian.co.uk/technology/2011/dec/12/modern-warfare-3-breaks-1bn-barrier). Projections at the time of this writing by Wall Street investment firm Sterne Agee put *Grand Theft Auto V*, expected to release in the first quarter of 2013 could sell as many as 25 million copies in its first year (http://gamasutra.com/view/news/165750/Analyst_Grand Theft Auto_V_likely_to_launch_in_early_2013.php).

We see the stylistic importance of video games in how their look and feel has crept into the production design of major motion pictures and television programs, where the comparison is often made derogatorily, but tellingly, that the production was targeted at the "video game generation." That said, while motion pictures based directly on video game franchises have generally met with only poor to mixed critical and box office success, it is important to note the roughly $450-million-dollar worldwide revenue of the *Tomb Raider* movie series and the $673-million-dollar worldwide revenue of the *Resident Evil* franchise (http://www.boxofficemojo.com) The fifth film, *Resident Evil: Retribution* was released in September of 2012. Additionally, a second fully computer-animated feature, *Resident Evil: Damnation*, was released in 2012 as well. The home video release of the original, *Resident Evil: Degeneration*, in November 2010 resulted in sales of more than 1.6 million copies worldwide.

Even the generally reviled *Mortal Kombat* films (*Mortal Kombat*, 1995 and *Mortal Kombat: Annihilation*, 1997) managed to bring in combined worldwide revenue of roughly $170 million (ibid.). (The 1998 *Mortal Kombat: Conquest* television series managed to only eke out a single season, some would say appropriately.) It is important to note that in all of these cases the motion picture adaptation of the video game was conceived of long after the conception and production of the original game. A production company licensed the rights to produce the video game as a motion picture, usually without the input of the original creative team or rights-holders (obviously, how much script, casting, or production say the original rights-holder retains varies with the licensing contract) and created an adaptation that was, in some cases, little more than "inspired" by the original source material. Frankly, for most of the video game source material that is completely understandable, since with the exception of more modern narrative-driven games the content and quality of game storytelling has been somewhat lacking, in a grander sense. Many video games have been licensed as motion pictures in an effort to take advantage of the brand notoriety of the original material rather than the narrative quality. Many video game fans complain that when they do go to the theatre to see the film version of their favorite games, what is up there on the big screen is barely recognizable as being derived from the game, with the exception of character and location names and some general plot points. Video game fans, however, are not expecting literal translations of the game to the screen, but they are expecting more faithful and more respectful translations of the original material. This is the same concern that fans of novels or other creative works express when they hear that a favored property is being adapted. Peter Jackson's adaptation of J. R. R. Tolkein's classic *Lord of the Rings* trilogy shows the kind of respect for the integrity of the original work, while not being a literal translation, that fans appreciate. A comparison of the history of adaptations from various Marvel Comic's properties shows how important respect and integrity to the original material is. With Marvel Studio's *Marvel's The Avengers* being one of the highest-grossing motion pictures of all time, and the success of its lead-ins *Iron Man*, *Thor*, and *Captain America: The First Avenger*, Fox Studios must be lamenting its missed opportunities with *The Fantastic Four*, *X-Men: The Last Stand*, and *X-Men Origins: Wolverine* that faired so poorly in comparison. Fox clearly learned, however, from Marvel Studio's success with its production of

X-Men: First Class which crafted a new take on the origins of the super-hero team that was not a direct adaptation of any one piece of X-Men material but yet felt true to the original material.

Participatory Content, for the Win

In terms of transmedia storytelling, video games hold an important position in that they allow a participant in the property to engage with it in a unique manner – interactively. Motion pictures and television programs are inherently *passive* mediums in that the viewer sits quietly by (or not so quietly by in the case of those who like to yell at the screen) and watches the story unfold as scripted, every time. No matter how many times one sees *Casino Royale* in theatres or watches it at home, the story always plays out the same way. Play the *Casino Royale* video game, however, and the player gets to decide how James Bond solves the immediate problem, albeit within a strictly defined set of choices predetermined in the game design. Despite those limited choices, video games allow a viewer to go beyond merely sympathizing with a character on-screen and instead become that character for a time, solving problems in a way that is appropriate (hopefully) for that character. While most games focus on re-creating physical problem-solving (running, shooting, punching, etc.) many promote social or intellectual problem-solving, with each area appropriately empowering for different kinds of players. Note that we use the term "player-character" to refer to the hybrid interaction between the player of the game and the character he plays. For example, while it is the character that performs the actions in the game (the player certainly isn't), it is the player who ultimately makes the decisions and pulls the puppet-strings, if you will.

We mentioned a moment ago that the stories in motion pictures and television shows play out the same each time viewed, and truth-be-told most story-driven games are structured similarly. While the environments may be interactive (via gameplay in terms of things that you can knock over, open or close, kick, drive, shoot and so on …) the story the player-character moves through is pre-set and linear, with each play-through of the game producing the exact same sequence of key plot events and character interactions, and ultimately the same finale. The player-character may have literally driven to the plot event via a different road or run through a different set of doors to get there, but the order of the key plot events remains the same even if the details of the progress from one to the next varies from play-through to play-through. It is important to point out that some games do have more interactive plot structures, but even these are more narrowly defined than they appear. We'll go into the particulars of video game plot structure shortly.

Few games allow players to truly affect the story or plot through their interactions, but many allow significant variations in subplots that relate to the main plot in ways that color the player's emotional reaction to the story. Additionally, in the way the gameplay and plot events are structured in many games, there is a great deal of non-linearity in terms of *how* the plot plays out, but ultimately the *what* of the plot remains essentially the same. For example, Electronic Arts/Bioware's hugely popular *Mass Effect 2* video game has a main plot that plays out very linearly throughout the course of the roughly 35 hours of gameplay. Key plot and story sequences become available periodically throughout the course of the game, and though some of the sequences can be played in varying order (based on the desire of the player) the story itself remains effectively unchanged. In the game, the player-character has a team of companions who must be individually recruited (via their own dedicated subplots/side-quests) and then participate in the climactic battle at the end of the game. Depending on how the player-character interacts with these companions they can become rivals, friends, or even lovers. During the final battle sequence, however, the player's own decisions and subsequent actions directly affect which of the companions involved live or die. Given the attachment the game allows the player in creating those characters, their survival (or lack thereof) can significantly alter the emotional outcome of the game. It is worth noting that *Mass Effect 2* included some decision-points that while somewhat impactful during the current game have significant influence on the events of *Mass Effect 3* released in March of 2012. As a side note, *Mass Effect* was optioned by Legendary Pictures, Warner Bros., in May of 2010 as feature film. Very little information has been available since, except for a Comic Con 2011 panel which included screenwriter Mark Protosevich (*I Am Legend, Thor*) and producers telling the audience that the film would follow the story of the first film. Additionally, Funimation Entertainment and studio T.O. Entertainment produced an anime film adaptation of the series that released in late 2012.

Interactive storytelling produces an interesting quandary for the property creator. How much influence can the player really be given toward how the story plays out? For example, if *Star Wars: The Empire Strikes Back* had been an interactive game how would the plot have changed if Luke Skywalker (under the control of the player) had managed to kill Darth Vader at the climax of the film? Clearly, for the sake of the over-arching story of the *Star Wars* property killing Darth Vader then and there would have been a bad idea narratively... so how much influence can we give the player on the primary stories of the universe without jeopardizing its integrity and continuity? We'll return to this question later in this chapter.

The opportunities for video games as components of the transmedia property are tremendous in terms of extending and expanding the storytelling. Care has to be given, however, as to what is allowed to change and how much permanent impact a video game's story can have on the storyworld or story universe. These problems are not insurmountable, however, and we'll dig deeper into them following a quick primer on game storytelling and design.

Basics of Game Design and Storytelling

Games cannot be simply written only as linear storylines in the same way that motion pictures and television shows can. Consideration must be given for what the player does as an active participant, rather than just a passive observer. *Gameplay*, which is to say the things the player-character *does* is what drives a game forward. Gameplay-driven games require only light, to-the-point, story to motivate the player. Story-driven games, on the other hand, require *both* strong core gameplay and strong story. Story lures players to the game and acts as a strong motivator, but it is gameplay that keeps them there.

Traditionally, we say that motion pictures or television shows are *written*, however we say that games are *designed*. The difference is again the emphasis on gameplay. What the player can do – run, jump, shoot, argue, construct units, cast magic spells, seduce, collect items, and so on – are complex systems that have to be designed to insure that the game is fun to play and isn't too hard or too easy. Story-driven games require story, of course, and until somewhat recently the burden of crafting the story-dedicated elements, including the characters and their dialogue, fell to game designers rather than professional writers. More recently, writers familiar with game structure and gameplay are being hired by game projects to work with designers in interweaving gameplay and story. (Hybrid writer/game designers are increasingly referred to as narrative designers. For the rest of this section we assume that the writer and the designer are two different people, though we think that a narrative designer is the better solution.)

The most important point to take away is that story and gameplay have to work together to support each other. In a game, one cannot succeed without the other.

Gameplay and Story Working Together

It is imperative that the writer of a game's story understands what the gameplay is. As we just said, the story and the gameplay have to work together to create a great game; the story has to support the gameplay, and the gameplay has to support the story. For example, Square's extremely popular and successful 1997 game *Final Fantasy VII* had a significant and notable disconnect between gameplay and story. Throughout the course of the game the player-character has access to a special magic item (a "phoenix down") that lets them resurrect companion characters that fall in battle. This particular item is pretty common in the game so there is little, if any, risk of the player-character's teammates dying permanently. There comes a point when the game's story requires that a beloved teammate die permanently for both dramatic effect and to drive the plot forward. Suddenly, though the character dies in a way very similar to ways that same character has died before, the magical item no longer works *because the story requires that the character stay dead*. This is a fundamental disconnect between the gameplay (the ability to revive fallen teammates fairly easily) and the dramatic necessity of the story (a character must die). Fortunately for *FFVII*, the rest of the game was a triumph and the death so dramatic and traumatic, that the fact that the deceased character should have been revivable in accordance with the rules of the game slipped by many.

As another more obscure example, the 1994 Electronic Arts game *Noctropolis* places the player in the role of Batman-like dark avenger comic book hero known as "Darksheer." As presented in the game, Darksheer is a character that uses physical action and violence as tools to achieve his goals. Oddly, *Noctropolis* is not an action game that allows for extensive physical combat. At one point in the story, Darksheer must break into a secure location protected by a lone security guard. After trying to convince the security guard that he is a city inspector (while in full costume, by the way, which the guard conveniently ignores) the character has to recruit his sexy sidekick Stiletto to distract the guard while he sneaks in. Apparently, while hyped as a powerful Batman-esque hero, Darksheer is unable to deal with a single rent-a-cop himself. This is a disconnect between gameplay and story and, as might be expected, significantly detracts from the game experience because the player cannot actually be the character the game claims he is.

Disconnection between gameplay and story is not always so clear-cut, however. A more current example, and one still often discussed though the game is a few years old now, involves the Rockstar Game/Take-Two Interactive monster success *Grand Theft Auto IV* (22 million+ copies sold by the end of 2011) ("Latest *Grand Theft Auto* IV sales figures revealed," accessed May 17, 2012, http://www.msxbox-world.com/news/article/16404/latest-gta-iv-sales-figures-revealed.html). The story of *Grand Theft Auto IV* involves the player-character of Niko Belic, a criminal and military veteran from some unnamed Eastern European country haunted by his past and trying to make a new life in Liberty City (somewhat based on New York City.) Niko, through the game's dialogue, continually talks about becoming a better man and his efforts to change his ways, but the narrative and gameplay choices afforded the player only allow him to pursue violent (some brutally so) solutions and continue the very life he professes to reject. Some critics of the game point to this disconnect as a failure of the game in that the player's actions cannot support the desire expressed by the character. Niko says he rejects violence and wants to be a better man, but the game requires the player to find violent solutions and follow a plotline that presents Niko as a brutal criminal. Others, however, view this "disconnection" as a revelation of character – Niko *says* he wants to be a better man, but it is not in his nature and so he cannot be a better man, or make better choices, so the game does not present them.

Let's pause a moment and consider this last possibility. Novels, films, and television are full of stories of protagonists who struggle with being better than they currently are. Sometimes they succeed, sometimes they do not. The struggle is the story, is the drama. Whether the character overcomes his demons or not is in the hands of the writer (though sometimes the ending is ambiguous and leaves things to the reader or viewer to interpret). In *Grand Theft AutoIV*, regardless of your interpretation of the gameplay/story disconnect, Niko fails to become a better man and continues his life of violence. The player, by the limited number of options afforded, must push Niko down this bloody path, and if we say that action reveals character these choices show us who Niko really is. This takes us directly into the issue in games of *static* vs. *dynamic* characters, which we will deal with more directly in a few sections. For now, let's move on to a review of how games present story but leave the question lingering in the air. Using *Grand Theft AutoIV* as the example, should the game's player have the ability to make choices that make Niko closer to the kind of man he says he wants to be (or the player wants him to be), or is who Niko is predefined and the player's choices appropriately constrained?

Game – Story – Game – Story is a Familiar Pattern

For quite some time games have had, and some still do, a structure of non-interactive movie sequences (known as cut-scenes) interspersed between segments of gameplay. This created an interesting split between different kinds of players who played video games for different reasons. Players who were primarily there for the story often found the gameplay sequences interspersed between the cut-scenes to be "busy-work" before the payoff of the next movie sequence. Players who were there for the gameplay found the cut-scenes distracting and would skip them (if the game allowed them to, or complain loudly if it did not) so that they could get back to the gameplay.

This storytelling structure was a production necessity in that early game engines were incapable of displaying complex scenes, animations or visual effects in real-time, which meant these scenes needed to be pre-generated and played back as movies rather than in real-time using the game engine software. The term "game engine" refers to the software that creates or plays back the graphics, sound, animations, visuals effects and so on of the game. Some games use an engine programmed specifically for that game, while others use commercially available game engine packages. Different games engines tend to do particular kinds of game very well.

Game engines render their game worlds in "real-time" usually somewhere around 60 frames per second (compared to playback rates of 24 fps for film and 30 fps for television). Complex scenes that are rendered using 3D graphics software for television or film can take many minutes to render, per frames. Game engines have to do similar at a lower resolution and complexity up to 60 times per second.

While the cut-scenes were dramatically effective, they were produced with the same 3D software used to produce motion picture special effect sequences and were at a higher quality and fidelity and so often looked significantly different than the gameplay sequences, which tended to be quite jarring and sometimes distracting. The start of a cut-scenes also takes control away from the player, forcing them into a passive, linear experience, which seems to defeat the purpose of using a game as a storytelling medium.

Nowadays, game engines are powerful enough that complex dramatic sequences can be constructed and played back in real-time and blended seamlessly with gameplay action. The *Half-Life* series of games from Valve Corporation are noted as successful examples of integrating storytelling in gameplay, both in crafting a deep, immersive world and integrating scenes that would normally be cut-scenes directly into gameplay and the game world. Some of these scenes play out as the player-character moves through them, but sometimes control is still taken away from the player, forcing them to watch the scene play out. This is usually done for dramatically or narratively critical scenes that contain information or an end-result that has to happen. This technique is also used extensively for dialogue or exposition sequences where, it is generally assumed, the player can do nothing but talk.

When we talk about characters and dialogue in an upcoming section we're going to specifically talk about the various methods used to create interactive dialogue, and specifically the system built for the *Mass Effect* series of games which allows for interaction during long dialogue scenes.

Sometimes, for technical reasons (such as the technical demands of the content exceed the real-time capabilities of the game engine), pre-rendered cut-scenes are still used, but more often than not dramatic non-interactive scenes are played back in the game engine itself. This means that story and gameplay can be effectively interwoven without having to interrupt one for the other. This also cements the concept that the story and gameplay have to be considered, and developed, side-by-side rather than tacked one onto the other.

The ability of video games to render believable, realistic characters has increased dramatically in recent years. The 2011 release of the Take-Two Interactive/Rockstar Games release *LA Noir* included breakthrough facial animation techniques that captured both the facial appearance and performance of the actor cast in the role and allowed their playback in the game engine. The performance capture technology used was so effective that a critical part of gameplay in *LA Noir* involved the player reading the expression on a character's face in the game and determining if they were lying or not.

Interestingly, one of the results of the application of this technology in *LA Noir* was a blending between the film/television and video game experiences. Viewers of film and television are used to seeing familiar actors appear in different roles as different characters. Video games have, for many years, sometimes cast famous actors as the voice of game characters, sometimes recognizably and sometimes not. Occasionally, efforts were made to have the in-game character resemble the actor providing the voice, but usually not. With the face and performance capture technology presented in *LA Noir* when the character of detective Cole Phelps appears on screen, fans of the television series *Mad Men* immediately recognize actor Aaron Staton. Similarly, when the character of Leland Monroe appears, he is clearly played by actor John Noble (*Lord of the Rings: the Return of the King* and *Fringe* (Fox TV)). This creates some interesting implications for the question of who is playing the player-character – the player or Andrew Staton – or is it clear enough that the character of Cole Phelps simply looks and sounds like Staton, but Phelps really is the player's to control. It's an intriguing question.

Key Transmedia Elements and Video Games

Earlier in this book, we talked about a set of key elements of transmedia storytelling property: *theme/story*, *plot*, *character*, *setting*, and *style/tone*. These elements are as important in a game development as any other media, but manifest in different ways. Let's take a brief look at each of them in the context of story-driven video games.

Theme/Story

The expression of theme and story in a video game is very similar to other visual media. Stories can be epic tales of the fate of humanity punctuated by the player-character having to make a decision that affects the fertility of an entire species (*Mass Effect 2*) or personal when a serial killer taunts and tests men to see if they are "worthy" to be fathers to their children (Sony/Quantic Dream's 2010 *Heavy Rain*). Key to successful integration is how the player-character's actions – again, the gameplay – and their choices reflect the themes and story. In games, themes and story elements that exist as subtext are not as effective as ones that are directly involved in the player's choices. Earlier we considered the possible gameplay/story disconnect in *Grand Theft Auto IV*, but it is important to now consider that it may be a theme/gameplay disconnect … maybe.

Spinning the story of a criminal immigrant come to Liberty City to build a new life, *Grand Theft Auto IV* deals with the false-promise of the American Dream, brotherhood, trust, and betrayal. Additionally, the story makes frequent references to the pasts of various characters, and how decisions from years ago have shaped their lives now. If those characters are locked into patterns based on who and what they were before, why not Niko? Perhaps one of *Grand Theft Auto IV's* themes is that we are who we are and cannot truly change, in which case there is no gameplay/thematic disconnect at all. But, one of the things that makes a video game different from a novel, film, or television show is the interactivity – the ability to change things. If who Niko Belic is cannot change, then *Grand Theft Auto IV* isn't character-driven narrative, but rather action- or plot-driven narrative. Why isn't he the main character in a novel instead?

In a subsequent Rockstar game, *Red Dead Redemption* (2010), the main character, John Marston, is written as a former hard man who separated from his old life and settled down to build a family. Like in *Grand Theft Auto IV*, however, Marston cannot escape his past and is forced back into a life of violence by government agents who kidnap Marston's wife and son in order to get him to hunt down some of the gang he used to be a part of. One of *Red Dead Redemption's* themes, though, is clearly that a man cannot escape his past. Marston himself says "People don't forget. Nothing is forgiven." It is also a time of change in *Red Dead Redemption* – the classic Old West is ending and what was once the American frontier is becoming conglomerated into the American nation. Marston is clearly a remnant of the "old world" being used by the agents of the "new world" to bring Marston's world to an end. Ultimately, Marston must pay for the sins of his past, but the player has the agency to control the man he is now. By structuring the game's themes this way *Red Dead Redemption* avoids *Grand Theft Auto IV's* perceived gameplay/theme/story disconnect (or conflict). Interestingly, Dan Houser of Rockstart Games was a primary writer on both *Grand Theft Auto IV* and *Red Dead Redemption*.

Plot

The sequences of events that play out the story in a video game are also more effective when focused on the player-character. A common cinematic technique used to build tension and drama involves cutting away from the main character to show what other characters are doing or saying. Since the player effectively inhabits the main character in a video game this tends to be more jarring than dramatic (and again serves to remove control from the player.) Often in film, this technique is used to build tension and drama where the audience is made aware of some action of the antagonist or a plot element unknown to the main character(s) and the thrill comes from seeing how the two will intersect or collide. In games, this technique has to be used much more carefully since the audience is the protagonist and the result may be a loss of tension due to too much fore-knowledge.

In story-driven games, the player usually has one primary character that they control. Often there are one or more secondary or companion-characters that the player has some degree of control over, usually for fight sequences. The player-character often has to recruit these companion characters during the course of the game and his actions often affect the relationship with that companion character either positively or negatively. For example in 2009's *Dragon Age: Origins* from Bioware/EA, the player-character has the opportunity to pursue a romantic connection with his companions. One of those characters is the bard, Leliana, who has a very particular world-view and if the player-character takes actions throughout the plot that Leliana approves of, there is an increased chance of romance. Make choices she disapproves of and the chance slips away.

Video game plots are usually comprised of a main plot, which supports the primary themes and story of the game, and one or more subplots – often referred to as side-stories or sometimes "side missions." While subplots are not uncommon in fiction, it is again important to understand that they must all involve the main character in some way, shape, or form, through goals, desires, relationships, or backstory. While it is not imperative that each of the subplots reflect the game's themes and key story elements, they often do and can be used to expand or extend the player's understanding of the main story.

Character

The main character – the player-character – in games is very different from those in other visual narrative media. We devote an entire section later in this chapter to the issues surrounding video game player-characters, but we'll touch on it here. A key indication that there are differences we've already mentioned is the use of the term "player-character" which recognizes an amalgam of the player and the main character. Ultimately, it is the player making decisions for the character and since games can only provide a narrowly defined palette of actions, whose consequences must be pre-determined, there is a great deal of doubt as to whether or not the options available to the player should tightly align with the choices a strongly defined character would take, or if the player should be allowed to make their own decisions for the character, thereby redefining the character as the game plays out. We mentioned this earlier with *Grand Theft Auto: IV*'s Niko Belic who is very strongly defined, and the options available to the player in the game are very tightly aligned with the decisions that Niko, with his characteristics, would make. This, however, removes a layer of choice from the player who cannot decide to show mercy on an enemy of Niko's because the only choices the game presents are about how Niko kills him. Some players reacted very positively to the strongly-defined Niko and specifically acknowledged that they thought about the choices presented to them in terms of "What would Niko do?", but others felt very limited by the choices presented. Bioware games such as *Mass Effect* and *Dragon Age* provide much more weakly defined main characters allowing the player to define the character through their actions. These games (and others) also allow the player to customize the appearance of their character in the game, including gender, race (or species), and cultural background. When the player can alter these fundamental characteristics and then define the character's personality as he goes along through action and dialogue choices, it becomes easier to see how the fundamental relationship of character to story (as expressed in other narrative media) becomes very difficult in game writing.

Some video games have multiple main characters that the player controls one at a time. For example, *LA Noir* uses Cole Phelps as the main character for most of the story, but then switches to Jack Kelso for the final portion. *Red Dead Redemption*, building on the theme of the old West giving way to the new order changes protagonists at the very end from John Marston to his son, Jack. Other games, particularly adventure games, use swapping between characters as a key part of their storytelling structure.

Setting

The setting in a video game can also be as elaborate or simple as necessary. Large, sprawling fantasy worlds like those of the *Dragon Age* or *Elder Scrolls* series or the science fiction expanse of *Mass Effect* are very common, and for many the norm. *LA Noir*, set in 1940s Los Angeles, presents a somewhat historically respectful impression of that city, whereas the *Grand Theft Auto* series of games are set in clearly fictionalized depictions of major American cities, including New York City, Miami, Los Angeles, San Francisco and Las Vegas. The upcoming *Grand Theft Auto V* (release date to be announced) is reported to take place in Los Santos, a fictionalized version of Southern California and the Los Angeles area. The popular *Call of Duty* and *Battlefield* series, on the other hand, both depict historical, modern, or near-future military storylines in various products and provide just enough story and setting information to drive the plot forward.

Like in film and television, the critical information the player needs about the settings has to be on screen and communicated diagetically (within the world) in small, easily absorbable chunks rather than available through secondary sources. Players do not read game manuals and will skip information screens or dialogue screens that contain too much information. Writers of game stories also have to resist the urge to dump huge chunks of required information about the world and game story through in-game texts, books or data sources. While some players will eagerly devour every bit of information ("lore") that the game presents, some ignore it entirely. This means that the game writer cannot present critical information through those channels. Long chunks of exposition also tend to get skipped or ignored, as they do in film or television.

Style/Tone

Video games encompass all forms of style and tone, with some easier to depict than others. Given how well games recreate physical actions, action-adventure style games are plentiful, as are suspense driven games. Comedy is difficult, for all of the usual reasons, plus the need to sustain the level of humor for 20+ hours of content. So-called "survival horror" games are plentiful as well, but these are not real horror stories in the truest sense (despite the proliferation of zombies and other unnatural things of all types) but rather action-suspense games. Real horror strives to generate honest fear, and scares are few and far between. A relatively recent title from 2010, THQ's *Amnesia: The Dark Descent* is a notable exception in its ability to generate an authentic sense of fear through its manipulation of the environment, the player's ability to perceive the world, and manipulations of the player-character's ability to protect himself.

We doubt there is much dispute that video games can handle action well, but there's a wide range or tone associated with action. The tone of the *Grand Theft Auto* series has grown increasingly real and serious with each entry in the series, whereas the *Saints Row* (THQ, 2006–present) series, which started out as a counterpart to the *Grand Theft Auto* series, has grown more and more outlandish. The original Word War II set *Call of Duty* franchise games included sequences of tension and drama that have been favorably compared to the best moments of *Saving Private Ryan* (DreamWorks, 1998).

Video Game Storytelling Structure

We've touched some on the storytelling structure of video games prior to this, but now we're going to go into it in more detail, building from simple to complex. First, let's revisit two terms and how we're using them, *plot* and *story*. Traditionally, the *plot* is the sequence of events that make up the *story*. While this is true, it is also implies a very simple relationship that is actually more complex. The plot is indeed the sequence of events – the things that happen – but the *story* is the emotional sum of all that happens because of what occurs throughout the plot. When we talk about storytelling, the terms plot and story tend to get interchanged and the lines between the two pretty blurry. As with motion pictures and television, it is very important that we make a clear delineation between plot and story in video games as well.

Standard, linear story structure involves moving from Plot Point A to Plot Point B and onward in a direct sequence, beginning to middle to end. Plot Point B always follows Plot Point A, and so on. What goes on from Plot Point A to Plot Point B can involve reverse time, alternative dimensions, flashback, flashforwards, and any number of nonlinear depictions of time and place, but the *storytelling structure* remains linear.

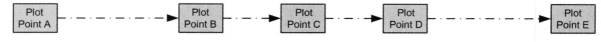

Figure 6.1 *Vanilla plot structure.*

It is very easy to layer this roughly over a traditional three-act structure.

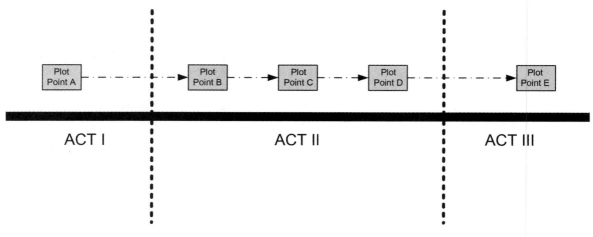

Figure 6.2 *The Three-Act Structure.*

As we mentioned, story-driven video games share this same structure, but intersperse interactive gameplay sequences between the plot points, like this:

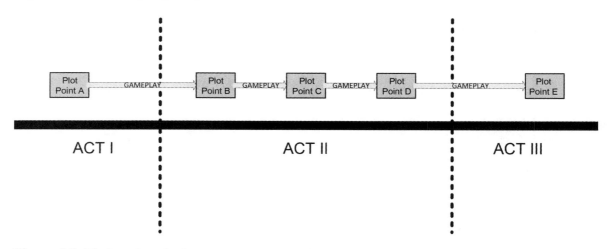

Figure 6.3 *The Story-Gameplay Structure.*

It is very important to understand that games that are structured like this *are not* interactive stories. They are interactive experiences, some may even say interactive narratives (depending on how one wishes to define narrative … more on that in a moment), but they are not interactive stories.

Some of our readers are undoubtedly squinting their eyes, making little sounds of disagreement, or even going so far as to say "Hey now ..." at this point, and understandably so. At the start of this section we mentioned the blurring of the terms plot and story, and here's where the terms story and story become blurry.

The Story Written vs. The Story Played

In a video game, there are two stories: the *story written* and the *story played*. The *story written* is, in some ways, the traditional plot/story — it is the one the authors crafted and represents the story backbone of the game. In *Mass Effect 3*, it is the story of how Commander Shepard builds the interstellar coalition force needed to defend Earth from the invading Reapers, and whether or not he succeeds. The *Mass Effect 3* writers created all the characters, plot points, scenes, dialogue and choices necessary for the player to move through the story, from inciting incident to denouement, but they had no way of knowing exactly how the story would play out. Shepard may, in a given scene, have the option of letting an opponent escape or not ... and that choice is pre-built into the story and game design ... but the writers have no way of knowing if the player chose to bring the companion character Garrus (who will argue that the opponent cannot be allowed to escape) or Liara (who will argue that the opponent must be allowed to escape) with Shepard for that scene. From the player's perspective, Garrus or Liara arguing for or against Shepard's decision is as much part of the story as anything else.

The game's writers and designers have to craft all the possible player options when building the story. They have to account for a version of the story where Garrus is present, or where Liara is present, or where any one of another half-dozen companion characters could be there. Some may have an opinion on the situation, some may not. Some may have *very* strong opinions. And some companion characters may have particular reactions after the completion of the scene. All of these possibilities make up the story played, including any gameplay that may have led up to the scene.

Continuing our example, Sheppard and companion(s) are in pursuit of our unnamed opponent. To get to him, they have to fight their way through a secret base filled with enemy guards. That movement through the secret base, and the fight to defeat the guards, makes up the gameplay of the scene. What if the fight is brutal, and hard won? What if Shepard's team barely makes it to the confrontation scene alive? Or, what if it was a cake-walk ... they were able to chew their way through the defenders with barely a scratch. Either one of these outcomes could color the *player's* emotional stake in the confrontation scene and change how they have Shepard respond. Garrus might (effectively) have an easier time of his arguments if the fight was a difficult one, whereas Liara's argument may be easier to accept if the fight wasn't as difficult. Whether the fight was hard, or not, is circumstantial and depends a great deal on the player's skill, any special abilities the player chose for the characters, what weapons or equipment were brought along, and the choices made during the actual combat. All of these possibilities must be accounted for by the game's writers and designers, but they have no way of knowing how it will all play out, so everything has to be written to account for everything that could occur.

Perhaps it is best to refer to the *story written* as the *story planned*. Ultimately, however, the real story, when all is said and done, is the story played, which is a combination of the story planned, plus all of the decisions made during the game. We're going to call that the *narrative*, and we're going to call the story written/planned the *master story*. Why narrative? To narrate is to tell a story. When we include story + gameplay + decisions, who's really telling the story ... the writers and designers or the player? We argue the player. The writers and designers craft the boundaries and possibilities, but it is the player who navigates the character through that space. When a viewer talks about *The Dark Knight* (Warner Brothers, 2008) they'll talk about how "Batman did this ... and then Batman did that..." When a player of *Batman: Arkham Asylum* (Rocksteady Studios/Eidos Interactive, 2009) talks about playing Batman in the game they say "I did this … and then I did that …" The identification is clear, and it is clear that the narrative is theirs. Additionally, while every viewing of *The Dark Knight* tells the same story, every playthrough of *Batman: Arkham Asylum* is a potentially different story.

So, getting back to the original point, not all games are interactive stories (some are) but all games are interactive narratives.

Interactive Stories

Some games are interactive stories, and by that we mean that the choices the player makes in the game affect the story. A choice is made and things turn out differently, depending on the choice. How great the effect is can vary significantly. It can affect who the enemies are, which characters are friends, where particular parts of the plot take place, and ultimately how the story resolves, and so on. The effect of these changes can be very narrow in scope or effect (help the woman who's been knocked down and she'll point you in the direction of the fleeing villain), or they can be cumulative (to romance the woman, the player-character has to perform multiple actions that slowly endear her to him). In a game like *Mass Effect 3*, which is allegedly tracking and processing over a thousand decisions made over the course of the games in the trilogy, it can affect the lives of billions and the rescue or destruction of an entire planet. The level of complexity in an interactive story is limited only by the designers' and writers' ability to conceive of and execute all the interconnected actions, and the practicality of implementation (which we'll get back to in a moment.)

A great deal of attention is given to how many endings a game's story has, and in truth even those games that are considered to have a highly interactive story have relatively few different endings. Those that do tend to have endings that are what could be considered "theme and variation" endings, meaning that all of the endings are very similar with relatively minor differences between them. Let's explore why that is …

The Complexities of Branching Stories

Before we dig into this, there is a caveat. We are, admittedly, dealing with very broad strokes in this section and the subsequent ones, and we're talking about very large plot decision points on the scope of "Assassinate the Dictator" vs. "Don't Assassinate the Dictator," which in and of themselves have a significant list of consequences, large and small. It is much more likely that the decision making is much more granular, small scale, and more frequent. We'll deal with those granular decisions in a few sections, but we first wanted it to be clear that we are consciously simplifying the scale/scope of decision points for the sake of the discussion, and for the sake of being able to diagram them usefully.

Earlier we looked at this simple diagram of plot/story structure:

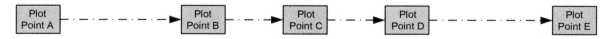

Figure 6.4 *Vanilla plot structure.*

As we said, this is the basic structure of movies, television, novels, comic books, and most video games (in terms of the master story.) If we turn this structure into an interactive story, we can look at each plot point as a potential decision point where the player gets to make a choice that takes the story in a different direction. Let's map out a story that has only one major decision point, and if we assume it occurs late in the game's story it could look something like this (and remember that the journey between the plot points could have as much interactive gameplay of running, shooting, talking, climbing, romancing, or what have you as you can cram in):

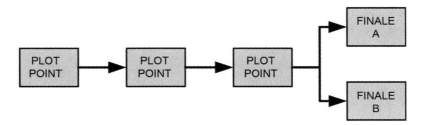

Figure 6.5 *Simple branched structure.*

Based on the way the diagram splits it starts to resemble a tree and branches we call this a *branching story*. This is a very simple execution with one branch, which seems reasonable enough, but consider the fact that depending on how the story is written the content of each ending could be completely different. Imagine if Finale A is the hero heading off on his own to live in a cabin in the wilderness and Finale B is the hero reuniting with his lost love and going off to live in the big city. This results in two very different environments, casts of characters, and circumstances to create the content for. If, instead, we create a "theme and variation" ending where the hero's lost love approaches him and either stops to stand with him, or continues walking past him, ignoring him (as in the classic motion picture *The Third Man* (British Lion Films, 1949)), the scope of the content (whether live-action or computer graphics) becomes much more manageable. Now imagine if we allow multiple decision points, with multiple branches. We could quickly end up with something that looks like this:

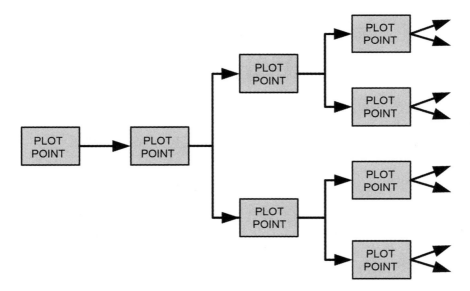

Figure 6.6 *Complex branched structure.*

If each of the nodes on each of the branches was significantly different from the others in the story progression, the scope of the content production clearly gets out of hand quickly. This is the fundamental danger, and failing, of large-scale interactive stories. Writers and designers of interactive stories have to rein in the understandable impulse to make every decision result in completely and highly significant differences.

A common variation of the branching structure makes use of what are called "chokepoints" to pull a branched story back into a single trunk. The advantage of this structure is that the story can make use of a significant branch to make a particular decision meaningful but not have to worry (as much) about the story branching out continuously into ever-increasing complexity as in the diagram above. This is what a branched structure with chokepoints looks like:

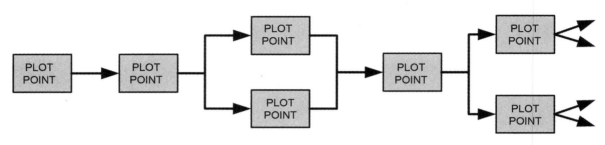

Figure 6.7 *Branch with chokepoints structure.*

As we said, this is a very popular compromise between allowing decision points with significant change and controlling escalating complexity. The downside is that a perceptive player who notices the structure will realize that since the chokepoint brings the plot back to a single trunk or path any decision before the chokepoint are, effectively, meaningless. Look again at the diagram above – neither choice ultimately matters because the chokepoint resets everything and nullifies what came before. The player-character could have taken either decision path prior to the chokepoint and it just doesn't matter after the chokepoint.

There are, of course, other types of interactive story structures out there. We're going to look at two of them before moving on – the *parallel structure* and the *non-linear structure*.

Parallel structure is built on the idea of theme and variation. The difference choices produce different but similar results. Let's look at parallel structure as used in the classic adventure game *Under a Killing Moon*. Here's a representation of the plot structure from that game:

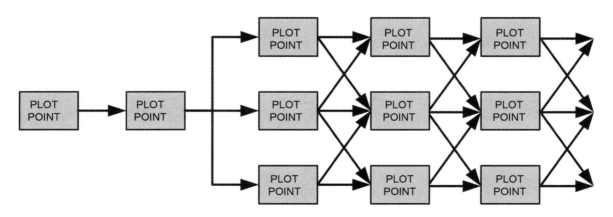

Figure 6.8 *Parallel Structure diagram.*

Each row, or tier, represents the different way the story plays through depending on the player-character's *attitude*. If the player's decisions reflect a more heroic, "white knight" mindset, the character progresses on the lowest tier and experiences the appropriate story progression. If the player's decisions represent a more cynical, bitter, world-view the player-character progresses through the top-most tier. The middle tier represents a "neutral" approach. The player-character's movement through the story can shift from tier to tier depending on the player's dialogue or action choices. In response, the tier the player-character is currently on only affects which characters like or dislike the player-character, how they speak to the main character, and what dialogue choices are available to the player during conversation scenes. The current tier can have significant consequences such as the police refusing to cooperate with him if he's on the cynical tier to criminal figures taking the opportunity to bush-whack him in a dark alley if he's on the white-knight tier. Some of the content on each tier is unique, but a large amount of it is a variation on the same content. So, if the player-character goes to a nightclub and interacts with the staff and patrons, the experience could be very different depending on which tier he's currently on and how he's treated.

Non-linear structure is the structure used in popular games like the *Grand Theft Auto* franchise, *Red Dead Redemption* and the *Mass Effect* franchise. In this structure, the player-character is able to explore the world as they wish. Depending on where the player-character is in the master story, different subplots or side missions can be discov-ered, usually in different locations. Some of these side missions may be related to the master story, but need not be. This sort of a structure is very difficult to diagram, but let's give it a shot.

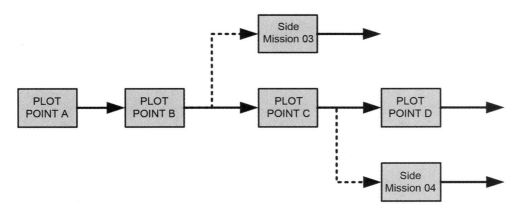

Figure 6.9 *Non-linear structure diagram.*

In the diagram above, as the player moves through the master plot, the different side missions (depicted as offshoots of the main plot) become available. So, until the player completes Plot Point B, Side Mission 03 cannot be accessed. The location in the game world may be accessible, but the side-mission may not be playable for some reason. For example, in the *Grand Theft Auto* series, buildings in the city are closed and inaccessible if the player-character finds them before the side-mission that uses that location is available.

Ideally, side-missions have their own beginning-middle-end plot structure, and often require visiting multiple locations (which is why it is logical to think of them as subplots). Sometimes, a side-mission can be started at a certain point in the main story, but cannot be completed until another, later point in the main story is reached.

We're not going to try and diagram it, but imagine blending the complex branching plot structure with the open world structure. Not only would the result be incredibly difficult to design and write, but it would take an insane amount of content creation to realize. Non-linear games usually have a simple main plot structure, or a branched one with chokepoints structure. That said, it is entirely possible that some number of the side-missions could have their own branched-with-chokepoints or complex-branching structure, with their smaller scale making the complexity more manageable.

The Concepts of Agency and Affordance

There are two very important concepts that need to be addressed when dealing with interactive narrative: *agency* and *affordance*. These are both fairly academic concepts, but they have real importance in video games and they have no equivalent in motion pictures, television shows, novels, or any other non-interactive medium. These two concepts are at the heart of the concept of interactive storytelling and get a little academic and esoteric, so bear with us.

Agency was defined by Janet Murray in her 1998 work *Hamlet on the Holodeck: The Future of Narrative in Cyberspace* (The MIT Press) when she wrote:

> *The more realized the immersive environment, the more active we want to be within it. When the things we do bring tangible results, we experience the second characteristic delight of electronic environments – the sense of agency. Agency is the satisfying power to take meaningful action and see the results of our decisions and choices.*

Understanding agency is important when we think about interactive narrative in story-driven games because it is a fundamental expectation, often subconsciously, of video game players. When they do something meaningful, they expect there to be a meaningful consequence. Murray's use of the term "satisfying power" is important – games are empowering when choices are meaningful. Many video games are full of meaningless, or valueless, choices. The body count in many video games is tremendous – it is frightening to count the number of nameless security guards, enemy soldiers, monsters, or what-have-you that get killed in an action-oriented video game. Because the enemy is faceless, because there will be another two, or three, or ten monsters in the next room, choosing to kill any of them is effectively a meaningless decision. There can be meaning in *why* the player-character kills in a sufficiently character-driven story, but very often the enemies to overcome are simply obstacles or effectively a puzzle to solve in order to progress through the story.

This isn't to say that this kind of gameplay shouldn't be in a video game – hardly – but if this is the only kind of interaction, the only kind of agency, present, the player is going feel the lack of meaningfulness as the game grinds on and on. This kind of gameplay can be present, but must be interspersed with more meaningful gameplay – choices that have real consequences – in order for the game to have substance.

Quantic Dream's *Heavy Rain*, released by Sony Computer Entertainment in 2010 presents agency in a different way. The game's storyline focuses on four different characters – all playable – who are involved with the mystery of the serial killer who has kidnapped the son of one of the protagonists. Much of *Heavy Rain*'s early interactivity (it is difficult to call it gameplay) is mundane and focused on tasks common in everyday life – cooking, cleaning, and so on. The emphasis on these seemingly meaningless choices and interactivity serves to actually enhance the importance of other certain seemingly mundane choices by amplifying their importance. For example, at one point in the story it is the birthday of one of Ethan's two sons. At the party, the player must decide which of Ethan's two children to play with, and how, and the meaningfulness of this decision as a metaphor for a father's life-long interaction with his children brings significant gravitas to the decision.

Affordance is related to agency, but it specifically relates to those action possibilities her player perceives as achievable – and likely – within the environment, and by the player-character. The term came to prominence in the 1988 book by Donald Norman, *The Design of Everyday Things* (Basic Books), which delved into how human beings interact with objects and systems and how the design of the object, as well as the potential user's desires, knowledge, and past experiences influence their fundamental, intuitive understanding of how to interact with that object. When playing a video game, there is a finite list of what a player-character can do, based on the design of the game. For example, a character in a video game cannot fly unless it has been somehow built into the game (designed, programmed, and the art, animation and sound effects for it all implemented). In the same manner, a player-character cannot open a cabinet or desk drawer unless this functionality has been specifically built into the game. While that affordance (the expectation and understanding that drawers have a particular shape, usually have knobs or handles, and can therefore be opened or operated in a certain manner) exists in real-life, video game players have learned that they have to discover what the possible actions and interactions are in a video game, usually through experimentation and trial-and-error. Inconsistent affordance is a bane of many video games, such as when the player learns that a particular object can be used logically in certain circumstances, but not in other equally logical circumstances. For example, the player-character is able to pick up and use a crowbar to open a locked trunk in the game, but it cannot be used to pry open a locked cabinet. Similarly, there may be a baseball bat in the game that can be used to break things open, or used as a weapon, but the similarly sized, shaped, and wielded crowbar cannot. This is a failure of affordance, and is all too common in video games.

Agency and Affordance and the Transmedia Property

Delving into the concepts of agency and affordance is perhaps a little too deep-thinking for a section that is ostensibly introductory to video games and game storytelling for the neophyte. That said, the reason these concepts are here, and the point that we've been building up to in the last few sections, is that they are critical for the success of a transmedia property that has video games as one of its mediums, especially those that have an expression in another medium as their mothership.

Why? Simply put, players have expectations. Players that have seen the James Bond film *Quantum of Solace* (2008) (and perhaps dozens of previous Bond films and read many of the novels) have a preconception of what James Bond is capable of. Having been exposed to James Bond in all of these forms, they have an understanding of the affordances reasonably attributable to Bond, and if the video game does not allow Bond to be Bond, it will fail. The same goes for a video game set in the *Star Wars* universe, or the *Harry Potter* universe. Certain kinds of actions and interactions are possible in the *Star Wars* or *Harry Potter* universes that must be possible in the game version, or that game will fail. Much earlier in this chapter, we talked about how it was important that adaptations of one work into another be respectful of the integrity of the original work – this is especially true for video games in that not only does the game have to be respectful of the story of the original work, but the affordances, or possible actions and interactions, of that work as well. Can you imagine the outcry of a *Harry Potter* video game where the main characters couldn't cast spells? An extreme example, perhaps, but one that clearly gets to the heart of the matter.

Does the video game version of a property have to completely model everything that exists or is possible in the mothership? Certainly not, but it must adhere to the core and spirit of the material. Video game players understand that not everything is possible in a video game, and can be very forgiving in that area (the rabble found on certain Internet discussion sites notwithstanding) but it has to be clear to them that an effort has been made to capture the spirits and feel of the property. Can you get away with doing a *Star Wars* game without there being Force powers?

Maybe, but players do not expect a game to completely and religiously simulate all the possible aspects of "the Force" seen in *Star Wars* movies, novels, comics, animated TV series, and even other video games. Compare the use of force powers in the *Star Wars: Knights of the Old Republic* (LucasArts, 2003) role-playing games, the *Star Wars: The Force Unleashed* (LucasArts, 2008) action games, and the *Star Wars: The Old Republic* (Electronic Arts/LucasArts, 2011) massively multiplayer game. All of them ostensibly have the same "Force" abilities at work, but each of them has slightly or somewhat difference affordances for those powers. Yet, each of them is *Star Wars*.

Could you have *Star Wars* without the Force at all? Lucasarts, the video game development company owned by Lucusfilm, the makers of the *Star Wars* films, is producing a video game entitled *Star Wars 1313* which is a cinematic action game set in the criminal underground beneath the surface of the Imperial homeworld, Coruscant. The main character of *Star Wars 1313* is a bounty hunter who uses an arsenal of exotic weapons in his quest to uncover a criminal conspiracy. The game shifts the emphasis in this kind of game from Jedi to bounty hunters and most likely away from Force powers in the hands of the player-character. At the time of writing, a release date had not been announced, so perhaps those reading this book will already know, or know soon enough, if a video game without Force powers can accepted as *Star Wars*. (Yes, we know about *X-Wing* and *Tie Fighter*, and various other vehicle-based *Star Wars* games, which is why we've said "this kind of game" enough times to be annoying (and to cover our butts.))

Character, Action, and the Expression of Character

Characters in games are tricky things. The more deeply defined a character is, the more restrictive it is, in some ways, for the player. We've already looked at the character of Niko Belic in *Grand Theft Auto IV* and if the choices presented in that game are narrow because they reflect the choices that Niko would make, not the ones the player might want to make. That game would be very different if Niko was, in fact, reformed, or on the path to redemption and the player had the choice to play him that way. The writers and designers had to make important decisions about the interaction opportunities available to the player in *Grand Theft Auto IV* since those choices, in very real ways, define the person Niko is. Exaggerating slightly, Niko cannot donate to charity, help an old lady across the street, give first-aid to an injured pedestrian, volunteer at a hospital or any number of other things the player might wish him to do, if they wished him to be something other than a thug. Niko is exactly the character that *Grand Theft Auto IV* allows him to be.

Grand Theft Auto IV, the *Uncharted* franchise, the *Tomb Raider* franchise, *Red Dead Redemption* and others are all examples of games with strongly-defined main characters, and the gameplay and interaction options in those games are built around the things the main character would do. Other games, such as *The Elder Scrolls: Skyrim* (Bethesda Softworks, 2011) and similar role-playing games, give the player complete customization control of the main character, including gender and a wide range of appearance options, as well as the option to name the main character. The player can also usually choose the background of the character (from a pre-defined list) and what type of character he or she is, such as warrior, priest, sorcerer, and so on. *Skyrim*, like other role-playing games in the same style, can only tailor the story to the character in the broadest strokes, or provide story based on one or more of the concrete decisions the player made during character creation. In the *Dragon Age* series of games from Bioware/Electronic Arts, the character's introduction to the master story varies with whether or not they are a warrior, magician or rogue/thief and whether they are human, or not. Specifics of the introductory story are reflected later on in the master story, and in the main character's interaction with other characters, but the character basically starts as an outsider to the main story and then becomes a greater part of it as the game progresses.

We say that characters in games like *Grand Theft Auto, Tomb Raider, Uncharted*, and others are strongly-defined because they have extensive backstories and fleshed-out personalities, and the interaction choices in the game are narrowly defined to represent the actions the main character would logically take. Characters in games like *Skyrim, Dragon Age, Half-Life, Halo, Mass Effect* and others are weakly-defined because their backstories are much thinner (sometimes non-existent), their personalities undefined or completely up to the player, and the interaction choices broadly defined because the player has the option to play the character as he or she chooses.

In the *Uncharted* series of games (*Uncharted: Drake's Fortune* (2007), *Uncharted: Among Thieves* (2009), and *Uncharted: Drake's Deception* (2011)), developed by Naughty Dog and published by Sony Computer Entertainment, the main character of Nathan Drake is strongly defined, and his personality, ethics, morality, and to some extent world-view are made clear in the game's dialogue and scenes. But here's the interesting thing: when a decision point comes up that does allow the player some choice it is the rare player that thinks "What would Nathan do here?" but rather thinks "What do I want to do here?"

The distinction is important because players project themselves onto (some would say into) the main character (again, that concept of player-character) and takes on the role of that character. Some players are very conscious of the personality of the main character, and act and react appropriately, but many simply play as an extension of themselves and act as they'd wish to. Some players, especially in games with weakly-defined characters, make conscious decisions to play in a specific way (heroic, evil, cowardly, brazen, reckless, etc.) and make a general personality decision during character creation, while others simply begin play and let the decisions in the game define the character throughout play.

Strongly-defined characters allow the game's writers to firmly link the character into the game's story. They know who the character is, what their backstory is, who their enemies and friends are, what moments in their past defined who and what they are, and so on. This allows the writers to create very character-driven stories. One would think, from this, that strongly-defined characters would dominate games, but the popularity of player-created main character games, and hugely successful games with weak anonymous or semi-anonymous characters such as *Half-Life, Halo,* or *Mass Effect* belie that.

Despite the fact that players do not think "What would Nathan do?" and project themselves into the situations and decisions that confront Nathan Drake, there is a sense that they are guiding the character through his adventure. The reflects back on our earlier point about *LA Noir* and the fact that the main character of Cole Phelps looks like the actor behind him, Aaron Staton. Cole Phelps is strongly defined, and so the player's job is to guide Cole Phelps through his story.

In game with weakly-defined characters (again, *Half-Life, Halo, Mass Effect* and others) the same perspective exists. Players of *Halo 3* guide Master Chief, whose face is never seen and name is never spoken, through his heroic adventure. Though academics, game theorists and fans alike will debate endlessly about strongly-defined characters vs. weakly defined characters it doesn't seem to matter to players. What seems to matter to players is that what the character *does* is compelling.

Action and Gameplay

We're going to draw a line in the sand, or plant our flag, or whatever metaphor you like, and say that games with bad gameplay *cannot* be saved by a good story, but that games with a bad story *can* be saved by good gameplay. The implications of this for your transmedia storytelling property are significant, and it means that you cannot just believe you have a great story and assume that you'll have a good, successful game because of it. Games are fundamentally about *gameplay* supported (and vice-versa) by a good story (or at least a good conceit for the gameplay).

What the player-character *does* in the game is gameplay, pure and simple. It could be running, jumping, shooting, dodging, building, destroying, talking, investigating, researching or any number of action verbs. Whatever those action verbs are, however, must be supported by the story, and vice-versa. You could create a James Bond game that was all about talking and researching (*007: Desk Job* anyone?) if you really wanted, but it would not be what people expect in a James Bond game. You could probably get away with that as a novelty short story, or an interlude in a game, but it wouldn't stand as the basis for entire game.

Gameplay does not mean action. Ubisoft's hugely successful line of games based on the CBS television series *CSI: Crime Scene Investigation* are relatively simple games that are all about investigation, research, and character interrogation. There's no action to be had, and yet they sell extremely well because the gameplay appeals to the *CSI* fan who wants to experience what it is like to be a crime scene investigator. Her Interactive's *Nancy Drew* game series are also hugely popular and have (basically) the same gameplay as the *CSI* games, but have a very different look and feel designed to appeal to fans of the Nancy Drew novels. (We'll have more to say about the *Nancy Drew* novels and games in Chapter 7.)

Gameplay also has to be executed well. There are many games that try and play like *Grand Theft Auto IV* with its open-world structure and "sandbox" gameplay, but most have failed because it takes a great deal of time and effort, and skill, to create good gameplay. "Sandbox" gameplay, by the way, refers to a style of gameplay found in games like the *Grand Theft Auto* series, the *Elder Scrolls* series, *Fallout*, and others, where a certain amount of the core gameplay is undirected and the player is free to roam the open world as he or she sees fit and engage in gameplay that is more environmentally-driven than story-driven. The term "sandbox" is often used synonymously with "open-world" incorrectly since the former refers to the gameplay mechanics in use and the latter to the story structure.

We talk about the realities of the game development process later in this chapter, but this is as good a time as any to stress that the development of good, core, gameplay takes time. A certain amount of the gameplay in any new game is influenced by the successful examples that have come before it, but even so it takes time and expertise to implement properly. Some of the gameplay also needs to be specific to the property and requires even more time and effort to get right. Again, we strongly advocate hiring professionals with experience in the area.

It is well out of the scope of this book to go into gameplay theory and execution, and a number of great books on the subject are listed in the appendix. The point that needs to be made here is that gameplay trumps story, but the story has to be strong and engaging, and that both need to work together to keep the player coming back for more.

Character Motivation

In an earlier section when we put forth that having a strongly-defined or weakly-defined character doesn't matter as much as what the character does, we deliberately left out the key element that any good storyteller knows. Why did we do this? Strongly-defined or weakly-defined, what matters is what the character does, and why.

The character's actions have to hook into his purpose. Stories in games are often – rightly so – criticized for their flatness. The reason for that flatness is that the "story" that compels the character to action is really just a conceit, a justification, for action, not a motivation and the story itself just a sketch of all the things that really matter in storytelling. For a long time, game stories were all about that simple conceit, but we can see that looking at the truly successful game franchises, particularly the story-driven ones, that compelling story is necessary for greatness.

Example: Halo: Combat Evolved

The original *Halo: Combat Evolved* video game developed by Bungie and published by Microsoft Game Studios in November of 2001 is an interesting case study. There is no question that the primary thrust of *Halo* was the combat gameplay (it's even in the name of the game), and in that area is succeeded magnificently. The story – particularly the motivation – of the main character appears, however, at first glance to be fairly thin (just a conceit) but it turns out to be far more than that.

The player-character, Master Chief Petty Officer John-117, is as weakly-defined a character (using the definition we put forth earlier) as they come – he's anonymous in that his face is never seen (ever); he's a man of few words, and his backstory is unknown in the game. In fact, while under player control he never speaks and his voice is only heard during cinematic cut-scenes. In the game, the character is only referred to as "Master Chief" and his full name is only known from the novel *Halo: The Fall of Reach* (Eric Nylund, Del Rey), which is a prequel to the video game and released about the same time as the game. The game in combination with the novel provides a true transmedia storytelling experience in that not only is the Master Chief's origin revealed, but the sequence of events leading up to the plot of the game is as well, providing additional information and emotional depth to the game's players. (Larry Hyrb of Microsoft's "Major Nelson" podcast on December 9, 2009 revealed that the *Halo: The Fall of Reach* novel has sold about a million copies by that date.)

We refer to Master Chief as "weakly-defined," but that does not mean he isn't a strong character. *TIME* Magazine looked at the character of Master Chief, the *Halo* franchise, and its creators in August 2007 in light of the upcoming release of *Halo 3*. The article makes note of the game's literary and lyrical touches, and its operatic, even Wagnerian, music and architecture. Writer Lev Grossman in the article says:

> *The face of the Master Chief is never revealed. His visor is solid reflective gold, like the faceplates of the Apollo astronauts. Halo's designers see the Master Chief's facelessness as a dramatic device, a way of allowing players to place themselves in the game's leading role, to map their own faces onto that of a blank protagonist. "If he takes off the helmet, he should be you," says Marty O'Donnell, Halo's audio director. "I mean, that's the big deal. Taking off the helmet is unacceptable." Engineering lead Chris Butcher agrees: "It's your experience. You have to be able to pour yourself into that icon." When nongamers look at the Master Chief's helmet, they see a forbidding, anonymous mask. But when gamers look at it, they see a mirror. They see themselves.*

Video Games: The Man in the Mask[2]

Despite this anonymity, Master Chief has been included in lists of top video game characters from websites like IGN, UGO, and others. He's also become the *de facto* iconic image for the X-Box gaming console and to some extent Microsoft Game Studios. Sure, his armor design is cool, but what makes the character that cool?

It's not just Master Chief – it's all the pieces around him. It's the imperatives in the superb storytelling, the classic imagery that elevates the tale to mythic status, and the gameplay that not only makes the player feel bad-ass as the Master Chief but integrates the environment and mission design into once cohesive whole. In the storytelling, it's the immediate threat of the covenant, the mystery and majesty of the alien artifact world that is the Halo itself, the discovery that the immediate threat against the Earth – the alien covenant – is the least of Earth's (and Master Chief's) problems, and its relationship between the Master Chief and the artificial intelligence Cortana that accompanies him. The dialogue between the Master Chief and Cortana serves to provide emotion and humanity to the Master Chief who, without this interaction, and due to his weakly-defined character could appear soulless (no insult to the player intended).

This is the important takeaway from looking at *Halo*, and it is a pattern that is repeated in successful game after successful game: where characters in motion pictures and television must be strongly-defined, characters in games

[2]accessed June 14, 2012, http://www.time.com/time/magazine/article/0,9171,1657825,00.html#ixzz1xDAMtvyu

can be weakly-defined, but if they are they must be supported by all of the other elements in the game, including theme, setting, other characters and especially the gameplay. Master Chief is an iconic hero for a generation of video game players because of what he does and how he does it – action expressing character – rather than who he is. Unless they've read the companion novels, gamers don't even know his name.

Dialogue and Conversation

We're going to touch briefly on dialogue and conversation even though it is really a game design and implementation decision and therefore outside the scope of this book. That said, and despite the imperative of "show, don't tell," because of the often complex plots and backstory of games, a great deal of exposition comes out through dialogue. Dialogue and conversation generally manifests in one of three forms in video games:

- **Non-interactive cinematics**: Characters appear and interact in these pre-rendered scenes, but the player has no control over what happens. Most games allow the player to skip these scenes with a simple key press, which is dangerous for storytelling because it means that players could easily miss some important piece of information. In terms of appearance and ease of production, this is the most schedule- and budget-friendly option, depending of course on scope and number.
- **Scripted scenes**: In many ways these are similar to non-interactive cinematics except that they occur in the game engine rather than being pre-rendered. Sometimes the player has control and can move around while the scene plays out, sometimes they are locked in place. The scene cannot be skipped, but in games that allow the player to retain movement it is possible for the player to move away and miss some of the content of the scene. Because they occur in the game environment, the player-character scripted scenes can often be interrupted or affected by the main character's presence. Very often, other characters in the game are involved in the scripted scene and if the player approaches and becomes involved either a non-interactive cinematic or interactive conversation activates.
- **Interactive conversation**: In an interactive conversation scene, the player has some degree of control over the conversation. Most video game conversation scenes are more like interrogations than conversations, in that the player gets to choose from a list of questions or responses and then hear the response from another character, and then repeat the process. The scenes are often very static with locked cameras and a few changes of camera positions. In games with weakly-defined characters, the player-character's voice and dialogue isn't heard, but the other characters react as if it was. Some video games, like the *Mass Effect* series have very complex and evolved conversations systems that control not only dialogue responses, but character actions as well. Let's take a closer look at the system used in *Mass Effect*.

Example: Mass Effect *Conversations*

The *Mass Effect* series of games introduced a sophisticated dialogue and action control system called the conversation wheel. The effect is that interactive conversations in *Mass Effect* play more like movie sequences than traditional static game dialogue scenes. As a conversation scene plays out, the player is able to control the main character, Commander Shepard's, dialogue choices in near real-time. The game presents the player with the dialogue line Shepard needs to respond to, and then multiple response choices.

Figure 6.10 *Master Effect conversation wheel.*

The different choices reflect different attitudes that Shepard can use in response. Looking at the conversation wheel image, the right side of the wheel includes direct responses to the previous line, while the left side is usually requests for specific information, and is only present at certain times. On the right side of the wheel, the top-most response ("Can I help?" in the example) is more straight-up heroic, white-knight response, the middle ("What's going on?") more neutral or inquiry-driven, and the bottom ("Only a dozen?") more wise-cracking,

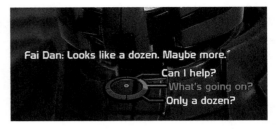

Figure 6.11 *Conversation wheel close-up.*

but still heroic. The player is sometimes given the option to perform an "interrupt" action which triggers an in-game action, like punching someone, pushing a button, or something similar, depending on the situation.

What makes the *Mass Effect* system very effective is how well it flows. The controls are responsive enough that the player can immediately respond to another character's line of dialogue, and the scene continues effectively uninterrupted and feeling like a movie scene or pre-rendered cinematic scene. It not only keeps the game moving, but gives the player a real feel of being in control of Command Shepard and constantly engaged in the decision-making process.

Game Production Realities

The video game production process is nothing like the production process in motion pictures or television. Both of those mediums share common technology, methodologies, production team structure (mostly), and postproduction techniques. Video game production, for the most part, shares none of these things with either medium. In some cases, technology is used in similar ways, but even then there are significant differences. In addition, the business end of video game development is very different from either motion pictures or television. The publication and distribution of video games is not very different from that of DVD/Blu-Ray products, but that's the very tail end of the production process and is, in many ways, the easiest part (marketing, advertising, and sales people will argue that last part, of course).

For a long time, video game tie-ins to motion pictures and television programs were considered marketing or advertising projects, and very often funded from those budgets. That is less true today, but the perception (somewhat understandably) still exists and the video game project is viewed as part of cross-media marketing effort in support of the primary medium. There is nothing inherently wrong with this approach, as long as such is understood by all parties and sufficient production time is allowed for a quality video game to be produced and not something that feels rushed. A video game project that is rushed through production will feel rushed because usually what is removed from the schedule in order to meet a shortened production cycle is the time at the end of the project needed to maximize gameplay, clean up any software bugs, and apply appropriate spit-and-polish to the art and audio.

It is important to understand that video game development is primarily a *software development* process, not a *media production* process. The requirements, realities, and pitfalls are vastly different and need to be considered appropriately. It is very easy to focus on the visual appearance of a game and therefore think of it in terms of traditional media production, but unlike motion pictures or television where the canvas is 35 mm film or high-definition video, both of which are known technological hurdles with solved problems, video game engines are crazy complex pieces of software that are, in great part, custom made for each video game project. We touched on video game engines a little earlier, and we will again, but the reality is that video game development is software development, and that's a different beast entirely.

Before we delve further into the realities of game production, let's first look at the single largest element that affects transmedia project development: timing.

Production Time and Timing

Games take a great deal of time to produce. Hopefully it is obvious, but the larger the project the more time it takes. How long? Of course that depends on the content of the game, but here's an overly-simplified breakdown in terms of time and project size:

	Time
Small mobile or web game	6–8 months
Large mobile or web game	8–12 months
XBLA/PSN/small PC game	8–14 months
Handheld system game	12–18 months
Large console/PC game	18–36 months
Massively multiple/online	36 months+

Generally speaking, the low end of the scale is a short-cycle (some would say rushed) and the high end of the scale the preferred (some would say generous) cycle time. Have successful games been made on shorter or longer production cycles? Of course. Your mileage may vary depending on a variety of factors including the scope and complexity of the game, the experience of the production team, the release requirements, whether or not the game is built with existing technology, or is a sequel using the same game engine, and so on.

The bottom line is that video game production takes time. If you have a motion picture property that you want to produce a companion game for, you need to start production early enough for the game to go through the production cycle and be ready for release with your motion picture. If we accept 24 months for a large console or home computer game, and look at the typical period from motion picture green-light to release, we see that the game has to be in production *before* the motion picture is contracted to begin production. Obviously, this is a scheduling issue that requires careful planning and preparation. Large summer blockbuster motion picture productions often have long postproduction cycles that can work to the benefit of trying to sync releases, but it can still be difficult to coordinate. This is one of the reasons, as we advocate elsewhere in this book, that is it important that transmedia storytelling properties be conceived *in toto* rather than piecemeal, or tacked together after the fact, if at all possible.

Production Methodologies

Again, there are entire books (and much better books) devoted to this topic, so we're only going to touch the surface here. There are three primary forms of game production methodologies that you'll encounter in the game development world, and which one used depends very much on the scale of the project and the particular development studio employed. We cover them briefly here because they include terms that are bound to come up in discussions of video game development production and schedules.

Agile Development

Agile development is a development practice that focuses on short production sub-cycles (known as sprints) within the larger project, and narrowly defined goals for each sprint. At the end of the sprint, the status of the project is reviewed, the results of the sprint thoroughly tested, and a set of goals generated for the next sprint. Agile is a very effective methodology better suited to smaller teams, and so is often used for mobile or web-delivered projects. It also requires an experienced team who are able to make extremely realistic and accurate decisions and time-to-completion estimates. The process is highly iterative, meaning that while general long-term goals are defined, production does not proceed on the assumption of what might work, or be effective, but rather in extensive testing of what is currently working and continual evaluation to determine any changes to the design or process to achieve those goals. Agile productions often have minimal documentation of design or technology plans as those decisions are made based on sprint iteration evaluations. This lack of documentation can make some producers very nervous, but that's a trust issue some producers have to get past. The Agile method requires a closer to real-time communication loop with the developers, certainly during the sprint evaluations, in order for the producer to stay in sync with the production. You'll often hear the terms SCRUM or extreme programming mentioned, which are variations of the basic Agile process.

Iterative Development (Cerny Method)

A criticism of the Agile method, and one of the reasons that it does not work well for large-scale productions, is that it defers certain decisions until they can be implemented, by one means or another, and then tested. With large-scale productions, especially those requiring a long art production cycle, some decisions cannot be put off as they would delay the entire production.

The iterative development model, sometimes referred to as the Cerny Method, advocates what is essentially an agile preproduction phase that transitions into a more highly-structured and scheduled production phase but also relies on a highly-iterative testing and verification process (especially for gameplay.) The Cerny Method is named after renowned game developer Mark Cerny (*Sonic the Hedgehog 2*, *Crash Bandicoot*, *Spyro the Dragon*, *Ratchet and Clank*, and so on) who became so much a primary advocate of the methodology that it is now referred to by his name. The Cerny Method also advocates more documentation and planning during the production phase than the Agile method as it recognizes that not every decision can, or should be, an Agile one. The Cerny Method has been used on game development projects of all scales, scopes, and platforms.

Waterfall Model

This is the traditional development model used in video game production, and is a heavily documented, highly sequenced and planned process, with a great deal of the decision-making occurring up-front, including a week-by-week, or sometimes a day-by-day project/task schedule built to cover the duration of the project. One of the reasons for the popularity of the waterfall model is that there are so many stakeholders involved in the development process that extensive up-front documentation is needed to confirm buy-in and direction prior to production funding. Also, large video game productions projects are so large, some with hundreds of team members, that more iterative or agile methodologies are hard to maintain and synchronize across the entire project.

The waterfall method is often criticized, often rightly so, for being too regimented and inflexible, given that in gameplay and software development all of the problems are not known, and cannot be known, at the start of production. Alternatives like the Cerny Method, and even Agile, have arisen to provide more responsive methodologies.

The documentation we discuss in Appendix C, with the exception of the Game Vision Document, is most associated with the waterfall model as that is the method still in use at most development studios.

Developers and Publishers

Quick definitions:

Publisher: Funding, licensing, marketing, customer support, and distribution is handled by publishers in the video game industry. Publishers hire development studios (see following) to create the video game project. Some publishers own their own development studios or have exclusive (or near exclusive) deals with them, some involving partial ownership. Self-publishing is becoming more and more common, especially in the mobile and web-delivered markets. Also, as digital distribution becomes more and more common, smaller development studios are making their own deals with distributors, effectively becoming publishers themselves as well. Publishers have varying (but significant) approval rights with regard to the final product, and in the case of licensed projects are responsible for managing all licensing and licensing approval requirements. (We're going to look at licensing in more detail in the next section.) Most large media conglomerates, such as Warner Brothers, Disney, Paramount, and so on have their own publishers and in most cases wholly or partially-owned development studios.

Examples of publishers include Activision Blizzard, Electronic Arts, Microsoft, Nintendo, Sony, THQ, Bethesda/ZeniMax and Ubisoft. For a pretty complete listing of video game industry publishers, go to www.gamedevmap.com.

Developer: The developer, or development studio, is responsible for the production, programming, art, design, sound, music, testing, and patching/bug fixing. Developers are hired by publishers, usually on a contracted, project-by-project basis, to produce a specific title within a specified timeframe for the negotiated price. Some developers are owned outright by publishers and other have very specific production agreements with certain publishers. The larger the development studio, the greater the likelihood that the house has a significant relationship with a publisher.

Examples of developers include BioWare (EA), Blizzard Entertainment (Activision Blizzard), Day 1 Studios (Independent), Disney Interactive Studios (Disney), Double Fine Productions (Independent), Gearbox (Independent), Naughty Dog (Sony), Netherrealms (Warner Bros) and 343 Studios (Microsoft). For a pretty complete listing of video game industry developers, go to www.gamedevmap.com.

> **First party developer:** *A first party developer is a development studio that is working directly for one of the big console game hardware manufacturers: Microsoft (Xbox 360), Nintendo (Nintendo Wii, DS/DSi, and the Wii U) or Sony (Playstation 3, or Playstation Vita). In this case, the hardware manufacturer is also the publisher.*

> **Third party developer:** *A third party developer is a development studio that is working for a publisher on a console game who is not Microsoft, Nintendo or Sony.*

> **Independent developer:** *A developer who is not owned wholly or in part by a publisher. There are fewer and fewer independent developers who produce large-scale games, primarily because ownership or a formalized relationship with a publisher streamlines funding and mitigates risk. The term "indie developer" has come to refer to small, independent development studios that produce games for the mobile, web-delivered, or the Xbox Live Arcade or Sony Playstation Network distribution channels.*

Licensing

We talk about transmedia property licensing in another chapter in this book, and there is little difference when it comes to video game licensing, whether it is from another medium for making a video game tie-in or in licensing a video game property.

When a publisher/developer is licensed to produce a video game tie-in it is on a contractual basis. Even if the rights-holder has a relationship with a publisher and/or developer, there is still some level of formal agreement and rights review and approval process put into place. As a normal part of the video game development process, periodic "builds" representing the current state of the project are sent to the publisher and/or rights-holder for approval. Usually, the contracted payment to the developer (or some other accounting transaction depending on the relationship between all the parties involved) is contingent upon successful approval of that build of the game. The particulars for approval are written into the development contract.

Also written into the contract are particulars related to who owns what. Rights are retained by the rights-holder and permission specifically given for the production of the licensed product. Generally, all materials produced, including any writing or art is owned by the rights-holder or in some cases the publisher, depending on the agreement, and copies are turned over to whomever the contract specifies at the end of the project. In many cases, the programming used to create the game is also owned by the contractor, but not in all cases. This is especially true if the development studio has a proprietary game engine that they created prior to the current contract. Most often in this case any programming created specifically for the contracted project is owned by the contractor, but the developer retains the rights to the underlying game engine.

The Game Production Process

The general structure of the video game production process is not dissimilar to the structure of film or television productions. In those mediums, the majority of the production effort is focused on the "shoot days" when the production is live on set or location and the bulk of material is created. Big-budget visual effects (VFX) intensive productions can have significantly more VFX production time scheduled than live-action time, but the VFX production time is traditionally scheduled as part of the postproduction process. An interesting aside, director Andrew Stanton (*Finding Nemo*, *WALL-E*) who was making his first live-action film with Disney's *John Carter* broke his production time into "live-action" and "digital production," acknowledging that the digital effects process had become so much a part of production that it made no sense to classify it as a "postproduction" effort when so much of the film relied on it.

There are no "shoot days" in video game production. There are specific, often monthly, "milestone" deliverables that represent the current snapshot of the game's state, and some milestones are categorized as more critical than others, but there is no window of time when the bulk of the game is created. Creation occurs somewhat equally across the entirety of the production schedule, more or less. In the next section entitled Game Production Scheduling and Milestones we'll categorize some of those milestones and talk about their importance internally to the production, and externally to the publishers and rights-holders.

Video game production is broken into three primary phases: *preproduction*, *production* and *postproduction*. The overwhelming amount of time is spent in production, with preproduction allocated anywhere from 10 to 15% of the production schedule, and postproduction a similar amount, though sometimes less. We'll talk about each of those phases in the next sections.

Game Production Scheduling and Milestones

Smaller games need less formal scheduling than larger ones. Large, complicated, home computer or game console titles need schedules so detailed that there are members of some teams whose job it is just to track who needs to do what when. The game project schedule also serves as a tool to ensure that the project is progressing on schedule and that the right tasks are getting done. There are multiple methodologies for project tracking, and some work better than others for different scale games. There are some wonderful books out there specifically about game project management and tracking, and the scope of such is too big for this book to cover, so we'll refer you the Appendix instead.

What we will go over here is the concept of milestones in the schedule. Milestones are contractually defined deliverables that occur regularly throughout the contract time. The definition of the particular deliverable varies, but it is basically a snapshot of the current state of the game, and includes a working version of the game (if the game is at that stage of development), current copies of documentation, a copy of the current schedule, copies of current artwork and sound, and so on. The contents of this deliverable go to the publisher, and perhaps the rights-holder, not just so that they can be updated on the progress of the game, but for them to approve. How much needs to be approved, and how often, varies by contract, but there is almost always a formal review process in place. A key element of the milestone and review process is that it is directly connected to the funding of the project. Usually, the contract specifies that a particular amount of the project funding is released from the publisher to the developer when certain milestones are approved. It is therefore, from a funding standpoint, important to the developer that any submitted milestone be approved promptly so that they can be paid. Likewise it is important for the publisher and any rights-holder to provide any feedback or comments on the milestone deliverable as soon as possible since development on the project continues. The schedule does not allow the developer to have the team sit idle waiting for feedback so work goes on. So it is in the best interest of the publisher or rights-holder to get their approval and feedback to the development studio as soon as possible.

Pre-preproduction

The preproduction process technically begins before any contracts are signed. Publishers either hold the intellectual property rights to a concept themselves, or are approached by another entity that hold the rights (or sub-licenses them from the rights-holder), and then decide who they want the project's development studio to be. If the development studio is in-house (wholly or partially owned) the process could be direct and take little time. If the publisher needs an out-of-house development studio (or wishes their in-house studios to compete for the project) they will issue a project specification or request-for-proposal (RFP) to the development studios they think may be interested. Interested development studios then have a deadline for submitting their proposal for the project, which is usually a less than ten-page concept document that outlines their vision for the project, why they are the right development studio for the job, and a rough schedule and proposed budget. Some proposals include a proof-of-concept video or example made using an existing game-engine. These are usually a combination of a sample of the intended art direction for the project and its gameplay. Some of these proofs-of-concept can be quite elaborate.

Note that the majority of project ideas flow from publishers to developers, but that is not always the case. Often, developers propose ideas they have been cultivating in-house to a publisher they have a relationship with, or use the new proposal as an opportunity to foster a relationship with a new publisher. As might be expected, these proposals are often very elaborate in terms of documentation and proof-of-concept presentations.

Once the RFP time is up, the publisher narrows down the candidate development studios and usually requests more detailed schedules and budgets. Often they have questions or feedback about the game concept document and require additional information or clarification on the art direction and gameplay. They also often ask very pointed questions about the development studio's ability to produce the project, especially if it is a studio they do not have a track record with.

Once the publisher chooses a development studio, contract negotiation begins. Hopefully, these negotiations take as little time as possible as, very often, the final delivery date has already been set by the publisher who has taken into account marketing, distribution, and financial concerns. Unfortunately, the negotiation time for the contract (especially with independent developers) eats into the production time and few developers are willing to launch into production without having a signed contract and its associated financial guarantees.

Preproduction

When preproduction kicks off at the development studio, a core team is assembled to start planning production. Usually this team consists of a producer (responsible for coordination, scheduling and communication with the publisher), and a lead designer, artist and programmer. Each may also have a junior member of the team to assist them.

During this stage of production it is the team's responsibility to lay the groundwork for the rest of the production and flesh out the design, art and technical documentation that the team will follow once production begins. Often, they begin work on a prototype or sample level that's used as an additional proof-of-concept for gameplay, art styles and technical issues.

During this phase of production (and again, varying on the contract) the project only has preliminary funding, which can be suspended almost at any time. In many ways, it is the job of the preproduction team to prove that this is a viable, achievable project to the publisher and that it's going to produce a great game. The team (via the producer) is in constant contact with the publisher and any rights-holders involved to insure that the project is proceeding as conceived.

The amount of the budget allocated and expended during preproduction is a fraction of the total budget, and publishers tend to use this phase as a determination of whether or not to proceed with the project. At the end of the preproduction phase a "go/no-go" or "green light" decision is made to fund the remainder of the project. When that happens, the remainder of the production team is hired, or allocated from the development studio's existing staff, and production begins.

A phrase you may hear is "ramping into production," which refers to the period of time when, at the start of production and the groundwork is being laid, there's not enough work to support the full-sized team, so team members are gradually added to the project, as needed. If the project is being staffed from within the development studio, these team members are most likely ramping off a previous project. If the development studio needs to hire from outside, time has to be built into the schedule to recruit, hire the new team members, and acclimatize them to the new company and new project. As a project reaches its end, team members are ramped off of a project as well as there becomes less and less for certain members of the team to do.

Production

Production is, well, production. Simplistically, and hopefully unnecessarily, this is when the game gets made. We've stressed this many times, but it takes time for a game to get made. And it comes together slowly. There are no dailies or rushes to look at after the first shoot day; depending on the scope of the production, it could be months before anything is reviewable, and it could be even longer before it starts to resemble the final product. This can be somewhat disconcerting to the publisher and approval coordinators such as the rights-holder, even though everyone understands this is how it is. There's so much money on the line that everyone is eager for the first taste of the game to make sure things are proceeding the way they're supposed to, that the game looks good, is fun to play, and is respectful of the intellectual property. Development studios often feel pressured to provide an example of how the final game will look and play as soon as possible, and this can create enormous stress between the studio, the publisher and the rights-holder.

Game design, finding the fun and gameplay, is what is called an "iterative" process. This means that the gameplay goes through much iteration where some part of the design is implemented, tested, and iterated to improve the gameplay. Lather, rinse, repeat.

For those outside the industry (and even for some within), that the gameplay isn't implemented and fun the first time it appears in the game is inexplicable. The thinking is that if the game has been designed properly, and the gameplay is implemented as designed, why isn't it "fun" immediately? The reasons are three-fold:

- No piece of gameplay is an island. If the design was done correctly, most, if not all, of the gameplay elements should work together. Not all of the gameplay elements appear in the game at the same time, so it's hard to evaluate a portion of the gameplay when the other elements aren't there yet. That said, it should be possible to see and understand *how* a particular element of gameplay will be fun in-and-of-itself when the rest of the design is in place. Still, it is difficult to see that sometimes.
- It may take a few technical iterations to get the implementation working properly. Game software is insanely complicated and it takes some work to get a particular piece of functionality working exactly as specified. So even though a piece of gameplay may be in the game, it may not be immediately working as designed.
- In order for a game to not feel like a knock-off, or rip-off, of another game that plays similarly, the gameplay has to be finessed to be right for *this game*. Again, that takes time and effort, and iteration.

All of these reasons involve implementation, testing and iteration. If you are looking for a metaphor from the film or television production cycles, you can think of these early iterations as "rehearsals" for the final implementation. On a shooting set, it takes a number of acting and blocking rehearsals, light tests, and camera run-throughs to get everything working together smoothly, and even then it may require a few takes to have all the parts working together. It is similar to this in video game production, but due to the complex technical nature of the development process the iterations can take days or weeks, or longer. And this iteration occurs continuously right up to nearly the end of the production phase. This "tweaking" is also an expected and necessary part of production, especially when the user-testing phase begins and the game starts getting into the hands of testers who have no prior exposure to the game (and perhaps no prior knowledge) and therefore no expectations for the game. Everyone associated with the game in production, from the publisher on down to the members of the development team, can develop tunnel vision for a project, and it is imperative that user testing occur as soon as there is a version of the gameplay that is fairly testable.

Sometimes the term "user testing" becomes confused with "focus testing." An alternative term to user testing is "play testing," but that's not entirely accurate since it is not always gameplay that is being tested. User testing in the video game industry is all about how the user reacts to the interface of the game, its gameplay and its storytelling in a very practical manner. Can the user navigate the game's control screens? Can they do so intuitively? Is the game story clear enough? And so on. Focus testing is a marketing process that looks at how a potential customer reacts to the imaging and branding of the project. Both are necessary, but they are different processes.

A video game project in development gradually takes shape, and it has to be allowed to. There are too many horror stories of publishers (who should know better) or those external to the process seeing early versions of the game while in development and panicking that it looks horrible and plays even worse. Yes, it will – at first. As the production phase continues, the game should get better and better looking, and start to play more and more like the final game is intended to. The time to be concerned is if the progress of the game seems stalled: it's not getting better looking or playing better. It's also time to be concerned if it looks like the direction of the game is veering off from what was originally proposed in the game concept document or in the documentation assembled during preproduction. Change will occur – this is natural, and part of the iterative process. A careful eye has to be kept that the change is for the better, but the communication between the development studio, the publisher and the rights-holders should be open and continuous enough that no one is surprised by any significant changes that develop. If anyone is surprised, the communication pipeline is failing, usually on the developer's end as they're not properly communicating the state of the game to all the stakeholders involved. This is why it is important for the stakeholder to keep an eye on the project as sometimes the developers, neck-deep in production and working as quickly as they can, don't realize the deviation from the intended final project.

Localization

Few, if any, large video game projects release in only one language any more. The term "localization" refers to the process of not only translating the games written and dialogue content into one or more additional languages, but making any necessary modification to the content as appropriate for the local market. For example, some countries and regions have strict limitations on certain symbols or references to topics that are considered unacceptable, and so those must be altered or replaced in the game in order to release it in that market. The localization process is usually spearheaded by a localization team affiliated with the publisher and based in, or near to, the region the game's to be released in.

First Playable Milestone

Many video game development contracts specify as one of the early production milestones something called "first playable." First playable is pretty much what it sounds like – it's the first time the gameplay exists in an evaluable form. Gameplay is usually in a very rough form and the art in the game equally so, so it can be difficult to actually perform the evaluation. But, if the development studio and the publisher and anyone else who has to evaluate or approve the first-playable deliverable are all on the same page about the project, and have been communicating, there should be no surprises. A version of this milestone, which may or may not exist as a separate milestone in the project, is referred to as a "vertical slice," which is focused on having demonstrable functionality in all the core areas of the project. What defines the first-playable and/or the vertical slice will be specifically defined in the milestone.

Alpha Milestone

The Alpha milestone is a critical production milestone that occurs as the project is nearing the end. Bug testing has already commenced and some of the team may be ramping off as certain large tasks and systems are completed. The definition of the Alpha milestone varies somewhat, but it traditionally marks the point where no additional features can be added to the game and the only work done on the game code from this point forward has to do with optimization (making the game run better) and bug fixing. Art can still be added to the game, and existing gameplay elements can be tweaked, but no new gameplay features can be added to the game.

Beta Milestone

When a game reaches Beta the only work on the game code permitted is to fix bugs – no further system optimization or modifications are permitted. Additionally, all art must be present in the game. Some of the art pieces may still be in a draft form, but there has to be a representation of every piece of art that is going to be in the game in the Beta build. Gameplay bug fixing is permitted, but no additional modifications are permitted. A significant portion of the team begins to ramp off as there becomes less and less for them to do.

An important point to be made is that, technically, at any point after Beta is reached the publisher could declare the game "done" and choose to release. If this is possible, it will be stipulated in the project contract. Bug testing is still continuing and everyone on the team looks forward to the day when more bugs are being closed than opened in a single day. This is often called the "crossover point" and some game publishers have sophisticated tracking methodologies that allow them to predict when a game will be done based on the day the project reaches the crossover point.

Certification Milestone

Video game projects to be released on console platforms have to be submitted to the console manufacturer for certification that it meets their standards for quality, content, interface, and so on. Every console manufacturer has strict certification requirements that must be adhered to. If a project fails certification it is bounced back to the developer to fix the problems. Once those problems are remedied the project must be re-submitted for certification and the process begun again. Given that the process can potentially take weeks, failing a certification submission can have serious impact on the release schedule.

Release Candidate Milestone

In some contracts, only a release candidate game build can be sent for certification, and this makes sense because the release candidate build is supposed to be one that the developer is confident could be released for production (hence the name). The publisher has the final say, and release candidate submissions are put through rigorous final testing to assure that it meets the necessary quality standards. Often, multiple release candidates are submitted to the publisher before the publisher agrees that the game is ready. When the publisher accepts the release candidate as ready for production it is called the "gold master" release. (The term comes from the early days of CD-ROM games when the final version of the game to be sent to the disk duplication manufacturer was burned onto a gold-toned disk.)

Post-Production and Post-Release Support

Technically, production ends with the Beta milestone when all content and features are in place and only bug-testing and fixing occurs going forward. The bulk of the team has ramped off by this point, or is in the process of moving on to other projects, which could be another game entirely, but could also be additional post-release content for the game (more about that in a moment).

The bug testing, reporting and fixing process is a complicated one. Care has to be taken that any changes made to the game at this point do not have unintended consequences. Despite being near to the end of production, the game is still in a fairly fragile state in that it is very easy, in the haste to fix bugs and get the game ready for release, to break parts of the game.

Invariably, when the publisher accepts a release candidate build as read for publication there are still some outstanding bugs that remain unfixed. Many of these bugs are minor or trivial and will never be noticed by the consumer.

Some of them occur in circumstances so particular that they affect only a small fraction of the consumers and so are allowed to remain. Recently it has become all but common place for a bug list to be compiled at the time of the release candidate for fixing after the game has been sent to manufacturing. This after-release fixing is done through the application of "patches," which are small software applications that are downloaded by the user (sometimes automatically by the game itself) and apply the fixes to the commercially sold version of the game.

In the previous generation of game consoles post-release patches were impossible since the game existed wholly on a disk or cartridge that could not be modified. Some of the current generation of game consoles (Microsoft Xbox and Sony Playstation 3) have hard drives that allow for patches, but the Nintendo Wii does not. So, as with the last generation, games released for the Wii have be extremely rigorously tested prior to release since there is no way to fix or update the game once it reaches manufacturing.

Customer Support

When a game goes through testing it's viewed by a couple of hundred players, at best, plus the members of the team. Within weeks of its release it could be in the hands of thousands of players, if not tens-of-thousands ... and if you're really lucky, millions. One result of this is players will be talking about your game (we talk about community building and management in another chapter), and needing help. The publisher is responsible for short- and long-term customer support, including online forums as well as customer and technical support phone lines (a rarity these days). Because video games are so complicated, because the hardware the game runs on can vary so much, and because there are now considerably more eyes looking at your project than ever before, problems will be noticed and discovered that were missed before.

A significant benefit of producing for a game console (Xbox, PlayStation, Wii) is that for the most part every single unit is identical. There are some variations (hard drive size, etc.) but those are relatively insignificant compared to the components that really matter, like the main processor, the video graphics, and the sound hardware. On any of the consoles, even between different versions of the same machine, those components are the same. This means that developers building a game for those machines can target one profile and be confident that it will run on all machines. This is so not true for home computers. There is no hardware standard for a personal computer, and there are multitudes of different processors, video cards, motherboards, memory chips, network connectors and sound cards. Some PCs come with integrated video and audio right on the motherboard, but many don't. The end result is that the total number of possible combinations of individual hardware components is so astronomically high that it is physically impossible to test all possible combinations. It cannot be done ... and that doesn't even consider the fact that the software the end-user chooses to install on their machine (or in some cases is installed without their knowledge) can create all sorts of unexpected issues. In this sense, personal computer development is a nightmare.

It is expected that problems will be found post-release, and so some of the game's team remains on the project in order to address these problems. These post-release teams are generally larger, and retained longer, for personal computer projects than for console projects. Depending on the scope of the release, game projects for mobile platforms sometimes have post-release teams, but for smaller projects or independent developers the burden usually falls to team members who are already working on other things. For larger projects, this post-release coverage – the size of the team and their duration – is part of the original project contract. If significant problems are found, the support team may be retained for longer than expected, but this often requires negotiation with the publisher over who is paying for their time, and for how long.

Downloadable and Post-Release Content

Post-release content, usually in the form of boxed expansion products or online downloadable content (DLC), is becoming more and more prevalent as a tactic to prolong the "shelf life" of a property. With the game space becoming more and more competitive for consumer dollars and shelf space (physical or virtual), it is becoming more and more important for a property to stay active and current in the minds of buyers, and post-release content is one way to do so. Additionally, with one year to 18 months between product releases in a franchise, publishers see post-release content sales as a way to continue to generate a revenue stream from a particular property.

Sometimes, post-release content is built into the original project contract, but sometimes it is covered by an additional contract drafted while the main product is in production. Often, members of the main project team roll onto producing the post-release content, but not always. For example, the downloadable content "From Ashes" for *Mass Effect 3* was created by a separate team following the main game reaching its Beta milestone.

Post-release content is a great way of not only extending the brand life of a project, but also extending its story. Staying the with *Mass Effect* series as an example, the "Lair of the Shadow Broker" DLC for *Mass Effect 2* was released in September of 2010, seven months after the release of the main game on Xbox and PC. The storyline focuses on one of the companion characters from the main game and serves to deepen the player's knowledge and understanding of that character and her backstory. The extremely positive reviews for the content invariably refer to how, in addition to the great gameplay additions, the DLC expands and builds on the story and characterization (http://www.metacritic.com/game/xbox-360/mass-effect-2-lair-of-the-shadow-broker/critic-reviews).

Video Games and Transmedia

Elsewhere we suggested visiting your favorite bookstore – real or virtual – and reviewing the shelves of video game and role-playing game novel and graphic-novel tie-ins. The shear linear feet of content there makes a persuasive argument that, shy of *Star Trek* and *Star Wars*, video games have made the most extensive use of fiction as a storytelling extension than any other medium. We'll touch more on them, but video games have also seen effective extensions with short and longer-form live-action and animation projects, such as *Dead Space: Aftermath* (Electronic Arts, 2011), the *Halo: Legends* (Warner Brothers, 2010) anime, the *Mass Effect: Paragon Lost* (Funimation, 2012) anime, and the *Dragon Age* live-action web shorts *Dragon Age: Redemption* (Bioware, 2011) and anime *Dragon Age: Dawn of the Seeker* (Oxybot, 2012). There have also been significant motion picture productions based on video games, such as *Tomb Raider*, *Resident Evil*, *Silent Hill*, *Max Payne* and others, though we'd be hard pressed to refer to any of these as transmedia storytelling. Before we look at the current state of video games and transmedia, let's look back a little way to another kind of games, table-top role-playing games, and how they laid much of the groundwork for the narrative extensions we see in video games today.

Role-Playing Games, World Building and Story Extension

The most famous of all role-playing games is undoubtedly *Dungeons and Dragons* (TSR, 1974), in all its myriad forms and rules editions. At their core, all role-playing games are essentially the same in that they are a primarily improvisational exercise in group storytelling. The terms change from game to game, but in most cases (excepting some experimental games) a group of players is led through a story by a "game master" who describes the circumstances and challenges, and the players respond by explaining how their characters respond to the scene before them. In the case of *Dungeons and Dragons*, imagine *The Lord of the Rings*, except that each of the actors portraying, Frodo, Sam, Merry, Pippen, Aragorn, Legolas and Gimli have the freedom to decide how their character responds rather than follow the script. The game master then processes what the players want to do, and with some help from the game rules that quantify how strong, agile or persuasive a character is, or what their powers do, tells the players what happens based on their actions. The players then respond to the revised situation and the story continues. This kind of spontaneous, highly-interactive narrative under the guidance of a game master with great storytelling skills can be brilliant. Play in a group with distracted or inconsiderate players, or with a game master with poor or misguided storytelling skills or goals, and it can be the most painful steaming pile of crap imaginable.

Despite our reference to *Dungeons and Dragons* and our use of *The Lord of the Rings* as an example, role-playing games are not only fantasy-based. Popular role-playing games include hard-core science fiction and science fantasy, horror, cyberpunk and steampunk, cartoon mayhem, fairy tales, and pretty much any setting or genre you can think of, including some based on popular media properties like *Game of Thrones*, *Star Wars*, *Star Trek*, *Indiana Jones*, *Battlestar Galactica* and others. Settings for table-top role-playing games are potentially limitless, since the production scale, scope, cast of characters and special effects are limited only by the game master's ability to describe them verbally and the players' ability to imagine.

Role-playing games of this type emerged in the late 1970s and many early video games were attempts to emulate the style and feel of these kinds of games, often referred to as table-top or face-to-face role-playing games to differentiate the fact that players are usually seated around a table in the same room. Without a living, breathing, creative, spontaneous, human game master, however, it is all but impossible to recreate a table-top role-playing game experience in all but the most tactical sense, which is why many so-called role-playing video games are really just hack-and-slash or shoot-and-dodge combat games with story filler.

All that said, table-top role-playing games are all about world building. Some players will go on for days about the flexibility or coolness of one rules system over another. What brings players to these kinds of games is the very same thing that brings us back to a transmedia storytelling property – the world and the stories told within it. Many companies that produce face-to-face role-playing games sell tons of books about the world (or worlds) their game is set in, and the majority of the sales for those companies come from these projects, often referred to as sourcebooks. Some groups of players use these sourcebooks and their worlds as written; some make up their own from scratch, and some mix-and-match story and setting elements from different sourcebooks, different games, and fairly often from other media, like popular novel series, motion pictures, television series and even video games. Worlds created for role-playing games are often incredibly complex and detailed, and their documentation can take thousands of pages.

We're very familiar with world building for role-playing games as one of this book's authors was very involved in the creation and oversight of a very popular role-playing game line in the late 1980s, early 1990s. (You can probably guess which one from the author bios.) When the *Shadowrun* role-playing game world was created by FASA Corporation in the late 1980s by Robert Charrette, Paul Hume, Tom Dowd, Jordan Weisman and others, it was decided early on that novels and other forms of media would be used as narrative extensions for the game fiction. Role-playing game rulebooks and sourcebooks can do a great job of getting across key elements like story and themes, plot, characters, setting and even style and tone, but it is very difficult sometimes to present the world cohesively, which is a strength of other media.

TSR Hobbies had in many ways pioneered the use of novels to support their *Dungeon and Dragons* game world years before, and the *Shadowrun* creators decided to follow that path, as the company had in prior years with support for their *BattleTech* game of giant robot combat. A trilogy of novels, written by Robert Charrette, were released around the same time as the role-playing game to provide players with an evocative and detailed example of what the world of *Shadowrun* was really like, what kind of stories could be told, and what the world felt like.

An important decision was made that contents of all the published novels would be canon in the *Shadowrun* universe, which made the novels in some ways as important as anything else for the players, or just casual readers (and there were many of those who read the novels but didn't play the game), to stay current with what was going on in the world. The connection between the novels and the mothership – the role-playing game itself – was strong, with one narratively driving the other, and vice-versa. This wasn't just brand extension; this was transmedia storytelling in the truest sense. The game plus the novels constituted the entirety of the experience. You could read the novels without ever having read or played the game, and enjoy them, but you'd miss out on details and connections. You could play the game without reading the novels, but the same would be true.

Ultimately, this is the goal of true transmedia storytelling. Each platform, each expression, continues the story creating a giant narrative web.

Video Games and Other Media

Video games have a long history with transmedia marketing and storytelling, with varied success. The strongest success, with a few exceptions, has been in extension of the property though novels and graphic novels. Interestingly, the medium has had the least success when extended or adapted into other visual media. In this section we're going to look at some examples of that adaptation, and consider what the problems might be, and afterward we're going to look at issues around extending other media, such as television or motion pictures into video games.

Motion Picture Adaptations of Video Games

First, let's get something out of the way – we can't think of a single motion picture based on a video game that was true transmedia storytelling. In each case, they were either vague or somewhat respectful adaptations of the original property, or what Kamilla Elliot refers to in *Narrative Across Media: The Languages of Storytelling* (University of Nebraska Press, 2004, edited by Marie-Laure Ryan) as the "psychic concept of adaptation," which refers to the desire or the insistence that an adaptation must retain the "spirit" of the original material. In the case of video game adaptations, it seems to be feast or famine where the motion picture is positively haunted by the original property, to its own detriment, or it feels as if someone performed an exorcism prior to it reaching the screen.

If you define success by critical reception, then the most successful video game motion picture adaptation was *Final Fantasy: The Spirits Within* (Columbia Pictures, 2001), which scored an aggregated 43% ("rotten") score on the film review tracking site Rotten Tomatoes (http://www.rottentomatoes.com). It also had nothing to do with the successful Eidos/Square Enix *Final Fantasy* game series, except for its name and the fact that the film's 3D animation was created by one of the teams that created the 3D animation cinema scenes for the games.

If you define success by box office, then the most successful video game motion picture adaptation has been the *Resident Evil* series of films. We mentioned the success of the series earlier in this chapter so all we'll do is repeat the worldwide box office take for the series, the $673 million. While based on elements from many different *Resident Evil* video games, none of them, even the first, are direct adaptations of any one game. Instead, they follow a storyline similar to the games, with liberal injection of jargon, creatures, characters, locations and corporation names familiar to fans of the game. Some scenes and sequences in the films are even directly inspired by events in the games, but little is taken directly from them.

If you define success by faithfulness to the original material you have to figure out a way to answer the question of what that means. Does it mean respect for the story/theme, for the plot, for the characters, the setting, or the style/theme? All of the above, or some combination? Is a psychic or spiritual adaptation sufficient, or do you have to find some way to translate the game's interactive experience to cinema?

Clearly this has been a tough nut to crack, and we'd argue that the shell remains unbroken. Even Peter Jackson who has unarguable success filming the un-filmable *Lord of the Rings* trilogy and has moved on to its prequel *The Hobbit*, had to walk away from a long-indevelopment adaptation of Microsoft's *Halo* game, ostensibly due to a loss of financial backing, but rumors had been long-swirling that Jackson and the rights-holder Microsoft couldn't come to an agreement on the direction of the project's screenplay. Given that the interest in a *Halo* motion picture is one of the few sure things out there, the issues working against the project must have been formidable, and insurmountable.

For a time, super-heroes and comic books were the unfilmable, insurmountable genre that motion pictures would never get right. Oh how times have changed. Avi Arad, one of the producers key to guiding Marvel Studios to its success in translating high-intensity action comic books to the big screen told the Independent Film Channel (IFC) in an interview that he'd passed on trying to acquire the rights to *Halo*, saying:

> *"My problem with the "Halo" games was that there was no face anywhere." he said of his decision not to pursue a big-screen version of the wildly popular Halo franchise. "I didn't know what to do with it. I thought about it a lot, because commercially it was huge. But when I look at things like 'Metal Gear Solid' and I'm reading the bible for it, and there's this Cain and Able story and all this shit, I'm like "Now, there's a movie!""*

Avi Arad on the 'Uncharted' movie and why he passed on 'Halo'[3]

What Arad was referring to when he said "…there's no face anywhere." is the fact that in *Halo*, the protagonist of the video games, Master Chief, is only ever seen wearing a helmet with his face fully-covered. Microsoft made this design decision, as we noted earlier, so as to keep the character more anonymous and therefore easier for the game player to project their own personality onto him. Was this one of the difficulties that Peter Jackson and his team had with their efforts on *Halo*? Can a big screen motion picture be carried by a heroic lead whose face is never seen? (Lionsgate's 2012 *Dredd* revisit may partially answer the question, though Dredd is an anti-hero at best.)

Clearly, this is an issue unique in some ways to *Halo*, but it does allude to the problem of weakly-defined main characters in video games. But is that really the problem? Frankly, most video game protagonists seem about as strongly-defined as the heroes of modern summer blockbusters, so surely that can't be the only obstacle.

We're going to go out on a limb and say that the biggest obstacle to creating a successful video game adaptation or extension in motion pictures is the commitment to creating a quality product. We've noted that for years and years the idea of there being a quality super-hero film was laughed at … even though Richard Donner did it with the original *Superman* in 1978, and Tim Burton did again with the original *Batman* in 1989. The same held true for big-budget fantasy-drive titles, until *The Lord of the Rings* and *Harry Potter* changed things.

In each of those cases pointed out directly above, there was a commitment to go above and beyond in creating the motion picture(s). It seems, most times, that the motion picture writers and producers are willing to place their cinematic bet purely on the marketing punch of the brand association, and are willing to let a weak script, casting, or production design slide by. Even as super-hero films were finding their groove, for every *X-Men* (20th Century Fox, 2000) there was a *Fantastic Four* (20th Century Fox, 2005) or *Catwoman* (Warner Brothers, 2004). And 2011's

[3] accessed June 27, 2012, htt://www.ifc.com/fix/2012/06/uncharted-movie-halo-avi-arad

Green Lantern (Warner Brothers) shows that even with clear examples Hollywood is still trying to figure out the super-hero adaptation puzzle, so is it any wonder video games aren't quite there yet?

Bottom line: if you want a great video game adaptation motion picture, make a great motion picture.

Video Game Adaptations of Motion Pictures

As bad as motion picture adaptations of video games are, video games extensions of motion pictures are nearly as bad, with a few exceptions. In most of these cases, however, the reasons are pretty clear … they're bad games. At the end of the previous section we put forth the somewhat obvious assertion that in order to make a good adaptation of a video game you had to make a good motion picture, and the inverse is even more so true here.

Games live or die, succeed or fail, based on whether or not they're good games. The brand connection to the motion picture may help their initial sales, but ultimately if the game isn't very good it isn't going to succeed. Let's take a quick look at four video game adaptations of motion pictures, in chronological order.

GoldenEye 007 *(Nintendo, 1997)*

Developed by Rare, *GoldenEye 007* is directly based on the 1995 *James Bond* film *GoldenEye*, released by United Artists. The game is considered a classic in the first-person shooter video game genre for its pioneering gameplay and its competitive multiplayer features. So much so, that the game was reimagined (the plot updated to fall in line with the current *James Bond* film series with Daniel Craig) and updated in 2010–2011 with modern graphics and gameplay and released on the Nintendo Wii, Sony Playstation 3, Xbox 360, and a handheld version created for the Nintendo DS.

According to "The Making of *GoldenEye*" at NOW Gamer (http://www.nowgamer.com/features/921602/the_ making_of_goldeneye.html, access July 28, 2012) production on the video game began in 1994, but the game wasn't released until 1997, two years after the motion picture it was tied to debuted. This extra time allowed the game's developers to fine-tune the gameplay and polish the presentation and create a classic video game adaptation. The lesson here: games take time to make. Give the developer the time to make it.

Blade Runner *(Virgin Interactive Entertainment, 1997)*

Loosely based on the Ridley Scott film of the same name (Warner Brothers, 1982), the video game *Blade Runner* occurs parallel to the events of the motion picture, and occasionally overlaps with them, but the game is not an adaptation of the story. The game had cutting edge (for its day) 3D graphics and 13 possible endings that were constructed from the player's decision through the game. It won the Academy of Interactive Arts and Sciences (AIAS) Interactive Achievement Award for Best PC Adventure Game, as well as other "best of" awards that year. The game was particularly praised for its reproduction of the production design aesthetic of the original film, and gameplay that supported the feel of the movie and game, an investigative procedural. Here's clearly an adaptation that got all the pieces right that made it feel like *Blade Runner* and had great gameplay.

Chronicles of Riddick: Escape from Butcher's Bay *(Vivendi Games, 2004)*

Chronicles of Riddick: Escape from Butcher's Bay is a prequel to the 2004 motion picture *Chronicles of Riddick* and developed by Starbreeze Studios and Tigon Studios, a game development studio owned by *Riddick* star Vin Diesel. Some claim that this is one of the few cases of the game being better than the motion picture it was based on. We're not going to go there, but there's no question the game succeeded at its goals, which was to create a transmedia storytelling connection to the *Chronicles of Riddick* create a bridge between that film and its prequel *Pitch Black* (USA Films/Gramercy Pictures, 2000) and provide engaging gameplay. Critics at the IGN website had this to say about Developer's Cut (PC/Windows version) late in 2004:

> The game is simply steeped in atmosphere from the moment Riddick walks into the dank, dingy maximum security prison. It's dark, not only metaphorically, but actually physically dark, which aside from being moody, plays heavily into gameplay. You can almost smell the thick stink of Butcher Bay and its inhabitants from the grime on the walls, dirty clothes of the inmates, and environmental textures. This places oozes with style and creates sense of reality in which it's easy to become immersed.
>
> **The Chronicles of Riddick: Escape From Butcher Bay – Developer's Cut**[4]

In 2007 IGN named *Chronicles of Riddick: Escape from Butcher's Bay* #12 on its "Top 25 Xbox Games of All Time," stating

> With the exception of GoldenEye 007, no game has so outshined its big-screen counterparts as The Chronicles of Riddick: Escape from Butcher Bay. It's all true. The game was way better than the movie sequel.
>
> **The Top 25 Xbox Games of All Time**[5]

High praise, good company, and another example of the time being taken to make a great game, with great gameplay.

Harry Potter and the Deathly Hallows, Part 2 *(Electronic Arts, 2011)*

A contrast to the previous three games, this game is, by all accounts, terrible. As an example, its aggregated Metacritic review score for the Xbox 360 was only 44 out of 100 ("Harry Potter and the Deathly Hallows, Part 2 Xbox 360," accessed June 27, 2012, http://www.metacritic.com/game/xbox-360/harry-potter-and-the-deathly-hallows-part-2). Frankly, this is embarrassing and inexcusable for a property as successful as the *Harry Potter* franchise. How does this happen?

It's hard to say, but the game seems to have been hampered by a significantly compressed development schedule that forced the game's creators to hamstring the storytelling, which one would think would be a cornerstone of a *Harry Potter* game. For a franchise with the prominence and success of *Harry Potter*, it makes little sense why those involved in setting the schedule for the game's production would short-change it so badly that it produced a product that is embarrassing to the property. Fortunately, it's *Harry Potter*, and the games are secondary.

The *Harry Potter* franchise can, and has, survived a bad video game (or a series of them), but that's because the mothership of the novel series (or has it become the motion pictures?) is so strong. Up-and-coming transmedia properties, especially original intellectual properties, cannot afford to have a potential key entry point be anything other than effective. It would seem that in the grand scheme of everything the *Harry Potter* video games were seen as simple brand extension and the benefit coming from the marketing synergy of having the brand prominent everywhere at the time of the final motion picture's release. This is a valid marketing strategy, but far from the best use of the potential of transmedia storytelling.

Video Games and Television

The relationship between video games and television has not been as extensive as between it and motion pictures. The majority of extensions or adaptations from video games to television have been anime or animated programs aimed at children, such as *Adventures of Sonic the Hedgehog* (syndicated, 1993–1996), *Devil May Cry: The Animated*

---

[4] accessed June 27, 2012, http://pc.ign.com/articles/573/573228p1.html
[5] access June 27, 2012, http://xbox.ign.com/articles/772/772315p3.html

Series (WOWOW TV Japan, 2007), *The Legend of Zelda* (syndication, 1989), *Pac-Man: The Adventure Begins* (Disney XD, 2013), *Wing Commander Academy* (USA Network, 1996), and many others. The heyday for these programs seems to have been the late 1980s and through the 1990s.

There have been significantly fewer live-action television series, but the most notable being the single season of *Mortal Kombat: Konquest* (syndication/TNT, 1998–1999), based on the *Mortal Kombat* fighting video game series. The most successful, in terms of longevity, is probably *Maniac Mansion* (The Family Channel/YTV, 1990–1993), loosely based on the LucasArts video game from 1987.

Two recent web series come close enough to television series that they warrant a look here, as do a number of other projects:

Mortal Kombat: Legacy *(NetherRealm Studio/Warner Brothers Interactive Entertainment, 2001)*

Based on and inspired by a 2010 unofficial live-action short film called *Mortal Kombat: Rebirth*, this nine-part web-series was a "reimagining" of the *Mortal Kombat* game universe that was more realistic and downplayed the original's more outrageous and supernatural elements. Director Kevin Tancharoen's original short was produced as a proof-of-concept piece to show to Warner Brothers as a possible direction for future *Mortal Kombat* films. Warner Brothers declined to back a motion picture project, but funded Tancharoen to create the web series, deciding on the venture after witnessing the video game fan base's strongly-voiced positive reaction to the short. While not canon, this is a great example of fan-produced content making a significant impact on the property and helping to strengthen the overall property.

Dragon Age: Redemption *(Bioware, 2011)*

Based on the Bioware video game series *Dragon Age*, the six-part web series premiered via Machnima.com and YouTube in December 2011. It was written by and starred Felicia Day, an actress and producer who created and stars in *The Guild* (YouTube), a very popular web series that premiered in 2007 and has been running on Microsoft Xbox Live and related services since. Day, who has a has a Twitter following of nearly 2 million, is an avid gamer and a fan-favorite. By effectively linking their brand with Day's, Bioware and Electronic Arts were able to extend the excitement for the *Dragon Age II* product, which was nearing nine-months old at the time of the webseries release. Additionally, the live-action webseries was linked to a downloadable add-on to *Dragon Age II* called "Mark of the Assassin" that released on October 11 and focused on the same character that Day portrayed in the webseries. This produced a clearly successful one-two punch of transmedia marketing and storytelling.

CSI: Crime Scene Investigation *Games and Similar*

A quick perusal of current video games based on a television series shows the popularity of investigation-related video games, with a few unexpected surprises. The majority of television series-related video games focus on properties like *CSI: Crime Scene Investigation* (CBS, 2000–present), *CSI: Miami* (CBS, 2002–2012), *CSI: New York* (CBS, 2004–present), *Criminal Minds* (CBS, 2005–present), *Law and Order* (NBC, 1990–2010), *Law and Order: Criminal Intent* (NBC, 2001–2011), *NCIS* (CBS, 2003–present), all of which are police procedurals. In these similarly-styled games, which are aimed at fans of the series who were also casual gamers (rather than hardcore gamers), players take on the role of the detectives and solve crimes in the style of the shows. The *CSI*-branded games made, for a time at least, regular appearances on best-seller charts for personal computer games.

The three unexpected stand outs are *House, M.D.* (Legacy Interactive, 2010), the even more surprising *Grey's Anatomy: The Video Game* (Ubisoft, 2009), which was available for Windows PC, Nintendo Wii, and the Nintendo

DS, and the even more even more surprising *Desperate Housewives: The Game* (Disney Interactive Studios, 2006). Unsurprisingly, all three games received terrible overall reviews and appropriately poor sales, but hopefully at least produced really interesting target market discussions. With the exception of the *CSI*-branded video games, no television-series-connected video game has sold well.

We can't end this little section without mentioning the iPhone/iPad game released in late 2010 based on the Showtime television series *Dexter* (Showtime, 2006–present) where you control the titular serial killer of serial killers going about his work. Do Dexter's job right, and you can torture other serial killers to confess their crimes, and then kill them. Mess up and Dexter could be exposed. Well regarded on its initial release, versions of the game for other platforms never materialized.

Red Faction: Origins

Produced jointly by game publisher THQ and Universal Cable Productions, *Red Faction: Origins* was a television series pilot that bridged the narrative between the video games *Red Faction: Guerilla* (THQ, 2009) and *Red Faction: Armageddon* (THQ, 2011) and aired on the SyFy channel just days before the latter game's release. The production of the series pilot marked a wider partnership between the game publisher and the genre-drive network, and though well-reviewed by television critics and fans of the *Red Faction* game series, the show has not been picked up as a series as of the time of this writing, though is allegedly still under consideration. The online game news and review site GameZone said this about the production:

> In the end, THQ and SyFy did a solid with this one. Red Faction: Origins *doesn't feel like a cheap, slapdash film*, and it certainly *fits the feel of the franchise*. Fans of the games should definitely take a peek this Saturday when Red Faction: Origins premieres on the SyFy network.

Red Faction: Origins Review[6]

The quote above includes our underlined text of the important points. Again, quality (even by SyFy network television movie standards) wins the day, as does a solid integration with the game property. This faithfulness to the property is undoubtedly due to the involvement of then THQ Executive Vice President of Games, Danny Bilson, a specialist in transmedia productions and writer of motion pictures (*The Rocketeer*, Walt Disney Pictures, 1991) and television (*The Flash*, CBS, 1990–1991), who crafted the story with his writing partner Paul De Meo.) Bilson, a multi-disciplinarian with a knowledge of both video games and television, was able to find a successful blending of the two where so many before had failed.

The Walking Dead *(TellTale Games, 2012)*

AMC's successful adaptation of Robert Kirkman's popular comic book series *The Walking Dead* (Image Comics, 2003–present) became a transmedia storytelling property with the release of Episode 1 of the episodic video game series in April 2012. The story presented in the video game parallels the start of the comic and television series and provides a somewhat different perspective on events, and includes characters seen previously in the fiction. PC Gamer said this about the game:

> I barely felt challenged. I died once. But I did feel entirely engaged. What dominates the first episode is the sense that you're plant-ing seeds in a zombie garden that you actually care about. Relatable characters are the basis of that connection. You encounter ordinary people dealing with unbelievable circumstances that are made believable by grounded dramatic writing. I wanted to know more about someone's wife. I felt suspicious of strangers. I rooted for a brave IT guy. Telltale doesn't clone existing archetypes from

[6] accessed June 28, 2012, http://www.gamezone.com/reviews/red_faction_origins

the Walking Dead *fiction (although Glenn and the Greene family make cameos); Lee, the main character in this spin-off, is as likeable and imperfect as Rick Grimes or Dale Horvath.*

The Walking Dead Review[7]

The review above, and others, stress the impact of the story/theme of the game, as well as the plot, characters, setting, and style/tone, thereby succeeding in all of the areas we noted in Chapter 2 as necessary elements of a transmedia property. The video game sold over a million copies in its first two weeks of sales on all non-iOS platforms, making it the developer's fastest selling game ever ("The Walking Dead soars past 1 million sales," accessed June 30, 2012, http://www.computerandvideogames.com/348163/the-walking-dead-soars-past-1-million-sales/). The game has also received high accolades from game critics, scoring an average review rating of 82% for the *The Walking Dead: Episode 1 – A New Day* across the personal computer, Xbox360 and Playstation 3 platforms. A total of five episodes were released, with game players able to purchase each episode individually or pay in advance for the entire "season."

Defiance *(SyFy and Trion Worlds)*

Currently in production for an April 2013 unveiling, *Defiance* is a joint massively-multiplayer online (MMO) video game and linked television series. The television series, written by Rockne S. O'Bannon (*Farscape, Alien Nation, seaQuest DSV*) and produced by Universal Cable Productions for the SyFy Channel, follows life in the former city of St. Louis, which is now a refugee town known as "Defiance" following an invasion of aliens intent on occupying Earth. The MMO shooter is being developed by Trion Worlds (*Rift, End of Nations*) is a combat-driven game set in and around Marin County near San Francisco. The plans for the transmedia experience are ambitious:

Those two very different experiences might sound hard to tie together meaningfully, but there are some ways in which taking part in one side of the "transmedia experience" can help add to the other. The creators gave an example of an in-game quest where players work with non-player characters to rescue a gem from a group of aliens. Those characters end up stealing the gem for themselves and driving off from the game's setting of San Francisco. In the opening scene of the first episode of the show, you see those same two characters driving into the show's setting of St. Louis, stolen gems in tow.

The idea is that playing the game isn't absolutely necessary to understand the show, but that it can help make the experience richer. "If you think about it from the perspective of someone who just watched the pilot, two characters that clearly have something stolen, driving at breakneck speed, clearly they're being chased – it sets the beginning of the show really really well," Trion Worlds Head of Development Nick Beliaeff told Ars Technica. "If you played the game, though, you know why."

Building a sci-fi TV show through an MMO (and vice-versa)[8]

The continual narrative interplay between the online video game and the television series has never been attempted before and is rife with possibilities, and narrative dangers. Will the players of the game need to see the television series to understand the game's plot, or will viewers of the television show need to play the game to understand as well? Will the actual integration be meaningful enough to matter, or will it seem superficial and pointless? The execution will be telling, but it's an exciting leap forward for true transmedia storytelling, and we hope a harbinger of things to come.

Interview: Jordan Weisman

Jordan Weisman has been the creative force behind several interactive entertainment companies, including his latest ventures: Harebrained-Schemes LLC and Go Go Kiddo Inc. Along the way, he created *MechWarrior, Shadowrun*

[7] accessed June 30, 2012, http://www.pcgamer.com/review/the-walking-dead-game-review/
[8] accessed June 29, 2012, http://arstechnica.com/gaming/2012/05/building-a-sci-fi-tv-show-through-an-mmo-and-vice-versa/

and *Crimson Skies*, three of the longest running franchises in the game industry.

Weisman got his start in the paper game industry founding FASA Corporation in 1980, where he created *Battle Tech/Mech Warrior* and *Shadowrun*. He pioneered publicly accessible virtual reality at his second company, Virtual World Entertainment, which he sold to the Disney family in 1992.

Jordan founded FASA Interactive to develop his properties for PC and sold the company to Microsoft in 1998. After the acquisition, Jordan became the Creative Director for Microsoft's Games Division where he oversaw the first two years of all Xbox titles, including the launch of the *Halo* franchise.

In 2000 Weisman founded Wizkids when he invented the collectable miniature figure game format for *MageKnight*, *MechWarrior* and *HeroClix*. Wizkids grew quickly and was acquired by Topps Inc. in 2003.

Figure 6.1.1 *Jordan Weisman.*

After Wizkids, Jordan co-founded 42 Entertainment to build upon the pioneering transmedia experience he created with Steven Spielberg for the film *A.I. Artificial Intelligence* which spawned the new genre of alternate reality games. As Chief Creative Officer of 42 Entertainment, Jordan oversaw the creation of *I Love Bees*, for the launch of *Halo 2*, *Why So Serious*, for Dark Knight, *Year Zero*, for Nine Inch Nails, along with many other landmark ARGs.

Harebrained Schemes, Jordan's latest company, is focused on raising the quality bar in mobile entertainment. Their inaugural release, partnering with Bungie, was the critically-acclaimed and best-selling title *Crimson Steam Pirates* and their second game, *Strikefleet Omega* became an instant success, placing Harebrained Schemes firmly on the list of studios to watch.

Weisman is a *New York Times* bestselling fiction author, winner of the Northwest E&Y Entrepreneur of the Year award, *TIME* Magazine's Ten Best Ideas, and dozens of design awards. He is an adjunct professor at USC's School of Cinematic Arts and co-founder of the Center for Serious Play at the University of Washington.

Jordan recently made headlines when Harebrained Schemes ran one of the most successful Kickstarter.com projects in history to bring back one of his favorite game worlds, *Shadowrun*.

Jordan Weisman was interviewed by the authors in early summer 2012 specifically for this book.

Interviewer(s): Your work with *I Love Bees* and *The Beast* and other projects clearly puts you in the position of a pioneer in transmedia storytelling. What we're hoping to do with our book is produce a more practical look at the subject that is much more focused on transmedia storytelling – not the marketing aspects of transmedia, because that's really cross-media, 360 marketing or whatever you want to call it. But really this is the process of telling one master story across multiple iterations, or multiple properties, depending on how you want to look at it.

Jordan Weisman: I guess that's the question that I've got – how are you defining transmedia? Jeff Gomez and (Henry) Jenkins are kind of on the same page, right? They define it as what we used to call multimedia, which is, I have a universe and then I have lots of exploitations of that universe across multiple media. That's not what I intended when I coined the term was which was, I'm going to tell a greater story by using lots of media and subservient methods and in total tell a larger story.

Interviewer(s): And we're pushing that perspective with this book. It kind of falls in line with the Producers Guild of America definition of it which we refer to often.

Jordan Weisman: Right but that's different. That's basically saying I have a novel and a comic book and a game all set in the same universe, right? That would qualify underneath their definition.

Interviewer(s): Yes it would. That sense of it being very discrete pieces.

Jordan Weisman: Right what I'm saying, to me transmedia has an additional component which is that if you read the book, played the game, read the comic book, that all of those contained elements of a larger story which only comes into view when all of the elements are combined.

Interviewer(s): So, it's kind of a found story.

Jordan Weisman: Yes. Each are individual pieces of a larger arc or contained pieces of a larger arc. This is not a revolutionary concept. I mean look at any kind of serialized television show, *The X Files*. A one-hour show and it was set up kind of 80/20–80% of the plot is devoted to resolving this week's monster, then 20% is reserved to feed into the larger arc. And so all my concept was simply why is that constrained into one media? Why can't we take that concept and apply it to everything from scraps of paper that you find on the floor to billboards to, novels, to plays, to advertising, to whatever else to just weave altogether into this larger arc.

Interviewer(s): Clearly that's what attracted you – or however you want to phrase it – to the ARGs because, that's really their grammar, right?

Jordan Weisman: Yeah. An ARG when I originally pitched the concept was basically just a role-playing game played on the world's largest fucking kitchen table.

Interviewer(s): Right.

Jordan Weisman: I mean it's what we always did; it's collaborative storytelling. It's just I'm going to take advantage of the three legs that I kind of based it on which was one, that collaborative story telling part. Two, what I call "the world is the medium." Every form of communication should be used to carry parts of the story. And three that it required a heightened mind to solve because you had to disseminate it, the stories, so widely and fracture it so small. I use the analogy of an archeologist who finds shards of pottery. If she finds enough shards, she can reassemble not just the pot but the entire society. So it was kind of mixing all three of those concepts together.

Interviewer(s): Did you have that vision going in, or did that evolve as you started putting together those early projects?

Jordan Weisman: No, I mean that was the original pitch. The original pitch had all three of those components. And if you look at the first one we did, *The Beast*, it contained all of those elements for better or for worse because, you know because in retrospect some of those things, they make the art form very limited but it did contain all of those elements initially.

Interviewer(s): Who do you think is doing this kind of storytelling well right now?

Jordan Weisman: It's become very broad. I think the techniques that we pioneered in that thing are used extensively by everybody from Bad Robot and everything they've ever done. It's funny because I've consulted with those guys a bunch over the years and they just keep constantly getting surprised by these things. The power of the hive mind.

Interviewer(s): We interviewed Carlton Cuse for the book as well and talked about the hive mind. We also asked him the questions that I just interrupted with. Who do you think is doing this really well right now? He was stumped. He couldn't really come up with anything. So I'm curious as to what your perspective is on this.

Jordan Weisman: Well I have to admit that I haven't followed it too much recently, but I've seen a huge amount of dissemination of the techniques, as we were saying. My old company 42, I think continues to do interesting work. I haven't worked there in three years, but I think they continue to do interesting things. Campfire does interesting stuff. I'd have to really go out and look.

Interviewer(s): It's interesting that there isn't anything that is kind of on the tip of your tongue. When *LOST* was at its peak, the people that were into it were talking about the *LOST* experience, and then there were the guys doing *Heroes*, and obviously were restricted to primarily electronic mediums.

Jordan Weisman: Yeah, and it had picked up a small percentage of the kind of techniques and stuff we had done and the more aggressive things like Nine Inch Nails or the Batman films and so on, you know. I think one of the challenges is, all my old, my basically protégé team which has a company called Forth Wall, is trying to address head on right now, the challenge is how do you monetize these things.

Interviewer(s): Sure.

Jordan Weisman: In truth you can't kind of take this transmedia experience and directly monetize it – it's in a subservient role to other media because it can only be used to market that other media. Once it actually has appeal of its own then I'll think you'll start to see it come into its own. That was my first attempt with *Cathy's Book*. How do we take this concept and apply it? Well *Cathy's Book* was an experiment on two levels: one, can we use an old form of monetization to pay for this, and two, can we take the same ideas and apply them to an individual rather than the hive mind. Because the hive mind is a very cool thing. It's like awe-inspiring when it comes together and what it's capable of. It just blows you away constantly. On the other hand it is, it's a very limiting thing because it's like a rock concert. You have to interrupt your life to go participate in it when it's happening because there is just no replay value. It's like an organic living thing and if you're not part of it when it's living, it's just really not that interesting to look back on it.

Interviewer(s): It's a once and done.

Jordan Weisman: Exactly. And so that inherently is very limited as an art form. It's performance art. It's very hard to make that a scalable, economically viable art form. And so with *Cathy's*, what I was trying to do was like well, if we make it individual and we make it more intimate and we make it so it runs on your time so you can do it anytime you want, how does that work? That worked well and really that's become the format that so many people followed afterwards and 4th Wall is trying to push much further on that. It is individual experiences and it runs on your time cycle, but it contains all the transmedia storytelling components. So, we'll see. I'm like one your students who has serious ADD [attention deficit disorder]. After four years of fucking around with it, OK that was fun. Let's go on to something else. And really, I did the keynote at StoryWord last year and it was funny seeing the Twitter feed afterwards. Basically what it talked about was that I held up an iPad and said, "Alright guys hold on. Everything that transmedia was supposed to do ten years ago when I came up with this wacky idea, was to mix every form of storytelling together that we've ever created into one story. That all happens in this device now." Every form of storytelling we've ever created is in one place. In one UI. And you know what? They're still artificially separated. Why is that? This is the new frontier. This is where we should be experimenting. We don't have to send people crawling through alleyways to find things we left there for them. Here we have a laboratory that allows us to figure out how you mix film and comics and story and game and novels and web comics and you mix it all together into a new form of storytelling. It's all in this one place. This is where we should be all playing. That's why I moved into mobile. I was just trying to play in those places and start to learn different techniques there. So to me I think there is a very interesting opportunity. What we've been trying to work on as an authoring system will allow people to do that without getting engineers involved. The engineer just slows down the experimentation.

Interviewer(s): There really isn't anything out there that lets you craft that. There's what, like Max on the PC but it's kind of been appropriated for that more than anything else.

Jordan Weisman: We're trying to figure out how to get that funded. But we'd love to put this in the hands of students. That's what I want to do.

Interviewer(s): Yeah, absolutely. Besides, you'd get such unexpected responses. Students don't know what they can't do.

Jordan Weisman: Exactly. And that's what I love.

Interviewer(s): They're going to push it and they're going to try it and we're just going to stand there are go, "Oh, look at that."

Jordan Weisman: Yeah, I totally agree.

Interviewer(s): You kind of answered one of my other questions, which was that you kind of moved away from the transmedia stuff into this other area and you explained why. But in a way you really haven't. You kind of laid the groundwork for continuing on in the near future is what it sounds like.

Jordan Weisman: Yeah. I think, to me as you look at our careers, you and I kind of walk down similar paths; there's always been that merging, that intersection between story and game. And right, really there's a third access because game inherently includes socialization. So it's the combination of social story and game. To me that's always been really exciting. Admittedly I've jumped from every different medium I could imagine to explore that space. I think that as the mobile smart phones and tablets developed, I just saw that as such an opportunity for pushing that kind of thing forward. It deserved to be explored.

Interviewer(s): Let's reflect back for a second on this definition of transmedia. Because obviously you have a very, very particular definition that's not the mainstream definition.

Jordan Weisman: Oh yeah. I've lost this battle. Henry's won. His message has been heard the loudest.

Interviewer(s): You could take him out back.

Jordan Weisman: Well maybe that's true. When I coined the term, I was trying to reflect something that's new and instead the term has come to mean something that previously existed. I mean, you go back, you can go back to the entire history of popular culture and what they've defined as transmedia has existed since the beginning of popular culture. It's nothing new. You go back to *Buck Rogers* in the 30s. You go back to the *Wizard of Oz* where he had plays and novels and movies all coming out simultaneously, all set in the same universe, right? So this is not new stuff. Now admittedly if you take some of the stuff that I was basing my work on, it's been around for a long time, too. I mean obviously there's the John Lennon/Beatles reference. But go back to Conan Doyle.

Interviewer(s): Right, yes.

Jordan Weisman: With his first published work which was, he claims, unintentionally a hoax about the Mary Celeste. Are you familiar with that story?

Interviewer(s): Yes.

Jordan Weisman: And how he published *Lost World* by creating all the photographs of him and his associates and really pretending that it was a real journal. Those are all techniques that I totally lifted. The only thing that I was introducing on top of that was taking advantage of, which didn't exist, was the ability for giant communities to form relatively instantaneously across the web. That was the only new element I was really adding and putting it on the global scale. But yeah, I guess what's disappointing to me is that we had taken a term which was trying to do something new and it became turned around to mean something that had been around for a long time. That's what mainstream means I guess, right?

Interviewer(s): They spend a lot of time trying to define things. When everybody notices that all the pieces are fitting together a certain way, they need to have some way to describe it and this came closest, I guess. So it kind of got picked up. I know that, when we've been talking about the book a comment that has come back to us has been, in fact it just came back to me in an email earlier today, was how little some parts of established media industry understand about this, about how transmedia works, however you want to define it. By your definition, by Henry's definition, by even kind of the simplest multimedia definition, they just functionally don't get it.

Jordan Weisman: Well why would they say that? By Henry's definition, it's the business that Walt Disney has been in since he created the studio.

Interviewer(s): I understand. And we wondered that too – and I suspect the idea of a master story with pieces scattered in different media is the culprit. But the response we hear is "Oh this book will be great because I want to give it to so and so because he doesn't get it." We'll see, but it's an interesting response.

Jordan Weisman: Yeah, well that's just the classic ignorance of our society, right? I mean history, to most of America, is what they had for breakfast. They just have no context. And that's just disturbing on many levels but unfortunately, constantly re-affirmed.

Interviewer(s): So through a lot of this, we've been interested in the chicken and egg process of some of this creation. So you're doing the TV series and the game Which comes first? Who's leading who? How is that all coming about? How is everybody working together? That's got to be really different for some of these entrenched organizations.

Jordan Weisman: Oh yeah. One of the things that I lecture on a lot, everybody from game companies to studios to the Academy of Motion Picture Arts and Sciences.

Interviewer(s): Yeah, yeah.

Jordan Weisman: I've talked at their events this idea of what I call "Planned Parenthood vs. a happy mistake." And the majority of the industry still goes in the happy mistake side. They craft in individual exercise, the film, the game, the comic book, and then after it's a big hit, then they have to kind of back-fill. Create the world around what they've already written. And they find out in most cases there isn't a good world to be had there because they wrote a very linear execution, which then produces just terrible sequels. Something Jeff (Gomez) has made a business out of is to try to take those linear worlds and fill backfill behind them. My whole point is if you're looking at producing any of those things, a graphic novel, which is a now a $100,000+ experience, any kind of console game or a movie which are multi-millions in dollars, it will cost you what, $25–50 grand to produce a great world bible right up front. And then craft your story within that? Should it succeed, you now have a real basis to work from. But it's like no, we'd rather spend that on a lunch budget.

Interviewer(s): That's very much what we advocate. What we're writing is build the world first and then figure out how you want to tell those stories.

Jordan Weisman: Oh yeah.

Interviewer(s): Will anyone listen? Who knows, but it's worth the shot.

Jordan Weisman: Well I think it's well worth giving it a shot. It's obviously a message I constantly preach on as well so we are on the same page. The most common talk I do is about world building and the process of world building. Which a lot of people seem, it's a less common thing. You go through your writing degree at university and they never talk about building the world; they talk about making the plot or creating the character, which are all obviously critical, but this is bigger than that.

Interviewer(s): Right. Create the environment that creates these motivations and let the characters react to those motivations and create your plot. But you've got to create all those dramatic forces if you will that are going to allow that to happen. It's a different way of looking at it.

Jordan Weisman: Yes absolutely.

Chapter 7
Other Forms of Storytelling

Though we often think of film, television and/or video games as the primary sources for (and expressions of) transmedia properties, there are many other platforms that can be used for storytelling, some we have a long history with and others that are more recent or even on the horizon. These can be analog or digital, producer-created or fan-created. They can exist as part of canon, or take an intellectual property in some bizarre and unsettling direction. These other forms of storytelling can be the starting place for a story or where the story universe finds its expression outside the traditional paths.

We can approach these forms in two ways, as first, an intellectual property that started as a novel, comics, or new media, and as second, intellectual properties that started as either film, television or video games and had a substantial or transformational existence in other media. Understanding the effect that other forms of storytelling and audience engagement can have on the core intellectual property is very important in creating and maintaining a successful transmedia property.

Intellectual Properties that Started as Novels, Comics or New Media

Why would a producer choose something from one of these other forms? Putting aside notion of passion for a particular narrative, these existing properties have inherent value because they have been "developed" in some sense. A blueprint exists to a certain level, depending on the type of other media; each has elements and form unique to both the variety of expressions and the individual property. To understand why to look beyond film, television or video games as a starting point, you must first look at what are both the typical and non-typical expressions and how historically they have been used as a starting point. The analysis begins by looking at each broad category and then addressing a series of the basic questions concerning the strengths and weaknesses of the transformation of that particular media.

Novels

While a complete exploration would require a book unto itself, at its most basic, a novel is a long narrative in literary prose form whose tradition dates back hundreds of years. The novel has historical roots both in the fields of the medieval and early modern romance, and in the tradition of the novella. Clearly defined in the 18th century, it became the cultural standard-bearer for encoding and sharing the stories of the time. While other media gained traction in the last century and a half, the novel attained a unique position as both a high culture and low culture artifact. Novels have also been in the position of first off the bench as other media look to adapt stories for their media: film, television, theatre, radio, etc.

For the novel, the basic media is words on a printed page. The language of novels has changed over time depending on many variables – genre, format, fashion of the time – but ultimately it goes back to words on the page and the imagination of both the writer and the reader. Through time, and at the various stages in the development of the form, there have been many efforts to redefine the novel, with success only limited by the physical nature of a book itself, until the last ten years, where changes to distribution and the additional possibilities afforded by technology are bringing about varying levels of change.

Strengths/Weaknesses of Novels

Tradition: When trying to sort out the strength and weaknesses of the novel as a launching point the simple fact that it brings with it hundreds of years of tradition and cultural acceptance makes for a natural starting point. It has proven over time the ability to build audience and achieved a weight in the culture that no other mass medium has.

Universe: The novel has always inherently had the ability to hold a story universe. It has only increased over time due to exploration by writers who find new and exciting ways to speak to their audience. Even more so when technology allowed and culture demanded the inexpensive mass production of books and encouraged multi-book series that create a larger universe. A recent example is, of course, *Harry Potter*. Note, however, that novels, and especially novel series, tend to have very dense and detailed story universes. It can be difficult to produce an expression of a dense novel story universe in a narratively "simpler" medium such as motion pictures or television.

Expression of the internal: No medium surpasses the novel's ability to reveal the interior of the human mind. Novels for centuries have delved into the human psyche with some astonishing results from Marcel Proust to Dashiell Hammett. That said, novels that are built around the expression of the internal thinking of the characters may be difficult to express in other media.

Action: The dynamic of words and actions has always been a challenge with some amazing results. Novelists have painted pictures with words depicting the great battles of mankind from Waterloo to D-Day. The dynamic of words describing actions, however has never been a perfect one and has faced new challenges as other media emerged with the ability to imagine and express unfettered by the limitation of words on a page. With each passing year this has only intensified as technology can imagine and create at a grander scale. The opening of the motion picture *Saving Private Ryan* (DreamWorks, 1998) does what may not be possible for a wide audience through the written word.

"Comics" (Comics, Graphic Novels, Manga)

Multiple terms are used to describe what is basically the same thing – a narrative work in which the story is conveyed to the reader using sequential art, in either an experimental design or in a traditional comic format. The term can be used to describe non-fiction works and thematically linked "short stories" as well as grand long-term narrative arcs often taking years to play out. This style/form of storytelling across a number of genres has an incredible history of evolution in the past 50 years, generating new forms and leaving the often dismissed "for kids only comics" as only a small portion of what is produced in this now expansive area of expression.

The basic components of comics have not changed much since their inception which is open to debate, but we consider the modern iteration – early 20th century multi-panel comics – as the starting point for this conversation. Clearly, however, the technique of blending images and words continues in an ever growing range of styles.

Strengths/Weaknesses of Comics

Culture/times: The history of comics in the United States is one filled with shame and persecution. Until the 1980s, the comic had a profound lack of stature and had risen very slowly beyond what would be thought of as a niche entertainment. In fact, comic books weren't just looked down on the 1950s, they were actively persecuted. My, how times have changed.

We list the impact of culture/times as both a strength and a weakness because, while it was clearly a blow to creativity in mainstream comics, in many ways, the marginalization of the comics and the repression of the form laid the groundwork for the adoption of comic books as a tool of the counter-culture in the 1960s. This in turn gave birth to what we know as graphic novels about a decade later. Without the outsider/rebel cachet, the graphic novel, and in turn comics themselves, may have not become the focus of mainstream culture that it has become.

Japan is a very different story with manga having a different genesis and place in the culture. Manga is the Japanese word for comics or cartoons, but is is predominantly used outside Japan to refer to comics published originally in Japan. It is a $5.5 billion business in Japan, with popularity increasing for locally-produced comics done in a "manga style" in many other nations, including the United States and the United Kingdom ("Comic Giants Battle for Readers," accessed June 27, 2012, http://www.bbc.co.uk/news/business-14526451). While manga has its share of superheroes, fantasy and science fiction content, it is also known for more soap-opera style stories of families and personal triumph and tragedy. Most manga in Japan are printed in black-and-white, and many find additional life as live-action or animated motion pictures or television series. Many popular Western properties end up with manga versions when released in Japan.

While a long complicated and interesting story, the takeaway is that manga has a very different place in Japanese culture and is a mainstream medium in a way comic books or graphic novel never have been in America. Its strength is in its place in the culture. However, it too is evolving due to the issues magazine publishing, the heart of manga culture, faces not just in Japan but around the world as electronic publishing tries to figure a path to viability.

Universe building: The ability to create a well-developed story universe particularly over time has been demonstrated again and again in the comics universe with many of the iconic cultural figures that were first brought to life in a comic book. A culture devoid of figures like Superman and Batman seems unimaginable. Comic story universes' and storyworlds' ability to be reimagined over and over allows comics to adapt and evolve with the times, but it does allow for many wrong turns in reconceptualization, though these can be relatively easily re-directed and then ignored. The industry tries to right the ship periodically. DC Comics' *The 52* effort is the most recent example, but ultimately comics have suffered for a long time with too many cooks and too many titles focused on the same character (count the number of current *Batman* or *Spider-Man* titles someday) and ultimately that means there can never be a truly coherent universe.

Action: The advancement in comics' ability over time to develop a sophisticated language that allows the authors to express action has been a real addition in the form's ability to tell a story. While initially limited by conventions, what has happened over time and as its place in the culture and the times changed is that the form was pushed by both the mainstream comics industry and underground comics to now have an incredible palette from which to express action.

Best of both worlds: Why have comics/graphics novels evolved in American culture from a 10-cent toss away in the back pocket of a 12 year old to a form that has a wide range of expression and large culture impact? In many ways it is simply because it was recognized as a complete storytelling form with a low entry cost dynamic. As a form that can both reveal the mindset and the thinking of its characters and also has developed a robust language for action, it has (when in the hands of talented artists and storytellers) become a place for a huge range of storytelling, from the strangest of humor to the most serious of topics with opportunities and — unlike film, television and games — the genuine possibility for a creator from outside the mainstream industry to reach a mass audience.

Comic Book as Pitch

In mainstream media, as the world gets more nervous about the money being spent of media properties (compare the failure of Disney's *John Carter* and the success of Marvel's *The Avengers*) it is inevitable that the comic would not just be a form of expression, but would become a means to an end. Pitches and scripts have no inherent value as objects, but a comic can both tell the story in a complete way and does have extrinsic value. It is an opportunity to "test" a story in a low-cost way and begin the process of generating a fan base. Bottom line, it is a great way to communicate or pitch a story because of the rich language of comics.

New Media Content (Internet-based)

New media, a broad term used in academia and media production circles, refers to a wide spectrum of current and archaic technologies. This book uses the term only in the narrow context of Internet-based expression occurring in the last 20 years. This limited definition of new media speaks to the change of access to content anytime, anywhere, on any digital device, as well as interactive user feedback and creative participation and community formation around the media content. New media technology allowed an explosion of authorship by a wide variety of participants who are able to both discern and reach an audience for the media in a manner unimaginable 25 years ago.

The raw materials for the medium draw from a wide variety of potential elements, forms and sources – some unique, particularly in the area of interactivity, but still more often a reflection of some intersection with the big three media sources we address – film, television and video games. While many elements influenced the growth of new media, we must view that history through a filter of technology, both of senders (broadcasters, media producers) and receivers (audience.) The explosion, while ostensibly one of content, is an explosion that is lit and re-lit by technological advances.

Strengths/Weaknesses of "New Media"

Audience: While once the playground of the few and the overtly geeky, the Internet has become "THE INTERNET", a culture-shaping, society-transforming economic engine. As a storytelling medium we sit at the same moment that Thomas Edison did running those early films though the first kinetoscope viewers. New media simply have the huge potential to engage a broad audience through their incredible reach that is, most interestingly, unrestrained by traditional media gatekeepers.

Potential for universe building: As technology matures and evolves, the potential for a huge storytelling canvas incorporating a wide range of elements is clear and therefore its potential as the framework for a huge complex story universe or storyworld is obvious. However, we have yet to see this potential fully exploited.

Tends to be niche: How can the most mass of mass media generate a niche audience? Finding an audience amidst the chaos of the Internet often requires a very narrow focus; you have to be niche to get started. Launching large-scale or broad intellectual properties not tied to another medium hasn't yielded widespread success outside children's media. Efforts often yield a story framework or characters that aren't a complete intellectual property due to budget and format limitations that affect the manner in which these intellectual properties are generated. Another issue is similar to the challenges games face because of the audience/user's need for interaction that often comes in conflict with a storyteller's need for control, particularly at the launching of a large-scale intellectual property. The YouTube model leveraging a single property into multiple channels has had some success but still has yet to achieve a success where that property loses that "YouTube" identification.

Can New Media Even be a Core Intellectual Property?

The previous point brings us to that very interesting question. There are many challenges including, what shape a new property takes in new media when constructed. For example, new media intellectual properties often use the television model as a starting point in that they choose a serial narrative structure. New media-based property structures often model more traditional forms in some manner of execution. This of course begs the question whether it is different at all, or just a variant of the big three, perhaps a distribution channel. The profound answer for the moment is "yeah, sorta." The possibilities that new media bring to storytelling are only at the beginning stages. The answer will eventually be an emphatic, yes.

The Strange Case of The Mongoliad

A synthesis of a variety of forms, *The Mongoliad* is a fictional narrative that follows the exploits of a small group of fighters and mystics in medieval Europe around the time of the Mongol conquests. Developed and told in the form of a serialized collaboration between multiple authors, most notably novelists Neal Stephenson (*Snow Crash*, *Cryptonomicon* and most recently *Reamde*), and Greg Bear (*Darwin's Radio*, *Blood Music*), it is available both on the Internet (http://mongoliad.com/) and as an app for mobile platforms. In April of 2012, the creators released a book form that pulled together some of the elements created and released in a digital format including video, images and maps. The serialized digital edition was intended as a new model for publishing storytelling, pulling together a wide variety of media including fan-generated content that would be included in the universe's canon. What is really important to us is that it was constructed as a storytelling collaboration between filmmakers, computer programmers, graphic artists, martial artists and combat choreographers, video game designers, and others. While on the surface it has the appearance of a "novel," much of the content of *The Mongoliad* is other than text and includes a wide array of fiction and non-fiction media, all in the service of the core narrative. This synthesis points in the direction of what is possible with new media and both the initial authors and engaged fans of the work contributing, expanding and enriching the narrative and the fictional universe. *The Mongoliad* really appears to be the first step in a true "new medium" intellectual property, distinct from simple translations of form, the big three we have been seeing over the last decade.

Cultural Artifacts

Some stories originate in ways that are more difficult to attribute to a simple media category; though they are at times quantifiable that way, they are instead better described as cultural artifacts. It almost doesn't matter where they come from, but rather that they exist. The questions raised by such sources for an intellectual property can at times blur the line between transmedia storytelling and transmedia marketing. Why an intellectual property kernel of some artifacts (and not others) resonates with an audience and achieves a foothold has to do with a specific moment in time and culture and the recognition by the creator that there is an opportunity to extend the property beyond its original footprint.

Toys, Food, Advertising and News as a Source

Cultural memes happen and producers often think they can bottle that. To look at the odd assortment of intellectual properties that emerge out of nowhere to become mainstream requires a degree of blindness to what some might describe as "quality." These are not *The Sopranos* or *Game of Thrones* of their eras, but it doesn't mean they don't loom large. By definition they can take the form of a wide variety of intellectual property objects – expected and unexpected.

California Raisins

The *California Raisins* (California Raisin Advisory Board, 1986) were a fictional rhythm and blues musical group that started life as an ad campaign and quickly turned into a multi-media extravaganza. The *California Raisins* concept experienced high popularity in the late 1980s, principally because of the claymation television commercials and animated specials but soon expanded in a variety of areas including a television series, music releases and every imaginable medium, including clothing, lunch boxes, costumes, and even a six-issue comic book series.

GEICO Cavemen

The GEICO Cavemen are characters created by the GEICO auto-insurance company that were used in a series of television advertisements that started airing in 2004. The premise of the commercials is that using the GEICO website is "so easy, a caveman could do it" and features Neanderthal-like cavemen in contemporary settings. The additional twist is that this slogan offends several sophisticated cavemen who not only still exist in modern society but prosper. The commercials were very successful and prompted an ill-conceived attempt to extend the property and turn the characters into a situation comedy. The show, *Cavemen*, aired on ABC in 2007 and flopped. Go figure. (Remember, not everything should be transmedia.)

Transformers

On the other hand, *Transformers* is an entertainment franchise that began with the Hasbro *Transformers* toy line which was based on molds from an unrelated Japanese toy line, which was then brought to market as a universe centered on two factions of warring alien robots respectively called the Autobots and the Decepticons. In its history, the franchise has expanded to encompass comic books, animation, video games and films. While this franchise has been successful from a money-making standpoint, it has always been viewed as a hollow intellectual property that receives much negative critical attention for its lack of depth. Yet even with the negative critical environment, there is a community that shows enthusiasm for the Transformers universe and tracks the property through all its expressions. This of course includes in addition to the feature films that have the largest profile, the multiple animated series, comic books and novels that have explored the property in differing ways. In fact the Transformer wiki deals with the issue with the concept of a "continuity family." A continuity family speaks to the fact that Transformers does not have a great deal of continuity from property to property but instead is measured by how many common elements a storyline might share to the point where it is seen as a new continuity. The wiki and the fans deal with their universe in a way that allows them to make sense of a successful but chaotic property.

Strength/Weakness of Cultural Artifacts

Most of the time these intellectual properties are just marketing turned storytelling. The first expression is typically a marketing exercise, and it is hard to rise above that. Occasionally, properties do have a real life after their conception but more often than not their history becomes a search for authenticity.

Don't Underestimate the Toys

Toys have always been a part of media marketing but have also taken on a new level of importance as they add to the worlds imagined by the story's creator and become a part of the discussion of what is canon and what isn't. Toys made George Lucas a rich man …

Does Anybody Just Make a Universe for the Hell of it?

Yes, but typically creators of an intellectual property take a conventional approach because of the cultural pressures and a desire to reach an audience. Pure universe construction, however, can take some very interesting twists. The best examples of universe construction without an overriding desire to reach an audience are in what is called "outsider art." By definition, it is art that is created outside the typical structures of the "art world" by artists who are typically self-taught and often work in isolation. A great example of this was Henry Darger Jr., a custodian from Chicago, who upon his death was discovered to be the author of a 15,000 page fantasy manuscript called *The Story of the Vivian Girls in What is Known as the Realms of the Unreal, of the Glandeco-Angelinian War Storm, Caused by the Child Slave Rebellion.* His life work also included several hundred watercolors and drawings. The grand vision he expressed is a great example of universe building and at the same time, possibly an expression of his mental instability.

Other Forms of Narrative Extension

Many intellectual properties have had interesting forums outside their traditional expression. This has only increased over the past decade with the possibility of expression expanding through the Internet and with both creators and fans taking full advantage of the opportunity to expand the story universe of "their" story. The most obvious is material that fills the Internet in a wide variety of forums from YouTube to personal blogs to websites dedicated to a particular property. Looking at these can give an indication of the general life of that property and more importantly, the connection the property has to its most ardent fans, fans that can often mean whether a property has an ingoing existence. The other interesting aspects of these additional expressions of the intellectual properties are dependent on culture, though that distinction has been less in the last ten years with the increasing globalization of the media marketplace.

Conventional Additions
Fan Fiction

Fan fiction is a broadly defined term for work in various genres that fans create based on existing intellectual properties that can take shape in a number of ways. The starting point is typically a beloved intellectual property that a fan chooses to expand or extend in some way. The work for the most part is not condoned in any way by the intellectual property's creators and exists in a grey area from a legal standpoint because it's typically a non-commercial endeavor. However, the work can also take some startling turns and explore relationships or storylines not in line with canon. The work is seen as by fans for fans and lives for the most part in a universe unto itself.

Media scholar Henry Jenkins explains the correlation between transmedia storytelling and fan fiction:

> *The encyclopedic ambitions of transmedia texts often result in what might be seen as gaps or excesses in the unfolding of the story: that is, they introduce potential plots which cannot be fully told or extra details which hint at more than can be revealed. Readers, thus, have a strong incentive to continue to elaborate on these story elements, working them over through their speculations, until they take on a life of their own. Fan fiction can be seen as an unauthorized expansion of these media franchises into new directions which reflect the reader's desire to "fill in the gaps" they have discovered in the commercially produced material.*

Transmedia Storytelling 101[1]

Cosplay

Cosplay, short for "costume play," is another expression of fan culture in which participants don costumes and accessories to represent a specific character or idea. Characters are often drawn from popular fiction in Japan, where this expression began but recent trends have included American cartoons and science fiction such as Disney. Favorite sources include manga, anime, comic books, graphic novels, video games, hentai and fantasy movies. This activity, too, exists as a niche culture with a small group of fans devoting time, money and commitment that outsiders rarely see except in fan conventions.

Fan Conventions

A fan convention or con is an event in which fans of a particular film, television series, comic book, actor, or an entire genre of entertainment such as science fiction or anime and manga, gather to participate and hold programs and other events, and to meet experts, famous personalities, and each other. This is not a new activity given that these activities have been around for most of the 20th century often tied to award presentations but has taken a dramatic upturn since the 1970s with more and more proprieties able to draw a crowd so that it becomes more than just fans getting together but instead a financially viable model for building a fanbase and maintaining (or launching) properties. Elements can include everything from appearances by stars, writers, and producers as well as cosplay activities including costume competitions. Trading cards, toys, large lectures, film trailers and teases: fan conventions have become a centerpiece for the media industry to test concepts and set trends.

Unconventional Additions
Slash Fiction/Fan Media Pornography

Slash fiction is a genre of fan fiction that focuses on the depiction of romantic or sexual relationships between fictional characters of the same sex. While initially focused on male characters it has broadened to a wide assortment of combinations. It has become an active community producing a creative and often shocking array of topics and challenges to conventional thinking about characters and canon.

Fan "Canon" Videos ...

This is a very odd category and a phenomenon that has evolved due to technology more than anything else. It happens because it can. Old school fan videos (compilations, tribute songs and the unending list of blogs, commentaries and critiques that are generated) are now a normal part of the ongoing conversations that creators, fans and their community have. But Fan "Canon" Videos go far beyond response or mashup, instead trying to create

---

[1] accessed July 25, 2012, http://www.henryjenkins.org/2007/03/transmedia_storytelling_101.html

new content, content that is meant to be consumed as a substitute for "legitimate" material often no longer available for a variety of reasons. Looking back, two of the most profound and important examples are:

Doctor Who: *Wilderness Videos*

During the darkest times of the intellectual property when the BBC itself had rejected it as a viable property (or just plain too embarrassing to produce) various fan supported/fan generated elements kept the property not just financially viable but truly alive with new "stories" being generated both in novel and comic form. The most interesting material generated during the wilderness were low budget "professionally" made videos using elements that were available due to the BBC's unique intellectual property policy (writers owned original material that was generated even in a work-for-hire scheme) that meant that characters and often the actors who played the role were able to carry on in new stories as long as they stayed away from BBC-owned material. This went even further to some degree with a series of videos produced by Bill Baggs in 1991. It was a commercial enterprise founded to serve *Doctor Who* fans who were starved of content during this time of abandonment.

Towards this end, it heavily used *Doctor Who* actors and, when possible, characters. Even earlier, *Wartime* was a short science fiction film produced direct to video in 1987 by Reeltime Pictures. It was the first professionally produced, authorized independent spin-off of *Doctor Who*, and the only such production to be made while the originating television series was still on the air. Produced and directed by Keith Barnfather, *Wartime* told the story of Warrant Officer John Benton of the United Nations Intelligence Taskforce also known as UNIT. During a mission for UNIT leader Brigadier Lethbridge-Stewart, Benton visits his childhood home where his past literally haunts him. John Levene, who played Benton in *Doctor Who* reprises the role in the production. These productions, while not the real thing, did keep the property alive in an era where doing just that was more challenging than it is today given the support found on the Internet. It went a long way in maintaining a fertile intellectual property culture that was the foundation when *Doctor Who* finally remerged as a vital worldwide property.

Star Trek

Unlike the *Doctor Who* videos of more than a decade earlier, the *Star Trek* videos are the product of a very different environment and intellectual property ownership. *Star Trek New Voyages: Phase II* is a fan-created science fiction series set in the *Star Trek* universe. James Cawley and Jack Marshall created the series in 2003. An Internet distributed series, its goal was to continue the original *Star Trek* beginning with the year following the real world cancelation, to continue the starship *Enterprise's* five-year mission. The first episode of the series was released in January 2004, with new episodes being released about one per year, with the hope of a more ongoing production schedule. Paramount/CBS, which owns the legal rights to the *Star Trek* franchise, allows the distribution of fan-created material as long as no attempt is made to profit from it without official authorization, and *Phase II* enjoys the same tolerance. In fact, it has seen contribution both before the camera and behind the scenes from a variety of individuals connected to the original series. It is a continuing reminder of the fact that the culture and the fans love *Star Trek* in some profound way, achieving a universal status few properties achieve.

It can be argued that fan connection, no matter what the nature, is more important than protecting a particular articulation of the intellectual property over the long haul. These kinds of activities described here as alternative forms can be strange and often seem to twist the intellectual property or fly in the face of canon but fans can distinguish what the main meal is and what the side dishes are. These other activities keep the connection with the hard-core fans strong and as history has already demonstrated, this small part of the larger audience can be a means to keep a property viable over an extended time frame.

Batman and *Naruto* Face the Challenges of Size and Longevity

The various topics in this chapter really highlight the complexity of the issues surrounding using other media outside film, TV and games as the core intellectual property. These other media often follow a relatively similar development process to those core intellectual properties with standard processes that are already in motion in their respective industries. Given that development is always a trial-and-error process, what is more challenging is the relationship and management of the other expressions to existing and expanding transmedia intellectual properties as they extend beyond and interact with the big three. Is it inevitable that all the possibilities shape or distort the core story? How do they change the relationship of the audience to the property? How do other media transcend being a marketing tool and really emerge as another story engine on equal/complementary footing with the mothership and other large-scale story extensions? It is clear that the other media really do have an effect in some circumstances in relation to a really complex core intellectual property and that depends on how the core intellectual property is being managed. Does it require a strong hand on the tiller or does some level of chaos serve to keep the intellectual property alive and relevant? What happens over an extended time frame and can an intellectual property exist with no core? To address the varied circumstances it will be useful to compare two intellectual properties with similar starting points but very different paths and existences. Both began as "comics" and each has generated a huge universe in their home country, Japan and the United States. *Naruto* vs. *Batman* sounds like a video game but the comparison should answer many of the questions asked.

Naruto/Naruto Shippuden
Origin: Manga

Masashi Kishimoto's *Naruto* manga series is the story of Naruto Uzumaki and his journey to gain the respect of his village and the position of Hokage, its leader. Originally published as a single-issue manga in 1997, it was relaunched in 1999 in *Shonen Jump* magazine and is still in publication with over 600 chapters and counting. At over 70 million books sold, *Naruto* is the company's best-selling manga series.

The story of *Naruto* has covered a huge section of his life as he matured from a young boy to a confident adolescent, including a wilderness years section that allowed the story to jump ahead in time and bring us to what seems to be the ultimate conflict between Naruto and his boyhood friend/competition, Sasuke. To express it in this manner is to simplify what is a huge complex story universe that's true focus is the nature of a hero in a world filled with shades of gray and the power of friendship.

Anime

Even though it began sometime after the manga, the anime quickly caught up, since one anime episode usually covers one or two manga chapters. To prevent overlapping, the anime's producers tend to organize content from the manga chapters into long, uneventful sections followed by short bursts of action, sometimes adding filler content in between. However, the anime is also used to explore story and character threads that would slow the momentum of the manga but enrich the story. Overall, the anime generally remains true to the manga, usually changing only minor details, with the manga perceived as the core intellectual property.

Films

The intellectual property has also spawned five animated feature films, situated both before after the wilderness trip which tell stories that aren't part of the large arc but do exist as canon. They have been successfully released to a Japanese audience.

Video Games

Nearly every game console has seen one or more *Naruto* games, and the majority of them are fighting games. Using techniques and fighting styles taken directly from the anime and manga, the *Naruto* video games allow their players a way to directly interact with the universe and its characters. The next *Naruto* video game release is expected to be *Naruto Shippuden: Ultimate Ninja Storm 3*, slated for Spring 2013 release for the Sony Playstation 3 and Microsoft Xbox 360.

All Sorts of Alternative Media

Music CDs, OVA or original video animation (animated films and series made especially for release in home-video formats or in American terms "straight to video"), pre-teen novels aimed at children aged seven to ten years old, a trading card game, art and guidebooks, clothes, posters, action figures … A cursory web search yields something for everyone; adults and kids, boys, girls and even babies. This kind of gear is an industry unto itself all hinged on the continuing production of the core narrative.

Why has Naruto *been so Successful?*

Few narratives reach the size of *Naruto* and maintain the internal consistency, quality and overall unified vision. Size and auxiliary media are an incredible issue for any core narrative that expands over an extended time frame. The question then really becomes "Why *Naruto*?" It has elements that are common to many stories of boy manga/anime. Many of the familiar elements are present mixing historical pieces like samurai, ninja and politics of the past with modern almost sci-fi elements all flavored with a religious/mystical worldview. It is a classic mixture of action/humor/heroism and yet has its unique elements. It has much in common with many other similar stories in its genre (ninja tales) as well as other genres it shares many storytelling elements with. The question then becomes again "Why *Naruto*?"

Naruto's *Core Story/Arc Dynamics*

To reduce the core elements to its most basic story dynamics, *Naruto* is the story of an immensely powerful demon trapped in the body of a boy with no family. The manga explores that boy/young man's commitment to his community as his love for his friends, village, and nation translates into a series of action filled chapters/episodes that are ultimately about Naruto's path/dream to become Hokage (the leader of his village) and protector of all its inhabitants.

His world is a complicated one filled with a wide variety of multifaceted characters with complex motivations, but the storylines all lead back to the same place. His all-consuming focus is about protecting his friends/village at any cost, even his life. A profound notion of self-sacrifice places his love of community well ahead of love of self, a quality that matches the ideal of Japanese culture. This dynamic creates a tension that appeals to Japanese across a broad realm of Japanese society. An astonishingly direct and powerful metaphor speaks to its audience both on the printed page and in electronic form.

Generating long-term but consistent story arcs is a complex challenge under the best of circumstance but to add the issues related to the dynamic of stories that are created in manga then transition to anime challenges the author to deal with the consuming nature of a "live" medium versus the printed page. The anime series has dealt with it by adding filler storylines that do not affect the core storyline but at the same time match the core narrative in every way. This has led to some bumpy patches and fan complaints but in general the material is strong enough to retain the fan interest while the promise of the core narrative stays in the wings.

Sometime internal storytelling issues need to be resolved as well with a reboot along the continuing timeline. *Naruto* saw a jump in the storyline aging the central character two and a half years and bringing to a head both the threat to the village and Saskue's relationship with Orochimaru. As these issues get sorted out what is amazing to think about is that the core character is still in his teens and a long way from reaching the final goal of becoming Hokage and the leader of his village. The vision for *Naruto* has always been very focused and in its own way, singular. Even with the immense of amount of story generated, the consistency of the universe has been maintained.

Batman
Origins: Comics
Created by comic book artist Bob Kane and writer Bill Finger, the character of the Batman made his appearance in issue #27 of *Detective Comics* in 1939 and changed comics forever. Since then, the story of the Batman has appeared in nearly every form of media, and his origins told and retold so many times that it has become a part of American (and world) folklore. Batman is an iconic figure, "The World's Greatest Detective," and next to Superman perhaps the most recognizable superhero ever.

First Transformation
Inspired by the success as a comic book, *Batman* became a 15-chapter serial, released in 1943 by Columbia Pictures. The serial starred Lewis Wilson as Batman and Douglas Croft as Robin. The plot involved Batman – as a US government agent – attempting to defeat the Japanese agent Doctor Daka, at the height of World War II. The film is really only notable for being the first filmed appearance of Batman, and for debuting story details that became permanent parts of the Batman myth, for example the Batcave and Alfred's appearance. These quickly appeared in the comic. It was followed by another serial in 1949 with new actors. After Hollywood took its shot, the comic maintained its popularity as one of industry's leading titles but *Batman* like all comics was subject to the challenges and pressures of the 1950s. It caused some strange twists and turns and unlikely elements to become part of the *Batman* universe.

Re-Emergence into Mainstream Popular Culture
1960s: Television and the Hipness Factor
During the 1960s *Batman* became an American television series, loosely based on the DC comic book. It stared Adam West as Batman and Burt Ward as Robin. It aired on ABC for two and a half seasons starting in 1966 with a total of 120 episodes produced. It was originally conceived as a kid's adventure show, much like the *Adventures of Superman* (Syndicated, 1952–1958) that had preceded it by nearly a decade. When that production fell through, ABC Television obtained the rights and elected to produce an over-the-top send-up of comic book stories, rather than follow the more serious tone of the comics themselves. Remarkably, the series became hugely popular, produced a money-making merchandising machine, and made its star – Adam West – a household name. It also moved *Batman* back to front and center in the cultural landscape, and though it wasn't the Batman of the comics, it was a Batman that everyone remembered. The down-side, however, was clear – the somewhat serious nature of what had been the intellectual property for most of its 20-year-plus existence had now become the source for humor and silliness.

The 1980s: New Comics, Animations and Movies
The 1980s finally saw the repercussion of the 1960s transformation recede. What occurred through the decade were lots of different thoughts and perspectives about Batman. From a comic book standpoint and in many

respects from a Batman-culture standpoint, the turning point was the publication of *Batman: The Dark Knight Returns* as a four-issue comic book limited series comprising *The Dark Knight Returns*, *The Dark Knight Triumphant*, *Hunt the Dark Knight* and *The Dark Knight Falls*, written and drawn by Frank Miller, published by DC Comics in 1986. It tells the story of a 55-year-old Bruce Wayne who comes out of retirement to fight crime, only to face opposition from the Gotham City police force and the United States government. This iteration was a revelation to readers and reshaped the perception of Batman as a character making it seemingly OK for adults again to engage with the Batman universe. What followed was the continued renaissance of the character with both a new feature film and cartoon series.

Batman was the 1989 film directed by Tim Burton. The film stars Michael Keaton, an unlikely choice, in the title role, as well as Jack Nicholson as the Joker. In the capable hands of Tim Burton with his unique storytelling perspective in full force, *Batman* became a huge hit and again introduced the Batman character as one that had impact in the larger culture. It was an adult Batman that was described by Burton and generated enough excitement that a film series was to follow but unfortunately Burton soon moved on leaving it to lesser hands and unraveling what was started.

The moment also inspired *Batman: The Animated Series*, paving the way for the DC Animated Universe, and has influenced Hollywood's modern marketing and development techniques of the superhero film genre. The series won multiple Emmy Awards using top of the line voice talent and was noted for its thematic complexity, dark tone, and high artistic quality. It received both critical acclaim and a enthusiastic fan base. It was seen as a faithful to the more serious elements of the adaptation of the character.

So What Happened to the Movies?

Although *Batman Returns* was a financial success, Warner Brothers thought the film didn't live up to expectations set by *Batman*. The studio decided to change the direction of the *Batman* film series to be more mainstream. Joel Schumacher replaced Tim Burton as director, while Burton decided to stay on as producer. However, Michael Keaton did not like the new direction the film series was heading in, and was replaced by Val Kilmer. Chris O'Donnell was introduced as Robin. Jim Carrey starred as the Riddler, while Tommy Lee Jones starred as Two-Face. Filming started in September 1994, and Schumacher encountered problems communicating with Kilmer and Jones. *Batman Forever* was released on June 16, 1995 with financial success, earning over $350 million worldwide and three Academy Award nominations, but the film had mixed reviews from critics. More importantly, fans of the intellectual property as opposed to the casual moviegoer felt that what had been a promising start had drifted to a revisit of *Batman* by people who don't get or who hate *Batman*. As flexible an intellectual property as it is, making itself a joke or too campy or really drifting from canon was unacceptable. While in the short term it may work with a mass audience, losing the hardcore fans is typically the beginning of the end for a property. That end for this run of *Batman* was called *Batman and Robin*.

Development for *Batman and Robin* started immediately as a fourth and final installment after *Batman Forever*, and Warner Brothers put it on a fast track for a summer 1997 release. Val Kilmer did not return, because of scheduling conflicts and was replaced by George Clooney. A solid cast was assembled including Arnold Schwarzenegger, Uma Thurman, Alicia Silverstone, and Chris O'Donnell reprised his role as Robin. It was critically panned for its campy approach, and for homosexual innuendos added by Schumacher. (The Batman suit had nipples?) Still, the film was a financial success, but now Batman was clearly a property in decline with this film the least financially successful of any of the series. It has earned a reputation as one of the worst superhero films made because of over-the-top tone that undercut the core of what had grown into a serious property at least among the hard-core fans.

Dark Knight Movies and More Dark Batman (mostly...)

Batman begins, and he wasn't kidding … *Batman Begins* was a radical departure from the last time we had seen *Batman* on the big screen. The 2005 movie directed by Christopher Nolan, staring Christian Bale as Batman, along with Michael Caine, Liam Neeson, Katie Holmes, Gary Oldman, Cillian Murphy, Morgan Freeman, Ken Watanabe, Tom Wilkinson, and Rutger Hauer screamed "we are a serious *Batman* film" and it truly was. Drawing from much of the darker retelling of the stories, it starts at the beginning and gives a very particular view on Batman as a troubled complex hero living in a complex post 9/11 world.

Batman Begins was both critically and commercially successful. Critics noted that fear was a common theme throughout the film, and remarked that it had a darker tone compared with previous *Batman* films. It really plugged into a world that had been laid out in the comics over the last 20 years, a more serious *Batman* world that due to social climate and expert storytelling became a universal story that *Batman* hadn't been for a while. The film would begin Nolan's *Batman* trilogy, each subsequent installment a highly anticipated event. As the series concludes, it begs the question what will be next on the big screen. How do you follow such an intellectual property defining moment? Time will tell but it is a very safe bet that someone will come along and try to redefine *Batman* just as they have done a *SpiderMan* reboot shortly after a successful run.

In the meantime, what will be going on with *Batman*? The answer is tons of other stuff … The intellectual property has seen an abundance of retellings in comics including a re-launch as part of DC's revision of all its properties, *The 52*. There are currently multiple *Batman* animated series with the launch of another currently scheduled for 2013. There too has been a plethora of choices for gamers starting in the 1980s with Batman being a consistent presence on a variety of computers, console and hand-held devices, often with a tie to whatever was the current media (film or TV) propriety that was at the forefront. However, in the last few years with most notably the critical and financial success of the *Batman: Arkham Asylum* game in 2009 followed by Batman arriving on multiple platforms including the iPad tied to the very successful film series, Batman has achieved a stronger place in the game industry than ever before. The sequel *Batman: Arkham City* established for gamers what had always been true culturally, that Batman was one of the premier media characters. It is a reminder that no matter how successful a television series or feature film is at any particular time, there will always be an underlying relationship between Batman and his core audience.

Why has Batman been so Successful?

A simple answer is that he is our Sherlock Holmes, a character that touched on an essential cultural nerve at launch and managed to implant himself into our psyche through the minds of generation after generation of pre-pubescent boys. Batman, like Superman, is a cultural icon but the difference is that we can never be an alien from another planet but at some level we all think we can be Batman. What has happened by accident, with the occasional profound artistic expression and changing cultural and market pressures, has become a rich multi-verse where there are multiple Batmans and no one cares, with the right Batman coming at the right time and sometimes not. At this point we seemingly can tolerate it because that's how it's been for a long time, just like we can have multiple Sherlock Holmeses telling different versions of the same story and no one seems to mind. Is it something unique in the American psyche that allows the rapid change in characters and story without rejecting the story just because of its unfamiliarity? At this point it would just be conjecture to try and answer the question but what is clear is that this pattern affords opportunity from both a storytelling perspective and a financial one.

Lesson Learned

This analysis is meant to illuminate the challenge of a long-term comic-based intellectual property with a huge universe. In many respects it also illuminates a variety of cultural differences between Japan and America that directly affects the shape and management of an intellectual property. The shorthand way to look at this is that different history, culture and industries have translated into very different practices. What it means is one tends to produce a coherent defined universe while the other produces a less defined multi-verse that uses characters/mythology to anchor the property but after that things evolve in the "moment," producing a universe that captures cultural zeitgeist, for good and bad. Americans seem to love a reboot and have no problem seeing their stories retold in a new way, at least some of the time, while the Japanese seem to prefer the well-tended carefully managed property. Though the simple explanation doesn't express all the subtleties of the reasons why differently structured and managed properties can grow to such expanse and remain culturally relevant, it should be remembered the comparison isn't a perfect apple to apple example. *Naruto* is a huge narrative but all of its storytelling has been done in a relatively short timeline. It begs the question what it would look like in 20 or 30 years' time. Even trying to take these examples and apply them to other media with different originating intellectual properties may be challenging especially when you layer in the challenges tied to the globalization of media that has occurred with the rise of the Internet. Comics have their own existence but ultimately the lessons learned can be applied to any big intellectual property. It really boils down to a simple baseball metaphor. Do you want to hit for average or hit home runs? A more tightly managed intellectual property by its nature tends to stay connected to a core audience while a less controlled intellectual property swings for the fences every time out. There are exceptions like *Star Trek*, which has had a unique life in the culture but these kinds of questions will arise more and more as an increasing amount of producers try to extend both the story and shelf life of their intellectual properties. What is clear is there are two distinct approaches (and lots of gray in between) and that both choices have merit and will yield results.

Figure 7.1.1 *Anthony Del Col.*

Interview: Anthony Del Col

Anthony Del Col has a wide range of experience in the comic, music, film and television industries. He has produced two independent feature films and served as a manager for international pop star Nelly Furtado, helping to supervise her 2007 "Loose World Tour." He is the co-creator and co-writer of *Kill Shakespeare*, the acclaimed IDW Publishing comic book series that has been profiled by the *New York Times*, *Washington Post*, *Publisher's Weekly*, the BBC and CBC.

The series has been nominated for a Harvey Award for Best New Series and a Joe Shuster Award for Outstanding Comic Book Writing. Working with co-creator Conor McCreery, Del Col co-wrote the theatrical stage show *Kill Shakespeare: The Live Stage Reading*, which debuted in 2011 with Toronto's Soulpepper Theatre and is currently overseeing the property's film development.

Anthony Del Col was interviewed by the authors in late spring 2012 specifically for this book.

Interviewer(s): The big picture topic of what we are trying to grapple with is, what the hell's going on in the world at this point in terms of storytelling, transmedia, multiple media, marketing, the whole bit. So, can you just fill us in a little bit about your own background?

Anthony Del Col: Yeah, my background is a mixed-media business background. Went to business school here in Canada. So majored in business, minored in film, but my heart was always in film and TV. I discovered that about half way through my university education, when I realized when I open up a newspaper, I don't go to the business section right away or the news or the sports, I go to film and entertainment. So that's really where my heart lies. But I decided to stick through business school so that I could apply the lessons I learned to my own ventures, which is exactly what's happened with *Kill Shakespeare*. I mean I've got various things: I've produced two feature films here in Canada, had a couple of development deals on the television front, worked for about 4.5–5 years in the music industry, where I helped manage Nelly Furtado and a number of other clients. And with *Kill Shakespeare*, Connor [McCreery] and I have been working on this full time for about 3.5 years. We left our jobs at that point. We raised private equity, private funding to get this up and running, as I talked about back at C2E2 [Chicago comics/media convention]. Raised private funding, then went to the publishers, got five publishers interested in the idea, and here we are. We have 12 issues out, two graphic novels, and we're starting this week on the first of another five-issue arc. We have a stage play; we have a feature film in development, a mobile game prototype that's going to go into production in the next month or two, and a bunch of other things.

Interviewer(s): Can you go back to the nugget, the moment? Was it in a bar, was it in the bathroom? What led you to *Kill Shakespeare*? Was it inspiration, perspiration? What was it?

Anthony Del Col: It was brainstorming. Connor and I were actually just hanging out one day. At that point Connor and I were working on some other projects. We had a television series that we had optioned and were developing with a Toronto production company, and there were a bunch of other things that we had worked on. We got development funding to work on a feature film script or two here in Canada. We were just kind of sitting around brainstorming ideas for video games, and the title *Kill Bill* came up, one of the Quentin Tarantino films, and we thought, wow that would make a great video game, but I'm sure someone has already done it. Or if not, I'm sure it's in development right now. And then somehow we went from David Carradine to Bill Shakespeare. So what if it instead of David Carradine, it was *Kill Bill Shakespeare* and we send all these characters on this quest to track him down and kill him. Oh my God, that's the coolest idea ever. And so immediately, within a minute or two, we started to suppose that instead of a video game – even though it could be like a massive online role-playing game, a console game, all sorts of variations like that – that maybe it is more of *Lord of the Rings*. So maybe it is feature film, video game, merchandise, comic books. This was about eight or nine years ago, 2003, 2004 maybe? And I had actually been reading up a lot about the theories, the early, early theories of transmedia at the time with Wachowski's and Star Light Runner, *Matrix* and that sort of thing. So I immediately thought this could be like a transmedia thing where we developed this really cool world and use the feature and the video game and everything else. That's kind of where we sat back and over the next probably about 8–12 months, well maybe six months or so, Connor and I sat down and we wrote a 20-page treatment of what the story was for *Kill Shakespeare*, which is pretty similar to what it is today. When I say treatment, I'm talking like for a feature film. And then we shelved it for a while and things got really busy in the music industry for me. Connor wanted to do some traveling, so we went to Africa for a while, and then he was also in broadcast journalism. But *Kill Shakespeare* was the one idea that kept gnawing away at us. It's like, oh my God there's something here; we need to get this done. And actually back around the time we came up with the idea, Connor was doing some part-time work at one of the comic book stores here in Toronto called the Silver Snail, and that's when he introduced comics to me. Up until then I thought, oh they're just super heroes and men in tights and that sort of thing. I was like, that doesn't seem very interesting to me. And then he said, well there are other titles, too. So he put *Fables* in my hand, *League of Extraordinary Gentlemen, Blankets*, those types of titles. And I started to realize, wow there is some really great stuff being told in comic books today. I remember I was traveling through Europe for two weeks. I was going through Cannes, and the Cannes Film Festival was on at the time, so in 2007, and I remember looking around and going, OK what projects do I have that can get here? You know, what's the most sellable? And I knew, *Kill Shakespeare*, and well what's the best way to bring it to the market to establish that brand in the first place? And it kind of just hit on me where hey, what if we did it as a comic book? When I came back, I pitched it to Connor, and he was kind of skeptical and like, I don't know, there aren't that many successful comics that deal with that sort of subject, not necessarily Shakespeare but more of the sword and sorcery; there's Conan but other than that there's not much in the marketplace. But I eventually convinced him, and here we are today.

Interviewer(s): You got to the comic book. But it becomes that question, why the comic book? What factors did you isolate that made you think comic book? Was it the accessibility of production? Was it the serialized storytelling? What was it that was clearly the first connection and why?

Anthony Del Col: There are a number of things. One was it's the most cost efficient way of development. Instead of trying to raise a million or millions of dollars to do a film or six or seven figures to put together a video game, and the amount of money to put together a theatrical show with a lot of resources in terms of people, I realized that for a fraction of the cost of a feature film, we can do the comic book, produce it. And also it gives you that creative freedom where you're able, within 22 pages or 32 pages, however long the issue is, to put together a huge pirate battle that not even Shakespeare could demonstrate in *Hamlet*. In *Hamlet* they talk about a pirate attack, but you never see it because that would just take too much. It happens offstage. But you can see that attack in the very first issue. It was also the trend in Hollywood that comic books were really, really hot, and obviously that's continuing today. I would just read in *Variety* and *Hollywood Reporter* at the time, and it seemed all you have to do was publish a comic book and it got optioned.

Interviewer(s): Yes …

Anthony Del Col: Not that we wanted to option it immediately, but it's a way of getting it out there, and also another key thing is that comic books really target the influencers of entertainment today. It's the geeks; the geeks are the influencers of entertainment especially in Hollywood in all forms and all mediums. Whether every geek reads them, they are at least aware of comic books. And so you kind of make a title or subject that appeals to that demographic or to that sector. It just helps build your brand. And the other thing that was kind of cool for us was, and this is perhaps more from a marketing perspective, but we thought it was just really cool that Shakespeare was always perceived to be very highbrow, and comic books are always perceived to be kind of a lowbrow type thing. You know, stuff for kids and for those who don't know how to read properly. So it was kind of poetic that way, that we were taking Shakespeare to the masses, from highbrow to a lowbrow type of medium.

Interviewer(s): Do you get push back from Shakespeare people ever?

Anthony Del Col: Very few and far between. It's funny. One of the conventions we attended this past spring as part of our "world-com marketing tours" we called it, was the Shakespeare Association Annual Conference in Boston. That was the week before C2E2. I remember going in and thinking, are they going to like us? There have been a lot of Shakespeare fans and scholars that have appreciated this, but I had no idea that we would become rock stars. We were set up there to sell books and t-shirts. We sold out of so many of those things, but more importantly we actually are starting to be analyzed by academics now. Unbeknownst to us there were at least three papers presented over the course of the weekend about *Kill Shakespeare* including the keynote address. The keynote was by Dr. Peter Holland from the University of Notre Dame. He used to run the Shakespeare Institute in Stratford-upon-Avon [United Kingdom]. But he's a huge fan. He analyzed three pieces of work where Shakespeare is a character himself with his other characters. So he looked at the Shakespeare episode of *Doctor Who*, at a very meta-production of *Macbeth* in Africa, like a stage show, and then *Kill Shakespeare*. This was on the keynote address on the opening morning, so you had 1,300 people that were there for the convention that heard all about us. Those that didn't know about us found out about us, and we were treated as rock stars for the rest of the weekend, which was great. There are some Shakespeare scholars who are purists, and they kind of look at this and go, well I like what you are trying to do in terms of getting people excited and stoked about Shakespeare, but some people think we are ignoring the language because we write in a hybrid where it's modern day meets Middle English or Elizabethan English. To some people, the essence of Shakespeare is the language. I can appreciate that and I can respect that, but we are focusing more on the characters and getting the readers and audiences excited about those characters so that when they are reading the play or watching a play of Shakespeare and they would normally get caught up in the language, and therefore not really be able to grasp what's happening, they have a better understanding of who these characters are. But yes, we've had Shakespeare scholars like the Peter Holland of course. Sir Tom Stoppard, co-writer of *Shakespeare in Love*, and won the Oscar for it, he's a fan of *Kill Shakespeare*; I have over here a personal note of congrats from him that I have with me from C2E2. Julie Taymor, who's directed Shakespeare productions. So a number of people that know their Shakespeare are really excited about this. Those that know their Shakespeare. And Shakespeare's been around for over 400 years, and there have been so many adaptations and reinterpretations of Shakespeare, that it's a very welcoming crowd.

Interviewer(s): That's interesting; Tom Stoppard is the perfect person to hear from because of *Rosencrantz and Guildenstern Are Dead*. It's 40 plus years ago now.

Anthony Del Col: Exactly, and his screenplay for *Shakespeare in Love* to me is one of the best screenplays of all time. He was just able to make something very accessible and very modern and yet thrown in so many Easter eggs and references for those who know their Shakespeare. It's so smart. He is one of the influences for us for *Kill Shakespeare*.

Interviewer(s): Have you ever read anything from an academic perspective about how to engage a fan culture that's helped you?

Anthony Del Col: Not specifically. I haven't delved into any academic papers on the subject because my fear was that they would be very, very theoretical and not very practical at all. No, I haven't really done much reading on it. I mean I've always been a student of marketing in general, so I kind of just follow my gut instinct on a lot of levels like that. There are a lot of creators who don't even understand marketing, and when I say marketing I don't mean, hey this is what a poster looks like or something like that. Marketing at its purest is, what is your product and why is someone going to consume it, whether it's a good or a service or whatever it is. A comic book is entertainment product. So what makes your entertainment product different from any other? If it takes them a half hour to read an issue or a couple hours to read a graphic novel, why would they spend those two hours reading what you've written versus reading another book, another graphic novel, watching a television show or a movie, that sort of thing? That's one of the things that I'm going to be focusing on to better understand in the next six months or so, because we want to grow our fan base and need to be able to tap into wider demographics or other niche demographics that we just haven't been able to hit yet. It's really tough. We're very fortunate, and it's also kind of strategic too, in that with our product, the comic series and the graphic novel, we had instant, well, brand awareness. I mean you have millions of people around the world that have heard of these characters. We could tap into that, but more importantly you had hundreds of thousands if not millions of people in North America and in the world all over that love their Shakespeare, as opposed to other comics that are launching or have launched. I mean we knew we had that specific marketplace of those that know their Shakespeare and love Shakespeare. So when you go to conventions, we have the banners up and people walk by and they're like, "Shakespeare, oh I'm a huge fan of Shakespeare." "I go see these productions of Shakespeare in the Park," and that sort of thing, so we knew we could tap into that. There's the literary market. In comics there are people who like comics but literary stuff like the *Sandman* and *the Fables* and those sorts, so we knew we could appeal to that, so we try to target those demos. Then there's the mash-up; the literary mash-up is kind of a new genre unto itself of late so we knew, that kind of taps into the literary but it also taps into the genre of marketing as well.

Interviewer(s): You're kind of the king of the Venn Diagram now that you've said it. It really is true. I start drawing the circles, and I'm going there's a good chunk of overlap here if you're in the right place at the right time. You've created multiple engagement points just in the very nature of what you do, the very nature of the property.

Anthony Del Col: That's one of the reasons why it got me so excited that there was market potential of those individual segments.

Interviewer(s): The graphic novels have now existed long enough that you can look back at them. You're about to do another one. What was your favorite thing about the first runs of the graphic novels and your least favorite thing. We're going for 20/20 hindsight.

Anthony Del Col: The favorite things about the graphic novel, the favorite things about the process, has actually been directly with the fans. That's the thing that I enjoy the most about the comic book industry in general, having spent time in TV, film and music, where it's really tough for a fan to interact directly with the creator or the artists. There's always that velvet rope in between the VIP section and the regular section for the regular people. Comic books and the conventions take down that rope. You can go up to any of your favorite creators or you can email them or talk to them and just have a conversation about what you like or what you don't like, specifically with what they do or what we do or just about Shakespeare in general. I have so many people that come up and haven't read *Kill Shakespeare* but often they see the title, and they get really excited, and they talk to me about for 15–20 minutes about Shakespeare and their favorite production and that sort of thing. It's really great to get that instant feedback. Like, "Oh I really like this, I love this character, this one, eh, I'm not that excited about." So we were actually able to slightly alter some of the plot lines or story lines in our series as it went on, based on the initial reaction.

Interviewer(s): But that's good. So what kind of alterations did you do? What kind of adjustments?

Anthony Del Col: There wasn't anything major, because the story was kind of set in stone in terms of the overall arc, but just small little moments. We knew that the [readers] really liked Iago. So we actually tried to play up his story a bit more in the second half. Those types of things, and Falstaff as well. People really like Falstaff. We already knew what the ending of his story was going to be, but we wanted to build it up a little more based on that initial reaction. And taking into consideration the reaction that we've got thus far, that's what we are incorporating into our story now. So our story has slightly altered because of the readers' reactions to the first story.

Interviewer(s): Is there anything looking back that you wish you could have changed?

Anthony Del Col: Oh yeah, of course. There are always little things along the way. I mean I could talk about the marketing. I would have done some things differently on the marketing perspective in terms of release dates and that sort of thing.

Interviewer(s): That's an interesting question, because one of the things we are trying to sort out in the course of this book is how we talk about "timetable." How a production timetable has story impact because story reads differently in June than sometimes in August. So what timetable would you have changed, just out of curiosity?

Anthony Del Col: The release was fine because the first issue came out in April, the second one in May of 2010, third one came out in July and that was a publisher decision; they wanted to give that month break or a two-month break in between the second and third, based on how well the first had sold, which we were fine with. I wanted it done differently, where we released the first six issues. We really rushed to put out the first trade, the first collected edition. I would have released that a bit later, say a couple of months later. It came out November 2010. I would have released it in maybe February or March to let people discover the first six issues and kind of build up that way. I would release the second six a bit later, because issue 6 was released in September or October; the next month we put out the trade and then issue 7 immediately followed in December. So what I would have done was held back on the issue of 7 and 8 until the new year in 2011 to let people kind of discover *Kill Shakespeare* bit more before the release of the second six because that would have helped out with sales. So in terms of timeline, that's the major thing I would say, but the fact that it's monthly is challenging. We really pushed to hit that monthly, that monthly cycle. The last few were a little late but that was more of the artist, because he was just putting everything into it; he actually broke his wrist and all sorts of things along the way.

Interviewer(s): Let's leave the *Kill Shakespeare* topic for a moment. What properties interest you today? When you look, I mean you're obviously devoted to your own. But when you pick your head up and look to see what's going on in the world, what properties interest you? Is it comics? Is it games? Is it films? Is it TV? Is it a little bit of … what?

Anthony Del Col: There's all sorts. My biggest passion is probably film. So that's probably the first thing I look at in terms of IP, like the IPs that really interest me. Because if we are talking transmedia or even just entertainment overall, film is still the major primary driver. It's still the premier or the prestige medium out of them all. So I think that's why I gravitate toward that still, I mean the ability to tell an interesting story. An IP that interests me these days, oh God, I mean there's all sorts. *The Hunger Games* is really interesting. I read the first two books. The first book I really enjoyed, the second one just seemed really repetitive. The feature film was good, not great, but that is a franchise. I'm very intrigued by all the YA [young adult]. I mean all the YA stories, that's a huge driver now in the publishing industry. It's really interesting because they have seemed to have tapped into that demographic, like the teen demographic. But I think it's because the concepts are just so high. They are all high concepts. I mean *Hunger Games* is just a great concept. Of course it's *Battle Royale*. But no, I mean those kinds of things are really piquing my interest. And it will be interesting to see what they do with *Ender's Game*.

Interviewer(s): You mention *Enders Game*, which I find fascinating. After all these years, a film is finally getting made.

Anthony Del Col: Yeah, Hollywood has been trying to make it for years. It's got the possibility of being like a *Tron*, if it had been done properly. Both as a film and a transmedia property, I mean *Ender's Game* could be very similar to that. We have the feature film, but more importantly we have an overall experience where people could actually get involved in the game. You can create an interactive type of game. And when I say game, I don't mean specifically a video game, but you could do something more interactive almost like an arcade type of experience. And that's actually one of the things we are trying to look at in *Kill Shakespeare*, to do an interactive theatre piece with it. I've spoken with another creator that's done interactive theater here in Toronto, and he actually just sent me a script, this 250–300 page script. We were talking about ways of creating the theatre experience so that it's interactive, because in that production, you're basically part of the masquerade ball, but you're just observing the main characters. I'd like to be able to come up with a way where you're involved; it's interactive, and you can actually decide the path of the story. So you might go to one where Richard III ends up winning the day, or you might go to one where Hamlet wins at the end of the day, and that's all decided through the actual audience and consumers. It's very, very theoretical. You'd probably have to include smart-phone technology. I'm guessing. But we are trying to come up with some sort of way for that. But that's really early, early stages. It's just conceptual right now.

Interviewer(s): What technologies interest you? Because really, what you're talking about is the merging of technology and storytelling, and we're seeing more and more attempts to do that.

Anthony Del Col: I know. I'm not a huge tech geek. But that's why I'm going to switch over to the iPad and the iPhone later this year. I'm waiting for the iPhone 5 to see what happens. Because I feel it's necessary. I'm missing out on a lot of apps and a lot of programs that people are creating for entertainment, for information, for everything. There is so much potential there. For some of the properties I've been developing that are outside of *Kill Shakespeare*, one of the first things I think of is, OK, what can I do on the digital or the mobile front? Like, how can I tell this story and adapt it to the iPhone? There's one property right now in particular where I've got the general idea for the characters, and the general world, like the theory of the world, but one of my first thoughts is, well it's either TV or film on the big screen format, and I definitely see it as a comic, but more importantly I think there's a lot of potential for it as a mobile app. Sort of like a game experience where you actually get involved in the game and you can actually kind of direct what happens. So you feel as though you really are involved as one of the main characters in the experience. Even comics moving forward; first of all comics look great on the iPad. *Kill Shakespeare* looks better on the iPad than it does in print because you don't have those printing errors that the printing company makes.

Interviewer(s): Like the misprint, the extra page in my copy of *Kill Shakespeare*.

Anthony Del Col: Yeah, exactly. But it's not being tapped into like the way it should be. We've actually received funding here in Canada to do a prototype of an enhanced graphic novel and that's what we are trying to do. So you'll have additional content. What we would do is take an issue of *Kill Shakespeare*, say issue number one of the new series, and then there would be a bunch of underlying content. Interviews with us, with Andy Belanger the artist, interviews with a

Shakespeare scholar or director or an actor like Kenneth Branagh or something. You can actually see real Shakespeare companies, *Romeo and Juliet* or something, and a mobile game. Of course there are things like that but for me, we should be taking that next step further, where the actual content itself is designed specifically for the iPad, not necessarily choose-your-own-adventure though a choose-your-own-adventure would be kind of an interim step, and you can create some sort of … I don't know; this is all very, very conceptual, but something that involves more than just the one-way interaction. So we are pushing the content towards you and then you decide what parts you want to experience, so there's that give and take as they help you out while the content is created.

Interviewer(s): We are at an exciting moment.

Anthony Del Col: We are, we are, but I feel like I'm throwing this back to you now, on the fact that we still haven't had a mainstream true success story yet. I'm really curious to see what that's going to be. *The Matrix* is the one I always looked to as "kind of," when people ask me about transmedia. Well that's the first attempt at it, but it wasn't full-fledged from the ground floor. *Matrix* is the first one where they actually put together the theory of transmedia and started to apply it in the second film, the third film and then *Animatrix* and whatever the video game was called. That's where the Wachowski siblings actually kind of came together. But unfortunately those films kind of ruined the IP for them. But I'm really interested to see what that first true mainstream success story is going to be.

Interviewer(s): *LOST* had a lot of elements of the success. It doesn't have the feature film but in terms of generating a universe and engaging fans, it had a huge amount of success.

Anthony Del Col: It had a huge amount of success. My thing with *LOST* is that it wasn't able to expand into other major mediums. You have the TV series and for me, you don't need the film when you've got the TV, but there's the video game. Even some of the writers on the video game basically acknowledged OK, we tried but it really wasn't there. I mean unfortunately, you could do an ARG route; they probably tried or did something along the way.

Interviewer(s): They did have a couple of ARGs, but what I find interesting is how much fan generated material that was really embraced by their universe. It's like their world got away from them in a good way.

Anthony Del Col: And that's what I really learned at the Sundance Lab last year. Transmedia is really about world building and building open worlds that you as creators can tap into, but then you open up for other users to experience and to create, kind of like a *Sims* game or something. That's really what it's all about. In hindsight, when talking about *Kill Shakespeare*, I would say if I would have known then what I know now, I would have tried to build up that world a little more, even such things as the geography. As we write the feature film at the moment, one of the things that's really come into play is you really need to know what the backstory is and what the rules of the world are. The rules of the world, that's huge. Something like *Game of Thrones* is so successful now, partly because George R. R. Martin was so specific on that world. He created the maps himself. This is Winterfell and all the different areas. At first it used to be just the geeks that used to be into that, but now it's getting into more of a mainstream audience. But yeah, building the world and the rules of the world, that's what transmedia is, right there.

Interviewer(s): Does the story dictate the medium or is that an old concept?

Anthony Del Col: Yes and no, it depends on the IP; it depends on the property. Something that is genre based or something that's like fantasy, sci-fi genre, like in *Kill Shakespeare*, you can do that in multiple mediums. A romantic comedy is tough to do in a kind of game space or interactive type of space. So it's more of the genre that determines the medium I'd say, or mediums.

Interviewer(s): Do we spend way too much time talking about genre material? It's a challenge at times. I mean that's why no doubt *Kill Shakespeare* reaches a group of people who normally wouldn't be pulled by graphic novels, just because it is. But typically when you talk about transmedia, you are so often stuck in the world of science fiction and fantasy.

Anthony Del Col: You know the answer to this. I mean that's where the fan bases are, and those are the people who are willing to embrace those technologies. They are willing to embrace the graphic novels or the mobile games or the massive online roll-playing games and those sorts of things. I mean, it's going to be tough to take that romantic comedy or comedy or simple dramas and make those into transmedia; that's going to be a challenge. Maybe that will be the first real success story, when you take something that's outside of genre and can come up with a way of doing that. A romantic comedy? You can do as a TV series, or you can do it as a film. That's quite easy. Comic book? You can do it, yeah. Your story is basically the same. Take something like the short-lived – the twice short-lived – series *Cupid*. Your TV series or film could focus on the main character. On the comic book front, you focus on a different person's story, and he or she is the Cupid, the Cupid master or love master or whatever it is. Then on the digital front, the mobile front, how can you tell a story on that? I mean you could have it as the Cupid gives advice. I'm sure you could come up with some sort of way. That one is where the medium dictates what the story is. Or the other way around.

Interviewer(s): As you're looking at the *Kill Shakespeare* film and developing that material, are you imagining that as more of an adaptation of the comics that you've already developed or are you creating a whole new story within that world? Are we allowed to ask that question?

Anthony Del Col: That's what's causing us to bang our heads against the wall on a daily basis when we work on the script. Fortunately I haven't been doing much head banging in the last couple of months, because we've been busy traveling. But no, we are looking it as an adaptation because as we move on, we've discovered how different the mediums are, so you have to adapt your story to it. On the film, I'd say right now in the current draft we are working on, I'd say about 35–45% of the content in the film is directly from the comic. The majority, so 60–65%, is actually new. The actual storyline, like Hamlet washing ashore on the beach and meeting all these characters, having to track down Shakespeare to kill or not to kill, that sort of storyline, that's exactly the same. It's just the way that he gets there that's different. We've discovered several things along the way, such as the fact that you really need to establish the rules of the world, which we've talked about. Also, we're altering Hamlet's character. In the comic book, he's very, very passive. And that's another one of those, going back to your question about changes you want to make in hindsight; we'd make him more active. Hamlet in the comic? He's a little too emo. He's a little too passive. He lets everybody dictate what he's going to do in the adventure, where as he should be saying no, I'm going to be doing this, this and this. He's going to make mistakes along the way; he's going to second guess himself, because that's what Hamlet is all about. I've actually analyzed the play, and people say he is very inactive, he can't make a choice. Yes, but he's actually actively trying to try to make a choice. He can't promise to try, he'll try to try. One of my favorite quotes from *The Simpsons*: "I can't promise to try, Dad, but I'll try to try." The stuff you do in a comic, you do that in a feature film would be 4.5–5 hours. You need to streamline that down to 2–2.5 hours. Because unfortunately we are not Peter Jackson yet in our careers and say, oh it's going to be three hours each. So it's just a lot of streamlining. The characters are still there. We are changing situations. We are changing environments. We are changing settings. But the main through line is still exactly the same. And it's great. I mean I love adapting it because I can kind of go back and see what worked in the comic, what didn't work in the comic and how we can alter that for the screen. Then also, how does that process work with respect to creating something for the screen? Again this comes back to the interaction with readers in that in some sense you can almost treat the comic as a prototype for the feature film. So you get your story out there, see what works and what doesn't work, and then you can kind of alter your next product to suit that.

Chapter 8
Choosing Properties and Forms

Given the wide range of content ready to develop from both the expected and more unusual sources it is good to ask, why this property? With a property that already has a significant life in other media the motivations appear clear, but history proves again and again that successful intellectual properties don't always move easily from one form to another. The primary reasons seem to be base incompatibilities between the source medium's storytelling language and those of the targeted medium, but that's not the sole reason. Any attempt to break down the reasons for choosing an intellectual property over another, outside passion for a particular story, touches on a complex web of cultural and financial motivations with unpredictable results.

When looking at good examples it must be noted that the reasons for choosing any particular property are not mutually exclusive. The motivation behind a property's development often includes many of the following elements.

Fan Base

Properties are chosen because they have already generated interest. There is good and bad in this. A fan base is important but can also be brutal in its judgment of the development and expression of "their" intellectual property. Fans can be very supportive but can also be anally critical of every little casting, production, or scheduling decision. We've touched on this before and the best approach seems to be opening and maintaining direct lines of communication with the existing fan base early and being really responsive to them, whether it's through a community manager of some kind or direct contact with the development team(s).

Wizard of Oz

The Wonderful Wizard of Oz is a children's novel written by L. Frank Baum and published in 1900. You probably know it as simply *The Wizard of Oz*, which was the name of the 1902 play and the 1939 motion picture. The fact that the name of the book changed is an important point about how the focal point of a property can shift.

In the story, Dorothy Gale of Kansas is magically transported into the Land of Oz, where she has many adventures. The success of the novels and the first 1902 musical adaptation encouraged Baum to explore the *Oz* universe through 13 additional novels. Though the novels were hugely successful, it was the 1939 MGM movie that transformed it into one of the best known stories in American popular culture. In 1956 the original story entered the public domain and has since seen a series of reinventions and translations to all forms of media.

While the intellectual property clearly began as a product of its time, it also has evolved with the times. In addition to the iconic film, the book has inspired the hugely successful 2003 Broadway musical (*Wicked*), the Gregory Maguire novel series the musical was based on (*Wicked: The Life and Times of the Wicked Witch of the West* (1995), *Son of a Witch* (2005), *A Lion Among Men* (2008) and *Out of Oz* (2011), as well as new television (*Tin Man*, SciFi Channel, 2007)) and motion picture (*Oz: The Great and Powerful*, Walt Disney Pictures, 2013) versions in just the past decade. The question always is what the property looks like going forward and what the next iteration will be. In many respects because Baum engaged in universe building, the property has retained some level of integrity and consistency, unlike other transmedia expressions based on similar novel series.

In this case, *The Wizard of Oz* is an example of a property with a seemingly evergreen fan base that is willing to accept the transformation of the property through its various incarnations and accept experimentation. We believe the fan base for *The Wizard of Oz* remains strong and accepting because the other expressions have always led back to the books and Baum's universe with a degree of faithfulness and respect, which has provided an ongoing foundation for generation after generation.

Nancy Drew

Nancy Drew is the original girl detective who burst on the scene in the Depression and continues solving crimes to this day. The first *Nancy Drew* novel appeared in 1930 from publisher Grosset & Dunlap, and though created by Edward Stratemeyer, founder of the Stratemeyer Syndicate book-packaging firm, the books were ghostwritten by a number of authors and published under the Carolyn Keene pseudonym. However, it should be noted that the first ghostwriter, Mildred Wirt Benson, set a tone that was unusual for its time, giving Nancy abilities and a personality that fell outside the cultural norms. Nancy had "moxie."

A 1959 revision (ostensibly to update the era of the books and correct racial and culturally sensitive elements) removed that characteristic, toning down the heroine's original, outspoken character and making her more docile, conventional, and demure. Since the 1959 revision, multiple versions of *Nancy Drew* have appeared in print, such as the 1980 *The Nancy Drew Files*. A new series, *Nancy Drew: Girl Detective* was launched in 2004 and presented an updated, hip version of Nancy. Additionally, there have been multiple versions in motion pictures (1930s and 2007), television (1970s, 1990s and 2000s) and a thriving video game existence under developer Her Interactive since 1998, each doing their particular spin on the timeless girl detective.

Nancy Drew is a property that has generated an incredible amount of fan interest through its core expression, the novels, and extension into motion pictures, television and video games. However, decisions made by those controlling the property began the process of losing the essence of what connected Nancy and her audience. An icon in our culture for many years, its current existence has begun a slow wind down in impact and while we see a strong ongoing presence in video games, it is rapidly becoming lost in the crowded young adult publishing field.

While the most recent attempt to re-launch the property, a feature film in 2007 (*Nancy Drew*, Warner Brothers), was a modest success, there was no follow up by the studio, and Nancy Drew is no longer the Nancy Drew of the past in terms of its presence in the culture. The property also has issues of connection with the core of the intellectual property, what there is left of it, given the repeated dramatic re-direction the property has seen since the 1950s.

Except for the fact that mom or grandma may have some connection to the brand, Nancy Drew is a young girl detective not all that different from a slew of others.

There is still significant recognition of the property, and an older fan base, but it is an example of where we may be seeing a shift in the growing portion of the fan base, from the reading young adult market to the game-playing young adult market. It is important to understand that the fan focus of a property can (and some might say will) shift, and it is vital to properly review the past, present and future of the property before investing in it.

Fred

American actor Lucas Cruikshank created the web series *Fred* and used YouTube as the platform to launch what has become a hugely successful media property, with its first YouTube episode having over 18.5 million views to date. The character of Fred Figglehorn is a six-year-old boy (portrayed by the teen/adult Lucas whose voice is digitally altered) with a complicated family life and appropriately immature perspective. Fred became a phenomenon and generated interest outside the YouTube community, which resulted in a television series on Nickelodeon and a series of television movies (*Fred: The Movie*, Lionsgate, 2010, *Fred 2: Night of the Living Fred*, Lionsgate, 2011 and *Fred 3: Fred Camp*, Lionsgate, 2012). The fact that the feature films aired on Nickelodeon instead of in theatres is an example of the challenge of translating a new media intellectual property, and particularly a YouTube property, into wider success.

Fred is a recent example of how to leverage a fan base into property expansion, in this case from new media into motion pictures, television and music. While the fan base was clearly established by the sheer number of views, the translation out of the narrow intellectual property that often works in that arena means that in order to "grow" the audience, the intellectual property has to change, and once that happens the connections to the audience are less clear. For example, the conceit that the young adult Cruikshank could play the six-year-old Fred in the web series is accepted, given the nature of the medium. For a television series and movies, the point of suspension of disbelief is different; the character became a teenager, which completely changes the dynamics of the property. There has clearly been a significant level of acceptance and transference from the web series to the television/film series, but it remains to be seen how long it can endure.

Developed Universe

Sometimes properties are chosen because it *seems* as if much of the work is already done. It is clear that large, existent, fully developed universes can be a very enticing choice, but careful analysis has to occur to ensure that the universe can support multiple iterations and become a true transmedia narrative property. This is especially true for properties that have already existed for some time, and creation of new material for the property may have stopped some time ago (often due to the original author's death.) With a true transmedia narrative property the goal is that current expressions *add* to the canon of the property, and that may not be possible or feasible for pre-existing developed universes. More possibilities exist, clearly, for ongoing pre-existing universes, but those that have become cultural touchstones over time may effectively be closed universes.

The Wizard of Oz, previously mentioned, is an interesting example because the core book(s) of the property have become public domain, which has allowed additional authors and creators to elaborate and expand on the *Oz* mythos, and thereby add to the unofficial canon. While many of the more recent projects have worked to remain faithful to the original works, inconsistencies between their interpretations have appeared. But it also seems apparent that *The Wizard of Oz* is, in some ways, beyond caring, which is perhaps an indication of the depth of penetration of the property into culture, but also perhaps an indication of how the property has been managed (or not, since it is in the public domain) and comes in clear contrast to the next property we're going to discuss.

Lord of the Rings

Oxford professor J. R. R. Tolkien's *The Lord of the Rings* is perhaps *the* classic of fantasy literature. Tolkien wrote it as a sequel to his earlier children's fantasy novel *The Hobbit* (1937), but as he expanded on the stories and mythologies therein, it grew to become the major portion of his body of work. With over 150 million copies sold, it is behind only Dickens' *A Tale of Two Cities* and Saint-Exupéry's *The Little Prince* as the best-selling book of all times. (Confusingly, perhaps, it was published originally as one book in three volumes).

Tolkien created a universe filled with good and evil: hobbits, humans, elves, dwarf warriors and most importantly wizards, very powerful wizards. It is a tale of the pursuit of the One Ring, the ultimate weapon in Tolkien's world. Middle Earth is a world that holds a very special place in the world of fantasy devotees, being discovered and re-discovered by subsequent generations of readers.

Cracking the nut that is *The Lord of the Rings* was no small achievement; successfully translating it to a wider audience remains an example of how to balance the factors of staying true to a universe that has an almost "religious" fan base and bringing the intellectual property to a wider audience. *The Lord of the Rings* is a property that had a very well developed universe, as well as a good deal of scholarship attached to it.

The challenge going forward for the property is to look beyond the existing universe as now defined by the movies for the mass audience. Like many other long-term properties (and especially true of one that has been taken so seriously in the culture) that have had a breakthrough presence in a media other than their origination, the question is now whether the center of the intellectual property shifted away from the books and to the movies and what that means for future lives of the property.

Unlike *The Wizard of Oz*, *The Lord of the Rings* and Tolkien's other related works are carefully managed. The licensing realities of the rights for these works are messy, to say the least, with Middle-earth Enterprises (formerly known as Tolkien Enterprises though it has nothing to do with Tolkien or his estate and is a division of the Saul Zaentz Company) owning the international rights (exclusively) to *The Hobbit* and *The Lord of the Rings* and their respective content, and the Tolkien Estate controlling the rights to everything else the author created. The content of what Middle-earth Enterprises has the rights to and what the Tolkien Estate controls overlaps somewhat and can result in some muddy licensing issues. The control the Tolkien Estate exerts over the bulk of the Tolkien material, and the particulars of the existing licenses, means that nothing is being added to the canon by any new productions. Reading *The Silmarillion* (controlled by the Tolkien Estate) does add notable insight to a reading or viewing of *Lord of the Rings*, so it fulfills the requirements of being a transmedia narrative property, but it is not a growing one. Original material was created in the 1990s by Iron Crown Enterprises for its Middle-earth set table-top role-playing games, but it was never considered to be part of the canon.

The Walking Dead

The Walking Dead is a comic book series depicting life in a post-zombiepocalypse American South and tells the story of former sheriff Rick Grimes and his family as they struggle to survive. First issued in 2003 by publisher Image Comics, the comic was created by writer Robert Kirkman and artist Tony Moore. An award-winning series, it transitioned from comic niche to mainstream culture when AMC television adapted the comics into the 2010 television series *The Walking Dead*. The television program inspired a Kirkman-approved full-length novel (*The Walking Dead: Rise of the Governor*, St. Martin's Press, 2011) that acts as a prologue to the comic book's timeline, as well as web series and a set of video games. The makers of the 2012 episodic role-playing adventure game, Telltale Games, claim the game is different from previous zombie games as it focuses more on characters and less on mass slaughter. The story in the game takes place prior to the comic book and allows the player to interact with several of the characters from the original comic series.

From successful graphic novel to breakout television series, *The Walking Dead* uses a now very familiar genre landscape – post-zombified United States – to tell a very particular story of a group of survivors and their journey. Zombies are now a cultural staple like vampires and superheroes, but it is this particular take on that often-told story that has achieved extension beyond the normal niche fandom and has become a piece of popular culture (the Season 2 finale had an unprecedented audience, 9 million viewers, for its network, AMC). While not a unique universe, it uses a familiar universe to tell character-based stories which goes to its current success in all its forms.

Chronicles of Narnia

C. S. Lewis' *The Chronicles of Narnia* is another classic of children's literature with millions of copies sold in a wide variety of languages. Set in Narnia, a magical place where animals act like people and of course, good battles evil, the novels use various children magically transported to Narnia as the center-point of epic battles and magical quests all in the name of maintaining stability in the realm.

Written between 1949 and 1954, *The Chronicles of Narnia* has been adapted for a wide assortment of media including radio, television, the stage, film and now even video games. The religious nature of the subtext has always made it an attractive property for adaptation and media extension, but the continued reboots have met with mixed financial and critical results.

Fantasy and science fiction universes create an interesting dynamic for transmedia translations. With each passing decade, new reboots of many classic properties have become a more technology-focused exercise because of the rapid evolution of visual effects industry. Comparisons of the BBC's *Narnia* series produced in the late 1980s and the most recent film series is less about film versus television and more about computers, software and the digital wizards that now rule the media universe. While this particular storytelling universe maintains its place in the culture, the presentation evolves dramatically. Is there an end to this cycle? Yes, and what does it mean for the long-term possibilities of the property. Once vision and technology line up, do we come to the end of the easy media extension? When the current film series comes to an end either by completing the series or because of the financial/critical pressure (each film has declined in both box office and critical acclaim), it is hard to determine when we might next see a large-scale reimagining of Narnia.

His Dark Materials

His Dark Materials is a trilogy of fantasy novels by Philip Pullman, published starting in 1995 by Scholastic and concluded in 2000. It follows the coming-of-age of two children, Lyra Belacqua and Will Parry, as they wander through a series of parallel universes against a backdrop of epic events. An award-winning series whose popularity in Britain translated to buzz and similar interest in the United States, the story includes a wide array of fantasy elements like witches and armored polar bears, and touches on a variety of ideas from fields that include physics, philosophy and theology. The trilogy functions at a very complex philosophical level for a book that gained its popularity as a young adult novel. Much discussion has been made of its underlying philosophy and reading as an anti-religious diatribe, but its success as a book series is indisputable.

The failure of the feature film, no matter how well imagined and executed, reminds all potential producers that there are real challenges in taking a success from one area at a particular moment in time and expanding the intellectual property. The inability to take a cultural phenomenon in one media and parlay it into larger audience and multiple media seemed impossible. At that time, we were living in a *Harry Potter* world and the possibility of another British intellectual property invasion seemed to make sense, but things happen (9/11 being the most obvious) and what worked for a bunch of wizards, matching and syncing with larger cultural and technological trends, failed for armored polar bears. It is interesting to ponder whether down the road, this could have grown beyond the almost pure adaptation path of *Harry Potter*, and if success could allow the real expansion of the universe.

Economic Factors

Sometimes, the path of least resistance is the answer. A property from another source is chosen because most of the work is done and an opportunity has arisen due to the market, another property's success or resonant events within the culture. The pieces have been created by someone else, allowing for a simplified or shortened development path based on some preconceived notion of success.

The Graphic Novel Craze

A graphic novel is a narrative work in which the story is conveyed to the reader using sequential art in either an experimental design or in a traditional comics format. The term describes a wide variety of storytelling modes and genres. Graphic novels, in recent times, have seen both non-fiction and fiction works and is a term that can be used to describe work intended and produced in that manner as well as collected works of "comics" that are bound together in a volume for sale, typically targeting different buyers and institutions, specifically libraries. When discussing the craze the topic must also include manga, the culturally unique version with wide cultural acceptance in Japan and that has its roots in both deeply seated visual storytelling traditions as well as the American comics that became common during the post-World War II presence of American troops. "Picture and words in a strip form" now is the most basic description of a wide variety of stories that remain niche and youth-focused in most cultures (America and Europe) but central and cross generational in others (Asia). Mainstream American media awareness of comics as a viable storytelling form came as "fanboy" culture began to produce tangible results as a source and was utilized in the promotion of the properties.

The craze expressed in the rapid if not "gold-rush" mentality of licensing and developing graphic novels has its roots in both fashion as well as logic. In an honest appraisal of the craze, it makes sense for a variety of reasons. Graphic novels when well executed offer a ready-made universe that can often easily be adapted to other forms, especially moving images. Because the intellectual property is both words and pictures, it can be a clear and distinct articulation of the universe which gives the producer a blueprint for moving forward. The value of the property can also be judged to some degree because it has already been fan tested and fan approved if successful. It is an unusual opportunity for a "proof of concept" for the intellectual property with a certain and often fickle audience. The pursuit and purchase of graphic novels now functions as a form of a pitch. They are written and evolved not as an expression unto themselves but instead as the opportunity to bring attention to an intellectual property with the hope of a motion picture, television series or video game in its future. This practice has had mixed results for a variety of reasons. Success with the fanboys is not always the best measure of widespread cultural interest; fanboys are different and can both support and undermine a property's emergence into mainstream culture.

As mainstream media has become increasingly entwined with this longstanding but niche geek culture (look at Hollywood's presence at Comic-Con), in-authenticity has crept into the mix. Devotion to the form has always been part of its value, particularly in America where comics came under such an attack and were reborn as a part of the counter culture. Using the medium to propel the intellectual property, which to outsiders seems harmless, to insiders may seem like a violation of the imagined oath concerning the purity of the community. This transition while continuing to be an important part of the evolution of transmedia might not be the imagined "bargain" that got the ball rolling.

The Internet Craze

Another trend that emerged in the last decade is the process of mining the Internet for the next big "thing." This craze is defined by the often-sighted meme of Los Angeles, talent agencies with rooms full of young people trolling the "interwebs" looking for the next big thing. While more mythology than reality, looking to the web became a normal process for people looking to jump-start their development process.

The interesting part is that it doesn't seem to work for a variety of reasons. The very nature of the success in one may prevent success in the other. As the interest grew in new media and views across the Internet exploded, the industry immediately thought that numbers of views meant success and the market had spoken. It was quite natural to make that assumption given there was no basis for understanding such a new dynamic and that the most rudimentary of measurements seemed to drive that conclusion. Views simply don't translate into success, in addition to which the transaction between viewer and creator is unique and personal in many ways that doesn't translate to a different medium. Similarly, fanboy issues arise as well as the flat-out rejection of mainstream media.

Cheap has Value

The new over-arching role economics plays in transmedia is tied to a new aesthetic that allows for the value of low budget. Historically, big budget seemed to make the most sense. The big success balances the books for all the failures, except that approach has not served the film industry well – blockbuster or tent pole mentality. So another value system/methodology is beginning to replace it.

Simply put, new audience equals new rules. While a variety of factors and dynamics affect viewing and audience experience, getting something completed, available and most important fresh is a value that is growing with new audiences… Budget is often overlooked in favor of ideas (not necessarily good ones, but different ones) because of the niche audiences of the vast majority of these intellectual properties. If someone is seemingly addressing "you" much can be forgiven, but this doesn't work when addressing a larger audience. It makes you wonder whether the desire to make it look like mainstream media might actually alienate the audience. These issues are being played out right now, particularly with the younger audiences.

Author's Pull

Sometimes an author has had enough success that he or she can drive the process simply by commitment to a property. This occurs at both ends of the spectrum, as in a new author who retains control as the process begins or a successful author who has enough traction in their industry/media to make the call.

Stephen King

He is the author of a wide variety of genre novels including horror, fantasy, suspense, and science fiction. As one of the most well-known authors of our times, with hundreds of millions of books sold, there are few who do not know Stephen King through his novels or adapted motion pictures, television movies and series, comic books, and even video games. King, a prolific and popular writer, has been able to balance the world of mainstream success and commitment to genre and niche audiences.

Because of his success early in his career as a popular novelist and experiences seeing his work adapted, King exerted his control and has often had direct participation in the adaptation process. As the technological progression transformed storytelling possibilities in the last 20 years, his work has seen some very well crafted expressions into other media but has never launched a universe. Though he has clearly had ambitions for his *Dark Tower* series (hints of connections to the *Dark Tower* are scattered throughout a number of his books) he has been unable to develop that expression (motion pictures or television) that will launch it into mainstream culture. At the time of the writing of this book, herculean efforts are underway to attempt to launch a combination television series/motion picture adaptation of the *Dark Tower* saga, but it currently looks to be too ambitious and too expensive to get backing. This is an example, perhaps, of the ambition of a property getting in the way of its transmedia success.

George R. R. Martin

He is an American author and television writer with produced works in a multiple genres including science fiction, fantasy, and horror. He the author of the epic fantasy series *A Song of Ice and Fire* adapted by HBO for their very successful *Game of Thrones* series. Martin has had success in writing novels and for television, but until *Game of Thrones* he did not have the broad-based cultural recognition he now has. Using the television series as a basis, he has seen an upswing in readership for the series as well as renewed energy for adaptation into video games.

The example of *A Song of Ice and Fire* and *Game of Thrones* is an interesting one in that the novel series is clearly the mothership, but the entry point into the intellectual property is quickly shifting to the television series. This could be problematic for a bottom-up planned property, but could be anticipated and profited-from for a top-down planned property operating under the prediction of the shift in dominance. With the success of the television series, the vision/marketing has to change, which in turn affects other expressions of the intellectual property. Unless carefully managed, this could result in brand confusion or friction between the television and novel fan bases. (Interestingly, Internet discussions of the television series often have to stipulate that they are about the events depicted in the television episodes and should include omitted or different elements from the novel series.) Fortunately, Martin clearly has an active hand in the television property which helps keep the peace and helps balance the shifting focus.

Orson Scott Card

He is an American author and critic, whose areas of interest are far ranging. He writes in many genres, but is best known for his award winning science fiction novels, in particular *Ender's Game* (Tor Books, 1985) and its many sequels and prequels. Its vivid storytelling and depiction of violence among its protagonists made it a controversial novel generating much commentary both pro and con.

It is interesting that it took the industry more than 25 years to look to what is an incredibly strong series of novels/universe populated by well-developed young characters with a very dramatic story. Only the last few years, following the success of multiple properties mining similar dynamics (young people in peril), has the project moved forward. A feature film is in production as of 2012 with a projected premiere in fall 2013. What will be interesting is to see how it is handled and what steps are to follow. Will the film become the center of the property? How will a very extensive universe be managed going forward if big success happens?

J. K. Rowling

She is the author of the *Harry Potter* series of insanely popular fantasy novels that, with over 400 million copies sold, have become the best-selling book series in history. The novels have been adapted into an extremely successful series of motion pictures, somewhat less successful video games, and various other books focusing on the world she authored as well as inspiring a wide assortment of merchandise and even theme-park rides.

When expanding a property, just like in comedy, timing is everything. The *Harry Potter* universe has been a huge success on multiple fronts leaving its mark as a cultural icon for the beginning of the 21st century. It will have an ongoing life in multiple media for the foreseeable future, with the recent addition of the *Pottermore* website being a first attempt to open what has always been a very tightly controlled intellectual property to its fan base. Given that only a handful of properties have achieved this kind of success, it is interesting that this property, due to circumstance, has had an unusual amount of author control. Rowling had overall approval on the film scripts as well as maintaining creative control by serving as a producer on the final installment. She was in sync with technological changes and responded to opportunities in a very organic fashion. In addition, her position as keeper of the flame allowed her to influence a wide variety of the scattered pieces of the intellectual property. An unusual convergence of circumstances that will be challenging to repeat given the industry's newfound awareness of what transmedia can mean to the bottom line and life of a property.

Final Thoughts on an Existing Property

You have to ask why the author or creator of a specific story would let you turn their universe into a transmedia property. In the acquisition of a property, it is inevitable that multiple factors will come into play when acquiring these intellectual properties. While motion pictures, television series and video games are complex, expensive and require a team to produce, many of the other forms of storytelling we've been talking about in the previous chapter are often the product of a solitary author who has ownership and the ability to move the universe forward as he so chooses. Once a property is chosen for transmedia development, what comes next is a complex dynamic of translation and adaptation that can disrupt any creative/business relationship and can turn an otherwise beloved property into a creature that can't be recognized. Let's return to the original question. Why would an existing medium's author let you turn their universe into a transmedia property? The simple answer is because the author believes the vision will survive or they are paid enough not to care …

The Expectation and Impact of Extension and Expansion

A wide variety of alternative media sources for the core intellectual property has become a normal part of the industry development strategy at this point. In fact, the audience almost expects that their favorite (fill in the blank) will eventually be translated into one or more films, television series or video games. The question becomes not if, but when, once a property reaches a certain level of saturation, and then the discussion shifts to how it will be handled. The ultimate success of these properties swings wildly from bonanza to disaster and has become almost a spectator sport for interested parties: fans, academics and other industry types hoping to avoid the mistakes made by most and replicate the successes had by a few. (Wait, did we just describe us…?)

What is harder to measure at this point is the effect that moving the other way, extending the property into alternative forms, can have. It is reflexive to think that there can only be positive outcomes in extending or supporting your property with alternative forms, but that is not wholly the case.

We'll look at both, but let's start on the positive side:

- **Enliven the intellectual property:** Alternative forms can make the universe, and at the same time the audience, bigger. The novelization of properties in both film and television has been going on for decades, but the opportunities for alternative media expressions have exploded in the last 20 years. An extended universe can seat an intellectual property in the culture in a way that is as permanent as any cultural artifact can be. It essentially becomes too big to fail … This process has multiple aspects and affects different segments of the audience in different ways, but many of these activities are aimed at or generated by the hard core/committed fans of the property. Their commitment often expresses itself as a desire for multiple ways in which to engage the story, which also explains why they often engage in fan-generated media.

- **Commentary and conversation:** Other media as in the web: Twitter, Facebook and other forms of social media create opportunities for dialogue between fans and creators. This was unimaginable 50 years ago. What has occurred particularly in the last 15 years is a steady discussion/dialogue that allows for feedback directly to creators as well as levels of commentary that are shared among fans, reinforcing their commitment to the intellectual property. The old cultural image water-cooler conversations is now on steroids, and the impact of these conversations on the intellectual property has become profound, with far-reaching dialogues that often include the creators of the intellectual property and the real possibility of helping to shape the course of the story.

- **Keeping it alive:** There are many examples where the intellectual property holders may stagnate or even terminate an intellectual property, but other media end up maintaining and continuing to grow the property. *Doctor Who* and the Wilderness Years are an extreme example of the sorts of activities that effectively keep a property culturally alive, even to the extent that they can reinvigorate the intellectual property. Fan loyalty spurred on by autographs at conventions, fan fiction and video tributes do matter.

- **Sometime things get fixed:** As odd as it may seem, sometimes things get fixed in (or because of) the other universe. Are you unhappy that *Buffy the Vampire Slayer* ended? You get season 8 as a comic book. Didn't you like the ending of *LOST*? Write your own and share it with the world. Are you unhappy that the end of *Mass Effect 3* sucked? Make enough noise and it matters. "Save our Star Trek" may have been the first in the modern era of fans saving a television show, but it is now somewhat commonplace that huge wrong turns get more than just negative financial feedback. Fans tell producers what's wrong, and sometimes things get fixed.

- **Multiple access points:** Having lots of other media expressions allows for a wide variety of access points to a property. The simple truth: it's hard to miss a big target. Many access points (whether they are strictly in line with canon or not) mean possible fans have a greater opportunity to find the property. The entry points can all in some way be traced back to the story, and if your intro is in (fill in the blank) it grants you access to a particular audience and the world at large; at that point anything is possible. This change is incredibly important, because the range of media accesses has increasingly created a situation that has resulted in removing the gatekeepers that have traditionally controlled mainstream media and therefore popular culture. A new way of fans finding and engaging with properties is evolving as the technology pushes ahead.

The flip side is, of course, that there can be a downside:

- **Obscure the intellectual property:** Other media expressions can confuse the audience and dissipate an intellectual property's energy. The lack of coherence can move the intellectual property from center stage in the culture to a niche position through overexposure and internal narrative conflict.

- **Over analysis:** Fan boys can eat their own. Just as dialogue has an upside by generating and maintaining interest in an intellectual property, it can also have a downside. A certain level of negative criticism can support and enliven the discussion, but to have a property torn apart and ultimately ridiculed is at times a point of no return. When properties become a long-term negative target, they develop a different relationship with the audience that does hang around and enjoys the spectacle. However, it's not always easy to keep a property down: *Battlestar Galactica* is a great example, and in this day and age you never know.

- **Peer Gynt:** The central character of Ibsen's play is at one point described as an onion. Peel the layers and all you get is more layers: in other words a person with no core. When it comes to a large-scale property built around a core character, there is such a thing as too many iterations. Properties that have characters at the center can become an onion through repeated and unfocused reboots and offshoots. The irony of course is that history has shown us that a managed property vs. unmanaged property (often public domain) differs little in terms of this happening. Two clear examples are *Nancy Drew* and *Sherlock Holmes* – one that has wound down and the other having just seen its third major version in the last five years. The reason often seems to have more to do with other issues, like a crowded young adult market for Nancy and successful updating/re-inventing for Sherlock.

- **Fan rebellion:** Bad things happen when the fans reject the property. *Star Wars* took a while to recover from Chapters 1 through 3 of the saga. *Star Trek* fans were uncertain about *Enterprise*. And the Hulk took three times to get it right. What is different about today is that fans have a place to organize and express their hate and do actual damage to a property. This is not just a place to complain; it translates into actual action or lack of participation by the most core of the audience and if you lose the core, what do you get?

- **Universe contradiction:** Core fans like canon. They like thinking they understand the world they are investing in, so what happens when you contradict it too much? Chaos and more chaos breed discontent, and discontent breeds disengagement. Some properties have seemingly avoided this dynamic like *Batman*, but that is an exception. *Terminator* is a good example or *Spider-Man*. When the mothership gets rebooted or gets translated into other media and doesn't match the game ... which draws on the books rather than the original comic book... and older fans hate the new and the newer fans don't get the old ... because it all seems so different. Chaos can create an infertile ground for future storytelling and iterations.

A Final Thought: The Blurring of Ownership

The issue of ownership needs to be thought of in both the industry sense and in the modern fan sense. While the notion of fan "ownership" has become more and more real with the development and clear establishment of fan boy culture (with the back and forth chaos that entails), a property that is unruly doesn't always mean it degrades in some way. In fact, it has been proven again and again that a certain amount of chaos, often brought about by the fans and within the realm of the other media expressions, can maintain an intellectual property that has otherwise strayed or degraded until technology/culture/industry can in some way re-sync it with the market, allowing it to get re-launched in a significant way. At the core is a genuine sense that fans invest time, money and care into a property, that they own a piece of it and can in part "control" a piece of it. In a way, they do ...

Part 3

Managing the Story

Chapter 9
Managing the Transmedia Property

A transmedia property is essentially an expansive narrative engine constructed to deliver almost unlimited stories across multiple media platforms. Extensive universe and world building with deep character development are necessary to manufacture this immersive storytelling mechanism. Management of this "mega-franchise" begins at its conception and extends over the sales and marketing thresholds. If a brand is grounded in a strong immersive story engine, the consistency of brand identity will be easily realized over multiple media platforms, and transmedia expansion will always remain true to the core narrative.

Transmedia property managemfent is the management of multiple story arcs that often are running and in production simultaneously. The release of one story via one platform, because the story arcs intertwine across platforms, may have a direct effect on the ongoing story taking place in another platform. And so managing a transmedia property is really managing a branded transmedia story-network.

Maintaining the Brand

What is a brand? Simply put, a brand is a commercial identity. It is a visual, aural and intellectual way of communicating the core principles of a company or product. Brands are the commercial personae, the mask shown to the public and in marketing. This mask has a purpose, which is to attract consumers to spend time and money participating in whatever the brand represents.

In the case of entertainment, a brand is the maker of the content. J. J. Abrams production company Bad Robot is a brand but *LOST* and the 2010 *Star Trek* reboots are very much extensions of that brand identity, at the same time each of those properties is a brand unto itself, or part of a larger brand. The content, as a brand extension, is meant to satisfy a need by the target consumer to be entertained in a specific way. The Bad Robot audience expects a different experience than the Pixar audience. All consumers are not created equal and brands tend to create content for a specific consumer called the *target audience* or *target demographic*.

Demographics: Demographics are statistical characteristics of a particular group, referred to as a population. Demographic data is used to study target audiences and create a profile of a brand's consumer to help create content that attracts and maintains those consumers. Examples of target audiences include gender or age ranges, ethnicity, employment and location, alone or in combination. Erroneously, demographics are often associated with spending habits, lifestyle choices, values and other areas related to interest, activities, or opinions. These are actually part of a psychographic profile, which is often combined with demographic details, hence the confusion.

Niche audiences: Niches represent even smaller more fine-tuned or specific groups of target consumers such as dog owners, 14–35 year old males who play the blockbuster video game *Call of Duty* or single working women over 35 with kids. Interestingly, the idea of appealing to a niche audience, especially in media, was viewed as a negative. In television, for example, series that appealed to a "niche audience" were usually canceled quickly since, traditionally, niche meant low viewership. Today, however, more and more media projects of all kinds are targeted at niche audiences as those audiences become more and more selective of what they consume and when. The term "narrowcasting" has even been coined to refer to the practice of specifically targeting, through advertising and marketing, what not all that long ago would have been an undesirable niche audience.

Some larger brands, big studios and production companies, usually try to satisfy multiple demographic groups. Universal Pictures, for instance, is not known for distributing a specific genre of content created only for a narrow target audience. Universal makes everything from 2004's *Dawn of the Dead* remake to the upcoming *Woody Woodpecker* reboot. Walt Disney Studios, however, is synonymous with family entertainment and makes movies that range from *Pinocchio* (1940) to their most recent transmedia mega-partnership with Marvel Studios to distribute *Marvel's The Avengers*.

If Disney made *Dawn of the Dead*, fans around the globe would be up in arms, confused and ready to choke Mickey on sight. Why? Disney would have stepped out of brand and disappointed their core audience of kids and their parents and fans of Disney movies. Disney would have betrayed their unwritten contract with their audience, to remain "in-brand," to stay Disney and to continue to churn out, with the help of Pixar and Marvel, Disney Magic.

From that example we see that branding is about a relationship between two "entities," the brand and the consumer. For a moment let's think of these as people named "the Brand" and "the Consumer." These two people have established a relationship of expectation. The Consumer expects the Brand to offer continuous and uninterrupted supply of "in brand" products and to make the very same general type of product or content that they were making when the relationship was established. The Consumer comes to depend on the brand for their "special" type of product. It's OK to make different products, but they have to give the same type of satisfaction, and they have to satisfy the "need" created by the Consumer's liking of the original product offered and consumed. In turn, the Brand expects the Consumer to be loyal and continue to purchase brand products and not competitive brands.

A Brand to Consumer relationship is not unlike a human love relationship. "When I met you, Disney, you made me laugh and took me on countless trips and adventures to magical and fantastical lands … but now …you bring home Zombies who eat the flesh of screaming and terrified teens?" Next line …"I'm sorry but this isn't working out … I'm leaving you for DreamWorks." And just like that, the Brand consumer relationship is shattered. The consumer goes to another brand where they can find what they were used to getting from the previous brand.

So, a brand is maintained by paying tremendous attention to the needs and wants of the target audience. By understanding their "language," who they are, what they love, where they engage their media content and most importantly for a transmedia brand, figure what they see as the primary engagement of the property and give them more of it, piece by piece, across multiple media platforms. This model works best for brands like Marvel, who have an established interrelationship with their core audience.

Marvel and Story Extension

The expectations of the consumer for each storyworld extension, say *Captain America*, from the comics and animated television appearances, is that each extension honors the history, character and core narrative associated with the patriotic, moral and all-American hero. Indeed, when making the film they set the vast majority of it during World War II, an acknowledgment of the original setting for the franchise. Doing so, however, not only acknowledged the brand's origins (they could have easily updated it) but gave them a context to use Steve Rogers/Captain America to make a comment about patriotism when he awakens in the modern day after being frozen in ice for over 50 years.

The transition of Captain America from historic super-soldier to present day superhero is proof of the strength of *Captain America*'s transmedia storytelling power. In 2012's *Marvel's The Avengers* motion picture, Cap is the symbol of justice, the hero with no flaws, the virtuous good looking all-American boy, who keeps the likes of the smarmy, arrogant, girl-magnet, Tony Stark aka, Iron Man in balance. He is the moral high ground in contrast with the woman of questionable background, the Black Widow. Cap is the solid and dependable hero unlike the professor with the darkest of dark-sides, the Hulk. And his allegiance is unquestioned while the assassin turned hero, Hawkeye, has the look of an anti-hero. And Cap is the leader even when taking orders from the ominous military super-leader of SHIELD, Nick Fury. And while Thor is the outsider who finds us interesting and visits from time to time, Cap is the ultimate of us, having defended freedom in the 1940s against the worst-of-the-worst and returned miraculously to defend us again in the 21st century. Cap is the American dream personified, adding balance to our anti-heroes and holding the Avengers together. It was no accident that the preview for the *Avengers* film appeared at the end of the *Captain America* film.

Captain America survives the transmedia explosion into the 21st century because Joss Whedon and Marvel understand the relationship between *Captain America*, the brand, the intellectual property, and you, the consumer. *Captain America* is one of Marvel's brand identities. If *Captain America* appeared in 2012 using profanity, being sexually overt and impolite … he would disappear from the American mythological tapestry.

Feedback and Conversation

Feedback is a tent-pole of transmedia brand engagement. Unlike traditional mono-platform media, transmedia provides an opportunity for a "conversation." The conversation is between the brand or content and the consumer. It is a two-way multi-platform conversation taking place anytime and anywhere, at the leisure of the audience. Constant contact provides for constant branding via transmedia connections.

Comments, whether text or video, are the currency of trust between the brand and its target demographic. NBC's *Heroes*, as a result of transmedia engagement, migrated a character created for the web and that had only appeared there onto its network television show in answer to the positive comments of fans and interest in that character.

Transmedia allows for fans to participate in the storytelling process for a deepening of the brand-consumer relationship via this conversation, often through social networking. Trust is established through a sense of appreciation and value for the thoughts and opinions of the audience.

Brand Loyalty, Across Platforms

We believe in our brands. We trust our brands to deliver on their promise. To be loyal to us and we return the favor by buying what they're selling.

Transmedia provides an opportunity for a brand to engage the millennial consumer on every media platform simultaneously; the way the millennial already consumes their media. We jump from laptop to iPhone to television to iPad on a moment-to-moment basis. We go from Facebook to Tumblr on the way to the movie theatre and we expect *Captain America* to be on each device, in a slightly different way, but remaining true to the original Cap messaging, personality and brand identity.

A transmedia brand endures through the maintenance of a one-on-one relationship between the brand and the individual consumer. We've moved past mass media experiences like film and television where content is designed to go from one, the studio, to many, the audience, and the vast world of social media engagement where the relationship is one, the maker, to one … the individual consuming on-demand, usually alone, on his laptop or smartphone. Transmedia creatives must understand their "one" consumer. The one consumer who represents the millions of consumers who all speak the same language … the language of brand expectation established by the original brand identity or content offered to consummate the relationship.

ABC's *LOST*, a property known for its innate mysteries, puzzles within premise and unending minute-to-minute surprises in its mothership expression, extended itself to web and mobile while staying "in brand," providing online and real life ARG experiences that mirrored and indeed deepened the established brand to consumer relationship. For this, *LOST* is viewed as one of the first television series to use social media transmedia successfully. It was true to itself and true to its brand via each extension across different media platforms.

Loyalty is earned. This is true of all brand-to-consumer relationships, but transmedia entertainment properties need to be immersive and unending for the duration of the campaign or content life. For this to be achieved, transmedia franchise properties must be developed with vast storyworlds, able to provide content from multiple entry points satisfying multiple creative and distribution platform languages.

The Game of Thrones video game needs to give the *Game of Thrones* television audience what they expect by staying in brand, by giving the same types of characters, fantasy, action and romance that the HBO series is famous for. The video game must also satisfy the gamer, by having exciting but tonally in-brand game play and game story. If the brand remains loyal to itself, to its core narrative story, then the fans follow it across multiple platforms. The brand must mortgage the tent-pole story elements of the original story engine against the creative and distribution demands of each platform. It must maintain tone and texture form the mothership. If the rules of engagement created in the original brand-consumer relationship are honored and the covenant respected, millennials will seek the brand everywhere that they engage content, on television, in film, on the web and on their mobile phones. Simple. Give the audience what they want.

Release Schedule

Putting together a release schedule is really a convergence of production reality and market demands. Each medium has its own production process and timeline as well as its own marketing considerations. In particular, film and television have had fairly defined guidelines for timing releases, much more so than games and comics.

The classic timing for film is that serious dramas and Oscar contenders are released near the end of the year so that they'll be fresh in voter's minds for the Academy Awards. Big effects-laden escapist fare is usually timed for a summer release, and family-oriented films are scheduled for release during those times of the year when kids are out of school and families may be going to the movies together, such as the summer but especially major holidays like Thanksgiving or Christmas.

Historically, television series in the United States always premiered in the fall. As performance became assessed more quickly and struggling shows were cut from the TV schedule sooner, there gradually grew to be an unofficial second season of premieres that were called "midseason replacements." Gradually, this practice of launching new shows around January, along with cable networks creating more and more original series content that is modeled on the shorter seasons and launch timing of European television networks like the BBC, has dramatically changed the timing of TV show premieres.

Webisode releases are often timed to fill in or bridge the gaps between seasons of TV series, such as the three *Battlestar Galactica* webseries. In a similar way, radio programs of *Doctor Who* kept the fan base alive during the long interval when no TV episodes were being produced. The ARG, *The LOST Experience*, was released between seasons 3 and 4 to keep fans engaged in the show's rich mythology.

Additional considerations for all releases, including games, take into account what else is being released around the same time, especially similarly themed projects with which our release will be competing for audience, and whether the release allows for ample marketing, advertising and reviews or PR.

Putting aside the production issues for a moment, it is really about when – from a marketing perspective – the producers think they have the best chance of reaching the target audience to generate sales/box office/ad revenue.

Before transmedia, after a property had been launched, the question became about potential sequels (for film) or other media (such as novels, games, toys) and how best to keep an audience engaged with the hope of building on whatever previous success has been generated.

What was lacking in this approach was the larger perspective about how an IP's release schedule can and should act as a story integrator. With transmedia storytelling, our decisions regarding the sequence and dates of release are more story-driven and less marketing-driven to achieve the long-term goals of launching a large-scale property. Multiple factors come into play.

To develop a viable release schedule, consideration needs to be given to the production issues surrounding each of the component media in terms of the time needed to develop, produce and distribute that platform's iteration of the story and the expense involved. Next, the entry points for viewer/users need to be considered and balanced with concerns of the long arc of the story. How the property begins and what follows was at one time a really simple question of engagement, finding an audience and keeping them attached to the property. The complex nature of transmedia property has changed this, and a producer deals more now than ever with issues of not just multiple platforms but multiple audiences unique to specific platforms or types of story. Different elements of the same story universe could have very different audiences and would require different decisions to successfully engage them.

No matter which medium we can talk about, production tends to follow a certain structure. The process of development is followed by preproduction, production, postproduction and distribution/exhibition/marketing. Though this can make it sound like each step is discrete and completed before we move on to the next, in most projects these steps may overlap, with postproduction beginning while material is still in production or marketing beginning before the project if finished.

Factors in Scheduling the Release of a Television Series

In many respects, the process that leads to the broadcast of a network TV series is the most defined, timed and orderly of all the media. Concepts for pilots are pitched usually in the summer with scripts solicited for the most promising in the fall; in January, those scripts are narrowed down to the pilot episodes that are going to be made and production of the pilots has traditionally taken place between January and April. Finished pilots are presented to the networks who decide which series will be picked up to go into production; the selected series are introduced to advertisers during "upfronts" in May and ideally go into production for the fall schedule, roughly a year after they were first pitched. It is only because of the "industrial" nature of television, with its distinct production schedule, deadlines and professional practices developed over 50 plus years, that this process can move so quickly. While there are of course shows that vary from that timetable due to production deals with superstar showrunners or response to the market success of a particular genre or the fact that TV series no longer only premiere in the fall, the bottom line is that the timetable does have inherent markers along the way that require adherence to the schedule and systems in place to help achieve success.

Factors in Scheduling the Release of a Film

Film does not have as specific or precise a process as TV series. Studios and producers often have multiple film projects in development at any given time, knowing that the specific timing depends on a number of factors. The common wisdom is that the average length of time from option to screen is seven years in Hollywood, with most projects never getting made. To some degree, large studio releases are often scheduled with regard to the audience they're trying to reach, the type of film produced and the scheduled release of other films that might compete for the same audience. Because of the marketing campaigns and potentially long postproduction process for films that rely on digital effects, an ideal release date is set and the other landmarks of preproduction, production, postproduction and marketing are reverse engineered. Moving a film's release date after it's been scheduled and advertised can be costly, and this is why a major studio production going over schedule can be such a catastrophe. This becomes especially challenging for transmedia properties where a change in release date doesn't affect just the advertising that's been done for the film but may have a cascade effect on any subsequent releases that have to build on the story material of that film in order to keep the overall arc of the transmedia IP in order.

Factors in Scheduling the Release of a Game

Three factors primarily affect decision related to the release of a video game: development and approval, internal publisher and external market concerns. As with other media, the release schedule for a major commercial property is determined and schedule at the earliest stages of production. Smaller or independent productions are often more flexible, though the identification of a target release date is important for creating valid schedules and budgets.

The scope (production scale) obviously has the single greatest impact on the release schedule – a game that takes 18 months to produce is available for release 18 months after production starts. As discussed elsewhere, video game production is software development and can therefore be tricky to schedule accurately since not all of the risks or difficulties can be adequately assessed or planned for prior to production. Video games are often "over-scoped," which is to say that the production is trying to eat more cake than it can chew. Well-managed projects with a properly maintained production schedule can identify scope issues before they become a problem and either trim features, increase the team size, or pursue a shift in the final delivery and release date. That said, video games are notorious for seeing their release date slip, which produces numerous revenue-related difficulties for the development studio as well as the publisher.

Additionally, if the video game is intended for a game console, time has to be built into the schedule for the approval of the console's manufacturer. As their internal testing and approval process takes time, and they are usually processing multiple products through their pipeline, when a video game begins their process has to be scheduled with them well in advance. If the game is rejected (for whatever reason) it will need to be corrected and re-submitted, which restarts the clock on the approval process.

For the publisher, the factors include considerations of their financial calendar, allocation of internal resources, and external market and competition concerns. Large publishers carefully consider the impact the revenue of a new title will have on their quarterly financials and will often space releases proportionally throughout the financial year and the slippage of the release date of one project can often cause the shifting of the release of others, depending on the company's financial needs. Smaller companies and independent developer/producers may not have these concerns, but may have to consider when sales income is expected in order to pay the bills and keep the lights on or for longer-term tax considerations.

Games, especially large ones, need significant marketing support, and the marketing budget for a large, high-profile title can rival the production budget. A company that releases multiple titles a year has to budget its internal resources appropriately so that it's not trying to do everything for all of its titles at the same time. A company with a significant number of resource-heavy releases in the autumn may need to shift one or more of them to winter so that all of them can be properly, or at least adequately, supported. There may be other internal considerations as well that influence release timing, such as advertising budget and production capacity.

Lastly, market conditions obviously influence release schedules. Though the market for computer games is large and expanding, large high-profile releases tend (with notable exceptions) to release in the fourth quarter of the year, in time for Christmas, which is to say on shelves before Thanksgiving. The end of 2012 saw the release of *Resident Evil 6* (Capcom), *Halo 4* (Microsoft), *Assassins Creed III* (Ubisoft), *Call of Duty: Black Ops II* (Activision), *Hitman: Absolution* (Square Enix), *NBA 2K13* (2K Sports), *Borderlands 2* (2K Games), *Dishonored* (Bethesda), *Medal of Honor: Warfighter* (Electronic Arts) and others. That said, late spring is becoming a prime release period for high-profile video games. Independent and mobile games are less restricted by release schedule marketing concerns, though games produced as extensions of, or in support of, a larger property release (such as a film, book, or television series) will need to be on shelves at the same time as their mothership.

Factors in Scheduling the Release of a Graphic Novel

In some ways, comics have always had to deal with the discrepancies between production schedule and release schedule. A typical 22-page issue in a comic series is often released on a monthly basis, yet the artists may only be able to do a page or two per week.

In her "Seven Pointers on Comic Production," Emily Pohl-Weary identifies a number of major milestones for comic or graphic novel production, including:

- writing and proofreading the script
- producing rough sketches
- drawing pencils (detailed proofs) of the pages
- inking the final pages
- scanning and "touching up" the electronic image files
- laying out the pages (this includes adding on word balloons if this is being done on the computer)
- coming up with a few samples of potential cover art
- painting the final cover art

- packaging and shipping to the printer
- examining the printer's proofs
- receiving the published comic
- mailing copies to people who've pre-ordered, media and distributors

("Seven Pointers on Comic Production," accessed July 25, 2012, http://nomediakings.org/doityourself/seven_pointers_on_comic_production.html) This may help explain why many serial comics are fairly time limited or have multiple production teams at work simultaneously.

Release Sequence

Examples of release schedule successes and failures inevitably provoke a "what if" response. Many examples of release schedules seem to imply a decision-making process that seemed more reactive than intentional.

Did launching the *Avatar* game before the movie drive people to the theatres? Does the game even reach the same audience as the film? Because the game generated the same level of enthusiasm as the film, did it prevent people from going to the theatre?

The executives steering the *Game of Thrones* franchise decided to adjust the release of the video game in order to fall in line with the newly successful TV series, but again, is the audience the same for both iterations? Will that decision impact game sales?

Perhaps a more illustrative example is *X-Files*. Much planning went into the placement of the first *X-Files* movie (*Fight the Future*) within the series' timeline. Producers looked ahead over two years and set the film as a pivotal part of the ongoing universe. This required a serious commitment both financially and in terms of story to support the simultaneous development, preproduction and production of a feature that eventually would compose an important story element in a TV series that was ongoing. While at best a moderate success, what was achieved was important from the standpoint of managing both production and story elements.

The undisputed kings of the release schedule at the moment are the executives in charge of the Marvel universe. The Marvel vision has matured from its early attempts to launch individual motion picture properties based on the comic characters to the more complex integration of the Marvel universe through well-sequenced individual launches that maintain its characters in a feature film context that then culminates in 2012's *Avengers* film from which additional characters (Hawkeye and Black Widow) could begin new film series. From there, individual characters will return to individual films with the plan to bring some if not all of them back for a second *Avengers* film. As a result, Marvel is managing to maintain multiple storyworlds in a larger Marvel universe. While not perfectly in sync, there has been clear synergy between properties for a comic universe that has historically not been as culturally "center stage" as their main competitor (*Batman*, *Superman* and *Spider-Man*). What Marvel has created is the grand vision with the syncing of both production and story through a well-articulated release schedule that has enabled creating a larger transmedia universe with films, games, comics and all the other bits and pieces that amount to both a rich story universe and great financial success.

So how do you structure a release schedule so that it does more than simply achieve its business goals? Most properties would benefit from using the cornerstone as an anchor and then follow it with ongoing engagement that includes the appropriate expression of building the universe. The original property/platform typically places the audience in the world and the release schedule of the properties that follow should both maximize success in that platform and look to building the coalition of audiences that will support the property long-term across multiple media platforms.

In this chaotic media universe, it is too easy to lose an audience to new properties if fan expectations are not met. The plan should take into account complimentary dynamics and the potential overlap of audiences, using this to advantage as both the overall IP, cornerstone and other expressions are put in the larger schedule. Marvel again is a master at this; look at how the individual hero films were leveraged to launch the *Avengers* film by pulling in the different heroes' fans (yes different heroes have different fans) and now beginning the process of moving the story back to individual heroes' films. Add to this all the video game, comic book and *The Avengers: Earth's Mightiest Heroes* animated series releases and the IP is everywhere, reaching wide-ranging and diverse audiences.

Another important aspect to scheduling is to find a rhythm and use audience expectations to help keep momentum. *Harry Potter* maintained its momentum through a commitment to almost continual production that produced films at a somewhat predictable timetable, though there was an alternating of the film's release between a holiday or a summer release date.

No matter what market pressures exist, properly launching a transmedia property is not a marketing decision alone but involves storytelling decisions and commitment to the larger universe. This includes identifying the story elements that will sustain interest, but that is not always easy. Most properties don't have a Harry Potter to anchor everything, so identifying the primary story element that connects to the audience and will sustain brand identity is the real leverage going forward. *Harry Potter* is a good example of a property that requires balance of character and universe in a way a simple franchise doesn't.

Transmedia storytelling requires a high degree of coordination across the different medium expressions and iterations. Though the release schedule is thought of as an expression of industry realities, it is important not to lose sight of the fact that it is a storytelling opportunity that if taken can be leveraged into the long-term success of a property.

Marketing

Transmedia has been used most intensely by advertisers and marketers to sell branded products, goods and services. McDonalds is perhaps the king of transmedia advertising having managed to spread a single message "I'm Loving It" across television, radio, print, merchandising and social media seamlessly. But entertainment brands, being the masters of suspense and surprise, are reshaping transmedia marketing, quite literally, as storytelling.

Many have confused the transmedia experience as being only a marketing technique, selling something to someone across multiple media platforms to make a profit, but they are incorrect. Transmedia storytelling and marketing work hand in hand to bring rich storyworlds to audiences before, during and after the release of original property. In an interview with the Producers Guild of America, Jeff Gomez, Transmedia guru and CEO of Hollywood's most sought after transmedia development company, Starlight Runner Entertainment, has profound insight into the relationship between transmedia and marketing:

> **Interviewer:** Transmedia is often discussed in the context of marketing campaigns – for example, the signage, web sites, and additional video that enhanced the *District 9* universe as a lead-up to the movie's release. To what degree is it possible, at this point in time, to distinguish transmedia as separate from marketing? In your opinion, are the two disciplines more likely to grow closer together or further apart?

Jeff Gomez: I firmly believe that transmedia and marketing will grow closer together. Transmedia doesn't replace marketing, it is infused into it, turning marketers into storytellers who are helping to enrich and expand the franchise. So many good (and expensive!) potential movie franchises have failed right out of the gate, not because they were terrible but because sometimes mass audiences need to be indoctrinated into these exotic worlds.

Peter Jackson has a fundamental understanding of this. He reached out to a doubtful core fan base of the Tolkien novels through a single web site and he turned them into torchbearers who beaconed millions into the theaters during the run of the *Lord of the Rings* films. He did this not only by respecting the source material but by teaching the language, culture and mythos of Middle-Earth to them all.

More so, the film's campaign was infused with the essence of Tolkien's message of unity, diversity and making a stand against overwhelming odds. The marketing helped to tell the story, immersing audience members into this exotic world, generating true excitement for it, long before any of them purchased a ticket at the box office.

Jeff Gomez on Transmedia Producing[1]

The Gift of Fire

Ridley Scott and Scott Free entertainment took the transmedia storytelling and marketing relationship to the next level with virtual to live integration for its 2012 summer blockbuster, *Prometheus* (20th Century Fox). Alongside the movie's traditional marketing efforts, including a hot trailer, Ridley Scott and 20th Century Fox unexpectedly changed the movie marketing game.

You are probably familiar with the global TED conferences where innovators in various fields are given 18 minutes to present their world-changing ideas (https://www.ted.com). In February of 2012 a video appeared on the TED website, and at others, of the TED Talk given by Weyland Corporation CEO Peter Weyland. Weyland paced back and forth telling us of his vision for our future. His goal was to change the world. He spoke of all of the technological innovations beginning with fire. Fire was the first technology, gifted to us by *Prometheus* who incurred the wrath of the gods for his hubris.

Interesting, made doubly so since Peter Weyland is not real but is instead a character from the motion picture *Prometheus*, played there and in the video by a fiercely convincing Guy Pearce, giving his presentation from a TED conference in 2023. In the movie *Prometheus*, Peter Weyland is aged, an octogenarian at best, but in the 2023 video he is young, innovative and full of fiery promise. A masterful piece of a transmedia puzzle.

The TED2023 promotional video was released on the TED blog and went viral, garnering its own fan base and triggering social media conversations worldwide. Never once did Weyland try to "sell" *Prometheus*. Instead the transmedia tool gave audiences another slice of the *Prometheus* World, packaged as a real-world event.

Weyland Industries business cards were also planted at the 2012 WonderCon convention (http://www.youtube.com/watch?v = uEs99Nea5HQ). Those who were lucky enough to receive a business card were led to additional in-story-brand content on YouTube. The video was entitled "Big Things Have Small Beginnings" which is essentially an advertisement for Weyland Industries and their robots (http://www.youtube.com/watch?v = u5P0ZGhXQDQ). The look and feel is of a 2023 commercial for David, the new artificial intelligence. Not a hard sell for the movie, but

---

[1] accessed June 8, 2012, http://www.producersguild.org/default.asp?jeff_gomez

again an experience separate yet intimately connected to the film. And, interestingly, and perhaps coincidentally, or deliberately distracting, the tag line and title "Big Things Have Small Beginnings" is a quote from David Lean's *Lawrence of Arabia* (Columbia Pictures, 1962), who Peter Weyland references at the start of his TED2023 talk …

Ridley Scott has blurred the lines between what is real and what is of the storyworld. No longer are the characters and corporations contained within the constructed world of the movie but rather, through transmedia storytelling and marketing, they live in a symbiotic relationship to the film; platform independent yet story-dependent. They can live without one another but when viewed in tandem they create a deeper understanding of the core narrative property. This is transmedia, the seamless relationship between content and marketing…transmitted via multiple media platforms.

Licensing and Rights Management

We are not lawyers, nor do we play one on television or any other broadcast medium using technology currently in existence or yet to be invented. This section is intended to provide an overview of intellectual property rights and management and should in no way shape or form be taken as legal advice or counsel. That's what you pay your intellectual property lawyers for. Should you have an intellectual property lawyer? The answer is yes.

Trademarks and Copyright

Understanding trademarks and copyright is critical for managing your transmedia property. With any luck you are going to create a complex franchise consisting of multiple properties. You may be licensing your core property from the original rights-holder, or you may be working with an original intellectual property of your creation and working with licensees who are creating projects under your brand. Regardless, when all is said and done, you are going to end up with a web of licensing agreements that indicate who can do what, and when, with the various trademarks and copyrights involved.

First, let's go to the source and define trademark and copyright using the definitions and language from the World Intellectual Property Organization (WIPO), which is the United Nations agency created to (according to its own charter):

> *to encourage creative activity, to promote the protection of intellectual property throughout the world."* [2]

It should be pointed out that the World Intellectual Property Organization is a bit of a controversial organization, but its definitions are sufficient for the purposes of our discussions (and much easier to understand than some of the language in the various legal agreements). A good deal of the international discussion about intellectual property has been shifted to the World Trade Organization and is specifically covered by the 1994 Agreement on Trade Related Aspects of Intellectual Property Rights (TRIPS), which in its own ways is equally controversial. Your intellectual property lawyer is far better suited to detail the specific intellectual property laws in your legal jurisdiction.

> *Trademark: A trademark is a distinctive sign which identifies certain goods or services as those produced or provided by a specific person or enterprise. Its origin dates back to ancient times, when craftsmen reproduced their signatures, or "marks" on their artistic or utilitarian products. Over the years these marks evolved into today's system of trademark registration and protection. The system helps consumers identify and purchase a product or service because its nature and quality, indicated by its unique trademark, meets their needs.* [3]

[2] http://www.wipo.int
[3] http://www.wipo.int/trademarks/en/trademarks.html, accessed April 10, 2012

A trademark provides protection to the owner of the mark by ensuring the exclusive right to use it to identify goods or services, or to authorize another to use it in return for payment. The period of protection varies, but a trademark can be renewed indefinitely beyond the time limit on payment of additional fees. Trademark protection is enforced by the courts, which in most systems have the authority to block trademark infringement.[4]

Copyright: Copyright is a legal term describing rights given to creators for their literary and artistic works. The kinds of works covered by copyright include: literary works such as novels, poems, plays, reference works, newspapers and computer programs; databases; films, musical compositions, and choreography; artistic works such as paintings, drawings, photographs and sculpture; architecture; and advertisements, maps and technical drawings. The original creators of works protected by copyright, and their heirs, have certain basic rights. They hold the exclusive right to use or authorize others to use the work on agreed terms. The creator of a work can prohibit or authorize:

- *its reproduction in various forms, such as printed publication or sound recording;*
- *its public performance, as in a play or musical work;*
- *recordings of it, for example, in the form of compact discs, cassettes or videotapes;*
- *its broadcasting, by radio, cable or satellite;*
- *its translation into other languages, or its adaptation, such as a novel into a screenplay.*

Many creative works protected by copyright require mass distribution, communication and financial investment for their dissemination (for example, publications, sound recordings and films); hence, creators often sell the rights to their works to individuals or companies best able to market the works in return for payment. These payments are often made dependent on the actual use of the work, and are then referred to as royalties.

These economic rights have a time limit, according to the relevant WIPO treaties, of 50 years after the creator's death. National law may establish longer time-limits. This limit enables both creators and their heirs to benefit financially for a reasonable period of time. Copyright protection also includes moral rights, which involve the right to claim authorship of a work, and the right to oppose changes to it that could harm the creator's reputation.

The creator – or the owner of the copyright in a work – can enforce rights administratively and in the courts, by inspection of premises for evidence of production or possession of illegally made – "pirated" – goods related to protected works. The owner may obtain court orders to stop such activities, as well as seek damages for loss of financial rewards and recognition. Copyright protection extends only to expressions, and not to ideas, procedures, methods of operation or mathematical concepts as such.[5]

Filing for Copyrights and Trademarks

Most countries have some form of national copyright or trademark office that oversees the process of recording, reviewing, and acknowledging copyrights and trademarks. In the United States it is the Library of Congress Copyright Office for copyright (http://www.copyright.gov/) and the United States Patent and Trademark Office (http://www.uspto.gov/) for trademarks. (A full directory of international intellectual property offices can be found at http://www.wipo.int/directory/en/urls.jsp.)

Copyright, under the Berne Convention for the Protection of Literary and Artistic Works (1988), is automatically granted to the creator upon creation of the work with no need to file for a formal registration of the copyright. This is fine for casual and semi-professional creative works, but for your professional transmedia property you should be filing formal copyright registration (or require your licensee to do so in your name) for everything created. Formal registration creates a legal record of the copyright recognition and is fully recognized in a court of law. (Additionally, in the United States statutory damages, which is compensation for copyright infringement, is only awarded for works properly registered within three months of the first publication of the work, and prior to the infringement (http://www.law.cornell.edu/uscode/text/17/412).)

---

[4] http://www.wipo.int/trademarks/en/about_trademarks.html#function, accessed April 10, 2012
[5] http://www.wipo.int/copyright/en/general/about_copyright.html, accessed April 10, 2012

As with copyrights, if you are serious about your intellectual property you must register your trademarks. You can use the TM (™) symbol (signifying that you are claiming the trademark) whenever you wish to claim usage of a trademark. You can use this before filing for and receiving a registered trademark. You cannot, however, use the ® symbol until you have been awarded the registered trademark and you cannot use the symbol while the application is pending. You can also only use the ® symbol for the goods and services listed on your trademark application.

When you apply for your trademark, you will need to specify which goods and services your trademark covers. Coverage isn't blanket – trademarking "World of Vooosh" for Class 009 (audio books in the nature of novels), Class 16 (graphic novels, novels, printed materials, namely, novels and series of fiction books and short stories featuring scenes and characters based on video games, romance novels, and series of fiction works, namely, novels and books), and Class 041 (providing online non-downloadable comic books and graphic novels) does not allow you to use that trademark for motion pictures, television, video games, clothing, and so on. Each has to specifically be part of the trademark application.

Maintaining Copyright and Trademark

Once an item is copyright to its rights holder, that holder can do as they wish with it. They can do nothing, sell the rights outright, license it, and so on. The copyright remains there, for the duration specified by copyright law.

Trademarks, however, must be used. If you file for a trademark for a video game and then do not release a video game under that mark you run the risk of losing the trademark for non-use. Trademarks abandoned in this manner do not permanently become public domain but may be re-registered by anyone wishing to re-establish use of the mark. Similarly, if you become aware of an infringement of your trademark but then fail to take legal action to protect your trademark you risk losing the mark. Action against infringers of a registered trademark is much easier under the law than if the mark is unregistered.

Trademarks in active use remain registered indefinitely as long as their usage is current and the appropriate periodic paperwork is filed to prove continuous use. Note that the trademark usage does not have to be by the rights-holder, but could be maintained through a licensed product.

Again, please consult with your intellectual property attorney for specific maintenance concerns, especially concerning infringement and double-extra especially for trademark issues involving international issues.

Creative Commons Licenses

You may have heard about something called a Creative Commons license, specifically with regard to music, photographs, or works of fiction. You may have also seen the (CC) logo in use. The Creative Commons license is not part of the legal copyright process, but is rather language related to the existing copyright laws that allows a rights-holder to grant or defer the rights given to them by copyright law. So, for example, a photographer may release a photograph under a Creative Commons license that allows anyone to use the image for non-commercial purposes, but prohibits commercial use of any kind. The Creative Commons licenses are an effort by the US non-profit group Creative Commons to create formal, recognized, common language for the broad assignment (or denial) of various distribution, duplication, or reuse rights to copyright protected material.

Depending on how you want to engage your fan base, releasing some or all of your transmedia property under a Creative Common license may be an option. For example, if you wanted to encourage fan fiction and projects related to your transmedia property you could create a Creative Commons license for a specific set of characters, or a setting within your franchise that fans could use for their own projects. You could just tell fans that they can do exactly that … or elect not to pursue any infringements in those areas … but issuing a Creative Commons license sets out the exact rights you are assigning, deferring, or restricting. If nothing else, issuing the Creative Commons license makes your intentions clear.

Consult http://www.creativecommons.org for additional information, and again be sure to speak to your intellectual property lawyer.

Trademark and Copyright Licensing

When a trademark or copyright is licensed, the rights-owner (licensor) grants permission to a licensee to use the trademark or copyright, in whole or in part, under the agreed terms and conditions of the licensing contract. The contract or license agreement lays out the rights and obligations of all the parties involved, including use approval, the duration of the license, and the terms for termination of the license. Merchandising is the licensing of rights for the production of what are normally considered to be common goods (and sometimes services) using the trademarks, branding, story elements, and so on. So, if Hasbro wanted to make toys of your franchise (lucky you!) you would enter into a merchandising licensing agreement with them.

If you partnered with a leading book publisher to create a series of transmedia novel tie-ins to your property, you would also enter into a licensing agreement with them.

Entering into a license agreement is an involved and complicated process. You've heard our refrain too often – consult your intellectual property lawyers – but we're going to cover some of the high points below. The following information comes nearly exclusively from the IP PANORAMA project which was developed by the Korean Intellectual Property Office (KIPO), the Korea Intervention Promotion Association (KIPA), and the World Intellectual Property Organization (WIPO). The entire set of e-learning modules from the project can be found at http://www.wipo.int/sme/en/multimedia/.

When entering into a license, or any legal contract, there is a process known as due diligence where the parties involved in the contract investigate or audit each other in preparation for the transaction.

Things the Licensor Should Know About the Licensee

- *Organizational structure*: The legal structure of the licensee will affect the content of the license and will determine the need for warranties or guarantors as to the performance of the individual or individuals involved.
- *Goals of the licensee*: In many instances, it is important to determine what the licensee wishes to do and determine if that will work within the licensing program of the licensor.
- *Financial background*: Basic information such as the name of the bank or banks through which the licensee deals could be important in determining the ability of the licensee to provide and comply with the financial terms of the agreement.
- *Business history and licensing experience*: What experience does the licensee have in the relevant area? If the licensee was a former licensee to a third party, how did the relationship end and why? If the licensee is still operating under other license arrangements, is there a conflict or possible conflict or are the products or services complimentary? Can the proposed licensee manage two or more licenses and the financial and performance criteria of both? If complimentary, how is the proposed licensee performing under the license or licenses? In this regard, in terms of whether the proposed licensee has successfully licensed the products and/or services in other countries such information would be useful to the licensor.

- *Products and services of interest to the licensee*: The licensor would be well advised to determine what product areas and/or service areas are of interest to the proposed licensee in terms of the use of the trademark(s) or copyright. Based on the information obtained by the licensor concerning the proposed licensee, the licensor is better able to determine whether, in fact, the proposed licensee is capable, financially and business-wise, to bring the new products and/or services to market successfully.

Things the Licensor Should Know About the Licensee

- *Licensor's trademark rights*: First and foremost, the licensee needs to know whether the licensor is indeed the owner of the mark and/or has the right to license that mark.
- *Other licenses*: It would be useful for the licensee to know about other licenses in existence. Other licensee or former license experiences, past and present, with the licensor will be invaluable in the negotiation process.
- *Specify licensor licensing policy*: Does the licensor have a trademark licensing policy? Does it have a manual in this regard? Are there criteria set up for dealing with infringers of the rights being granted? Are there criteria for dealing with breaches or perceived breaches of the license by the licensee and are they fair? Is there any room for licensee creativity in terms of products, services, advertising and promotion? If so, what is the process and who ultimately owns that creative work.

Issues of Interest to Both Parties

- *Business plan of the licensee*: The licensee as well as the licensor must have a business plan relating to the prospective license agreement, including the timing of the different steps for bringing the goods and/or services to market in a particular region as well as, inter alia, the promotional methods to be used to obtain and maintain market share, financial requirements and methods of finance.
- *Promotional and marketing information*: Often the marketing plan for the licensee, the proposed manner in which a product or service is going to be marketed, advertised and/or promoted is of great importance to the licensor.
- *Sales territories*: Ultimately, an appropriate marketing territory will be mutually agreed upon by the parties. To determine the appropriate size of the territory, the assets and experience of the proposed licensee must be assessed in terms of his distribution facilities, manufacturing facilities and future expansion plans as well as the proposed licensee's business acumen.
- *General information*: Sources such as annual reports of the respective parties, government filings, credit ratings, existing sales catalogues for product lines or services, newspapers, magazines or trade journals, commentary on the respective parties and so forth can provide a wealth of information, as can the Internet.

Key License Points

- *Exclusive license*: An exclusive trademark license provides the licensee with the right to use trademark to the exclusion of all, including the licensor. Thus, the trademark or copyright owner cannot use the trademark or copyright himself nor can he license any rights to others. The licensee remains the only user of that mark in the relevant market. It may be seen as or deemed to be an assignment particularly where this is no termination date.
- *Non-exclusive license*: A non-exclusive license grants to the licensee the right to use a trademark or copyright according to the grant, the licensor may continue to use the trademark or copyright himself as well as grant other licenses. Any of the above licenses can also include other limitations or limited rights provisions. The most common of those limited license provisions is that the territory of the licensee is limited either as to the

products or services that can be provided in association with the trademark or copyright, the geographical territory within which the licensee can sell, the location or site from which the licensee can sell (site location) or the market sector to which they can sell and promote the licensed product or service.

- *Sub-license*: The licensee may be granted the right to sub-license some or all of the rights included within the license and the licensor may wish to be a party to any sub-license that the licensee enters into.
- *Term or duration*: In many license agreements, the term of the license is stated in terms of three-, five- or ten-year increments.
- *Reservation of rights*: The grant clause often includes not only the grant of the rights to the licensee but also an indication or reservation of rights to the licensor for future licensing opportunities or for the entry of the licensor itself into the marketplace. In addition, most sole, exclusive and even non-exclusive licenses set minimum sales objectives on a periodic basis.
- Payments and Royalties
  - *Lump sum payments*: These can take the form of fully paid up license agreements, where a lump sum is agreed to and paid at the time of the license right being granted. Lump sum payment may also be spread, periodically, over the term of the license.
  - *Royalties*: The most usual type of consideration is to provide for some sort of upfront fee as well as an ongoing royalty payment based on sales. In some cases an upfront fee is paid as against royalties. Once royalties to be paid exceed the upfront fee, then the royalty payments are paid on a monthly, quarterly or some other periodic payment basis. The amount of the royalty, in terms of percentage, may vary from product to product, service to service and industry to industry. The royalty is usually calculated on a defined "base" rate. In some cases, this might be net profit, net sales, gross profit or gross sales.

You knew it was coming, but your intellectual property and contract law legal counsel will know all the particulars of what needs to be in a license. The information preceding is provided to give you a base understanding on how such agreements work. We've included the sample trademark licensing agreement produced by IP PANORAMA in Appendix B.

The Approval Process

Whether you are the licensor or the licensee, the approval process is a critical step in the process. It allows the rights-holder to insure the quality of the work produced under their trademark or copyright, and it assures those producing the work that efforts are in line with the rights-holder and there will be no surprises (or fewer surprises) late in the project.

For the rights-holder it is important to maintain quality control. It is important that the rights-holder set standards for quality and then actively police those standards across the board. The work produced by the licensor has to be in-brand or match the style and feel already associated with the property and it is important that the rights-holder confirm that any additions to the property, whether canon or not, match the property. As a broad example, the *Star Trek* universe does not contain magic, or at least only contains "magic" that is ultimately explainable as science (even if science fantasy). Adding true magic (whatever that may be) runs counter to the established *Star Trek* universe. Similarly, the rights-holder has to insure that the behaviors of any characters are in accordance with the tenants of the property. It is the responsibility of the rights-holder to maintain the value of the property, and allowing anything in that runs counter to the property, creates controversy for or degrades the property ultimately reduces the value of the property.

As part of the licensing and approval process it is customary to provide the licensor with any intellectual property or franchise bibles, branding guidelines, color/palette standards, style sheets and so on that will aid them in matching the visual style of the property, and understanding what elements are or are not permitted. As another example, if the rights-holder wishes the property to basically be a "teen" property, certain adult topics or references should explicitly (pardon the pun) be called out in any franchise bibles or branding guidelines.

On the flip-side, the approval process should be welcomed by the licensor, rather than considered an inconvenience or necessary evil. Communication with the rights-holder is important to the licensee who needs to be certain that the work they are producing is in-line with the needs and wants of the property. It is also important to the licensee that the approval process occurs early and often, and frequently, during production. Waiting until the end to have the rights-holder review material is dangerous and risky if there are fundamental problems that now become cost and schedule prohibitive to correct. The license contract should be written to include regularly scheduled content approval reviews by the rights-holder (and other stakeholders, as appropriate), along with a very specific timetable for response and feedback from the rights-holder.

For example, in the video game industry monthly or bi-monthly milestone submissions include approval review by the rights-holder (among others). Standard in such contracts is a timeframe for an approval response since production does not stop while awaiting approval. If there is a problem with the material produced, it is important that the rights-holder notify the production team as quickly as possible to avoid having to go back and re-do work once the team has moved on.

The approval process must be very clearly and cleanly documented so there is no confusion. It is imperative that all parties involved understand when a for-approval submission is scheduled to occur, how it is to be submitted, and what the contracted timetable is for approval feedback. It is also important that some mechanism be in place to allow partial approval and feedback. For example, if an approvals submission includes a set of artwork for review, and a chunk of story/narrative text, there should be a way to decouple the feedback and approval processes for each, instead of dropping a litany of comments and feedback at the very end of the approval timetable. Some rights-holders will have a single approval/reviewer, which means that every part of the approval process, including preparation of useful and meaningful feedback, falls to them.

Consideration has to be made when setting up the approval submission schedule to the fact that one person has to review everything when it is submitted. If it seems unlikely that this single individual will be able to receive the submission, check it for completeness, review it (mostly likely manually cross-referencing it with prior work or the continuity bible), and then prepare a feedback report to send back to the submitter. Within the allotted time some other method must be put in place to facilitate the process. Perhaps the rights-holder needs to have multiple approver/reviewers, or perhaps the material to be reviewed needs to be submitted more often, in smaller chunks. The exact solution will depend on the nature of the production, the rights-holders involved, and exactly what material needs to be reviewed and approved.

Timeliness of feedback is very important, but so is insuring that everything that needs to be reviewed and approved is submitted in an equally timely manner. Be sure the rights-holder sees all concept art, for example, and don't wait for "final art" before sending it for approval. If there is a piece of critical material that needs reviewing, it may be worth communicating with the rights-holder to send it in for review and approval even though it is not yet officially due for submission.

Who's in Charge?

It is imperative that the management of the transmedia property is handled by a single individual, or group of individuals, who are in-sync with the universe and franchise goals of the property. This group has to be at or near the top of the property food chain (so to speak) in order to best manage all the aspects and expressions of the property. The group may be beholden to a rights-holder, and if so the management group needs to be sure they are in-sync with the goals of the master property.

What the transmedia property is, and where its management is located, will change the nature of this supervisory group. By that we mean that if the property is managed by a small company, the composition and nature of the supervisory group will be different in practice than if it lives as part of a larger media company. At a smaller company, the supervisory group may very well have direct production or creative responsibilities as well, whereas if part of a larger media company the supervisory group may in fact be comprised of representatives of different parts of the company and while responsible for the grand vision of the property may only have an oversight, guidance and internal approval role rather than one involved in actual production or creative output.

The odds are that you will be outsourcing the actual production of the different media elements of your transmedia production, but even if you are part of a larger media company where different wholly or partially-owned partners of the company are doing the work, the effect is the same. We talked in an earlier section about how someone on your team needs to be able to "talk-the-talk" in each of the media areas, and this is equally important for the supervisory group, even it requires bringing a consultant or two who keeps an eye on the unfamiliar medium but reports to the supervisory group. Having these core creative and production skill competencies close to the supervisory team is important for communication and expectations.

In some cases, the supervisory group may also be the creative/production team. In some ways this is ideal, but we clearly understand that in the case of big media properties or companies this may not be true. Key to either group should be someone who is effectively a communication coordinator and has the responsibility of making sure that the teams currently live (in preproduction, production, or postproduction) are appropriately in contact with each other and the supervisory group. Communication is a delicate balance in that on one end of the scale is the desire for complete and continual communication between all the stake-holders all the time, but this can lead to an overload of information that quickly becomes ignored. On the other end of the spectrum is the bunker mentality where a production team wants to just dig in and get their part of the job done and be left alone. Neither one is acceptable, so some middle ground needs to be found.

Whoever that communication coordinator is could be the approvals/continuity coordinator, and if they are not the same person they need to be working in very close partnership. Production teams don't necessarily know what needs to be communicated to other teams or to the supervising group beyond what needs to be formally sent in for approval, so someone has to keep an eye on everything that is going on and make sure that everyone who needs to know anything knows it, promptly. Additionally, keeping a constant eye on everything improves the chances of making synergistic connections between disparate parts that might not have been connected during planning.

It is important at this point to make a distinction between production authority and creative authority. If the skills sets line up — and we encourage teams to recruit members who have multidisciplinary experience — then both may fall with the same person or persons, but not necessarily. For example, the communication coordinator may or may not be the continuity manager, and may or may not have creative authority. If there are separate production and creative authorities, it is important that that right person be involved in the right conversations in a timely manner. For smaller projects and supervisory groups, sharing production and creative responsibilities can be effective and efficient, but as the size of the project grows, it makes more and more sense to separate the authority and responsibility into different individuals who remain in regular communication.

Fans, Fandom and Fan Culture

Over the past two decades much has been written about fan and fan culture in academic circles, but typically from a media analyst's point of view. The issue from a producer's standpoint is rarely discussed, nor are strategies discussed from a storytelling perspective rather than a marketing perspective, though that line is often hard to distinguish. In creating a transmedia property at this time, there need to be decisions made up front about the how and when a producer "deals" with fan and fandom. It is not a simple marketing decision as it might have been 20 years ago. Fans require an active strategy. In fact, it seems unlikely that a property can really take the culture by storm without a high level of fan engagement beyond a success with a casual audience. Every effort needs to be made to structure the engagement in different categories with elements targeted toward specific audiences. Even as a strategy is laid out, an over-arching concern must be with the most elusive element, authenticity.

Authenticity is the fan version of someone being described as having "star" quality – the old "you know it when you see it" explanation while convenient does little to really explain why George Clooney is George Clooney. Authenticity is that star quality that fans look for. It may be as simple as that authenticity is a product of a good story but that would discount some active strategies producers have taken over the years to engage the fans.

Marketing vs. storytelling is at the core of the question of authenticity. At this point there is a wide variety of media that is generated for many popular film, television and video game series as part of their ongoing lives. Various storytelling extensions with a variety of goals appear on a regular basis within the media environment. The goals of the media can vary widely from collecting an email address for updates to extending the lifetime of the property. Simple games or background information accessible on the web as well as more traditional extensions like novelizations can all extend the immersion time of the audience in the story universe.

Connections

In the current climate there is much activity but from a fan perspective, what medium is doing an interesting job connecting to its fans?

The environment is currently filled with web games, giveaways or pay-for-play games that use the brand as the hook. The challenge in many cases is a simple one. How do you monetize this other media that can be costly in both in terms of production and support? Many recent attempts have focused on the iPad, such as the *Doctor Who* spin-off connected game *Torchwood: Web of Lies* (BBC Worldwide, 2011) that told a different story in the same universe as the *Torchwood* television series, the *Mass Effect: Infiltrator* for iOS or Android game that allows you to affect the galaxy's "military readiness" in the *Mass Effect 3* console or personal computer game, or the extended story experience like HBO provides for its programming through its *HBOGO* app.

Each is an expression of engagement, of trying to connect with the fans yet it is hard to see a comprehensive approach to connecting with a specific fandom in any of these attempts. Most attempts seem to make the inaccurate assumption that all fans are alike. The industry and culture seems to be at a crossroads. Technology is just catching up to the imagination and the larger storytelling possibilities, while a financial model that accounts for the importance of connection to the fans, has to be re-defined.

Conversations

Video games based on feature films started as an advertising and marketing tool. Few would have envisioned how those first attempts could really lead to storytelling across multiple media that fans commit to engage on an ongoing and committed way. The possibility that fan culture would mature and become a force within mainstream media would have been hard to imagine standing amidst a *Star Trek* convention in the mid-1970s. It is now time for the industry side of the equation to mature in the same way.

The current attempts to engage the true fans seem to fall into several categories. Some producers engage in a dialogue with fans, dialogue that has been enhanced by the moving of that discussion to the Internet and in fact, those early user-groups, early adopters, define a dynamic that has evolved as new technologies have brought other formats for the discussion. The back and forth can take lots of forms – highly critical, earnestly devoted or even offering suggestions in trying to shape the narrative.

What is important is the engagement and the fact that fans have a forum for the opinions. Some producers have created various activities for their fan base, complex ones like ARGs (alternative reality games) or websites with simple games or activities where the participant is rewarded with special info or glimpses into the world not given in the primary medium.

Currently, the HBO series *Game of Thrones* is using an enhanced viewing experience to engage its audience if the episodes are watched on an iPad. This is another way of extending the engagement time and can be used to great advantage as a way of extending the storytelling. Fans engaging in the more complex activities can raise their level of involvement, like in the *LOST* ARG experiences, to incredibly high levels with producers finding that the small group of super engaged fans could help shape the course and quality of a property. The last piece is harder to quantify and is best described as "fan generated universe extension."

Interestingly, this has not been uncommon before the digital age, the most notable being the *Doctor Who* fans who continued telling *Doctor Who* stories while the BBC was no longer interested. This kind of activity can take a variety of forms from fan fiction, cos-play, video mash-ups, music videos or even original video productions. It transcends the audience's role and moves fans into the role of a co-creator. Reaction to this can be a wide gamut from cease-and-desist orders to reluctant toleration to enthusiastic support. It is the opportunity for fans to re-shape the intellectual property to their satisfaction using the original intellectual property as the foundation for their re-envisioning. For many fans this a powerful experience that can add energy to a universe, sustain the fan engagement in between iterations and in some cases call for a revival or reboot of a dormant property.

All these possibilities point to the simple fact that a decision should be made up front concerning resources committed to these various modes of engagement and an openness created to the positive effect these modes of engagement can have on the universe as a whole. While it may seem obvious, the producers should have respect for the devoted fans and understand at this point in time fan participation is intrinsic to transmedia storytelling and that all media creation is now a dialogue between the content and its most devoted fans.

Technical Management

We spent some time in various chapters and sections looking at issues of creation, coordination, and management from a conceptual standpoint, with a couple of practical details sprinkled here and there. This section addresses the technical side of managing the transmedia property, specifically how to handle internal documentation and files and how to share that information with others who may need constant or regular access to the information. The complexity of technical management rises geometrically with the size and complexity of the transmedia project, but even for small teams it can be an issue.

By its nature, transmedia storytelling properties have a lot to do with technology, and many of those involved are already technologically savvy. If you are one of those people we salute you and point you in the direction of Chapter 11 as this section is not for you. In fact, you'll probably roll your eyes at some of the over-simplification of process or giggle at the obvious nature of our particular recommendations for software or processes, and we'd probably roll our eyes at yours, so there's no reason to put either of us through that.

We encourage any transmedia production group to have core members who are technology geeks to handle technology issues internal to the team and production. These may be the self-same individuals who are in charge of your marketing/advertising/promotional website, but may not be. Know this, that a designated technology team member will, if not at the start, become invaluable to the success of the property. You also have to be careful of "casual" or "good enough" solutions that seem to do the job but do not scale well, or are insecure. Transmedia is by its definition, expansive and the primary tool of transmedia story expansion is technology.

Technical Solutions

Before we talk about solutions, we need to identify the problems we're solving.

Problem #1 – document management: Any transmedia project is going to produce lots of text documentation, including bibles, contracts, style sheets, contact lists, design and development docs, pre-vis and correspondence that have to be kept, maintained and organized in some manner. The more complex the franchise is, the greater the number of projects in development, and the longer it has gone on for, the greater the literal or virtual pile of documents, many of which will include media files, is going to grow. Also, once it becomes common practice to update certain documents (like bibles) it becomes important to insure that everyone has access to the most recent version, not just the one that's handy on their desk that was printed out four months ago. There are also issues when the documentation accumulated is a mix of physical paper and electronic documentation.

Problem #2 – non-document asset management: Text documentation isn't the only type of documentation that needs to be maintained. Any transmedia franchise that includes visual media elements is going to have to keep records of what things look like, including concept designs, character images or photographs, costume references, setting or object visual references and so on. These will all be image files of sufficient resolution that the fine detail is visible to anyone who has to approve or use them as reference for other work, which means their file sizes will be large. Physical photo prints could be kept for reference, but maintaining an electronic image file is easier for sending to licensees, and it can always be printed again. An archive of music and sound needs to be maintained as well, again for consistency across the franchise. Also, if computer graphic images – 3D CGI – are created for any of the projects, say for a video game or any kind of visual effects for television or motion pictures, those files will need to be catalogued and maintained as well, and again those files can be very large in size indeed.

Problem #3 – continuity management: Earlier in the book we talked about big transmedia properties like *LOST* and *Star Wars* maintaining databases for tracking continuity. This could be done on paper, but when you are talking about scores of television episodes, or multiple movies, and dozens of novels ... the amount of information that has to be cross-referenced becomes tremendous. So, for complex properties, large or small, you need some quick way to get at continuity-related information, and flipping endlessly through giant binders isn't the way to go.

Internal vs. External Needs

When considering solutions it is also important to understand whether these solutions need to be solely internally accessible or externally as well. What we mean by that is whether or not the document and asset storage and sharing, or the continuity database, needs to be accessed only by individuals physically within the group or by those outside, such as licensees. This also has to be considered if members of the core team will not be in the same location, such as writers or artists working remotely under contract.

Ultimately, what we're really talking about is network access. Any electronic solution will exit in one of two places – on the group's local computer network connected with their computers or out on the Internet in some accessible location. There are pros and cons to each.

Local Network

The odds are that if the group overseeing your transmedia franchise is working from the same physical location, such as an office, there's a network in existence for file sharing. Many of the document and asset sharing and storage solutions can exist quite easily and simply on a local network. Some of the more complicated ones can as well, but need a stand-alone dedicated computer to act as the server for the necessary software.

Things are simple and straightforward if everyone who needs to access the document and asset storage, or the continuity database, are all going to be in the office, and not in some remote location, working from home, or on a mobile device. If someone needs to access the information storage or databases off-site, a more sophisticated server and access solution is required and it's time to call in the professionals.

Simple document storage is achievable on a local network with just dedicated, shared storage space somewhere on the network, but there's little or no safety or security. It also relies on the dedication of those who use it to keep it organized in some sensible manner.

More complex solutions are available as well that run on the local network, such as Microsoft Sharepoint, but again knowledgeable technical support is needed.

Remote Access

With a remote access solution, the documents or the database exist outside the work network, and everyone can access it remotely across the Internet. The benefit of this is that whatever system is in use is configured for remote access, so if anyone needs to get at it from home or from an alternative work site or if licensees need direct access, the capability is always there. There are, of course, downsides. The first is that you are probably paying a monthly or yearly subscription fee for the service. The second is that the Internet can sometimes be spotty, even from reliable networks. And the last is that your valuable data exists on some other system outside your control.

Document Storage and Sharing

When it comes to document creation, there are really only two notable solutions: Microsoft Office (http://office. microsoft.com) and OpenOffice (http://www.openoffice.com). Both do essentially the same thing, and for many it becomes something of a political-religious argument as to which is best. A simple point to understand, however, is that most large companies use Microsoft Office and unless they are set up to handle OpenOffice documents they could have problems accessing anything you send them. (OpenOffice can save files in Microsoft Office compatible formats, but we don't recommend it.) There is also a web-based version of Microsoft Office now called Microsoft Office 365 (http://www.microsoft.com/Office3656).

For simple document storage and transfer with remote capabilities there are solutions like Dropbox (http://www. dropbox.com), Skydrive (http://www.skydrive.com) or iCloud (http://www.icloud.com) which all allow the storage of documents and files out on the Internet and access from multiple locations. These services are great because they sync the files they store with your computer, so when you want to work on them you just work on the file on your machine and when you are done the software automatically syncs the changed file back to the master storage. It is possible for different users to access the same file and make conflicting changes, and each of these services handles those conflicts slightly differently.

Another option is Google Docs, which at the time of this writing was to be integrated into Google Drive, which works similarly to Dropbox, Skydrive and iCloud mentioned earlier. Google Docs (http://docs.google.com) allows document creation and editing through a web interface and very slickly allows multiple users to edit the same document at the same time. There are some limits to the size and scope of documents that can be produced and edited in Google Docs. Similarly, Microsoft offers a product called OneNote (http://office.microsoft.com/ en-us/onenote) that is designed as a collaborative work tool but may suffice for smaller transmedia projects.

Legal Concerns

A point to consider, that may or may not be of concern, is that whenever using external solutions like those described above, your information is being stored and handled by a third party who may have access to your information. Google Docs and some other solutions, for example, are not considered sufficiently secure or private enough to fulfill the privacy requirements of the legal and medical professions. Whether this is a concern or not for your project is something you need to decide.

Database Software

There are really only two desktop databases to consider: Microsoft Access (which often comes as part of the Microsoft Office suite) (http://office.microsoft.com/en-us/access) and FileMaker Pro (http://www.filemaker.com). Both are relatively simple to use and set up, and both can be used to access more sophisticated enterprise databases such as SQL or Oracle systems. Even though they are both fairly simple and straightforward we recommend recruiting a team member with database experience (or willing to spend the time learning) in order to make the best use of either of these systems. Both are quite useful and can be set up to do sophisticated information cross-referencing in the right hands.

Wikis

Another option is the use of a "wiki" which is a website that allows multiple users to access document pages and add, remove, or edit the content. Pages can be easily cross-linked to each other, and the entire wiki site searched. The most famous wiki is Wikipedia, but it is worth noting that the *Star Trek* Memory Alpha site, as well as many fan-based continuity sites are based on wikis. There are many wiki hosting sites that you can make use of, and it is also possible to host a wiki site on your own network but it can get complicated. Popular wiki solutions include MediaWiki (http://www.mediawiki.org) and TWiki (http://twiki.org). Some larger solutions, like Microsoft Sharepoint, allow the creation of wikis as well as other functionality. (We'll talk about Sharepoint below.)

Project and Multipurpose Sites

A number of companies provide web-based project, collaboration and document management solutions for a subscription fee. One of these sites could be ideal for coordinating your transmedia project since they allow different levels of access, as well as collaboration tools, task management, project tracking, wikis, and other similar services. Probably the two most popular of these solutions is Basecamp (http://basecamp.com) and Zoho (http://www.zoho.com).

Basecamp is an optimized transmedia tool. Everyone involved in a project can work together on Basecamp. You have full control over who sees which project, and who sees each other. A story universe can be broken into individual story worlds, worked on individually, and then shared. All types of files from text to CGI composites can live on basecamp. You can also create groups to keep people on each team organized. Basecamp is web based and can be made private or made open to anyone worldwide.

Both Zoho and Basecamp provide similar functionality using slightly different approaches. Either of these could be an ideal solution for some of your content and project management solutions.

Microsoft Sharepoint (http://sharepoint.microsoft.com) is another sophisticated solution. You can find Internet-based Sharepoint hosting services, or you can choose to install it on your local network, with the potential for outside access. Sharepoint is very powerful and configurable, but it does require knowledgeable technical support to set up and maintain. If you've got that already you may want to look at Sharepoint.

Chapter 10
The Transmedia Intellectual Property Bible

When planning an intellectual property that will be developed and presented across multiple media streams, there is no way that we can directly oversee all the work ourselves. We are instead the guiding force behind a team of people (or many teams of people), each a specialist in a particular area of the transmedia process. To maintain canon and manage this complex process, we need a document or bible that is developed specifically for transmedia storytelling. Such a bible or guiding document is a critical tool for communicating not just with our current team members but future hires, archiving story developments and making sure that future story developments are consistent with the universe and storyworlds we have created.

We use the term *transmedia intellectual property bible* (sometimes shortened to transmedia bible or IP bible, and we will use these terms interchangeably) to identify the overall reference document that informs and underlies the development of all the various transmedia iterations of our larger story. This over-arching document (or super bible) can be so large that we often group related materials together and refer to those as bibles as well.

As we noted earlier in this chapter, the universe bible is comprised of those parts of the intellectual property bible specific to the over-arching story elements that inform all iterations of the property. Particularly complex properties then develop world bibles for smaller or more focused storyworlds within the larger universe. Both types of bibles include broad mythology, themes, conflicts, characters and dramatic action that drive the various stories we want to tell.

The franchise bible then is those portions of the intellectual property bible that relate to the distribution of story elements across multiple media expressions and the ways in which those various platforms interrelate and are made available to various audiences – in effect emphasizing branding, promotion and marketing issues. The technical and delivery specs that the production team will need are sometimes referred to as a production bible. And each of the individual platforms telling a story from our universe will have its own specific platform bible.

There is no one definitive way to create or present a transmedia IP bible, and these bibles – like story bibles for television series or a novelist's research – are often closely guarded. The *Halo* Story Bible developed by Starlight Runner Entertainment has been described as a black-and-silver loose-leaf binder with hundreds of pages. There are supposedly only four copies in existence, each kept under lock and key, and authors working on the *Halo* novels are given just the portions of the bible that are applicable to what they're writing about.

The challenge with *Halo*, though, was that Microsoft approached Starlight Runner Entertainment as the fourth game was being developed. This meant that writing the bible was a retroactive process – they had to go back and assemble a bible based on what already existed:

> *[343] and [Halo Franchise Development Director] Frank O'Connor have talked several times about the Halo mythology and the "super bible" we assembled for them, which contains, up until the point that we finished, the totality of the canonical Halo universe. And what's beautiful about the Halo universe is that you don't necessarily need Master Chief to tell a good Halo story.*
>
> **—Kevin Smith for Official Xbox Magazine Online**[1]

Starlight Runner's bible was designed to help define canon and ensure continuity among the franchise's branching fiction so that Microsoft would be able to confidently move forward in developing new stories and characters that would not contradict what had already been established. Gomez describes the process as not just studying the story elements of the games but also reading the novels and watching the television shows, fan films, user-generated content, music videos and commercials for the games.

Though they were able to create (or in some ways reconstruct) a bible for Microsoft from Bungie's (the original game developer) and 343's (the most recent game's developer) material as well as other pre-existing expressions of the *Halo* universe, we can see from this that it's better to control our intellectual property from the beginning. The more thoroughly we think things through at the intellectual property development stage, the easier things are down the road.

Building the Bible

As a document that summarizes, details and communicates our intentions and plans for the property, the transmedia intellectual property bible establishes a clear direction for the overall and individual components within the intellectual property as well as presents an understandable world in which our narratives will take place. With that said, we're best served if we think of the intellectual property bible as a living document, flexible enough to grow as new people, new ideas and new modes of expression or technologies come to the intellectual property.

The transmedia bible has to establish continuity, setting, character, the rules of the universe (and worlds) and other details that are important for creators working on various platforms to know in order to maintain believable consistency among the various expressions of story. This means laying out key story and design elements, but the bible may also provide logistical information such as an assessment of the technical issues inherent in each iteration of the property, goals as they relate to the overall intellectual property and to each individual iteration, and overviews of the business plan and marketing strategy. The intellectual property bible is the go-to comprehensive story, style and production reference guide for those responsible for any aspect of the property.

Story, Rules and Underlying Assumptions

The starting point is often the universe itself, the place in which our various stories will take place. The universe bible (or that portion of the transmedia bible that addresses larger story elements) will be the primary creative guidebook for the narrative (or story) aspects of the intellectual property. In our example earlier, we discussed how

---

[1] "Talking with the man who assembled the 'Halo Bible' for Microsoft," accessed June 16, 2012), http://www.oxmonline.com/talking-man-who-assembled-halo-bible-microsoft

Microsoft learned the necessity for such a book four *Halo* games in, and contracted with Starlight Runner to retroactively compile a universe bible (or story bible) that could then be used to guide future expansion of the *Halo* universe across multiple platforms and into other expressions of storytelling.

Novelists like Tolkien, Herbert, King, LeGuin or Martin create and compile great amounts of information and backstory about the world in which their stories take place, sometimes even drawing maps and making notes to themselves about historical, geological or biological events that have shaped that world's landscape and societies. The more interesting and immersive the universe, the more likely the audience is to suspend their disbelief and engage fully with the story. The best worlds in storytelling are those that resonate with and enhance the audience's understanding of the themes and conflict at play in the stories. In other words, the entire universe and/or world should have meaning and significance to the story. This ties in with the mythology and underlying mystery or quest of the intellectual property.

The temptation is to think that we don't need to do world building when our story is set in our society in the present day, but in fact, it may be even more important to clearly identify the parameters or rules of the universe in those cases. For example, all four of this book's writers live in the metro Chicago area, but if you asked us to describe Chicago, we would each describe it and its rules differently. Depending on where we live, we might have different city ordinances that affect us (such as parking restrictions) or those ordinances may be enforced differently from local precinct to local precinct. We're used to these small contradictions and differences in real life, but in a story they can start looking like inconsistencies or like the author doesn't remember what was established several pages ago. People usually think of world building as vitally important for fantasy and science fiction intellectual properties, partly because there are significant environments that do not resemble (at least at first glance) the world we live in. But don't underestimate the importance of world building for stories that seem closer to home. All stories reveal a worldview that results from certain rules or assumptions that underlie the story. Our theme is actually just one of those rules, such as "fate will guide us to our true love" or "life is meaningless," but there are many other rules that affect how our narrative will progress and how our characters will behave.

Characters are an important consideration as we build our universe and its individual storyworlds. We're not trying to figure out every character we might ever want to use in a story, but we do need an initial set of characters through which we (the audience) experience the universe. It is through the characters that we learn about the world and universe. Of course, as our intellectual property develops, we will probably add additional characters in the future, but in the early stages of our intellectual property's development, it's important to consider the initial characters the audience will encounter. One of our favorite quotes about storytelling is from our colleague Sue Mroz who says that an audience will follow the storyteller anywhere as long as there are humans there. Her point is that in stories, we attach not just to spectacle but to characters who are in some way recognizable to us. This doesn't mean they can't be an animal (like Bambi or Benji) or an alien, simply that part of our engagement with story is caring about one or more of the characters in the story, thereby caring about what happens to him or her.

The rules that we need to establish may apply to the universe or to the characters. For example, one of the rules in *The Walking Dead* is that animals are not and cannot become zombies. In *Avatar: The Last Airbender*, the world has no modern conveniences like electricity though the Fire Nation is in its industrial revolution, using steam-powered ships.

The idea of having an intellectual property bible, in particular a universe bible, comes from the use of story bibles in television that serve as a guide and touchstone for the multiple writers and producers who will work on the television series over the course of its run. Like those story bibles, the intellectual property's universe bible helps assure continuity by making sure that each person's part of the various projects is consistent with – and therefore a part of – the canon.

Authors

If the universe bible is the cornerstone of our transmedia intellectual property bible, then who creates the universe or at the least, lays a solid enough foundation that others can be added to or further developed down the road?

At first glance, having a single author for the universe bible would seem to more likely assure consistency and continuity, and it's not a bad idea to have a primary person responsible for creating the document if not the universe itself. Certainly Gene Roddenberry started with a very clear and singular foundation for *Star Trek* that initially existed only in his imagination.

But great additions or nuances to the universe can come from collaboration or shared conversations about the narrative aspects of the property both at the beginning and during the growth of the property. As the original *Star Trek* series went into production and other writers were brought in – and as other series developed from the *Star Trek* universe – Roddenberry had to share his vision, and these new writers and producers brought their own ideas to the material, adding to the universe bible.

In addition a universe can become so big (with so many iterations on different platforms) that one person cannot keep track of all its elements. Each platform or medium is going to have its own creative teams, and they will discover new material for the universe, and we want them to be part of a dynamic contribution to the primary universe. Of course this means that their contributions will potentially affect the story material being used by other creative teams in other media and vice versa. The universe will begin to take a life of its own, and that can be one of the most exciting aspects of this whole process:

Collaboration – or more accurately co-creation – is at the heart of transmedia.

The bible – rather than a single person – becomes our resource for all information about the universe or the intellectual property in its entirety. With that said, there does need to be a person or small team that's responsible for reviewing all new information generated within the universe to make sure that it is indeed consistent with what has come before and with the projected arc of where we want to go with the property in the future. Early on in the process, this person might be the transmedia property's creator or primary producer, but eventually this may need to handed off to another person (or team) much in the way that the creator of a television series will often eventually hand off the day-to-day further development and guardianship of the series' universe, canon and individual stories to a head writer.

Elements of the Bible

There is no one definitive template to use when creating a transmedia intellectual property bible. The bible can range from tens of pages to hundreds (if not thousands) of pages, depending on how fully each aspect is developed within the document. Because it is a living document, it might start relatively small but continue growing as new stories and characters are introduced to the storyworlds within the intellectual property, becoming a combination of archive and future plan.

The actual document may be a combination of prose, lists and images that include a description of the storyworld and assumptions (rules), diagrams of how the story breaks across different media, script or story excerpts, conceptual art, technical specs, creator goals, audience enticements, development schedules, mileposts, business plans and marketing strategies. No one intellectual property bible may have all of these; what's included will vary upon the type of intellectual property, its stage of development or production and its breadth across media. Also, depending on your intellectual property, you may structure or order the document differently from the order of elements presented below. At its barest, the bible defines the storyworld, characters and anticipated narratives. At its fullest, the bible expands to include information we might normally associate with a production bible.

As you create your intellectual property bible, choose the elements and their order that makes most sense for your projects.

Not all of the following elements are required, but in considering whether they apply to your specific intellectual property, you will be in a better position to create a bible that can serve as that comprehensive, consistent and cohesive resource guide for the producers and the creative and production teams.

Title Page

The title page should include the name of the overall transmedia intellectual property (such as *Halo* or *Avatar: The Last Airbender*), the name and/or logo of the intellectual property copyright holder and the words "intellectual property bible" ("I.P. bible") or "transmedia bible."

Table of Contents

All the info that was on the title page should be at the top of the table of contents page, followed by "Table of Contents" and a listing of all the individual sections that are contained in the document. It probably won't make sense to include page numbers for each section, because this is a document that will be added to. Better to treat the list of contents as simply section headings; the location of their content is then indicated by tabs, tags or dividers in the actual document.

Story Synopsis and Treatment (Universe Bible)

The story synopsis and treatment section summarizes our overall storyworld, including characters and underlying assumptions of how that world operates. This section includes a variety of different ways to describe your story and is the core document of our universe bible (or sub-bible). These descriptions could include any or all of the following:

Tagline: The tagline is basically best thought of as a one-sentence marketing slogan or enticement designed to generate excitement about the potential stories within the intellectual property universe. We are surrounded by taglines all the time – just look at any movie poster – but the trick here is to find a tagline evocative enough and broad enough to reflect not just one story such as we'd see in a single film but the entire intellectual property universe. One of the most famous taglines is from the *Alien* franchise: "In space, no one can hear you scream," but a better example of an intellectual property tagline is the *Transformers'* "More than meets the eye."

Premise or logline: Similar to the logline of a feature film, the premise or logline for our entire intellectual property is one sentence that indicates the tone, conflict, theme and core actions within the property's universe, an understanding that will inform all the creative decisions we make within that world. If we were going to create a logline or premise for the *Transformers* IP, it might look something like: "Sentient alien robots have brought their war to Earth, hiding among us, disguised as the cars we drive and the machines we use every day."

Theme: If there's an underlying point of view, truth or insight, you may want to state it in one or two sentences. Sometimes this might be a line of dialogue (or catchphrase) from the intellectual property itself or a famous quote or an original phrase that reflects the primary rule of the universe you have created (more on rules in a moment). It could also be a statement about human behavior – or at the least, the way humans behave in your intellectual property universe.

Backstory and context: We are all products of our time, our culture, our history, our families, our environment, our world. We'd expect nothing less of the characters in our intellectual property. For the intellectual property world to feel fully immersive, there needs to be a consistent and coherent impression of its existence before (and after) the actual events that form a particular story within that universe. This usually includes some sort of historical information about the societies and cultures within that universe as well as environments within the universe that impact the narratives that we want to tell. This section might include maps or event timelines or even information about family genealogies that are significant to the narratives we plan to build from the intellectual property. The idea here is to build a universe that feels as real and as lived in as our own.

Rules

There are rules that are implied in and underlie your entire backstory and context, but your teams will find it helpful to have them overtly listed in brief one or two sentence summations for quick and easy reference. For example, *Avatar: The Last Airbender* breaks down its rules into short subsections that then list two to 5 five points of information about each:

Bending
General rules of bending – followed by two to five rules for how bending works
Air bending – followed by several rules specific to air bending, basically defining how it's different from other kinds of bending
Water bending – with several rules specific to water bending
Earth bending – and its two to five rules that make earth bending different from other forms of bending
Fire bending – with, you guessed it, a list of two to five rules that are specific to fire bending

Characters
The bible then lists all of the main characters along with a brief one-paragraph description for each, particularly in terms of what personality traits or backstory governs their behavior and choices in the story. The Airbender bible has character biographies for Sokka, Katara, Aang, Appa, Momo, and Zuko

Environment
The physical world and environment of the story is governed by rules as well. We need to identify those. For example, gravity on an alien planet or the length of its day is most likely going to be different from what it is on earth.

Nations
In Airbender, *there are four major societies or groups of people: Water Tribe, Earth Kingdom, Air Nomads, and Fire Nation; each has its own laws and customs and rules that will affect the story and the characters from those particular nations.*

Animals
In stories like Airbender *or* The Walking Dead, *there are rules that specifically address how animals will or will not behave in the story. Those need to be identified.*

Spirit World
Because the spirit world is a significant presence in Airbender *(and many manga and anime stories), we need to identify the rules that apply to how that world can be perceived and interact with the non-spirit world or characters of our story.*

Language/Writing
Airbender *has very specific rules about how written language or signage can be used or shown within its stories. Obviously, this might not apply to every intellectual property, but from the list of areas that have rules in the* Airbender *universe, you can see how we might break down the rules for our own intellectual property.*

Highlights or Special Reference

If your world relies on special abilities, such as superhero powers, you may need a separate section that lays out those powers, their limitations, how they are used, what affects them, etc. This information will probably overlap with some of the details in your backstory section and your rules section, but the advantage to having it broken out in its own section as well is that it is easy to find and draws attention to those unique rules that form the core of your property and are the significant touchstone for all expressions of the intellectual property. From the example above, we might recap the key concepts about bending.

Synopsis

Synopses are often one page, but you may need more, depending on the complexity of your intellectual property. Even so, the goal is to be brief and to provide an overview of the over-arching narrative and/or the various smaller narratives that you anticipate telling within the larger intellectual property universe. You're not trying to tell each story comprehensively but rather provide a thumbnail sketch of each one, perhaps one paragraph per story, regardless of its platform or medium of expression.

These synopses can be grouped by those that share the same storyworld within the larger universe, forming the cornerstone of more detailed world bibles.

Plot Points

Because the larger story arc will cross multiple media, we need to list or diagram the key plot points of that larger story regardless of what medium they will occur in. Again, we're not trying to tell the comprehensive story in detail here but rather to lay out key narrative events in that story. You may want to actually create a chart that shows how these plot points are distributed across the various media that will be part of our transmedia story.

Characters

Stories are often only as interesting or believable as the characters that inhabit them. Characters are the way in which we experience the narratives and the intellectual property universe, so they are a critical element in our intellectual property development. The characters section identifies the key characters that will drive the narratives or explore the intellectual property universe.

Each key character is described in a character biography: a paragraph or two that describe distinguishing features or characteristics in three arenas that are or will prove to be narratively significant:

Physical (including appearance but also physical prowess, abilities and skills),

Psychological (including core values, insecurities, self-awareness), and

Sociological (in terms of their interactions with others and/or their roles within groups – as a member of a family, as a member of a larger society, and so forth).

Some characters may have a phrase that is specifically associated with them, perhaps something they say, such as "Up, up and away" for Superman or "Spoon!" for the Tick. If so, that should be included in this brief character description as well.

In addition, you may choose to include a found image – or once you're cast, photos of the actors – of a face or person to serve as further clarification or inspiration for the creative team.

Scripts

Examples of script writing or formatted documents illustrative of supporting material for the storyworld are recommended. This serves partly as a style guide and to assure that all written materials are consistent for ease with reading and ready identification of the medium they represent.

For example, we might include a scene in screenplay format for the feature film (roughly three pages), a scene in television format for the episodic series (roughly three to seven pages, depending on whether it's comedy, drama or the story genre), the equivalent of one page of a comic in comics script format for our graphic novel (one to three pages of script), a split script for webisodes (one page) or text materials for uploading to a website.

Audience

Describe in a few sentences the primary or target audience(s) for the overall transmedia intellectual property. If you are developing specific worlds within the universe or platforms for dispersing story that are aimed at different audiences, then you may want to identify those.

Because transmedia properties will have multiple ways in which viewer/users may enter or leave the story and require a certain degree of interactivity or cross platform involvement, it's not uncommon to create user-centric scenarios, identifying four hypothetical users and describing their chronological and individual routes through the service (including entry points) as well as their individual lifestyles and how the project is relevant to them.

Glossary

If the intellectual property has repurposed or created new words or uses existing specialized language in the dialogue or storyworld, you may want to provide a glossary of those. For example, in *Avatar: the Last Air Bender*, we may need to define "bender" and "bending" as well as other terms used in various iterations of the story. In the original *Star Trek* bible, this glossary would include definitions for "transporter," "tricorder," etc.

Expressions and Iterations (Platforms, Channels, Streams)

Each platform, format or medium needs to be expressly defined and described in terms of the necessary components for expressing the intellectual property in both linear and non-linear storytelling expressions. It's important to note any special features that might be of interest to the marketing team, innovations in content, execution or technology that might generate interest in the intellectual property.

Overview: The overview lists all anticipated platforms, channels and streams to be utilized, each with a brief (one or two sentences) description of how they are utilized in the intellectual property and what the content will be on each. This might include an overview of infrastructure needed for each platform or delivery service in the following subsection and whether we will be using existing services or needing to build our own. This information can be a diagram, list or text.

We may also want to consider the interface from a user perspective, especially for games, websites and apps. This info lays out some considerations for the first stages of level design, game mechanics, etc. As such, it may be more specific than you need for the initial intellectual property bible, but as you move into production, these kinds of considerations become increasingly important and can be archived here.

More importantly at the early stages, it is important to think about the audience/user's journey through the intellectual property universe and narratives. This may be best represented by a diagram, but the bottom line is that you want to demonstrate the range of routes and possibilities for intersection as a user maneuvers through the property. These routes are directly tied to the plot points and synopsis in the treatment section, and we should be able to see from this the relationship of each platform to other platforms and to those narrative plot points. In effect, we are identifying entry points (sometimes referred to as POEs for Points of Entry), calls to action (CTAs), service exits and key events.

We may want to itemize our treatment plot points again in this section but now add information that specifically indicates how each fits into the context of the overall narrative. The trick here is to find the best possible way to make that relationship between plot point, context and platform/delivery system clear, understandable and manageable. This may be where we consider whether the smaller story chunks are best thought of as chapters or episodes or seasons.

This relates directly to the issue of timelines: reverse engineering from when the content needs to be available to the viewer/user to when content needs to be created for delivery. Clear due dates and milestones will help with the management of content delivery to assure that our narrative is uninterrupted.

Finally, our overview will want to consider how branding and advertising fit within and change across the various platforms, how branding will integrate with the story and those unique elements that can entice or engage viewers/users.

Platform Specific Bibles

In previous chapters we talked about the story conventions and approaches unique to and shared among film, television, gaming, novels, comics, webseries and new media, and that information will help you choose which platforms are best for your transmedia property.

Once you have chosen the primary platforms that will convey aspects of your universe's narrative, you will then create a more specific bible for each one. Each medium has its own approach to story bibles (including no approach), and specific templates are in the appendices. However, we should note that none of the platforms have one tried-and-true format for story bibles, so all the templates are a range of possible inclusions in the platform specific bible that you will then pick and choose from to tailor the bible to your specific project.

Any platform specific bibles you develop become a part of this overall intellectual property bible and are usually inserted here. Depending on the mediums you choose to distribute your universe narrative across, the platform specific bibles included here might include a:

Film platform bible (see Appendix A for specific elements to include in this type of bible)
Television platform bible (see Appendix B for specific elements to include in this type of bible)
Game design guide (see Appendix C for specific elements to include in this type of bible)
Novel platform bible (see Appendix D for specific elements to include in this type of bible)
Graphic novel platform bible/comics platform bible (see Appendix D for specific elements to include in this type of bible)
Webseries platform bible (see Appendix D for specific elements to include in this type of bible)
New media platform bible (see Appendix D for specific elements to include in this type of bible)

Because each of these platform bibles can be a lengthy document in and of itself, the platform specific bibles will probably be separate files/folders or in separate binders. If that is the case, this section of your intellectual property bible will list and briefly describe the concept and basic story covered in each platform specific bible and then refer the reader to that particular bible for more detail.

If you are summarizing the platform bibles here rather than including them in their entirety, each bible summary should have a:

Title page: The title page will be a duplicate of the title page that is on the platform bible. This page ideally indicates the title of the story being told in this particular medium as well as the title of the larger intellectual property if it is different, the logo and/or name of the copyright holder of the property, the bible's author, the version number with date and a prominent label that says this is a platform specific bible. For example, the television story bible will be labeled television platform bible; the graphic novel bible will be labeled graphic novel platform bible. The list of different types of bibles above gives you a standard labeling strategy.

Table of contents: The table of contents page is a duplicate of the table of contents from the platform specific bible. Even though not all of the sections listed on it will be summarized here, it's important for the reader to know exactly what material is covered in the full document of the bible in order to know if the information they need is included there.

Concept: If your platform bible includes an overview and/or concept statement, include it here; if it doesn't, then write a brief overview for the purposes of this summary. The overview usually is just a couple of paragraphs that reiterate the premise of the intellectual property and specifically the portions of the intellectual property that will be expressed in that specific platform's version.

Primary audience: Identify the primary audience for the specific platform, or who you're targeting that part of the story to. Your audience will probably vary somewhat from platform to platform, so it's important to see that information right up front in the intellectual property bible's summary of the individual platform bibles.

Story synopsis: Include a brief synopsis of the story or stories that will be presented in the specific platform bible. You're not summarizing every episode of a TV show or providing an outline of all the plot points for a film; the synopsis should be succinct and can usually duplicate the short version or one- to two-page synopsis of the overarching story used in most platform bibles. An even more succinct synopsis of one to two paragraphs would be a viable alternative here.

Characters: Provide a brief description of the primary characters for this platform's story. You can duplicate the character section from the platform specific bible. If the characters have been detailed in the story synopsis and treatment section of this intellectual property bible, you can just list the name and refer the reader to that earlier section.

Sample pages: Rather than a full script or treatment, you may want to include an example of key art or a script excerpt (one or two scenes at most) that gives a sense of the approach being used to develop the material for that specific platform.

Design Specs

This section of the transmedia intellectual property bible will include information that will help guide the team working on any elements that relate to the actual production of iterations of the property. These design specs and the tech specs coming up in a couple of pages are sometimes referred to as the production bible.

Design aesthetics: The design aesthetics section provides a general philosophy or strategy for approaching all design considerations. This section is less about an itemization of specific requirements and more about the underlying approach to design, stressing mood, tone, atmosphere, psychological point of view.

Branding and design guidelines: Any issues related to branding or design elements that have to cross multiple or all platforms need to be itemized and described in this section.

Storyboards and concept art: Because nearly all the iterations of intellectual properties include some form of visual presentation, this section provides examples or mockup designs to give a sense of the "look and feel" of each iteration from the perspective of the viewer/user.

There should be an example for each and every one of the various release platforms that shows four or five key frames of each to give a clear sense of the aesthetic experience within that medium and its relationship to the aesthetic experience across all platforms. This might include a page of storyboards from the feature film or episodic screen story, a page of panels in sequence for the comic, concept art for the games, renderings of the website portals and pages, etc. As production begins, these drawings may give way to actual stills from the set or screenshots of work in progress.

Wireframes: To further assist with web, game and mobile app design, we may want to provide detailed interface maps or charts that give an indication of structural elements to a build prior to final assets and graphics being put in place. This might include additional information such as pixel coordinates, block references, etc.

Style guide, color and font specs: As we lock in the technical specs for our aesthetic choices, we will want to have them archived for future reference. This might include the color pallet along with technical specs such as the RGB values, textures, font and size, general frame composition guidelines, etc. Besides listing these specs, there should be visual references as well, such as key examples of these specs expressed in artwork or photography representative of the various iterations we will be developing for our intellectual property.

Media design styles: Our bible might include descriptions of the image, audio and musical styles to be utilized, including motion graphics and moving title sequences for trailers, videos or films. Seeing is sometimes better than reading, so this section may be a combination of text with embedded videos or links or still frames representing all the media elements to be utilized in order to create cohesion among all the visual elements.

Full assets list: We then need to create a hierarchical list of all the assets that need to be produced and that have a design need. We may need to give consideration to the different amounts of development time required for each medium and recognize that there is a difference between start time and delivery time, depending on the medium. This requires a larger view of how the intellectual property will be experienced by the viewer/user and might include or reference specific timelines and milestones.

You can see that most of these are providing broad references to design issues, but each platform will have more specific needs. These more platform-specific and detailed design specifications will be added to their respective platform bibles rather than expanding this section of the transmedia IP bible. Your decision for what info goes where or the level of detail needed here in the intellectual bible will probably be based on who needs what info and which bible is easiest for those people to find and utilize the information.

Technology Specs

As we move into production, things will run much smoother if we can anticipate and establish consistent technological specifications. As with the design specs we just talked about, the technology specifications included in the IP Bible are going to often be more general, an overview that is of value to all the production teams. More detailed specs for the technical development on specific platforms will be included as part of those platform specific bibles. The general tech specs to include here in the IP bible consist of any or all of the following:

Technology platform vision: a rationale for why certain platforms, devices or systems are being used for this intellectual property.

System architecture: a description or visual representation of how platforms and channels within them are interconnected, how content and data intertwines; this architecture needs to take into consideration the earlier aesthetic and narrative considerations detailed in storyboards or concept art and in the ways in which the viewer/user experiences the narrative through the various media.

Highlights: a listing of any aspects that are unique to the intellectual property or individual projects (and their platforms) within the intellectual property; these potentially can generate interest in the intellectual property and its various iterations.

Infrastructure: a listing of operating systems, coding environments, open source engines, client software, existing web services and media formats that are required for delivery of the intellectual property to viewer/users. This might also include consideration of third-party hosting of content and how media assets will be managed.

Devices: a discussion of any cross-platform considerations, such as the rationale for making decisions about limiting releases to particular devices (will our game be exclusive to PS3 or also available on Xbox or will we develop apps for Android but not iPhone).

User data: whether we will gather information about the viewer/users and if so, how that data will be collected, analyzed and fed back into our plans for future development of the intellectual property.

Coding and builds: any specific elements that need to be built from the ground up or modified from existing engines; this section should also include a time estimate for each part of the development.

Quality control: the timeline and criteria for assuring the completion of all the design builds.

Business Plan, Promotion and Marketing Strategies

While the story and design elements require an intensive investment in time and energy, our work only pays off if our intellectual property gets in front of viewers and users. Though this section comes near the end of our bible, the business plan, promotion and marketing strategies are actually some of the first things we consider when determining whether a particular intellectual property is viable for transmedia development.

Before we invest all that time and energy in developing the property, we need to know where it's going to go after it's created. The business plan with marketing strategies is the longer vision of the intellectual property's life after it leaves the creators' hands.

The business plan may be a set of documents that express a set of overall goals and strategies for the intellectual property, but you will often find that an intellectual property bible requires another layer of goals and strategies that are specific to the individual medium or iterations of the intellectual property.

Goals: Whether we are talking about the intellectual property's overall goals or the goals for a specific iteration (or platform), we need to consider at least three different sets of experiences for each in the business plan:

- Goals from the perspective of the user
- Goals from the perspective of the creative team
- Goals from the perspective of the investors

For example, our one-way website might have the goal to entice the viewer to go see our film or our virtual social world environment might encourage a viewer/user to comment on or contribute to a story in the intellectual property universe (both examples of a goal from the perspective of the viewer/user).

Our creative team may be generating specific content in order to reach a particular demographic, such as age group or gender, or the team may have a broad goal of increasing the overall audience – and it's hard to think of an intellectual property that is not going to have this as a goal from the perspective of the creative team, though it connects directly to the goals of the investors, whose goals are generally going to build around revenue generation and cross-promoting the intellectual property with other properties or products, such as McDonalds Happy Meals, with the hopes of generating additional interest in our intellectual property.

Success indicators: Of course, goals are only meaningful if we have a way to know whether we have achieved them. Therefore we need to identify clear measurable ways to assess our success.

Target audience and marketing: Though marketing is a part of each of the individual intellectual property iterations, in general we need to identify what audience is likely to be most interested in or eager to access our intellectual property whether through interactive, active or passive expressions. How will we attract these users or audience members? This section addresses those questions, but besides a written marketing strategy it may also include concept art and visual examples, such as a mockup of a one sheet (or poster) for a feature film or packaging for the games. It might also include proof of concept videos either embedded or via link to give a sense of what trailers, commercials and teasers might look like.

Business models: The section on business models deals specifically with how we anticipate generating the revenue needed to pay the costs of developing our intellectual property and its various iterations as well as how we anticipate making a profit from these endeavors. Even if we weren't talking about a transmedia property, it's rare for there to be a single business model that fits these goals of budget and profit. Our business plan will probably be a mix of business models ranging from advertising to transaction to product placement to … whatever will generate income. This might include how investment is handled and how shares in the property are distributed.

Projections, Budgeting and Timelines

Building off our business models, this may be one of the most important sections as our intellectual property bible becomes more akin to a production bible. This is where we budget the development and production costs, and this budget will generally be complex because it has to incorporate the budgets needed for each individual expression of the intellectual property and compile them into one comprehensive budget for the entire launch of our property. In other words, we're creating a series of smaller budgets that then are compiled into an overall budget for the intellectual property.

A huge factor in budgets is the schedule, and we need to clearly identify a timeline for when elements need to be completed, allowing the necessary time for them to be completed well. We often will set milestones that indicate the potential budget spent at each of those.

We may also estimate likely revenues or profits by doing comparisons, or looking at similar intellectual properties (either in terms of content or in terms of scale or in terms of platforms) and seeing how they've done. From these, we should be able to better estimate when our project(s) will break even and at what point we should start seeing profit.

Creative and Production Teams

So who's going to do all this work that we've been describing in our intellectual property bible? Who is responsible for what? What does our organizational chart look like for the production of this particular intellectual property? Those are the questions that get addressed in this section.

Generally, we want to break down each of the roles that has responsibilities in developing and producing our transmedia property. Often times, this might be divided up into several categories. We may initially express this as a chart or a flowchart and then have a separate section for the names and bios of specific (hired) team members, or we may combine our list of roles/responsibilities with the names and bios of the people who will be filling those. Either way, we will probably organize these roles and bios by each type of medium or platform we are developing for the intellectual property.

Our breakdown might start with a list of the overall intellectual property producing team and then organize each individual team around the platform for which it's responsible. We will have a separate team of people responsible for the graphic novel or comics, for example, from the team that oversees the social media aspects of our intellectual property or the team that produces our episodic television series.

Ideally, each team's members are listed by name with a brief (one-paragraph) bio that gives some sense of not just their talents or background but also their personality; these bios are usually accompanied by a photo as well.

This section personalizes all the work that needs to be done – these are our coworkers, colleagues and co-creators in the intellectual property universe that we have created.

Current Status

There should be a section set aside in the bible that is up to date with every aspect of the intellectual property development and production process. Most current updates should be at the top of this section and then in reverse chronological order, in effect archiving the previous updates. The challenge with transmedia is to be able to check the status of parallel project development, and you may want to have separate subsections for each transmedia platform or you may want to simply compile them all in one section. What is best for you as a producer will depend on your own working methods and the specific intellectual property you're working on.

Copyright and Licensing

There needs to be a small section in your bible that clearly identifies who owns the intellectual property or has been assigned the intellectual property copyright for development purposes as well as any plans for licensing to third parties portions of the intellectual property for further development or production.

Summary

Though an intellectual property bible doesn't necessarily need to end with a summary, because the document, file or book is so lengthy, it can be helpful to have the last page or two simply reiterate the basic concept in terms of its broad story, over-arching aesthetics, a sense of viewer/user experience and any aspects that are unique to the property.

Sharing the Bible

A final word about intellectual property bibles: remember that the goal here is to have a comprehensive but easy-to-use reference guide for your creative and production teams. Reading page after page of densely written material can defeat the purpose, which is why you'll notice that many of the elements in a bible are expressed as lists, diagrams or images and that when text is used, it is often broken down several ways and in various lengths (such as a one-sentence tagline, a one or two sentence premise, a one-page synopsis, a multi-page backstory, etc.). A reference guide is only valuable if you can find the information you need quickly. This is why some bibles will have both a table of contents at the front and an updatable index at the back.

Also, you'll see that much of the material in the intellectual property bible can be used to create pitch presentations for the overall intellectual property or individual expressions of the intellectual property. However if you use materials from the bible for a pitch, keep in mind that the goal of the bible is to provide a comprehensive reference guide for the creative and production teams. The goal of a pitch document or presentation is primarily centered on the story, characters and narrative world with a very general and broad overview of the design and business plan. The pitch is designed to entice and excite potential investors or partners, not bog them down in the level of detail that your creative and production teams will need. Therefore, adapt any materials from one type of document to the other with care.

Updating the Bible, Maintaining the Franchise

The transmedia intellectual property bible's importance is in defining and communicating the elements of the property that are shared between its various incarnations and that stand solely in one medium or another. This relates to the concepts of canon and continuity and as we've seen in previous chapters, the large transmedia franchises of *LOST* and *Star Wars* both had specific individuals who were in charge of monitoring continuity and maintaining a database of important characters, places, objects, events, references and so on, for the franchise. We've also noted the existence of fan-driven community repositories of the same continuity information maintained by the official gatekeepers at Bad Robot (*LOST*) and Lucasfilm Licensing (*Star Wars*), for properties like Stephen King's *Dark Tower* series, George R. R. Martin's *A Song of Ice and Fire*, and others.

All of these reflect a common goal of continued monitoring and maintenance of the property's continuity, which requires, for all intents and purposes, treating these various strategies as living processes or documents.

The Transmedia Intellectual Property Bible as a Static Document

There is a strong and natural desire to view the bibles as static reference documents created at the start of production and then simply referenced throughout its course. Television series showrunners know the value of, for all intents and purposes, creating a new bible for each new season. The new bible could, in some ways, be viewed as a continuation of the old bible, but it is also in many ways a "reset" of the previous season's bible. Sometimes it contains repeated information, sometimes it does not. Sometimes it is an expansion of the prior bible, and frankly we think this is the best approach. We'll get to why in a moment, but hopefully, with everything that's been said, it's beginning to becoming self-evident.

It is highly unlikely that the transmedia storytelling franchise you are working on is static. More than likely it is constantly evolving with each new property, product, expression, or tie-in created. New ideas surface and are absorbed, existing characters re-defined (perhaps even retconned), settings expanded, and so on. These new or revised elements could come from the creators of the mothership, or they could come from the creators of these ancillary projects. Regardless of the source, the common element is change. And change is good.

Fearing Change

We're going to resist our baser nature here to throw in quotes from *Star Wars* and *Dune* about fear, but a transmedia property requires a degree of openness that is unlike any other process, and quite frankly, can be pretty scary. We're leaving a discussion of the mechanics and process of managing the transmedia intellectual property bible and platform bibles to a different section of the book, but we wanted to take a little time to talk about the openness required from a conceptual and creative standpoint.

The approval process in franchise management exists to insure the consistency and integrity of the brand. Even though the *Star Trek* novel-verse stories aren't canon, the approval coordinators know to make sure that the material in the book will be inherently *Star Trek*. There's room for a variety of styles and tones within *Star Trek*, but there are things that feel like *Star Trek* and things that do not.

Licensees of a property historically have a great deal of flexibility within their universe, but have little in terms of the franchise. Very very rarely does the material created in ancillary or tie-in material contribute to the canon or official continuity of the franchise. It's a form of deniability – yes, that content in that video game was kinda cool, and maybe someone else will pick up on it, but unless it appears in the mothership (core property) it's not canon. Makes sense, right?

Here's the problem: In true transmedia storytelling, everything is canon.

Was that the sound of your sphincter tightening we heard? Most likely, and with good reason, but let's break this down.

We've said, an annoying number of times, that transmedia storytelling is the art of telling one story across many forms, across many stories – one story, many worlds. And we've been serious about that: one story. If you have multiple continuities, you have multiple worlds, multiple universes, multiple stories. There isn't a single master story running through all of your properties.

To have a true transmedia storytelling property there has to be one, single, master story that is told in all of these mediums, across all of these platforms, sequentially and in parallel, all the time. That means that every story, every character, every setting, every object, every event, every betrayal, every romance, every aside, every friendship, every snark, every culture, every creature, every … everything… is canon.

Now you can tighten that sphincter … and release.

Reality Sets in

"Everything is canon" is an ideal, probably not an achievable reality, especially for a giant transmedia property. For something relatively small scale, with a mothership/core property and a handful of ancillary releases a year it could be manageable. But for something potentially on the scale of *Star Trek* or *Star Wars*, it's probably not. For those giant properties the reality is that canon and continuity can be maintained within specific slices of the pie, but not overall. The shear logistics of managing all of the continuity elements, approving them, informing all the relevant licensees of any changes or updates in a timely manner, reconciling conflicts trivial and large … just process of continuity management itself is just too big. And that's just the management process … the creative review and approval process alone is an even more formidable task. Every addition to the canon needs to be reviewed and considered for its long-term and short-term impact, on its consistency and aesthetics, on its style and feel, and whether it simply makes sense or not.

And there's the question of who gets to decide if something becomes part of the canon or not? Where does that authority lie? We've left that to Chapter 7, and instead continue on here about the process.

The Bible as a Dynamic Digital Document

If we run with the idea that everything is canon, then nothing related to the guidance of the franchise can be static. With each new creation, the franchise expands. New elements are added constantly.

This means that the idea that the transmedia intellectual property bible is a thick manuscript that gets shuffled around on your desk with all of the other random bits of production paper is outdated. That probably works for the early days of the property, before production begins on multiple expressions of the property and new material, other than what was in the original version of the transmedia intellectual property bible, starts being created. Once things go live, the process has to change.

If you look at the transmedia intellectual property bible as the guidance creative document for the creation of the mothership/core property, and any subsequent properties, and the various universe and production bibles as guidance and direction for the implementation of those properties, you have to look at something we're going to call the continuity bible that represents the current state of the property, as a whole. When Gregg Nations or Leland Chee talk about what they do, they talk about a database as their primary tool, and there's a reason for that. Your continuity bible has to be a database, or something similar.

Big, thick paper documents are hard to work with. A good table of contents only gets you so far, and even a really well done index can be difficult to slog through. Digital databases are perfect for things like a continuity bible because they are searchable, easily updatable, and can be worked on by more than one person. Though it is well-concealed, the websites like Memory Alpha and *LOST*pedia are basically just online databases.

We've talked about the technical specifics of some of these options in Chapter 7, but for now let's just accept that the technology exists and that it is friendlier than you think. A well-constructed database is simple to search, and easy to update, and the current state of the "document" is accessible to everyone (or at least everyone that you want to give access to).

The hardest part, frankly, about maintaining a digital database as the continuity bible isn't the maintenance of the database itself, from a technology standpoint, but rather maintaining the data within in.

Maintaining the Continuity Bible Consistently

Whether you decide to go with a big single document or digital database continuity bible, the most difficult part in maintaining will be keeping the information inside it up to date. The reality is that unless it is someone's job to update the information nobody is going to do it.

It's not that they don't want to (some may), but for the most part everyone who is creating the information that needs to be added to the continuity bible is pretty much busy creating that information. They're also not creating it in a manner that makes it easy for them to just simply add the information to the continuity bible. The relevant information needs to be extracted from a screenplay, novel manuscript, game story document, or whatever kind of document it is, and compiled in a way that facilitates adding it to the continuity bible. For example, if whoever is entering the data is documenting an event, they need to generate a description of the event, indicate where the reference is coming from (what screenplay, which novel, etc.) including page number references, list which characters are present, where it happens, when it happens, and so on. That information then has to be physically added to the database in what is probably a multi-step process. Additionally, many databases support searchable "tags" (very much like the topic tags or keywords seen with articles on blogs or websites) that make it easy to locate information. So, a particular event could be tagged with "Rebel Victory," "Military Battle," "Major Death," or any number of appropriate tags.

With all due respect to writers, and we know of what we speak, not many writers think this way, and even more of them find the task of breaking down information (especially for their own writing) in this manner mind numbing and to be avoided at all costs. The right person needs to be recruited for this task and they need to show a degree of technical savvy, attention to detail, and a willingness to deconstruct the information and enter it in the database in as non-biased a manner as possible. What do we mean by that? Well, some of this kind of information, especially when it refers to mysteries, or character motivation, needs to be entered in as neutral a manner as possible, with no speculation or "spin" on the part of the enterer. They also need to have no creative stake in the process, again so that no bias slips in during data entry.

They do, however, have to be very knowledgeable about the property, and understand it, since (depending on the property) it could be quite fantastical, technical, jargon-filled, or just make no damn sense at all on the surface. This is a difficult balance in that they are ideally someone who is engaged with and passionate about the property, but doesn't have that bias we just mentioned and can resist the urge to interpret or inject themselves into the data.

Part 4

End Matters

Chapter 11
Wrap Up

This book is intended as a gateway drug. For those of you who haven't taken television seriously in the last decade, or thought video games were for adolescent boys only, or think good cinema is only made in Europe, this book should in part serve as an introduction to a broader culture and provide some perspective on the state of media today.

In order to think about a transmedia property you have to think in a very broad and eclectic terms. The journey this book begins is the process of reading and thinking about what lies at the heart of the most successful transmedia properties and how they manage to create a universe that supported a wide variety of expressions that connected to multiple audiences. Most of the successes have been, up to this point, at least part serendipity. That will always be true, but what producers and creatives can do is give themselves a better chance to develop, produce and manage a property in a way that has been informed by the past successes, by the present culture and by the emerging technologies. That's the real challenge of transmedia storytelling; it is like juggling chainsaws, really exciting but really dangerous.

The properties that stand out like *Star Trek*, *LOST*, *Harry Potter*, *Star Wars* and *Mass Effect* do so not just because of the quality and depth of storytelling/engagement but because of the commitment of their audiences and perhaps as importantly the commitment of their fans. How fans fit into this equation, and how industry decides to deal with them is one of the many interesting but unanswered questions going forward.

There are other questions, too. When will audiences have more choice in their narrative paths, just like a *Choose Your Own Adventure* book? Will other stories beyond the more nerdy genres rush into a transmedia storytelling space with some huge success? Is the act of conceptualizing and executing a multi-platform transmedia storytelling strategy from scratch just too ambitious for reality? How many years will it be before the blending of traditional, but contemporary media with transmedia storytelling and marketing techniques becomes so ubiquitous that anything that isn't transmedia is considered "out of touch"? And of course, who will make the next big transmedia storytelling property success and redefine all of the rules and show the rest of us how it's done?

You?

Appendix A
Motion Picture Platform Bible

Though traditionally they might have had narrowly focused bibles for a specific aspect of production (like a production design bible), film projects generally have not had *story* bibles. This is partly because the story within a single screenplay is small (compared to other media platforms), tightly focused and often initially written by one person (or perhaps two collaborators working together). In those cases where there are a number of writers on a project, they are usually rewriting or building off of previous script versions and also being closely guided via development notes from the producer.

As alluded to earlier, the idea of a bible as a guide for the development of consistent and cohesive character and story is a concept that first gained prominence in serialized storytelling, specifically in television. While a film's producers and writers may develop backstory, character bios and other materials that reflect their thinking and research on the film's story, these materials have rarely been formalized in any sort of guidebook. However, there have always been ways in which producers, writers and filmmakers document that material and research, such as the synopses, treatments, proposals, outlines and scripts (often multiple drafts) mentioned earlier.

In addition, the notes the writer receives from the development executive or producer shepherding the project can be an important document in the development of the storyworld. These notes are often written in memo form and distributed to those most closely associated with the project and/or their supervisors. The notes become a record of story decisions made and rationales for those, whether successful or not, so that if the development spans into years (which often happens in filmmaking and, yes, transmedia), there is less danger of reinventing the wheel or duplicating past mistakes.

The one place where we might traditionally find a formalized bible document in film is when we anticipate making a series of films. In this case, we might create what is often referred to in the film industry as a franchise bible, a guiding document for the producing, creative and marketing teams, and not surprisingly, this bible might look a bit like the story bible for television, treating each film in the franchise a bit like an episode of a TV series, with the crucial addition of sections that address how the film franchise will be marketed and promoted to its target audience. But historically, that's as close as we've gotten to a formal bible in filmmaking.

Transmedia is changing that, though, and developing a film platform bible for the film components of an intellectual property has become critical. With the development of the fourth "*Bourne*" film, Variety reported in June of 2010 that Tony Gilroy, the writer who wrote the first three films, had been contracted to write a franchise bible (another example of retroactive bible creation). This means that the studio is looking to tell other stories within that universe, as reflected in the description of the fourth film: "[*The Bourne Legacy* is] centered on a new CIA operative in the universe based on Robert Ludlum's novels." (http://www.imdb.com/title/tt1194173/ accessed 6/30/12). Though the studio is calling Gilroy's bible a franchise bible, and as the writer for the first four films, he's probably the next best guy after Ludlum to write it, it is in effect a film platform bible. Of course, its focus may be broader than just the films (past and future), in effect becoming something more akin to a universe or intellectual property bible, providing an over-arching guide to the backstory, rules, characters and possible future stories or storyworlds to be developed over multiple platforms, but for now, let's assume that the studio's use of franchise is film-centric – a film platform bible.

The film platform bible lays out a developed progression of narrative material for the films in our transmedia property – universe elements relevant to (or to be explored in) the movies, plot developments, and their placement over the series of individual films, identifying in particular story material that needs to be iterated in *each* movie. This includes narrative elements that set up future films, build off material from previous films, and that feed into – or out of – the other platforms' stories.

For example, if we could go back in time and create a film platform bible for the *X-Files* movies, we'd consider not just the stories to be told in the feature films but their relationship to the TV series and the games. In fact, though it may not have been formalized as a bible per se, those very considerations were taken into account for the first film (*Fight the Future*), carefully developing and placing it within the television series' plotline and timeline.

The film platform bible ideally establishes a clear relationship between the films and the story parts they need to convey. Such a bible might look very similar to a television story bible (Chapter 4) or an intellectual property bible (Chapter 2), with a description of the overall concept behind the films as a group, biographies for those characters who will appear in one, some or all of the films, a synopsis of the overall film series' narrative (or the larger story covered in the films as a group) plus additional story synopses or broad outlines for each individual film installment in the series.

As part of our intellectual property bible, the film platform bible summarizes key narrative and universe considerations for the films' producers and writers. We can draw from many of those documents that are traditionally created during the development of a feature film, but we can also draw elements from other platforms' bibles.

Each intellectual property's film series will have different and unique traits and requirements (for example, you may plan to make only one film in your transmedia property while another transmedia-maker plans to make ten films for his), so consider the following as a sort of starting point or a default template; your own project may be best expressed with fewer, more or different sections in its film platform bible:

Title Page
The title page should include the name that designates the overall film franchise, the name and logo for the copyright holder of the intellectual property, and the words "film platform bible" (or "film franchise bible"). Your title page might also include a tagline or logline.

You will want to make sure that it's clear the films are part of a larger intellectual property universe if it's not obvious from the property's film franchise name. This could be as simple as a distinguishing logo (if the intellectual property has one).

The title page might also include a tagline or even the image of a mocked up onesheet (or movie poster) for the film.

Table of Contents
All the info that was on the title page should be at the top of the table of contents page, followed by "Table of Contents" and a listing of all the individual sections that are contained in the document.

Overview
The bible might start with an overview of the film's context, a couple of paragraphs that reiterate the premise of the intellectual property and specifically the portions of the intellectual property that will be expressed in through the film franchise. In some ways, this might be a bit like the short version of the synopsis in the game platform bible – it's meant to spark our curiosity or enthusiasm for the project.

Concept
This section addresses the overall series of films and is a summary of the goals for the films as part of the larger transmedia story. You could include a discussion of how the films will fuel interest in other iterations of the intellectual property or the ways in which the films will resonate with or link to those other iterations. Much like a film proposal document, this is a one-page summary of the primary theme or themes (one sentence), primary goals and rationale (several paragraphs) and primary audience (one or two sentences) for the film series.

The Films
The title (or working title) of each film is listed, followed by a logline or one-sentence summary of that individual film's essential conflict and scenario, serving as a concise summary of the story's plot by identifying the protagonist, main conflict and if possible hinting at the resolution in approximately 25 words. You might even see thumbnail mockups of potential movie posters that provide a visual shorthand representation of each film.

Synopsis
For each film that we plan to make, we need to develop a four-paragraph one-page summary of that film's narrative. We do a synopsis for each film rather than a franchise synopsis because our films are not the sole expression of the larger intellectual property but rather intertwined with stories being told in other platforms. If we anticipate a number of films in the series, we might not try to synopsize all of them, but just those initial films that will go into production first, adding a more detailed synopsis for each of the series' later films as those are further developed.

Plot Points
In addition to a synopsis for each film, we will gradually add a labeled beat sheet, step outline or a diagram that lists key plot developments or turning points in the narrative for each film in the franchise. This allows us to see the

progression, scale and proportion of the film story. Some producers prefer treatments instead, but generally, the bible is meant to be a reference guide, so a beat sheet is more effective and easier to read and grasp quickly. The plot points for each film are probably best attached to or immediately following the individual synopsis for that film.

Backstory

Like other bibles, the backstory is an overview of the intellectual property's universe and storyworlds, especially those aspects (characters, settings, etc.) that are part of the film stories, and a summary of the rules that apply specifically to those stories, plus any additional rules or backstory information that will fill in and/or further develop the storyworld(s) of the films.

Highlights

Ideally, the bible includes a list or brief description of any element that is unique to each film's story and therefore a potential enticement for audiences of the larger transmedia property to see the film(s). Perhaps this particular film will reveal an important piece of backstory or character biography that will shape how the audience will view other platforms' iterations of the intellectual property. You may have highlights for the entire films series but ideally there is at least one property highlight in each individual film – otherwise, you're just treading water. There has to be a reason why an audience is going to want (or need) to move from the television series, to use *X-Files'* example, and to see the movie. Or they may want to see another film in the series, which *The Terminator* franchise has been pretty good at accomplishing (though the rumored original ending for *Terminator Salvation* would have been the highlight of all highlights).

One highlight is sufficient, and there might be two in any one of the films, but if you have more than three in a single film, you may be trying to do too much in terms of the scale and proportion of each feature film.

Marketing Strategy

Because film marketing is often linked with the studios that produce films, we may need to give some consideration of how a studio's marketing team will integrate with our larger intellectual property marketing strategy.

Appendix B
Television Platform Bible

Historically, television series have had what's called a show bible, a reference guide to assist the writers in maintaining narrative continuity and character consistency for episodic screen presentation of story. Though there is a general format and certain elements or sections that you'll find in all television story bibles, there is also room for a certain degree of variation and creativity; for example, the *Dark Skies* show bible looks like a top-secret file of conspiracy evidence including government memos, investigative reports, magazine covers and other cryptic documents. This made the actual show bible itself consistent with the universe and stories *Dark Skies* was telling.

Just as with the intellectual property bible covered earlier, the following elements may be sequenced differently or omitted depending on their relevance to your particular property. Do not think of this so much as a template, as a list of things to consider and then use those that help express your episodic story the best.

Title Page

The title page should include the name of the television series, the name and logo for the copyright holder of the intellectual property, and the words "television platform bible."

You may also want to include a tagline.

You may want to make sure that it's clear the series is part of a larger intellectual property universe; for example, we might say on the cover page of *The Sarah Connor Chronicles* that this is "A Terminator Series" (in the same way that *S. Darko* is identified as a Donnie Darko Story) or *Terminator: The Sarah Connor Chronicles*.

Table of Contents

Your table of contents page lists in order the main sections that comprise your television platform bible (or show bible) but it may not include page numbers, particularly if you anticipate regularly adding material to specific sections of the bible as the series progresses. All the info that was on the title page should be at the top of the table of contents page, followed by "Table of Contents" and your listing of the individual sections contained in the document.

Series Concept

The bible may start with a teaser or brief backstory and context (or world) for the series. If that's the case, this section might include the mythology, main characters for the series, the basic conflict and a hint of the mysteries and issues that will engage the audience. As with all things in media, brevity is encouraged, so this section may only be one to three pages maximum.

The concept section may end with a paragraph or two that places the television series or webseries in relationship to the audience's real world experiences: current cultural or historical events that might inform the audience's interpretation or enjoyment of the show. For example, the creators of a show like *Battlestar Galactica* might use these paragraphs to note the ways in which the series will reflect anxieties and ethical debates about the Iraq War.

Another approach uses the opening series concept section to describe the goals in presenting this series and then has a separate backstory section that lays out the world and backstory more fully either right before or right after the synopses (see the third element on backstory below).

Characters

Your bible usually includes biographies and backstories for each of the primary or regularly recurring characters. These bios can range from a paragraph to several pages, depending on the importance of the character and the type of story you're telling. The goal in creating the bio is to provide physical, psychological and sociological information about the characters that will inform their actions and behaviors within the storyworld. These are not arbitrary "facts" but rather traits or characteristics that will help keep the characters consistent and comprehensible for the audience (as well as the creative team). If the series runs for multiple seasons, you will need to add new information to these bios as events change their circumstances episode to episode.

Season Arcs and Episode Synopses

Next, your bible needs to include synopses of each projected season and a representative sample of specific episodes from the first season.

Season Synopsis

A season synopsis might read much like a film treatment, describing the over-arching story for an individual season as if it were a complete and (somewhat) self-contained story. In this case, each season may be given a title much like an author might title the chapters in a book. The audience will probably never know what these season titles are – they are a guide or focus for the writers and producers. For example, the *Dark Skies* television bible treated the two-hour pilot as a separate chapter of the story, "The Awakening," and then named season 1 "Official Denial," Season 2 "Progenitor" and Season 3 "Cloak of Fear." Each season's synopsis may be two to five pages long, depending on the complexity of the season's storylines.

Another approach is to break the season down into separate but intertwining arcs. The bible for *Battlestar Galactica* describes four major arcs for its first season that include specific plot developments (such as finding evidence of a place called Earth) and character arcs (such as Baltar's rise to power.)

Again, the approach you take will depend on your specific intellectual property and the story you are telling with episodic television.

Episode Synopsis

Each episode of the first half-season to first full-season, depending on how the project will air, is described in a couple of pages.

Early in the process, you may simply list each episode with a one- or two sentence *logline*. Episode loglines are slightly different in television than in other media because at the least, they must encapsulate both the A and B stories for that episode.

Eventually, though, you will probably expand that logline into a slightly longer summary of the episode's story – a one- or two-paragraph single-spaced summary of each episode's story.

Following the summary, there will be a short description for each of the relevant elements in the episode, such as:

Locations seen in the episode (not literally where the crew will film the show but where the story takes place).

Characters or the main characters featured in the episodes. Some series do not have every major character in every episode.

Secondary characters that may only be appearing in this episode or only appear in the series occasionally (sometimes labeled secondary cast).

Activities or the actions of the characters presented in the episode.

Costumes might be noted if these are critical for the story, such as a superhero costume.

Special highlights of the episode that tie in to what makes this world or these characters special; for example, *Avatar: The Last Air Bender*'s bible details the specific bending that will be seen in the episode.

Highlights or general set pieces, sequences or key plot points of the story, in effect, a brief summary – often presented as a detailed list – of the major story or plot information that has to be presented in this episode.

Animals that appear in the episode, especially if animals have a specific narrative or aesthetic role in the series.

Props seen in the episode, especially those that help propel the story forward.

Vehicles or modes of transportation that we see in the episode.

Guest talent or guest stars in the episode.

Quotes or sample dialogue, phrases that are significant to either the episode or the series, often with thematic or marketing implications, that must be included in the episode. Use this section sparingly; you're not trying to list all the dialogue, just a few lines that are important.

Now that you have one episode synopsized, you want to do this for the first set of episodes which will establish the series, at least half a season's worth. This collection of synopses will help your team see the general scale of story material per episode, where the story is going from episode to episode and how the season's arc is exemplified in each episode.

You are not trying to do an episode synopsis for the entire series, just the first season or a significant chunk of the first season, which is usually a minimum of six to 12 episodes and no more than 22 episodes, depending on what number of episodes constitute a complete season and how many of those you want (or the network requires you) to plan out before you start.

As your bible develops further, you may find that some of your episode synopses are followed by a scene outline or a summary of the episode comprised of brief descriptions of each scene in order as it will appear in the episode. This kind of outline might add another four to five pages, the exact length depending on whether your series is comprised of 30-minute, 1-hour, 90-minute or 2-hour episodes.

Backstory

If your bible began with a series concept section that did not include substantial storyworld information, you may want to have a section dedicated just to backstory for the world and characters. Depending on your intellectual property and specific series, you may want to put this backstory section before the season arcs and episode synopses section, especially if you feel the backstory information is crucial to know before reading about the season arcs and specific episodes. If the backstory section is not critical for understanding the season arcs or specific episodes, then it may make more sense to place it after the synopses.

Much of the television series' backstory information draws from the intellectual property bible's overall summary of backstory. Often times you also need to expand, further create or more fully develop certain aspects of that larger universe that are especially relevant for the episodic series. Of course, in doing this, you may need to go back to the original intellectual property bible and add your new material to it so that the producers of the other transmedia expressions maintain continuity with what you are doing in the television series. As you can see, the bibles are living documents but also at times interconnected with the bibles being used in other iterations of the intellectual property.

Rules

In this section of your Television Platform Bible, highlight key underlying assumptions or rules for the world that you've just described in your backstory. These rules are usually expressed as easy-to-read lists, quickly summing up important facts that affect the storyworld and how the characters interact within that world. Obviously these rules are informed by and may reiterate rules from the overall intellectual property. Any redundancy is okay, because the writers hired for the episodic series are going to refer to this Television Platform Bible and may not even see the larger Intellectual Property Bible.

Appendix C
Video Game Platform Bible

We may be creating a series of gaming experiences, ranging from the casual easy-in/easy-out to highly immersive extended narratives. Unlike television or film, where delivery formats, infrastructure and technological processes are pretty much predetermined, game design requires a host of considerations beyond just the story elements to be used. Traditionally, there's been nothing that is the equivalent of a game platform bible in game development, but there is a document that in some ways serves much the same purpose. We're going to introduce you to that document, the game vision guide, and then look at three other documents common to game development, the game design guide, the technical design guide, and the art style/production guide. Another way of looking at this would be to say that all four documents combined constitute the game platform bible. A really, really thick game platform bible… We're going to spend the most time with the game design guide because it tends to be the densest of all the documents.

The whole goal in creating a bible is to provide your creative and production teams a reference guide that they will actually want to use. Pages and pages of dense text and poor organization work against your teams' ability to quickly and easily find information relevant to their part of the game development. And more than just about any other platform bible, the game platform bible (in whatever its form) will have a lot of information to convey. Good organization, clearly marked sections that consist of lists, charts, diagrams, images and short blocks of text will ultimately be more useful. Unfortunately, how to put it all together is mostly up to you. There are no standard document templates in video game development because, well, quite frankly there is no one way to deliver a game experience.

Again, just to reiterate, the goal of this section like the rest of the chapter is not to teach you how to be a game designer or developer, but to expose you to working practices and methodologies so that you know what you are looking at and can have appropriate expectations and conversations. The goal is not to incorporate every single element listed below but to choose those that are relevant to the project. There will be times when new sections need to be created that are not listed below because none of the sections described adequately addresses the game experience being developed.

Note also that these are internal documents for the rights-holders and team-members, not the general public.

Game Vision Guide

The game vision guide is a high-level description of the story/theme, plot, characters, setting and style/tone of the game. Sound familiar? When we say high level, however, it's not as high level as describing the universe or world, but rather is focused on the video game itself. It should, of course, reflect the key story elements, but may not be as broad in its depiction. Also, the description of the elements need not be explicitly called out in their own sections, though often they are, but must be addressed in due course in the document as appropriate. Note that the vision document is a persuasive, rather than a technical document. For all intents and purposes its goal is to sell the reader on the absolute coolness of the game. All vision documents are different, but here are the usual sections:

Introduction/Prologue

The Introduction/Prologue sets up the narrative of the game, explaining the backstory in an evocative manner that leads up to the starting moment of the game.

Development/Property History

If the game has a legacy or inheritance, say it's the sequel to a best-seller, or is based on a notable intellectual property, describe that history here.

Game Overview

Next, describe the actual game and gameplay, not the story. What does the player do? What kind of characters are there? How does the environment or setting affect gameplay? What are some of the challenges the player-character has to overcome? Why will this be fun/engaging/exciting/scary/sexy/funny ... whatever the game is supposed to be?

Pillars

Literally think of the pillars as the most important elements that support the game. A pillar could be gameplay, setting, visual design, technology, character, or story related. The pillars are what make the game remarkable, notable, and different from the other games out there ... they're also the things that players should be excited about before the game's release, and talking about once they can play. In some ways, the pillars are also what the project is betting on will make the game the must-have game when it releases.

Game Story

What happens in the game? Describe the story that's played out as a narrative – tell it to the reader. If there are branching stories or alternative endings, tell one version and then talk about the alternatives. Don't hide anything here – lay it out for everyone to read and appreciate.

Note, however, that if this document is going to be released prior to the game, as a marketing tool perhaps, be sure to remove this section before distributing. You want your internal team to know what's going on, but not your audience.

Game Design Guide

First, a note about terminology: in the video game development industry the term *game design document* is that standard way to refer to this document. We're going to attempt to start a minor revolution here and advocate the use of the term *game design guide* for one simple reason. The term game design *document* sounds inflexible and unyielding, when in reality the contents of the document are a guide, a direction, for the production since the game design and associated gameplay *will change* as it is implemented, tested, and iterated and revised. We've seen too many projects fail because the game design document is viewed as an infallible, unalterable document, and that's a terrible mindset for a production to have. If you are laughing and shaking your head at our naiveté, feel free to pick up a pen and replace the word "guide" with "document" throughout the rest of this chapter.

Traditionally, the game design guide is created during preproduction and then updated and maintained throughout the course of production. Ideally, all questions related to the game design are answerable in the game design guide, but that is never the case (which is another reason we advocate guide over document). As the document is created, an attempt needs to be made at full inclusiveness because this is the document that is used to create the production and technical schedule, so in many ways if something isn't in the game design guide it's not in the game.

A final note before we get into the document itself ... it may not be a document. Different development studios use different technical solutions for creating and maintaining their documentation. Some create giant master documents and some create multiple documents that when combined create the master document. Some use collaborative documentation solutions, like a Wiki (which we talked about earlier), and others use even more esoteric methods. So, when we're talking about these documents we're talking more about the contents rather than any specific manuscript delivery mechanism.

Title Page

The title page includes the name of the game, and if it's not obvious from the game name, the title of the primary intellectual property, the name and logo for the copyright holder of the intellectual property, the name of the development studio and publisher and the title, "Game Design Guide." It also needs an indication of which version of the document this is. Hopefully there's some version numbering system in use so that stakeholders and team members know that they're not looking at an outdated version of the document.

You may also want to include a tagline and the primary author of the document on the title page.

Table of Contents

Your next page is a list of all the sections that make up the document in order of appearance. If the document is electronic, each entry should be a hyperlink that allows the reader to jump to that section. For paper documents you will probably want to create clear tabs or dividers that allow users to quickly flip to the section they need.

All the info that was on the title page should be at the top of the table of contents page, followed by "Table of Contents" and your listing of all the individual sections contained in the document.

Design History

Because there are so many elements at play (pun intended) in a game document, there will be multiple revisions throughout its development and production. A design history section can be an effective way to list any major changes in the document by listing each version number/date with a brief description of the changes made in that version, and who made that change. The listing should be in reverse-chronological order so that the most recent versions are noted first.

Game Overview

The overview concentrates on the tangible considerations, interactive features and the ways in which the player will experience the game rather than on story elements, which get discussed in more depth later in the document.

Sometimes, the game vision guide is dropped into the game design guide right up front. If not, the game overview section generally includes the following subsections:

- **Concept** or a brief overview of the key premise of the game, its story and appeal. This is sometimes referred to as a vision statement.
- **System requirements** (both minimal and optimal/recommended).
- **Genre** which in this case usually means the type of game rather than story genre, whether it's a puzzle game, a platform game, etc. If the narrative elements fit a particular story genre, you could make mention of it here but more likely you would include that info in the concept paragraph.
- **Target audience** or key demographic information for the primary audience you plan to market the game to.
- **Game flow summary** or a description of how the player will move through the game, both through the interface and the game itself.
- **Look and feel** or a description of the visual style of the game and the way in which the player might describe the sensory experience of playing the game.
- **Project scope** or a summary of the scale of the game, listing the number of locations, levels, non-player characters and/or weapons.

Gameplay and Mechanics

This section of the bible briefly describes the various elements that relate directly to how the player experiences playing the game. Gameplay includes elements like the game progression, the structure (whether mission, challenge, puzzle, etc.), objectives or goals for the player and how the player experiences the flow of the game (ingeniously called, game flow).

The mechanics part of this may be one of the larger sections in the bible, detailing both the explicit and implicit rules or underlying assumptions that guide the game both in terms of play and in terms of story. This might include discussion of physics or how the physical universe will work or be manifested in the game. Multiple subsections could address how movement, objects (picking up, carrying, dropping), actions (walking, running, shooting), talking, combat and menu screens look or operate.

In addition, mechanics would include replay and savings options as well as Easter eggs and/or cheats to add additional pleasure or a sense of discovery for the player.

Story Bible

This section of the game design guide summarizes those elements from the intellectual property universe that directly relate to the game's story, setting and characters. If the game design guide becomes so big as to be unwieldy, the story bible may be separated out into its own document. In that case, there would still be a section here in the general game design guide that succinctly addresses all the elements listed below and make note of the fact that there is more detail in the separate story bible volume.

Synopsis

There may be two different synopses for the game's narrative: a short description that describes the game in three or four sentences and a long description that is in effect a high-level written walkthrough that summarizes how the player will encounter and interact with other characters and locations, perform tasks and learn the story content.

Backstory

The game's backstory draws from the intellectual property bible and further develops those aspects of the universe that relate directly to the storyworld of the game. This backstory provides a context in which events in the game take place as well as help identify their relationship to narrative events in other media iterations of the intellectual property. Sometimes this information is referred to as the scenario, where the story takes place and the background and rules of that setting.

Plot Elements

In gaming especially, this might be a combination of diagram or graph and a list of major story events that indicates how they are connected to each other and potentially how they link to story events in other iterations of the intellectual property across multiple mediums.

Game Progression

As with plot elements, the game progression might be expressed as a flow chart or diagram rather than text. This becomes another way of seeing how the story is incorporated into or serves as a foundation for the overall game experience.

License Considerations

Any issues related to licensing or intellectual property rights or potential branding considerations are noted here; this section may tie directly to the overall Intellectual Property Bible and only include any considerations unique to the game's development.

Cut-Scenes

The content and preproduction work for any cut-scenes needs to be described in this section. Even though these cut-scenes are sometimes referred to as cinematics or in-game movies, they really are more like the scene in a film than a short film, only telling a small part of the story, advancing the plot and providing narrative information that connects to what has come before and what comes next. The cut-scenes hone in on a narrowly defined narrative event, a single building block in a larger story, and each cut-scene is usually broken down into subsections that address:

Characters: Often referred to as actors in game design documents, the term "actor" can be confusing because it means the person performing the role of the character in film, television and other media. Now that our story links with other mediums, and to make communication more consistent across the various teams in those mediums, we recommend using the term characters instead of actors when describing the key people, beings and creatures that populate the game's storyworld. In this section of our cut-scenes section, we want to identify those characters who will be in this particular scene.

Description: In a paragraph or two, this section details the story content that has to be delivered in the cut-scene and is almost like a mini-treatment, telling the story in third-person present tense in such a way that we can follow and understand "what happens" in the scene.

Storyboard: Just like films, cut-scenes are usually storyboarded in sequential panels, much like a graphic novel would look, in order to help the team fully visualize how the story material will be presented on screen to the player. The decisions about framing (sometimes referred to as camera placement), lighting, production design (background, costumes, color pallet, etc.) and other visual elements are all a part of the storyboarding process.

Script: Though it usually looks nothing like a film or television script, we still need to create a blueprint for how the story progresses for the viewer/user. Game scripts often look more like a flow chart or a combination of diagrams and text, with lists thrown in for good measure, than a master scene script or shooting script (used in film), but the intent is the same – communicate the story and narrative arc.

Once these steps for the first cut-scene are done, they will be repeated for every other cut-scene in the game, in order and numbered chronologically.

Game World

The game world section of the bible needs to detail the general look and feel of world itself, drawing from elements described in the intellectual property bible and expounding upon those to create as fully a realized game storyworld as possible. It will usually do these by setting or areas where the gameplay will take place. This might look like a series of descriptions for each environment, numbered in order. For example, it might label the first setting as area #1 and then follow that with a general description (or overview of the setting), physical characteristics (or specific details that relate to the look and feel of that setting), a list of levels that use that area and connections to other areas.

Once it's done that for area #1, it moves on to area #2 and continues describing the world environment by environment until all the settings for gameplay or character actions/interactions are listed and described.

Characters

Each major character of the game is then succinctly described in the equivalent of one to three paragraphs. The description usually touches on the most pertinent aspects of the character's backstory, personality or psychological traits, appearance and physical characteristics, animations, relevance to the game story, relationship to other characters and statistics.

For ease of use, this information is usually categorized, and you might see age, weight and height simply listed, two or three sentences labeled physical description, another four or five sentences labeled character description (including backstory specific to this character as well as personality traits), advantages or several skills the character has in the gameplay and disadvantages to the character in gameplay (such as low hit points or slow).

Depending on the complexity of the character or the game, it may decided that the character description should instead be divided into two sections, one on attributes (or personality traits) and the other labeled backstory (sometimes referred to as the character's background). It might also include a separate section in the character bios for weapons if the character is associated with or can only operate certain weapons in the game.

Levels

In a way, levels can be thought of as similar to episodes in a television series or web series (the *Doom* bible actually calls them episodes). Each level is summarized in terms of story materials and key elements needed for that level. The resulting synopsis for each episode may be several pages long, depending on the complexity of the level. Each of the elements below may start its own new page so that specific info is quick to find by simply scanning the label at the top of each page. The specific order of these elements or even which ones appear in the bible will depend on the game being created.

Synopsis

The synopsis may run anywhere from one to five paragraphs and summarizes the story events or character activities that take place in this particular level.

Characters

The main characters who appear in this level are listed first. This list may be text or it may be a picture of the character. Then other characters who will appear in this level are then listed. Some notes as to exactly how these characters are used may be included. These might include how other players will look in multiplayer games as well as all beings or creatures the player could encounter on this level.

Highlights

This section provides a listing and description of those elements that are unique to the particular episode or level. In the first level, this might be quite detailed because it's establishing the game's overall setting, which will not repeat in every level. In addition, its identifying cinematics, specific setting elements in this particular level (such as buildings or structures the player will encounter), a list of object graphics (such as weapons, gettable items, animations, walls, doors, etc.) and sounds needed for this level to be a fully realized experience for the player. Some of this info may be expounded upon or appear in a section on physical descriptions.

Introductory Material

This section describes or details the set up the player will experience at the start of the level or mission, providing a narrative context for the gameplay. This might be a cut-scene or a mission briefing or a prologue – whatever best serves as initial entry point into the game.

Objectives

The objectives for the player in this level need to be clearly identified.

Physical Description

This expounds upon or more thoroughly describes some of the information listed in the highlights section.

Map

Yep, this is an actual map of the level, providing an overview of where the player can roam in this episode and the placement of items or beings he or she can encounter.

Critical Path

This identifies the main progression of player actions to successfully complete this level.

Encounters

This section lists the possible encounters and interactions the player can experience on this level.

Level Walkthrough

This is a narrative walkthrough of the level as if through the eyes of the player-character.

Closing Material

Each level will generally have a closing sequence for when the player successfully completes the level and moves to the next episode or – in the last level – wins the game.

You'll see that there is a lot of story information included in the elements above, but that it is often presented in the form of lists, diagrams, images and succinct text. This allows for the document to have lots of white space, another way of saying that it feels open and easy to dip into, finding what information you need and being able to read it or understand it very quickly.

Drawing from all the levels elements we've just listed, a similar summary for each and every additional level to the game is created, numbering the levels sequentially.

Interface

The interface section describes the elements that will shape and define the sensory experience of playing the game. This section will usually address:

- Menus
- Rendering system
- Camera
- Lighting models
- Control system (or how the player controls the game)
- Audio
- Music
- Sound effects
- Help system

Artificial Intelligence

This section addresses how to design the various artificial intelligence systems that determine the way in which characters in the game interact with the player. In broad strokes, it might describe the design of the opponent AI (the active opponent that plays against the game player and therefore requires strategic decision making) and/or enemy AI (such as the villains and monsters the player might encounter) as well as non-combat characters, friendly characters and support AI (which might include player and collision detection and pathfinding).

Glossary

The glossary is a short compendium of special terminology or lingo used in the game as well as a quick reference to key creatures and beings that are unique to the game world. The glossary may include thumbnail images as well as text.

Appendices

In addition to the key elements described above, there is some logistical information that you will need to keep track of, and this is usually separated out at the end of the bible in order to be easy to find and to serve as a sort of checklist.

Asset List

The asset list is an itemization of those elements that are going to have to be created or produced for the game. These may include:

3D and 2D art: Art assets are all the visual elements that will have to be created for the game, and these assets are often further divided into a model and texture list, an animation list, a visual effects list, an interface art list and a cut-scene list, depending on the specific game that you're creating.

Sound effects: Comment assets needed in the game's sound design are environmental sounds, weapon sounds and interface sounds; each of these larger categories would then list all the specific sounds needed.

Music: The music section lists and describes the music to be created for the general background (ambient) as well as specific actions (action) or moments (victory, defeat) in the game.

Voice: This section lists each voice actor's lines along with unique identifying code for each line, and other production and recording related data. This is not written in anything resembling script format, but lists all the lines spoken in the game. It'll have a heading that says "Actor #1 lines" and then list all that character's dialogue that needs to be recorded. It will do this for each speaking role in the game. (Note that very often this section is a spreadsheet document maintained separately and then attached to the game design guide document.)

Technical Design Guide

The technical design guide is usually provided with the game design guide, but is usually a separate document because it is prepared by different team members on a different schedule.

Information often included in the technical design guide includes identification of the target hardware, development hardware and software tools, development procedures and standards, middleware, game engine, physics, graphics, networking, installation and update software, and scripting language. A large part of the technical design guide is devoted to technical implementation considerations of the elements presented in the game design guide. As such, the technical leads of the development team begin working on the technical design guide once they have a draft of the game design guide.

Art/Style Production Design Guide

The art/style production design guide is usually provided with game design guide, but it is usually a separate document because it is prepared by different team members on a different schedule.

The guide provides examples and references as the visuals for the game are created and built. Historically in game development, this has been referred to as an art bible, but teams working in film, television or webseries usually refer to this collection of images and documents as production design, and as transmedia producers, we are trying as much as possible to standardize the terms used from medium to medium so that our teams can easily communicate with each other, so we're splitting the difference somewhat.

This art/style production design guide is usually made up of:

- Concept art (examples of key settings, characters, objects or props, etc.)
- Style guides (general theoretic and tonal, as well as specific details to assure uniform look and feel in the game world)
- Characters (visual representations, not biographical info, including reference, sample, and preproduction art)
- Environments (visual representations, including reference, sample, and preproduction art)
- Cut-scenes (art and design elements specific to the cut-scenes as opposed to the general game environment)
- Production equipment and software requirements

- Production pipeline procedures and processes, such as the exact process required to get a modeled 3D asset into the game engine

A large part of the art/style production design guide is devoted to visual implementation considerations of the elements presented in the game design guide. As such, the art leads of the development team begin working on the art/style production design guide once they have a draft of the game design guide.

Appendix D

Platform Bibles for Other Forms of Storytelling

Though there is not a defined standard in developing platform bibles for novels, comics and new media, transmedia storytelling requires consideration of how to guide these various expressions of the narrative so that they maintain continuity with the other medium iterations and remain canonical. The following provide some possible guidelines to consider.

Novels

Traditionally, novel writing has been considered – more than any other medium we've discussed in this book – a solo endeavor. A bible to guide multiple writers or creative teams was not necessary because the single author could pretty much keep much of the continuity in his or her head. That's not to say that some novelists don't write stacks and stacks of documents as research and "thinking on paper" about the history of the world and characters in their novels; it's just that this material hasn't generally been shared with anyone or even much talked about.

Of course, there are times when novels do link with other properties. Initially, these were pretty straightforward adaptations – novelizations of movies especially – which didn't require a lot of consideration of continuity because the writer was in some ways transcribing the original script or film.

But what about those novels that don't adapt the material as much as insert episodes or events in to the larger storyline of the source material? As these tie-in novels became a more common practice, intellectual property holders realized that there needed to be some guidelines given to the authors of those books to help assure – or at least not substantially contradict – the continuity of the mothership.

Now with the advent of full-on transmedia storytelling, novels are not just tie-in marketing tools but ways in which specific story material or narrative events or plot points of the over-arching intellectual property universe and story get told. As a result we will see a growing need to develop guiding documents specifically for the novelists and prose writers of the property.

The current practice is to often hand the novelist excerpts from the larger intellectual property bible that apply directly to the story to be included in the novel. These novelists are often considered sort of work-for-hire who see proprietary material on a "need to know" basis.

If – or as – novels become more integrated in the larger story universe, the writers will probably need a more comprehensive view of the story material in order to contribute in meaningful ways to the larger story and its iterations across multiple platforms.

Until that time, the film platform bible may be a good starting point for considering the kinds of documentation that could be included in a novel platform bible but don't hesitate to look at all the bibles described in this book and pull the elements from any that seem most conducive to communicating the goals and story material of the narrative you want in novel form.

At the very least, you're going to want a title page, concept, synopsis, backstory and character descriptions similar to the ones used in other platform bibles.

Graphic Novels, Comics and Sequential Panel Art Expressions

More than with any of our other media, keeping things brief and highly visual in the bible and proposals for comics and graphic novels is critical. This particular bible is meant to be eye catching with lots of white space, in effect mimicking the experience of reading comics, which is after all a decidedly visual act. Your specific graphic novel bible might not incorporate all of the following elements or it may sequence them differently.

Title Page

The title page should include the name of the graphic novel or comic series, the name and logo for the copyright holder of the intellectual property, and the words "graphic novel platform bible" (or "comics platform bible"). Your title page might also include a tagline or logline.

You will want to make sure that it's clear the series is part of a larger intellectual property universe if it's not obvious from the title of the comic. For example, there's no doubt that the TV show and graphic novel *The Walking Dead* belong to the same larger intellectual property. Likewise, *Star Trek Ongoing* is clearly a part of the *Star Trek* universe. But if your title is more obscure or subtle, you may need to draw attention to the fact that this comic is indeed part of a larger story.

Table of Contents

You may not need a table of contents if your bible is really short, but for longer-running series, you may want to include one so that as the bible grows, it's easy to locate the information needed.

All the info that was on the title page should be at the top of the table of contents page, followed by "Table of Contents" and a listing of all the individual sections that are contained in the document in the order they appear.

Overview

The bible starts with an overview of the comic, a couple of paragraphs that reiterate the premise of the intellectual property and specifically the portions of the intellectual property that will be expressed in the comic version. In some ways, this might be a bit like the short version of the synopsis in the game platform bible – it's meant to tease us a bit, giving us just enough info to spark our curiosity or enthusiasm for the project.

Concept

The section about the concept is really just a summary of the goals for using a comics or graphic novel platform to tell this part of our transmedia story. You could include a discussion of how the comics will fuel interest in other iterations of the intellectual property or the ways in which the comics will resonate with those other iterations. You sometimes see this part of the bible called a project summary, but we prefer the label concept in order to be more consistent with the other platform bibles.

Synopsis

The bible will always have a brief synopsis or treatment of the story or stories that will be presented in comic form. This synopsis may be one to two pages, depending on the complexity of the overall narrative arc in the comics. For some comics, the format for a television platform bible may be more appropriate, with an overarching synopsis and then individual synopses for each "season" or in the language more commonly associated with comics, a "volume." This section generally just lays out the larger narrative of the series or the story arc for each volume; individual episode – or issue – synopses come later (see below).

Audience

Besides identifying the primary audience for the comics and graphic novel, you will want to give consideration to the ways in which this audience will participate in other iterations of the intellectual property. Are there overlaps between the comics audience and the primary audiences of other iterations, and if so, how can those be reinforced and rewarded.

Promotion

The promotion section includes not just traditional marketing strategies in the comics industry but also promotional activities such as attending comics conventions, posting to fan sites, doing interviews, etc. Comics' readers are an increasingly engaged and enthusiastic fan base, and comics-centric promotion of your intellectual property can encourage loyalty to – and interest in – other iterations of the universe besides the graphic novel or comic.

Characters

Each primary character is presented on their own single page. Rather than lengthy biographies in prose, the a comic bible's character pages have lots of white space with only a few lines or a very brief paragraph summarizing key psychological or sociological factors that determine the character's actions and behavior. Most of the page is a series of fully rendered drawings of the character, usually at least three, consisting of a full body shot, the character's face in profile and his or her face either from three-quarter view or full on.

Sample Pages

Rather than a script, script excerpt or treatment, the sample pages in a comics bible are actual artwork: a couple of pages of sequential panels that convey a particular scene, sequence or dramatic moment in the story. Depending on the narratives to be rendered in this medium, there might be several samples. For example, you may want one sample to be a sequence of panels that show our key characters in quieter moments, such as alone or in relatively calm interactions with other characters, and then another sample that portrays an action sequence.

Sample pages help your team understand the ways in which the visual aesthetics work and as importantly, the ways in which story material is compressed, expanded and portrayed in panels. Special consideration is given to the ways in which story material breaks at the end of each double-page spread, meaning the bottom of the right-hand page. How does that last row of panels encourage us to turn to the next page? For some of the more innovative digital comics, the concept of a double-page spread may be meaningless, but there are probably other transition or story bridging choices to be considered.

Issue Synopses

Much like a television series, comics are usually released in a series of episodes, or what we call issues, and graphic novels are divided into chapters. A single issue is usually 22 pages long, and the producers, writers and artists need to be aware of the scale of story that can be adequately conveyed in such a specific timeframe or page count. As we noted earlier, a series of issues that feel related because they follow one particular story arc are called a volume, whether they're literally bound together as a single volume or not. A volume in comics is similar to a season in a television series.

In terms of these synopses, you're not trying to summarize every single issue you plan to produce. You should provide synopses for no more than 12 issues, with each synopsis only a paragraph or two.

Web, Social and Viral Media Platform Bibles

Expressions of our intellectual property that are streamed through the Internet or wireless networks need to have bibles that are appropriate to their particular delivery system and the story content that is being delivered.

Webisodes

A webseries is another form of episodic screen storytelling. As such, its bible may look quite similar to a television platform bible. Elements of a webseries platform bible include:

Title Page

The title page should include the name of the webseries, the name and logo for the copyright holder of the intellectual property, and the words "webseries platform bible" (or "webisodes platform bible"). You can also include a tagline or logline for the webseries if doing so seems appropriate to your project.

You will want to make sure that it's clear the series is part of a larger intellectual property universe if it's not obvious from the title of the webseries.

Table of Contents

You may not need a table of contents if your bible is really short, but for more complex webseries or multiple series, you may want to include a listing of the sections that comprise the bible. For example, *Battlestar Galactica* created three distinctly different webseries to run during the summer breaks of the broadcast television series. Each series had different characters, different narrative structures and different relationships to the TV shows. Detailing each of these will create a more complex bible than if we are producing a webseries that has the same characters and time frame in all of its seasons or groups of episodes.

All the info that was on the title page should be at the top of the table of contents page, followed by "Table of Contents" and a listing of all the individual sections that are contained in the document.

Series Concept

The bible might start with a teaser or snippet of backstory and context (or world) for the series and a hint of the characters, conflict, mysteries and/or issues that will engage the audience. This is usually very brief – more of a hook than a comprehensive summary of those elements, which we will talk about in more detail later in the bible.

The concept section may also place the webseries in relationship to the other intellectual property iterations of the universe and describe the goals in presenting this particular story material in webisode format.

As with all things in media, brevity is encouraged, especially for shorter expressions of story like webseries. Your concept section will generally be two to three short paragraphs at the most and certainly less than one page for a webseries.

Characters

Like in other bibles, the webseries platform bible will include biographies and backstories for each of the primary or regularly recurring characters. These bios are usually shorter than those we might find in a television platform bible. It depends on the specific webseries, and character descriptions can range from a paragraph to a page or two per character, depending on the importance of the character, the number of episodes the character will appear in and the type of story you're telling.

Season Arcs and Episode Synopses

Your bible will include synopses of each projected season and a representative sample of specific episodes from the first season, or if your seasons will radically vary, maybe the first couple of webisodes for each season you have already thought through.

Season synopsis: Though webseries don't have seasons in the way that we talk about serialized television programming, there are still usually defined story arcs that bridge a set number of episodes. For all intents and purposes, these are the equivalent of a season and so we will use that term. The season synopsis might read much like a short film treatment, describing the over-arching story for an individual season as if it were a complete and (somewhat) self-contained narrative arc. Just as with television series, each season may be given its own title. Though the audience of a television series will probably never know what the season titles are, webseries sometimes clearly title their seasons so that the audience can clearly identify the different seasons and the webisodes that belong together. For example, *Battlestar Galactica* had three seasons of webisodes, but each season revealed a story arc distinct and discrete from the other two seasons; the three sets of webisodes were called *The Resistance*, *Razor Flashbacks* and *The Face of the Enemy*.

Again, the approach you take will depend on your specific intellectual property and the story you are telling with episodic television.

Episode synopsis: Each episode of the webseries or first season will be briefly described in a paragraph. Keep in mind that each webisode is only trying to convey three to seven minutes of story material – people are not likely to sit and watch a 30-minute webisode, especially if they're watching on mobile devices. Therefore, your synopses should reflect the fact that the story events and material in any one webisode is scaled way down and is more of a snack than a meal (assuming at 30-minute or 60-minute television show is equivalent to a meal).

As your platform bible begins to incorporate more aspects of a production bible, you may then add additional information to each of the episode synopses. This information might include:

Locations *seen in the webisode, not literally where the story will be filmed but where the story takes place.*

Characters *or the main characters featured in the webisodes. Some series do not have every major character in every episode.*

Secondary cast or characters *that may only be appearing in this webisode or only appear in the series occasionally. With both your characters and secondary cast, webseries require you to be as streamlined as possible. You are not going to have time to establish or follow more than one or two characters in any sort of dramatically meaningful way for a three- to five-minute webisode.*

Activities or the actions *of the characters that will be presented in the webisode. In a way, this serves as a beat sheet or plot point summary for the individual webisode.*

Costumes *might be noted if these are critical for the story, such as a superhero costume.*

Special highlights *of the episode that tie in to what makes this world or these characters unique.*

Props *seen in the episode, especially those that help propel the story forward or if they set up (or resonate with) narrative elements in other iterations of the intellectual property.*

Vehicles or modes of transportation *we see in the episode.*

Guest talent *if there's a guest star or someone who is not usually a part of the series.*

Quotes *or sample dialogue, phrases that are significant to either the episode or the series, often with thematic or marketing implications, that must be included in the episode. Use this section sparingly; you're not trying to list all the dialogue, just a few lines that are important. And webisodes are too short to have a lot of dialogue.*

You will flesh out these elements for each webisode that you synopsize. You and your team can now get a sense of the general scale of story material per webisode, where the story is going through this particular season of the webseries, and how the season's narrative arc (synopsized earlier in the season synopsis section of the bible) is exemplified in each webisode.

Because the scale of webseries is much smaller than traditional television series or even a graphic novel, if you know your story well enough, you can go ahead and lay out a general summary for each episode for several seasons.

As your bible develops further and you get deeper into the property's larger story, don't be afraid to rewrite the webisodes yet to be filmed. This section of your bible will change and grow as you and the story does. And as you move into more of a production bible, you will probably add a brief scene outline or a summary of the episode comprised of brief descriptions of each scene. Of course some episodes may be a single scene – if the average scene in film is three minutes and in television three to seven minutes, then most webisodes are going to only be a single scene or not much more than that.

Backstory

The backstory section of your bible will now expand on the teaser that was in your series concept section at the beginning of the document. This information will originate with ideas and information detailed in the intellectual property bible's summary of the backstory, but you will likely have further developed and added to that material in order to flesh out the world of the webisodes.

Rules

Underlying assumptions or rules for the world that you've just described in your backstory need to be explicitly identified in this section. These rules are usually expressed as easy-to-read lists, quickly summing up important facts that affect the storyworld and how the characters interact within it. Obviously these rules are informed by and may reiterate rules from the general intellectual property.

New Media

In terms of new media, we need to develop a guideline or general set of info to be utilized in the creation of content for social virtual worlds, the interaction of social media with moving image clips (for interaction with webisodes or with excerpts from the film and/or television iterations), community building, shared spaces for viewer/users to socialize and create their own stories as well as to contribute to ongoing socially based narratives in the larger intellectual property universe. In addition, we will want to consider the content for one-way websites. These elements for new media platform bibles are highly specific to the medium and the intellectual property, but in general they will include:

Title page *that includes the title of the project, the name of the larger intellectual property if it's not self-evident from the title of the project, the logo and/or name of the intellectual property copyright holder, the author and the version number with date. The title page should also clearly indicate that this is the new media platform bible.*

Table of contents *page, especially if the document is large enough that easily finding information in it is difficult. All the info that was on the title page should be at the top of the table of contents page, followed by "Table of Contents" and a listing of all the individual sections that are contained in the document.*

Concept statement *or a brief description of the viewer/user experience and the content delivery that results from that experience.*

Synopsis *as a brief summary of narrative content that will need to be developed for the various new media iterations, usually no more than one page and in many cases perhaps only a paragraph for each iteration – usually new media focus on very small or tightly focused narrative information which might be expressed as prompts for viewer/users to add to or work with as well as self-contained blocks of story for viewers/users to respond to or discuss.*

Aesthetic considerations *in the form of a brief summary of any key aesthetic elements that need to relate to the larger intellectual property's aesthetic design or to the design elements of other individual iterations of the intellectual property. We also need to be aware of branding considerations to be sure that there is resonance and consistency with other iterations of the intellectual property.*

Environment-specific expressions and iterations. *With increasing interest in geographic storytelling, or the ways in which narrative experiences from the intellectual property can be expressed as either physical installations (either with kiosks or scheduled events) or enhanced reality (the layering of digital elements over the real world using GPS systems), you may want to consider what parts of your intellectual property would be appropriate for this type of storytelling. Not all intellectual properties will be conducive to this form of expression.*

The specific order of these elements will vary from new media project to new media project. Feel free to sequence the elements differently from how we have ordered them above – do what makes most sense for your project (of course, a title page usually only makes sense as the first page, so don't get too crazy!).

Finally, as we've said before, there is no one right way to build a platform bible, so what's most important is that you use those elements that help you best conceive and share the story that you plan to tell in this particular medium. For many of us, the bible is one of the most exciting aspects of transmedia creation. The main thing to remember that bibles are meant to be quick and easy reference guides for the producers, creative teams and production teams with the express goal to help them with continuity, narrative coherence and canon.

Appendix E
Sample Trademark Licensing Agreement

This sample trademark licensing agreement was produced for the IP PANORAMA project developed jointly by the Korean Intellectual Property Office (KIPO), the Korea Invention Promotion Association (KIPA), and the World Intellectual Property Organization (WIPO). It is provided for reference and education only.

This Trademark License Agreement (the "Agreement") is entered into as of DATE by and between the following two parties.

The Licensor: [Person, position, company name and address, e-mail, fax number]

The Licensee: [Person, position, company name and address, e-mail, fax number]

WHEREAS, Licensor owns the registered trademark (the "TRADEMARKS") shown in Attachment 1 to this Agreement;

WHEREAS, Licensor wishes to license to Licensee and Licensee is desirous of acquiring a license to use the Marks on the conditions and restrictions contained in this Agreement;

NOW THEREFORE, the parties agree as follows:

1. Grant of License
    1.1 The Trademarks
    Upon the terms and conditions hereinafter set forth, the Licensor hereby grants a general license to the Licensee the registered trademarks as defined in Appendix 1, and the Licensee hereby accepts the general license to use the trademarks as defined in Appendix 1, including all the trademarks, any part of the trademarks, and any design, character, symbol, and visual representation of the trademarks (collectively the "Trademarks"). The license hereunder is non-exclusive.
    1.2 Scope
        1.2.1 The right to use the Trademark granted by this Agreement shall only be used in the business operated by Licensee. Licensee agrees not to directly or indirectly use or authorize any other party to

use the aforementioned Trademark in any other manner, unless there are contrary provisions in this Agreement.

1.2.2 The License granted by this Agreement to Licensee shall be valid in "TERRITORY" only. Licensee agrees not to directly or indirectly use or authorize any other party to use the aforementioned Trademark in any other region.

2. Terms of Payment

The Licensee agrees to pay to the Licensor a license fee and the details of license fee and the form of payment are set forth in Appendix 2.

3. Goodwill

The Licensee recognizes the value of the goodwill associated with the Trademarks, and acknowledges that the Trademarks and all intellectual property rights therein and goodwill pertaining thereto shall be the sole and exclusive property of the Licensor, and that the Trademarks have an underlying association with the Licensor by public perception.

4. Confidentiality

4.1 The Licensee shall protect and maintain the confidentiality of any and all confidential data and information acknowledged or received by the Licensee by accepting licensing of the Trademarks from the Licensor (collectively the "Confidential Information"). Upon termination or expiration of this Agreement, the Licensee shall, at the Licensor's option, return all and any documents, information or software including any of such Confidential Information to the Licensor or destroy it and delete the Confidential Information from any electronic devices and cease to use them. The Licensee shall not disclose, grant or transfer any Confidential Information to any third party without the Licensor's prior written consent.

4.2 It is agree that Section 4.1 shall survive any amendment expiration or termination of this Agreement.

5. Representations and Warranties

5.1 Licensor represents and warrants as follows:

5.1.1 Licensor is an enterprise legally registered and validly existing in accordance with Territory laws.

5.1.2 Licensor shall execute and perform this Agreement within the scope of its corporate authority and business; has taken necessary corporate actions to give appropriate authorization and to obtain the approval and permission from third parties and government authorities, and shall not violate restrictions by laws and contracts binding or having an effect thereon.

5.1.3 This Agreement shall constitute Licensor's legitimate, valid and binding obligations as soon as it is legally executed, and shall be enforceable against it.

5.1.4 Licensor has exclusive ownership of the Registered Trademark under this Agreement.

5.2 Licensee represents and warrants as follows:

5.2.1 Licensee is a company legally registered and validly existing in accordance with Territory laws.

6. The Licensor's Right of Licensing and Protection of the Licensor's Rights

6.1 The Licensee agrees that it will not during the term of this Agreement, or thereafter, challenge the right of licensing or any rights of the Licensor in and to the Trademarks or challenge the validity of this license or otherwise take or fail to take any action that impairs such rights or license.

6.2 The Licensee agrees to assist the Licensor to the extent necessary in the procurement of any protection or to protect any of the Licensor's rights to the Trademarks. In the event any third party lodges a claim concerning the Trademarks, the Licensor, if it so desires may commence or prosecute any claims or lawsuits in its own name or in the name of the Licensee or join the Licensee as a party thereto. In the event any third party infringes on the above mentioned Trademarks, the Licensee shall notify the Licensor in writing of any infringements or imitations by others of the Trademarks which may come to the Licensee's attention, and the Licensor shall have the sole right to determine whether or not any action shall be taken on account of any such infringements.

6.3   The Licensee further agrees to use the Trademarks only in accordance with this Agreement and shall not use such Trademarks in any way, which, in the opinion of the Licensor, is deceptive, misleading or in any way detrimental to such Trademarks or the reputation of the Licensor.

7.   Quality

7.1   Licensor authorizes Licensee to use the Marks in association with the Wares and/or Services so long as the use by Licensee is in accordance with the instructions, standards of quality and trade-mark specifications set by and approved by Licensor from time to time.

7.2   Licensee undertakes to use the Marks in strict accordance with the instructions, standards of quality and trade-mark specifications supplied by Licensor from time to time, and to use each of the Marks only in association with [the Wares and/or the Services] now set out in Schedule "A" which may be amended to add or delete Marks as Licensor in sole discretion shall decide.

7.3   For as long as Licensee uses the Marks, Licensor shall have the right to inspect the premises of Licensee from time to time during normal business hours, upon reasonable notice and to take samples, at Licensee's expense, of any Wares sold or to be sold in association with the Marks by Licensee. For as long as Licensee uses the Marks, Licensor shall have the right to inspect the premises of Licensee from time to time during normal business hours, upon reasonable notice, and to observe the performance of the Services.

8.   Promotion

In all cases where the Licensee produces promotional material involving the Trademarks, the production cost of such material thereof shall be borne by the Licensee. All copyrights or other intellectual property rights of such material concerning the Trademarks thereto shall be the sole and exclusive property of the Licensor whether developed by the Licensor or the Licensee. The Licensee agrees not to advertise or publicize any of the Trademarks on radio, television, papers, magazines, the Internet or otherwise without the prior written consent of the Licensor.

9.   Effective Date and Term

9.1   This Agreement has been duly executed by their authorized representatives as of the date first set forth above and shall be effective simultaneously. The term of this Agreement is ten (10) years unless earlier terminated as set forth below. However, the Licensor and the Licensee shall review this Agreement every 3 months to determine whether any amendment to the Agreement is necessary depending on the circumstances.

9.2   This Agreement may be extended for one year only if the Licensor gives the Licensee its written consent of the extension of this Agreement prior to the expiration of this Agreement. However, the Licensee has no right to confirm such extension.

10.   Record Filing

Within three (3) months after the execution of the Agreement, the Licensor shall make a record filing of the copy of the Agreement to the relevant trademark management authority of The Territory.

11.   Termination

11.1 Termination on Expiration.

This Agreement shall expire on the earlier date of the date due and the date when the Licensor's right of licensing is terminated, unless this Agreement is extended as set forth above.

11.2 Early Termination

Without prejudice to any legal or other rights or remedies of the party who asks for termination of this Agreement, any party has the right to terminate this Agreement immediately with written notice to the other party in the event the other party materially breaches this Agreement including but not limited to Section 6.1, 6.2 and 6.3 of this Agreement and fails to cure its breach within 30 days from the date it receives written notice of its breach from the non-breaching party. During the term of this Agreement, the Licensor may terminate this Agreement at any time with a written notice to the Licensee 30 days before such termination.

11.3 Survival.

Article 3, 4, 6 and 16 shall survive after the termination or expiration of this Agreement.

12. Force Majeure

12.1 Force Majeure, which includes but is not limited to acts of governments, acts of nature, fire, explosion, typhoon, flood, earthquake, tide, lightning and war, means any event that is beyond the party's reasonable control and cannot be prevented with reasonable care. However, any shortage of credit, capital or finance shall not be regarded as an event of Force Majeure. The party affected by Force Majeure shall notify the other party without delay.

12.2 In the event that the affected party is delayed in or prevented from performing its obligations under this Agreement by Force Majeure, only within the scope of such delay or prevention, the affected party will not be responsible for any damage by reason of such a failure or delay of performance. The affected party shall take appropriate measures to minimize or remove the effects of Force Majeure and attempt to resume performance of the obligations delayed or prevented by the event of Force Majeure. After the event of Force Majeure is removed, both parties agree to resume performance of this Agreement with their best efforts.

13. Notices

Notices or other communications required to be given by any party pursuant to this Agreement shall be written in English and Chinese and shall be deemed to be duly given when it is delivered personally or sent by registered mail or postage prepaid mail or by a recognized courier service or by facsimile transmission to the address of the relevant party or parties set forth below.

Party A: [Person, position, company name and address, e-mail, fax number]

Attention:

Party B: [Person, position, company name and address, e-mail, fax number]

Attention:

14. Assignment or Sublicense

The Licensee shall not assign, lease, pledge, sublicense, or in any other way transfer the rights or responsibilities Licensed pursuant to the Agreement to any third party/parties, or transfer the economic benefits of the license granted hereby or any portion of the rights included therein to any third party without the prior written consent of the Licensor.

15. Amendment and Supplement

The Agreement shall not be amended or modified except by a written instrument come into force only signed by both parties. The amendment and supplement duly executed by both parties shall be part of this Agreement and shall have the same legal effect as this Agreement.

16. Severability

    Any provision of this Agreement which is invalid or unenforceable due to the violation of the relevant laws in any jurisdiction shall be void of effectiveness and birding force within the relevant fields of such jurisdiction without affecting in any way the remaining provisions hereof.

17. Appendices

    The Appendices referred to in this Agreement are an integral part of this Agreement and have the same legal effect as this Agreement.

IN WITNESS THEREOF the parties hereto have caused this Agreement to be duly executed by a duly authorized representative each on behalf of the Party hereto as of the date first set forth above.

Licensor:

Representative: _____

Licensee:

Representative: _____

Appendix F

The Producers Guild of America "Code of Credits" Definition of Transmedia Producer

Producers Guild of America, Code of Credits – New Media[1]

Transmedia
Producer

A Transmedia Narrative project or franchise must consist of three (or more) narrative storylines existing within the same fictional universe on any of the following platforms: Film, Television, Short Film, Broadband, Publishing, Comics, Animation, Mobile, Special Venues, DVD/Blu-ray/CD-ROM, Narrative Commercial and Marketing rollouts, and other technologies that may or may not currently exist. These narrative extensions are NOT the same as repurposing material from one platform to be cut or repurposed to different platforms.

A Transmedia Producer credit is given to the person(s) responsible for a significant portion of a project's long-term planning, development, production, and/or maintenance of narrative continuity across multiple platforms, and creation of original storylines for new platforms. Transmedia producers also create and implement interactive endeavors to unite the audience of the property with the canonical narrative and this element should be considered as valid qualification for credit as long as they are related directly to the narrative presentation of a project.

Transmedia Producers may originate with a project or be brought in at any time during the long-term rollout of a project in order to analyze, create or facilitate the life of that project and may be responsible for all or only part of the content of the project. Transmedia Producers may also be hired by or partner with companies or entities, which develop software and other technologies and who wish to showcase these inventions with compelling, immersive, multi-platform content.

To qualify for this credit, a Transmedia Producer may or may not be publicly credited as part of a larger institution or company, but a titled employee of said institution must be able to confirm that the individual was an integral part of the production team for the project.

[1] accessed July 20, 2012, http://www.producersguild.org/?page=coc_nm#transmedia

Appendix G
Suggested Readings

Motion Pictures and Visual Storytelling

Block, Alex and Lucy Autrey Wilson, *George Lucas's Blockbusting: A Decade-by-Decade Survey of Timeless Movies Including Untold Secrets of Their Financial and Cultural Success*, It Books, 2010

Dancyger, Ken and Jeff Rush, *Alternative Scriptwriting, Fourth Edition: Rewriting the Hollywood Formula*, Focal Press, 2006

Katz, Steven D., *Film Directing Shot by Shot: Visualizing from Concept to Screen*, Michael Wiese Productions, 1991

McKee, Robert, *Story: Substance, Structure, Style and The Principles of Screenwriting*, Regan Books, 1997

Snyder, Blake, *Save The Cat! The Last Book on Screenwriting You'll Ever Need*, Michael Wiese Productions, 2005

Vogler, Christopher, *The Writer's Journey: Mythic Structure for Writers*, Michael Wiese Productions, 2007

Television and Serialized Storytelling

Blum, Richard A., *Television and Screen Writing: From Concept to Contract*, Focal Press, 2000

Blumenthal, Howard and Oliver Goodenough, *This Business of Television*, Billboard Books, 2006

Dimaggio, Madeline, *How To Write For Television*, Touchstone, 2008

Mittel, Jason, *Television and American Culture*, Oxford University Press, 2009

Sandler, Ellen, *The TV Writer's Workbook: A Creative Approach To Television Scripts*, Delta, 2007

Smith, Aaron, *Transmedia Storytelling in Television 2.0*, http://blogs.middlebury.edu/mediacp/

Video Games and Interactive Storytelling

Chandler, Heather Maxwell, *Game Production Handbook*, Jones and Bartlett Publishers, 2008

Despain, Wendy (editor), *Professional Techniques for Video Game Writing*, A. K. Peters, 2008

Despain, Wendy (editor), *Writing for Video Game Genres: From FPS to RPG*, A. K. Peters, 2009

Dille, Flint and John Zuur Platten, *The Ultimate Guide To Video Game Writing and Design*, Lone Eagle, 2008

Thompson, Jim and Barnaby Berbank-Green and Nic Cusworth, *Game Design: Principles, Practice, and Techniques – The Ultimate Guide for the Aspiring Game Designer*, Wiley, 2007

Transmedia and Transmedia Storytelling

Alexander, Bryan, *The New Digital Storytelling: Creating Narratives with New Media*, Praeger, 2011

Bernardo, Nuno, *The Producer's Guide to Transmedia: How to Develop, Fund, Produce and Distribute Compelling Stories Across Multiple Platforms*, Beactive Books, 2011

Dinehart, Stephen E., *The Narrative Design Explorer*, http://narrativedesign.org/

Jenkins, Henry, *Convergence Culture: Where Old and New Media Collide*, NYU Press, 2009

Miller, Carolyn Handler, *Digital Storytelling*, Focal Press, 2008

Phillips, Andrea, *A Creator's Guide to Transmedia Storytelling: How to Captivate and Engage Audiences across Multiple Platforms*, McGraw-Hill, 2012

Rose, Frank, The Art of Immersion: How the Digital Generation Is Remaking Hollywood, Madison Avenue, and the Way We Tell Stories, W. W. Norton & Company, 2012

Other

Card, Orson Scott, *The Writer's Digest Guide to Science Fiction and Fantasy*, Writer's Digest Books, 2010

Hajdu, David, *The Ten-Cent Plague: The Great Comic Book Scare and How It Changed America*, Picador, 2009

McCloud, Scott, *Reinventing Comics: How Imagination and Technology Are Revolutionizing an Art Form*, William Morrow Paperbacks, 2004

McCloud, Scott, *Understanding Comics: The Invisible Art*, William Morrow Paperbacks, 1994

Napier, Susan J., *Anime from Akira to Howl's Moving Castle, Updated Edition: Experiencing Contemporary Japanese Animation*, Palgrave Macmillan, 2005

Niven, Larry, *Playgrounds of the Mind*, Tor Science Fiction, 1992

Schodt, Frederik L., *Dreamland Japan: Writings on Modern Manga*, Stone Bridge Press, 1996

Tatsumi, Yoshihiro, *A Drifting Life*, Drawn and Quarterly, 2009

Verino, Jessie, *Fundamentals of World Building*, L & L Dreamspell, 2010

Wolk, Douglas, *Comic-Con Strikes Again!*, (Kindle Single) Amazon Digital Services, 2011

www.io9.com

Index

A

Abrams, J.J. 5, 27, 45–6, 134, 142, 239
act structure
   in a story 61
   in television 113–15
action lines 87
adaptation 22–3, 188
"additive comprehension" 5
advertising 98, 111–13, 127
Aeon Flux 102–5, 109
aesthetic treatments 93
affordance concept 168–9
AfterMash 131
agency concept 168–9
agile development 177–8
Airforce One 57
Alcatraz 12
Alien films 6, 23, 60, 267
"all is lost" moments 85–6
alpha milestones 183
Alphas 127
alternative reality games (ARGs) 19–20, 258
Amnesia: The Dark Descent 161
Angry Birds 37
anime 210
apps, mobile 17–18
Arad, Avi 189
arcs in storytelling 117–20, 129
Armageddon 83
aspect ratio 82
asset lists 273
asset management 259
associate producers 8
audience engagement 12, 18–19, 29–32, 65; *see also* target
   audiences
author's "pull" 231–3
Avatar 24–5, 44, 63–4, 246, 265, 268, 270

B

backstories 44–5, 85, 268–9
"bad guys" 51–2; *see also* villains

Bad Robot 19, 239
Bad Twin 137
Baggs, Bill 209
Bale, Christian 214
Barnfather, Keith 209
Basecamp service 262
Batman 68, 163–4, 189, 210–14, 235
Battlestar Galactica 23, 26, 28, 49, 66, 119–20, 124–5, 131, 235
Baum, L. Frank 225–6
Bear, Greg 205
The Beast 20, 30, 195-96
beat sheets 92
beginnings, middles and endings in film 62–6, 87–8
Belanger, Andy 221–2
Bender, Jack 144
Bennet, Harve 23
Benson, Mike 143–4, 147
Benson, Mildred Wirt 226
Benton, John 209
Bergman, Ingmar 79
Berne Convention for the Protection of Literary and
   Artistic Works (1988) 250
beta milestones 184
"bibles" 127, 255, 263–6, 271–80
   for different forms of storytelling 303–9
   as dynamic documents 279–80
   maintenance and updating of 277–80
   for motion picture projects 285–9
   platform-specific 271–3
   sharing of 277
   for television shows 289–92
   for video game projects 293–302
"big picture" vision 38–9
Bilson, Danny 193
Blade Runner 190
The Blair Witch Project 23
Blish, James 73
blockbusters 51, 81, 176
Boam, Jeffrey 141
Bollywood films 89
Bonanza 132
"bookending" 84

bottom-up and *top-down* development 36–8
Branagh, Kenneth 221–2
branching stories 164–8
branding 239–42, 255, 273
Braun, Lloyd 142
British Broadcasting Corporation (BBC) 209, 229, 243, 258
Brokeback Mountain 81
budgeting 10, 276
Buffy the Vampire Slayer 16, 24, 118, 124, 129, 234
bugs in video games 184–5
building blocks for storyworlds 42–3
Burton, Tim 189, 213
business models 275
business plans 94, 274–5

C

cable television 113
California Raisins 206
Call of Duty games 153, 161
cameos 130
Cameron, James 24, 44, 64
canonical material 72–4, 278–9
Captain America: The First Avenger 241–2
Card, Orson Scott 62, 232–3
Carrey, Jim 213
Carroll, Sean 146
Carter, Chris 50
Casino Royale 154
casts of characters 39–40
catalysts 85
Cathy's Book 32, 197
"causal chains" 86
Cavemen 206
Cawley, James 209
CBS Dramatic Universe proposal 139–41
CBS Studios 74
central question in film 83
Cerny, Mark (and Cerny method of game development) 177–8
character-driven stories 57–8
characters 39–40, 52–3, 89–90, 265, 269, 272
    motivation of 172–3
    strongly-defined and *weakly-defined* 171–4
    on television 116–20, 125, 128; *see also* player-characters
Charrette, Robert 188
Chayefski, Paddy 111

Chee, Leland 75, 279
chokepoints 166, 168
Chronicles of Narnia 229
Chronicles of Riddick 190–1
Chung, Peter 105
cinematographers 97
Clash of the Titans 107
cliffhangers 115, 123, 128
climaxes
    in film 60
    on television 114
Clooney, George 213, 257
coherence *see* narrative coherence
Coleridge, William Taylor 21
collective intelligence 30
Collider 9
comics 16, 71, 202–4, 212–13, 217–19, 223–4, 304
"coming full circle" 84
commercial breaks 113–14, 121
communication coordinators 256
Community 126
computer graphic imagery (CGI) 79
concept art 273
conflict between characters 25, 51, 118, 122
continuity 69–72, 259–60, 279
    retroactive 72
"conversation" between brand and consumer 241
coordinating producers 8
copyright 249–54, 278
core narratives 24
cornerstones 27–9, 63, 136, 246–47
cost of filmmaking 95
costume play ("cosplay") 208
crafting a transmedia property 38
creative authority 256–7
Creative Commons license 251–2
creative directors 8
creative producers 7
creative scope 9
"creatives" 20–1
Croft, Douglas 212
crossover
    between storyworlds 131
    in game production 184
Cruikshank, Lucas 227
CSI 130–1, 139–40, 147–8, 172, 192–3
cultural artifacts 205–7

culture and cultural impact 39, 44
Cupid 223
Curb Your Enthusiasm 131
Cuse, Carlton 27, 46, 141–51, 197
customer support 185
cut-scenes 157–8

D

Darger, Henry Jr. 207
The Dark Knight 20, 163–4, 195, 213–14
Dark Shadows 26
Dark Skies 289
The Dark Tower 69, 71, 101, 232
database software 260
databases, digital 279–80
David, Peter 74
Dawn of the Dead 240
Day, Felicia 192
decision points in stories 164–6
Deep Impact 83
Defiance 194
Del Col, Anthony 215–24
Del Rey (publishers) 70
De Meo, Paul 193
demographics 12, 29, 95, 127, 239–40
design aesthetics 273
design specs 273
Desperate Housewives 126
deus ex machina 46–7
development process
    for a film 96
    for a television show 120
    for transmedia 6–7, 35–8
    for a video game 178
Dexter 52, 193
dialogue (in video games) 174–5
Die Hard 58, 87
Diesel, Vin 190
Dietz, William C. 70
digital video recorders 14
directors
    of films 97
    of television shows 129
Dirty Work 32
Discordia 69
Disney, Walt 132–3, 199; *see also* Walt Disney Studios

Doctor Who 9, 41, 66, 72, 209, 234, 243, 258
document management 259–61
Donner, Richard 189
Doyle, Arthur Conan 46, 66, 72, 132
Dragon Age games 159, 170, 192
"dramedy" 123
Dredd 189
Dungeons and Dragons 186–7

E

economic aspects of transmedia 10, 39, 230–1
Edison, Thomas 204
The Elder Scrolls: Skyrim 170
Elliot, Kamilla 188
en medias res 88
Ender's Game 221, 232
entry points in film 63–5
episodic storytelling 14, 116
establishing shots 90
The Event 12, 37
executive producers 7–8
expansion of storyworlds 23
exposition 60
extension of intellectual property 23, 234

F

Fallout 3 52
Family Guy 130
fan base 225
"fan boy" culture 230–1, 235
fan "canon" videos 208–9
fan culture 208, 241, 257–8
fan fiction 207–8
fanwanking 72
Faulkner, William 89
Fiennes, Ralph 107
The 52 203, 214
films 13–15
    "bibles" for the making of 285–9
    duration and scale of 81
    levels in 88
    producers of 7
    related to other media 99–101
    scheduling of release 244
    and television 133

Final Fantasy games 156, 188
Finger, Bill 212
Flash Forward 37
flashbacks 84
format in television 121
frames 79–80
frames per second (fps) 80
framing 100
franchises 6, 99, 239, 278
   definition of 129
   in television 129–30
Fred 227
Furth, Robin 69

G

game consoles 13, 185
game engines 157–8
game masters 186–7
Game of Thrones 54, 65, 71, 133, 222, 232, 242, 246, 258
gameplay 155–8, 168, 182
   and action 171–2
Garden State 57
GEICO Cavemen 206
genres and genre types 57–60
   in television 113, 121, 123
Ghost World 81
Gigantic 33, 62
Gillis, Gregg 150
Glee 32
glossaries 270
goals of transmedia 36, 116, 275
GoldenEye 190
Gomez, Jeff 3, 30, 32, 199, 247–8, 264
Google Docs 260
Grand Theft Auto games 52, 153, 156–61, 167, 170, 172
graphic novels 16, 71, 203–4, 219, 230–1, 304
   scheduling of releases 245–6
"greenlighting" a project 96, 127
The Grey 84
Grossman, Lev 173
The Guild 192

H

Half-Life games 157
Halo games 19, 34, 173, 189, 263–5

Hamlet 217, 223
Harry Potter 39–40, 63–6, 95, 105, 169, 191, 202, 230, 233, 247, 283
Hawaii Five-0 26, 131
Hay, Phil 101–10
Heavy Rain 58, 158, 168
Heineken 148
Heroes 18, 37, 49, 116, 125, 133, 137–8, 197, 241
hiatus breaks 128
His Dark Materials 229–30
"hit movies" 37
The Hobbit 80, 95, 99, 189, 228
Holland, Peter 218
Hollywood films 82–3, 89, 95
Holocaust 133
Home for the Holidays 83
home movies 98
The House of Sand and Fog 84
Houser, Dan 159
The Hungry Games 39, 98, 220–1
Hyrb, Larry 173

I

I Love Bees 19, 195
In America 84
inciting incidents 85
independent film projects 95
intellectual property 9, 27–31, 35–9, 48, 129, 210, 233–5
   access points 234
   definition of 5–6
   originating in novels, comics or new media 201–5
interactive conversation scenes in video games 174
interactive stories 17–18, 164–5
interactive storytelling 155
Internet resources 18–19, 204, 207, 231, 260
The Invasion 84
The Invisible 89–90
iPhone/iPad game 193
iPod applications 257–8
iterative development of games 177
It's Always Sunny in Philadelphia 126

J

Jackson, Peter 153, 189, 248
James Bond character and films 55, 68, 169, 172

Japanese culture 203, 210, 215
Jason Bourne films and franchise 34, 286
Jenkins, Henry 4–5, 20, 30, 33, 208
jeopardy 49, 53, 114
John Carter 204
Jones, Tommy Lee 213

K

Kane, Bob 212
Karp, Jensen 150
Keaton, Michael 213
key story elements 48
key transmedia elements
    in television 124–5
    in video games 158–61
Kill Shakespeare 216–23
Kilmer, Val 213
King, Stephen 69, 71, 101, 232
Kirkman, Robert 193, 228–9
Kishimoto, Masashi 210
Kring, Tim 137
Krueger, Jacob 35
Kurtzman, Alex 19, 70, 74

L

LA Noir 158, 160, 171
Lars and the Real Girl 89–90
Law and Order 115–16, 148
Lean, David 249
LeBeouf, Shia 152
Lenkov, Peter M. 104–5
"letterboxing" 82
Levene, John 209
Levy, Pierre 30
Lewis, C.S. 229
licensing of intellectual property 139, 179, 228, 249–55, 277–8
    exclusive and *non-exclusive* 253–4
    sample agreement for 310–13
Lieber, Jeffrey 134
life cycle of a film 96–8
Lindelof, Damon 19, 134, 142, 146–8
line producers 7
local networks 260
localization of video games 183
loglines 91, 127, 267

The Lord of the Rings 52, 54, 99, 153, 186–9, 228, 248
Los Angeles 90
LOST 12, 20–1, 27, 30–1, 46–53, 58, 63–6, 69–71, 75, 117–20, 134–8, 142–50, 197, 222, 234, 239, 242, 277, 283
Lost World 199
Lucas, George 207

M

McCreery, Connor 216–17
McDonald's 247
McIntyre, Vonda N. 23
Mad Men 112
management of transmedia property 239–62
    supervisory groups for 256–7
    technical aspects of 258–61
Manfredi, Matt 101, 103
manga 203, 210
Manhunter 47
Maniac Mansion 192
manipulative nature of cinema 82
Mario Brothers 133
marketing 10–11, 97–8, 175–6, 207, 218–19, 243–8, 253
Marshall, Jack 209
Martin, George R.R. 54, 63, 65, 71, 222, 232
Marvel's The Avengers 41–2, 153, 204, 240–41, 246–47
Marvel Studios and Marvel Universe 31, 41–2, 153–4, 189, 204, 240–1, 246–7
Mass Effect games 9, 58, 61, 70, 154–5, 158, 163–4, 174–5, 186, 234, 283
master story
    of a transmedia property 278–9
    of a video game 163
The Matrix 4, 40–1, 52, 143, 222
media, definition of 6
Memory Alpha website 70, 75
merchandising 252
MICE Quotient 62
Microsoft company 264–5
Microsoft software 260–2
milestones, video games 179–80, 183–4, 255
Millennium 55
Miller, Frank 213
Miller, George (and Miller's Law) 47
miniseries 133
mise-en-scène 99–100

mobile frames 100
The Mongoliad 205
montages 92
Moore, Ronald 19, 66
Moore, Tony 228
Mortal Kombat 101, 133, 153, 192
motion pictures *see* films
motivation of characters 48
moviegoing, demographics of 29
Mroz, Sue 265
multiplayer gaming 16
Murray, Janet 168
Muybridge, Edward 80
My Best Friend's Wedding 57
My Sleep 84
mystery elements in transmedia 45–53, 117–20
mythology 44, 50, 117, 120

N

Nancy Drew games 172, 226–7, 235
narrative coherence 66–9
narrative designers 155
narrative gaps 50, 117
narrative treatments 93
narrative of a video game 163
Naruto 67, 210–12, 215
Nations, Gregg 70–1, 279
NCIS franchise 24, 139–40, 192
new media 204–5, 309
niche audiences 205, 240
Nicholson, Jack 213
Nike 148
Niven, Larry 106
Noble, John 158
Noctropolis 156
Nolan, Christopher 214
Norman, Donald 169
novels 16–18, 89, 201–2, 303–4

O

O'Bannon, Rockne S. 194
O'Donnell, Chris 213
The Office 148
on-demand viewing 14

OpenOffice software 260
Orci, Roberto 19, 70, 74
organization charts 276
outlines of scenes 91
"outsider art" 207
overseeing production 11
overviews 270–2

P

"pacing" of information 120
parallel structure in an interactive story 166
Paranormal Activity 9, 85
Pascale, Anthony 19
"patches" for software 185
Pearce, Guy 248
Pedowitz, Mark 144
Peer Gynt 235
pilots 117, 127
platforms 35–6, 40
    definition of 6, 12
player-characters 154, 159–60, 167–72
Pleasantville 83
plot 50, 57, 84–9
    as distinct from story 161
    on television 125
    of a video game 159–61
plot curves 84–7
plot-driven stories 57–8
plot points 61, 85, 269
plotlines 87
Pohl-Weary, Emily 245–6
post-production 97, 184
post-release content of video games 185
post-release teams for video games 185
premise of an intellectual property 88, 128, 267
pre-production 96–7, 180–1
previews on television 115
prime themes, *prime goals* and *prime audiences* 94–5
procedurals 120, 192
Producers Guild of America 3–4, 7–8, 102, 196
    "code of credits" 315–16
producers, transmedia 4, 7–11, 315
production designers 97
project websites 261–2
prologues 115

Prometheus 6, 18, 23–4, 106–7, 248
proposals 94–5
Protosevich, Mark 155
Provencio, Marla 143
Psycho 26
publishers of video games 178
Pullman, Philip 229

R

"ramping into production", video games 181
reality television 129–30
reboots 26, 131, 215
recaps 115
recognition scenes 85–6
Red Dead Redemption 52, 159–60
Red Faction: Origins 193
Reeves-Stevens, Judith and Garfield 74
ReGenesis 32
Reign of Fire 95
release schedules 242–7
remakes 25–6, 131
remote access to documents 260
requests-for-proposals (RFPs) 180
Resident Evil 153, 188
resolution in film 60
revivals on television 131
rights-holder's approval process 254–5, 278
rights in video games 179
RIPD 103–6
rising action and *falling action* 60–1, 84–5
Roddenberry, Gene 43, 68, 73–4, 266
role-playing games 170, 186–8
romantic comedy 58
Rose, Reginald 111
Ross, Gary 83
Rowling, J.K. 233
royalties 254
Rutledge, Pamela Brown 56

S

sales territories 253
"sandbox" gameplay 172
Saving Private Ryan 202
Saw 95

scenes in film 91–2
scheduling 10–11, 180, 242–7
Schnaubelt, Franz Joseph 73
Schumacher, Joel 213
science fiction 130
Scott, Ridley 18, 107, 190, 248–9
scripted scenes in video games 174
scripts 93–4
    examples of 270, 272
season planning 128
secondary characters 125, 130
"second-screen" experiences 13
sequels 99
sequences 92
serialised storytelling 116–17, 120, 148
Serling, Rod 111
setting 54, 90
    in television 126
    of a video game 160–1
Se7en 87
Shadowman 188
Shadowrun 187-88, 194-95
Shakespeare in Love 218
Shatner, William 74
Sherlock Holmes stories 46, 48, 66, 68, 72, 132, 214, 235
"shoot days" 179
short films 81
short stories 89
shot size and shot scale 82, 100
showrunners 8, 127–8, 278
side-missions, video games 160, 167–8
The Simpsons 113, 116, 125, 223
single-camera directing 129
situation comedies ("sitcoms") 115–16, 126
The Sixth Sense 47
slash fiction 208
Sleeping with the Enemy 83
Slide 32
Smallville 126–7
Smith, Kevin 264
Snakes on a Plane 57
soap operas 132
A Song of Ice and Fire 54, 71, 133, 232; *see also Game of Thrones*
Sonic the Hedgehog 133
Sophie's Choice 84
Sowards, Jack B. 23

specifications *see* design specs; technology specs
Spider-Man 235
spin-offs 130–1
spiral structure for movies 84
spirals of conflict 122
sponsor-driven model of television 113
"sprints" 177
Stanton, Andrew 179
star quality 257
Star Trek films and franchise 5, 19, 23–4, 27, 34, 43, 49–50, 67–75, 118, 130–4, 209, 215, 234, 239, 254, 266, 278–9, 283
Star Wars films and franchise 107, 109, 155, 169–70, 235, 277, 279, 283
Stargate 130
starting concepts 24–5
Staton, Aaron 158
step outlines 92
Stephenson, Neal 205
Stewart, Sean 30, 32
Stoppard, Tom 218
stories
    character-driven and *plot-driven* 57–8
    low-concept and *high-concept* 57–8, 90
    "size" of 81
    structure of 83–4
story-driven games 155, 159
story summaries 92–3
story written and *story played* 163
storyboards 273
storytelling 3–4, 7–10, 30, 34, 56–7, 82, 88–9
    different forms of 201
    on television 111–12, 121, 123; *see also* interactive storytelling; serialised storytelling; thematic storytelling; visual storytelling
storyworlds 21, 24–5, 41–3, 120, 128, 131, 265, 270
    as distinct from story universes 41–2
Straczynski, J. Michael 19
Stratemeyer, Edward 226
Strikefleet Omega 195
struggle in stories 118; *see also* conflict between characters
style guides 273
style in transmedia 54–5, 90–1, 126, 161; *see also* writing style
subplots 53, 87
subscriber-driven model of television 113
subtext 88

success indicators 275
Superman 189
Supernatural 115
"survival horror" games 161
synopses 92–3, 269, 272
system architecture 274

T

tagging of events 280
taglines 267
tags in sitcoms 115
Tancharoen, Kevin 192
Tarantino, Quentin 52
target audiences 127, 239, 270, 272, 275
Taymor, Julie 218
team-building 10
teases or *teasers* 115
technical management of transmedia property 258–61
technology specs 274
television 14–15, 37, 65, 81, 111–51
    "bibles" for 289–92
    and film 133
    producers in 8
    revenue models of 113
    scheduling of series releases 243–4
    show development in 120
    and transmedia 132–9
    and video games 191–4
    world events linked to 112
Terminator films 48, 50, 54, 67–8, 71–2, 101, 235
test screenings 97
text in film 88
thematic storytelling 49
"theme and variation" endings 164–6
themes and thematic shifts 88–9, 124, 158, 268
The Third Man 165
three-act structure 61, 85–8, 113, 121–2
timelines 271
timescale for producing games 176
Tolkein, J.R.R. 153, 228
Tomb Raider 153
tone
    in film 90–1
    in television 126–7
    in a video game 161

top-down development *see* bottom-up and top-down
        development
toys 207
Trade-Related Aspects of Intellectual Property Rights
        (TRIPS) agreement (1994) 249
trademarks 249–54
    sample licensing agreement 310–13
"traditional narrative" 83
Transformers 48, 133, 206, 267
transmedia
    definitions of 3–4, 102, 195–6
    and film 99–101
    history of 132–4
    and television 132–9, 139
    and video games 186–94; *see also* management of
        transmedia property
"treatments" 93
"trusting the audience" 89
turning points 61, 85
21 Jump Street 26
24 117
Twin Peaks 54

U

Uncharted games 171
Under a Killing Moon 166
universal human themes 24–5, 49
Universal Pictures 240
universe-building 203–4, 207, 226–8, 239, 265, 283
universe contradictions 235
user testing of video games 182
Uzumaki, Naruto 210

V

Van Sant, Gus 26
"vertical slices" 183
Vibes 81
video games 11, 15–16, 28–9, 32, 37, 51–2, 58, 65, 152–200,
        211
    adaptations of 188
    based on feature films 190, 258
    "bibles" for 293–302
    design 155–8
    producers of 8

production of 175–86
scheduling of releases 244–5
state of development of 152–4
storytelling structure of 161–8
and television 191–4
and transmedia 158–61, 186–94
villains 53; *see also* "bad guys"
viral marketing 19
viral storytelling 148
viral videos 18
visual stories 91–2, 99–100
visual storytelling 99–100, 129
Voyage to the Bottom of the Sea 133

W

The Walking Dead 193–4, 228–9, 265
Walt Disney Studios 145, 148, 204, 240
Ward, Burt 212
Wartime 209
waterfall model of game development 177–8
weaving the universe 38–41
webisodes 28, 243, 306
websites dealing with continuity 70–1; *see also* project
        websites
Weisman, Jordan 3, 19–20, 32, 194–200
West, Adam 212
"western narrative" 83
Whedon, Joss 241
"wikis" 261
Wilderness Years 234
Williams, Steven 144
Wilson, C.J. 149–50
Wilson, Lewis 212
The Winds of War 133
The Wire 126
wireframes 273
The Wizard of Oz 91, 198, 225–8
worldbuilding 21–2, 33–4, 39, 42, 51, 187, 239, 265
World Intellectual Property Organization (WIPO) 5,
        249–50
World Trade Organization 249
Wrede, Patricia C. 43
The Writer Guild of America 110
Writers Guild of Amreica West (WCAw) 128
writing style 128

X

Xbox SmartGlass 13
The X-Files 50–1, 55, 99, 101, 118, 246
The X-Men 52, 153–4

Y

Young, Neil 5
YouTube 18, 205
Yu-Gi-Oh 133

Z

Zoho 262